Hitler's Bureaucrats

Hitler's Bureaucrats

The Nazi Security Police and the Banality of Evil

Yaacov Lozowick

Translated by Haim Watzman

continuum
LONDON • NEW YORK

CONTINUUM

The Tower Building, 11 York Road, London, SE1 7NX

370 Lexington Avenue, New York, NY 10017–6503

First published in German as *Hitler's Bürokraten: Eichmann, seine willigen Vollstrecker und die Banalität des Bösen.*
© Pendo Verlag GmbH, Zurich 2000
English edition first published 2002 by Continuum in association with Leicester University Press.
Translated from the unpublished Hebrew version by Haim Watzman

English translation © Yaacov Lozowick 2000

British Library Cataloguing-in-Publication Data
A catalogue record for this book is available from the British Library.

ISBN 0–8264–5711–8 (hardback)

Library of Congress Cataloging-in-Publication Data
Lozowick, Yaacov.
    [Hitlers Bürokraten. English]
    Hitler's bureaucrats : the Nazi security police and the banality of evil / Yaacov
Lozowick ; translated by Haim Watzman.
      p. cm.
    Includes bibliographical references and index.
    ISBN 0–8264–5711–8
    1. Nazis—Biography. 2. War criminals—Germany—Psychology. 3. Holocaust, Jewish
(1939–1945) 4. Eichmann, Adolf, 1906–1962. 5. Bureaucracy—Germany—History—20th
century. 6. National socialism—Germany—Moral and ethical aspects. I. Watzman, Haim.
II. Title.

DD244 .L6413 2002
940.53′18—dc21

2001047405

Typeset by BookEns Ltd, Royston, Herts.
Printed and bound in Great Britain by Biddles Ltd, *www.biddles.co.uk*

Contents

Preface to the English Edition   vii
Archival Sources   x
Tables and Charts of SS Organization   xii

Introduction   1

1   From Theory to Practice: 1933–8   10

2   Documents in the Bureaucratic System   43

3   Toward the Final Solution   57

4   Executing the Final Solution in Germany   94

5   Holland   143

6   France   179

7   Hungary   238

8   Conclusion: Listening to the Screams   268

Bibliography   281
Index   293

Preface to the English Edition

Evil is powerful, palpable, and very real. Rationalism would wish to reduce it to a poetic expression of something else – social, psychological or perhaps economic stresses and currents. In our age of postmodern cacophonies of competing voices, narratives and viewpoints, evil seems a leftover, a relic of an earlier, religious age. Yet for me, the writing of this book has been accompanied by the growing awareness of the aridity of these explanations and, finally, of their futility. Having spent years watching Adolf Eichmann and his colleagues from as close as I dared, I was forced to re-evaluate the understanding with which I began my research; eventually, an honest appraisal of what I was finding forced me to recognize the evil in them.

Numerous people assisted me. At Yad Vashem, Esther Aran and Judith Levin showed me the documentation of the West German prosecutors which, alongside the documentation collected for the Eichmann trial, is the basis of the research; both repeatedly told me there was an important thesis in there. Once I was launched, Haddassah Modlinger offered her hospitality in the reading room, and kept an eye open for relevant documentation in unexpected files. Judith Kleiman gave me the run of her strongrooms. Shmuel Krakowski sent me to the Zentralle Stelle der Landesjustizverwaltungen in Ludwigsburg, armed with a letter of introduction stating that I was operating for the Yad Vashem Archives of which he was the director. Once at Ludwigsburg, Willi Dressen was a valuable guide.

Yehuda Bauer, under whose tuition the original thesis was written, granted me the large degree of freedom I needed, while offering valuable guidance. As my thesis grew away from what both of us had expected, he was both an important critic and an enthusiastic supporter.

In the 1960s Raul Hilberg was turned away from Yad Vashem. When he spent a week in the archives twenty-some years later, I fear that his main problem was that we pestered him all week, vying for his time and not letting him read. For me he was an eldorado; in a week of informal discussions I learnt much of what I know about the workings of the bureaucracy of the Third Reich. I don't know what he will make of this book, but I hope he will appreciate the attempt to understand the murder of the Jews through the memos of the murderers. Similarly, Christopher Browning, who also counts himself as a student of Hilberg, has been an important model. His own research, ever coherent and thought-provoking, is quoted often in the following pages; over the years we have repeatedly found occasion to discuss what we were doing. Often we have disagreed, but it has always been a pleasure to talk, and I would hope our ability to disagree amicably might be a model for others.

A number of colleagues gave me many hours to let me sound off my ideas, Daniel Blatman, David Silberklang and Robert Rozett foremost among them. Shalmi Barmore, at the time our boss in the Education Department at Yad Vashem, never accepted the direction I was moving in, and was a fascinating and tenacious adversary, forcing me to fight every sentence of my evolving understanding. I miss the atmosphere of intense intellectual fervor he managed to create around him.

A large number of German friends assisted me in understanding contemporary Germany, which, while radically different from the Germany I was studying, was not without its own value. A partial list of them would include Dierk Jülich, Karin Finsterbusch, Regina Schlegel and Hinrich Krahnstoever, Joachim Schütte and Katrin Volkmann with the perspective of the East, Jaqueline Gierre (an American who has spent her adult life in Germany) and of course Christoph Münz.

Not reading French or Dutch meant that I was not certain the chapters on France and the Netherlands were good enough; I was helped by Renée Poznanski and Josef Michman, who may not have always agreed with me but pointed out the occasional error so as to improve my accuracy. Haim Watzman translated the original Hebrew into English, while finding hundreds of pitfalls that needed clarification; Malka Lozowick then took his product and went over it again with a fine-tooth comb. She has been supportive of this project since its very beginning.

As I completed the research and should have sat down to writing I became director of the Yad Vashem Archives. I am greatly indebted to my deputy, Nomi Halpern, for taking upon herself parts of my tasks so that I could find the time needed to write. Another colleague, Efraim Kaye, regularly invited me to lecture to his groups of educators, thus supplying me with a critical sounding board for my evolving ideas.

The Jewish Memorial Foundation granted me two scholarships

while I was researching. Nonetheless, being the proud father of three meant that holding a full-time job always took priority over research and writing, much of which was done late at night. At one point, Meir, Nechama and Achikam were literally counting down to completion. My wife Sarah offered far more than support, she often added the necessary steel to my resolve to complete this project. For this, for her friendship and counsel, and for her love I am deeply grateful.

Yaacov Lozowick
Jerusalem
July 2001

Archival Sources

Most archival material upon which this research is based is to be found in the Yad Vashem Archives (YVA). This includes documentation from other archives, i.e. the Special Archive (Ossobi) in Moscow, and the Zentrale Stelle der Landesjustizverwaltungen in Ludwigsburg (ZSL), Germany. The single most important record group is that of the Eichmann Trial, as collected by Section 06 of the Israeli Police, in 1960–1. These document were culled from the Nuremberg Trial documents, from the German Foreign Ministry, and from other sources. Here, it has been quoted by its title in the YVA: TR.3.

Record groups

Eichmann Trial documents: YVA TR.3
Interrogation of Adolf Eichmann by Captain Avner Less of Section 06, prior to Eichmann's trial. Six volumes, YVA.
Nuremberg Documents; YVA TR.1, TR.2 (but quoted as Nuremberg Documents, not by YVA numbers).
West German NSG (Nationalsozialistische Gerichtsverfahren) are to be found in YVA primarily in TR.10. Much of this material reached YVA from the Zentrale Stelle der Landesjustizverwaltungen in Ludwigsburg; however, TR.10 includes also indictments and court decisions (verdicts, annulments, etc.) which were sent directly to YVA, not through the ZSL.

A number of TR.10 files appear repeatedly in this book, and are quoted by their YVA file numbers. The original Verfahern numbers of these files are as follows:

> TR.10-515 = Staatsanwaltschaft Wien, 15St 1416/61, Anklageschrift gegen Franz Novak, 3.6.64.
> TR.10-652 = Vermerk zur Anklageschrift gegen Fritz Wöhrn, 1 ks 1/69 (RSHA), 21.5.69.
> TR.10-767 = Vermerk über das Ergebnis der Staatsanwltlichen Ermittlung nach dem Stande von 30.4.1969 in den Ermittlungsverfahren

gegen Friedrich Bossshammer, Richard Hartmann, Otto Hunsche, Fritz Wöhrn, 1-Js-1/65 (RSHA).

TR.10-754 = 1-Js-1/65 (RSHA), Anklageschrift gegen Bosshammer, 23.4.1971.

TR.10-1277 = Zentrale Stelle der Landesverwaltungen in Ludwigsburg (ZSL), RSHA Vernehmungsniederschriften 415 AR 1310/63 E5.

United States National Archives, Captured German Documents (Alexandria): T-175; YVA JM 4710-4714

Berlin Document Center, Personnel Files: YVA O.68

German Documents: YVA O.51

Sonderarchiv (Ossobi), Moscow, record group 500: YVA O.51 (Ossobi)

Heiner Lichtenstein Collection: YVA P.26

United Restitution Organisation: in YVA O.48

Video-taped testimonies of Holocaust survivors: YVA O.3

YVA Film Archive

Tables and Charts of SS Organization

Table 1 Individuals and ranks

Name	SS rank	Position	Location
Abetz, Otto	(Brif.)	German Ambassador	France
Ahnert, Horst	O'Stubaf.	Staff of IV J	France
Baki, Laszlo		Hungarian high official dealing with Jews	Hungary
Becher, Kurt	Standartnf.	Himmler's negotiator	Hungary
Bene, Otto	(Brif.)	Top representative of German Foreign Office	Holland
Best, Dr Werner	O'Grupnf.	1. No. 3 in SD	Berlin
		2. Senior official in Paris	Paris
Blobel, Paul	Standartnf.	Chief eradicator of mass graves	Eastern Europe
Blohm	Hauptschrf.	Staff of dept.	Holland
Bohmker, Dr Hans		German official in Amsterdam	Holland
Bosshammer, Friedrich	Hauptstuf.	Staff of IV B 4	Berlin
Bousquet, René		Head of French police	France
Brunner, Alois	Hauptstuf.	Troubleshooter for Eichmann	France and elsewhere
Calmeyer, Dr Hans Georg		Official of German Dept. of Justice	Holland
Ciano, Galeazzo		Italian Foreign Minister	Italy
Daluege, Kurt	Oberstgrupnf.	Head of Orpo	Berlin
Dannecker, Theodor	Hauptstuf.	Longtime colleague of Eichmann	Berlin, France and elsewhere
Darquier de Pellepoix, Louis		Commissar for Jewish Affairs in France (Vichy)	France
Endre, Laszlo		Hungarian high official dealing with Jews	Hungary

Table 1 — *continued*

Name	SS rank	Position	Location
Ferenczy, Laszlo		Top Hungarian Gendarme in charge of deportation	Hungary
Fischböck, Dr Hans	(Brif.)	Commissioner for Economy and Finance	Holland
Frank, Hans		Nazi governor of Generalgouvernement	Poland
Fünten, Ferdinand aus der	Hauptstuf.	Commander of Central Office for Jewish Emigration	Holland
Gemmeker, Albert	Hauptstuf.	Commander of Westerbork	Holland
Geschke, Albert		Commander of Security Police forces (BdS)	Hungary
Grell, Theodor Horst		German Foreign Office	Hungary
Günther, Rolf	Stubaf.	Eichmann's deputy	Berlin
Hagen, Herbert	Stubaf.	Longtime colleague of Eichmann	Berlin, France
Harster, Dr Wilhelm	Grupnf.	Commander of Security Police forces (BdS)	Holland
Hartenberger, Richard	U'Strmf.	Staff member under Eichmann	Berlin
Hartmann, Richard	O'Strmf.	Staff member under Eichmann	Berlin
Heinrichsohn, Ernest		Staff member, Paris	France
Heydrich, Reinhard	O'Grupnf.	Commander of Security Police	Berlin
Hezinger, Adolf		German Foreign Office	Hungary
Himmler, Heinrich	RFSS	Commander of SS	Berlin
Hunsche, Otto	equivalent to Hauptstuf.	No. 3 under Eichmann	Berlin
Jänisch, Rudolf	O'Strmf.	Staff member under Eichmann	Berlin
Kaltenbrunner, Ernst	O'Grupnf.	Successor to Heydrich	Berlin
Klingenfuss, Karl		Foreign Ministry	Berlin
Knochen, Helmut	Standartnf.	Commander of Security Police forces (BdS)	France
Knolle, Dr Bodo	Hauptstuf.	Deputy to Harster	Holland

Table 1 — *continued*

Name	SS rank	Position	Location
Krumey, Hermann	Stubaf.	Deputy to Eichmann in Hungary	Hungary
Lages, Willy	Hauptstuf.	Fünten's deputy Prime Minister	France (Vichy)
Laval, Pierre		Prime Minister	France (Vichy)
Leguay, Jean		Bousquet's deputy	France
Lischka, Kurt	O'Stubaf.	Deputy to Knochen	France
Lösener, Bernhard		Expert on Jews, German Min. of Interior	Berlin
Lospinoso, Guido		Head of Italian police in France	France
Mös, Ernst	Hauptstuf.	Staff member under Eichmann	Berlin
Müller, Heinrich	Brif.	Head of Gestapo	Berlin
Naumann, Dr Eric	Brif.	Successor to Harster	Holland
Nebe, Arthur	Grupnf.	Head of Kripo	Berlin
Novak, Franz	Hauptstuf.	Train expert under Eichmann	Berlin
Oberg, Carl	O'Grupnf.	HSSPF France	France
Rademacher, Franz		Expert on Jews, Foreign Office	Berlin
Rajakowitz, Dr Erich	O'Strmf.	Longtime colleague of Eichmann	Holland
Rauter, Hans Albin	O'Grupnf.	Commissioner for Security and HSSPF	Holland
Röthke, Heinz	O'Strmf.	Expert on Jews, Paris	France
Schleier, Rudolf		Consul-general, German Embassy, Paris	France
Schöngarth, Dr Eberhard	Brif.	Successor to Harster	Holland
Schweblin, Jacques		Jewish Affairs police in France	France
Seyss-Inquart, Artur	(O'Grupnf.)	Nazi governor of Holland	Holland
Slotkke, Gertrud		Staff member, Amsterdam	Holland
Stulpnagel, Karl Heinrich von		Second military governor of France	France

Table 1 — *continued*

Name	SS rank	Position	Location
Stulpnagel, Otto von		Military governor of France	France
Stuschka, Franz	O'Stubaf.	Staff member under Eichmann	Berlin
Suhr, Friedrich	Stubaf.	No. 3 under Eichmann	Berlin
Thadden, Eberhard von		Expert on Jews, Foreign Ministry	Berlin
Vallat, Xavier		French commissar for Jewish Affairs	France
Veesenmayer, Dr Edmund	(Brif.)	Plenipotentiary in Hungary	Hungary
Wimmer, Dr Friedrich	(Brif.)	Commissioner for Management and Justice	Holland
Winkelmann, Otto	O'Grupnf.	HSSPF in Hungary	Hungary
Wislicency, Dieter	Hauptstuf.	Longtime colleague of Eichmann	Berlin, Slovakia, Hungary
Wöhrn, Fritz	Hauptstuf	Staff member under Eichmann	Berlin
Zeitschel, Karl-Theo		Expert on Jews, German Embassy, Paris	France
Zöpf, Wilhelm	Stubaf.	Expert on Jews, Holland	Holland

Notes:

SS ranks in (parenthesis) are honorary SS ranks.

Abbreviations: see Table 2: SS ranks and their US counterparts.

The positions described are approximations, not official titles.

Table 2: SS ranks and their US counterparts

SS	Abbreviation	US Army
Reichführer SS	RFSS	General of the Army
SS-Oberstgruppenführer	Oberstgrupnf.	General
SS-Obergruppenführer	O'Grupnf.	Lieutenant-General
SS-Gruppenführer	Grupnf.	Major-General
SS-Brigadeführer	Brif.	Brigadier-General
SS-Oberführer	O'fhr.	Senior Colonel
SS-Standartenführer	Standartnf.	Colonel
SS-Oberststurmbannführer	O'Stubaf.	Lieutenant-Colonel
SS-Sturmbannführer	Stubaf.	Major
SS-Hauptsturmführer	Hauptstuf.	Captain
SS-Obersturmführer	O'Strmf.	1st Lieutenant
SS-Untersturmführer	U'Strmf.	2nd Lieutenant
SS-Sturmscharführer	Strmf.	Sergeant-Major
SS-Hauptscharführer	Hauptschrf.	Master-Sergeant
SS-Oberscharführer	O'Schrf.	Technical Sergeant
SS-Scharführer	Schrf.	Staff Sergeant
SS-Unterscharführer	U'Schrf.	Sergeant
SS-Rottenführer	Rttnf.	Corporal
SS-Sturmmann		Corporal
SS-Oberschütze		Private 1st Class
SS-Schütze		Private

Tables and Charts

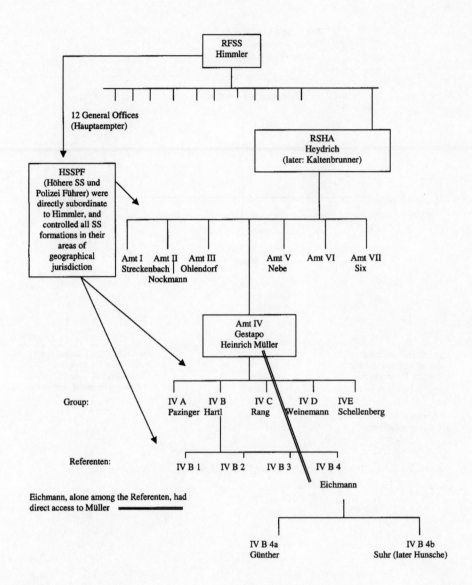

Chart 1 Department IV B 4 (Commander: Adolf Eichmann) in the structure of the SS during the Second World War

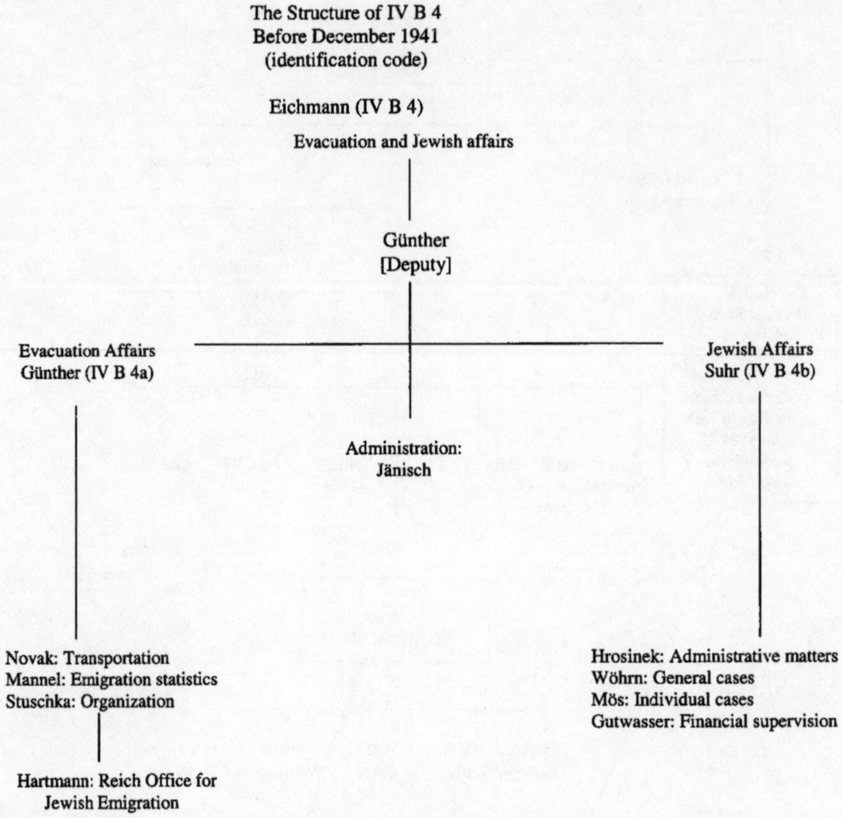

The Structure of IV B 4
Before December 1941
(identification code)

Eichmann (IV B 4)
Evacuation and Jewish affairs

Günther
[Deputy]

Evacuation Affairs
Günther (IV B 4a)

Jewish Affairs
Suhr (IV B 4b)

Administration:
Jänisch

Novak: Transportation
Mannel: Emigration statistics
Stuschka: Organization

Hrosinek: Administrative matters
Wöhrn: General cases
Mös: Individual cases
Gutwasser: Financial supervision

Hartmann: Reich Office for
Jewish Emigration

Chart 2 The structure of Department IV B 4 before December 1941
Source: TR.10-767, vol. 2, p. 248.

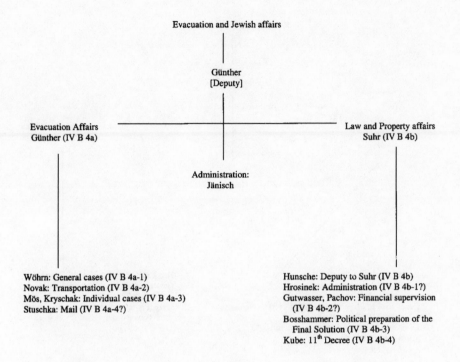

Evacuation and Jewish affairs

Günther
[Deputy]

Evacuation Affairs
Günther (IV B 4a)

Law and Property affairs
Suhr (IV B 4b)

Administration:
Jänisch

Wöhrn: General cases (IV B 4a-1)
Novak: Transportation (IV B 4a-2)
Mös, Kryschak: Individual cases (IV B 4a-3)
Stuschka: Mail (IV B 4a-4?)

Hunsche: Deputy to Suhr (IV B 4b)
Hrosinek: Administration (IV B 4b-1?)
Gutwasser, Pachov: Financial supervision
  (IV B 4b-2?)
Bosshammer: Political preparation of the
  Final Solution (IV B 4b-3)
Kube: 11th Decree (IV B 4b-4)

In November 1942 Suhr left the department. He was replaced by Hunsche. Bosshammer and
Kube, while retaining their identification codes, were subordinated to Günther

Chart 3 The structure of Department IV B 4 January–November 1942
Source: TR.10-767, vol. 1, pp. 250–1.

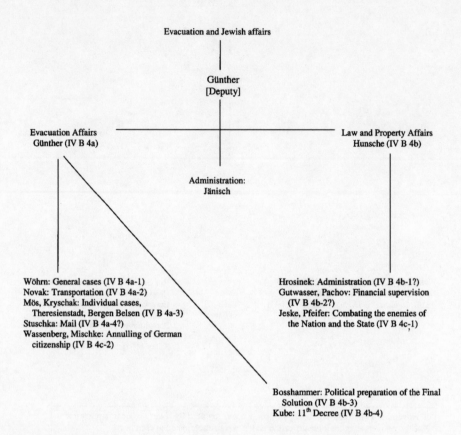

Evacuation and Jewish affairs

Günther
[Deputy]

Evacuation Affairs
Günther (IV B 4a)

Law and Property Affairs
Hunsche (IV B 4b)

Administration:
Jänisch

Wöhrn: General cases (IV B 4a-1)
Novak: Transportation (IV B 4a-2)
Mös, Kryschak: Individual cases,
  Theresienstadt, Bergen Belsen (IV B 4a-3)
Stuschka: Mail (IV B 4a-4?)
Wassenberg, Mischke: Annulling of German
  citizenship (IV B 4c-2)

Hrosinek: Administration (IV B 4b-1?)
Gutwasser, Pachov: Financial supervision
  (IV B 4b-2?)
Jeske, Pfeifer: Combating the enemies of
  the Nation and the State (IV B 4c-1)

Bosshammer: Political preparation of the Final
  Solution (IV B 4b-3)
Kube: 11th Decree (IV B 4b-4)

Chart 4 The structure of Department IV B 4 April 1943–March 1944
Source: TR.10-767, vol. 1, p. 252.

In memory of Avraham Lozowick,
who taught me to question accepted wisdom

Introduction

Jerusalem, ever a city to generate historical events, scored unusually well on the clear day in April 1961, when Adolf Eichmann was put on trial. The world over, people took note that a former SS officer accused of being a central figure in the Nazi policy of murdering the Jews of Europe was about to be tried by a court made up of Jews, in the capital of the Jewish state that had been founded after Germany's defeat. Any trial for a capital crime is dramatic, but this one promised to be historic.

And yet, as the weeks of proceedings turned into months, it became increasingly clear that the story of Adolf Eichmann fighting for his life was not the single event of significance nor even the main one. Of greater social and historical meaning was the parade of witnesses, survivors of the Shoah, who took the stand and riveted the attention of millions. Ordinary men and women, to whom no one had paid attention till then, described in subdued, deferential tones how, in face of adverse conditions the human mind can scarcely grasp, they had preserved considerably more human dignity than their tormentors ever possessed. Totally powerless, they continued to make choices: to die with one's children rather than letting them die alone; to keep going even where there could be no hope. The murder of the European Jews became suddenly the story of individuals, not huge numbers; and Israeli society would never be the same again.

But there was yet a third story born in the court in Jerusalem, even though it would become obvious and significant only years later: This was the clash between Gideon Hausner, the prosecutor, and Hannah Arendt, perhaps the most illustrious spectator. The conflict was about the essence of Eichmann: Was he a human monster or a petty bureaucrat?

Gideon Hausner was born in 1915 in Lemberg, a town then in Habsburg-ruled Galicia but which within a few years of turmoil and war would become Polish Lvov. His father, a rabbi, was a Zionist activist who brought his family to Palestine in 1927. Hausner himself shed his father's orthodoxy, yet remained in many ways similar to the Eastern European Jews murdered by the Nazis. During the proceedings he moved freely among all the various languages used by the survivors: Yiddish, Polish, German, English and of course Hebrew. But for the chance of having been brought out of Europe, he also would have been there. Is it surprising, then, that his understanding of Eichmann was quite simple? Here was one of the major perpetrators of the Final Solution, thus one of history's greatest murderers. By definition he must be a monster, else what does the word mean? "Eichmann," Hausner summed it up a few years later, "was the personification of satanic principles."[1]

Hannah Arendt was far more complex. Like Eichmann himself, she was born in Germany in 1906. By the age of 22 she had completed her doctoral thesis at the prestigious University of Heidelberg as a student of Martin Heidegger. A Jew fleeing from the Nazis, she reached the United States in 1941. She became in 1959 the first woman to be appointed a full professor at Princeton. By the time the *New Yorker* sent her to cover the Eichmann trial she was one of the most prominent political thinkers in the world, author of the seminal *Origins of Totalitarianism*.[2] This was no ordinary journalist.

Years of study of the totalitarian phenomenon had pre-conditioned her perspective on Eichmann. According to her theory, he was a building block in the totalitarian edifice, not a link in the ancient chain of Jew-haters. One of the most riveting chapters in her *Origins* describes "Totalitarian Organizations" as having a pyramidal structure. At the lowest tier are front organizations of volunteers and non-party members. Above them rise a series of party organizations beginning with mass formations and culminating in the secret, inaccessible, innermost group surrounding the Leader. Each level protects the purity of the one above it, drawing its own legitimacy and power from the proximity, but also shielding the higher-ups from reality. Thus, the top floors house the most powerful and dedicated individuals, who are also the furthest removed from what is really going on. Once the totalitarian movement comes to power, the whole society must be integrated into the pyramid; the party, now armed with total power, will do everything to ensure that, where reality and ideology clash, reality will be changed to fit ideological preconceptions.

1. Hausner, Gideon, *Justice in Jerusalem*, New York: Schocken, 1968, p. 13. The formulation is not Hausner's. It is a quotation from Bernhard Lösener, one of Eichmann's erstwhile colleagues, who fell out with him and with the policy of murder during the war. But it was Hausner's decision to use it.
2. Arendt, Hannah, *The Origins of Totalitarianism*, New York: Meridian Books, 1958.

Arendt would probably have placed Eichmann at a high level, though hardly at the pinnacle. The significant point for her, however, was that non-totalitarian criteria for judging reality, normality, not to mention morality, had lost their relevance for anyone inside the totalitarian system. Describing the total lack of communications between those inside and outside, she precluded the possibility that Eichmann's judges might have understood who he was:

> [Eichmann's] was no case of insane hatred of Jews, of fanatical anti-Semitism or indoctrination of any kind. He "personally" had never had anything whatever against Jews; on the contrary, he had plenty of "private reasons" for not being a Jew hater. ... Alas, nobody believed him. The prosecutor did not believe him, because that was not his job. Counsel for the defense paid no attention because he, unlike Eichmann, was, to all appearances, not interested in questions of conscience. And the judges did not believe him, because they were too good, and perhaps also too conscious of the very foundations of their profession, to admit that an average, "normal" person, neither feeble-minded nor indoctrinated nor simple, could be perfectly incapable of telling right from wrong. They preferred to conclude from occasional lies that he was a liar — and missed the greatest moral and even legal challenge of the whole case. Their case rested on the assumption that the defendant, like all "normal persons," must have been aware of the criminal nature of his acts, and Eichmann was indeed normal insofar as he was "no exception within the Nazi regime." However, under the conditions of the Third Reich only "exceptions" could be expected to react "normally." This simple truth of the matter created a dilemma for the judges which they could neither resolve nor escape.[3]

In other words, Arendt is telling us that ordinary people in a totalitarian state, and certainly its functionaries, naturally live by the precepts of their state; they lose touch with the standards of the non-totalitarian world. She summed up this concept in the powerful subtitle to her subsequent book about Eichmann's trial: "A Report on the Banality of Evil". In the postscript, written two years later in answer to detractors and published in all future editions, Arendt spelled out precisely, in plain clear English, what she meant:

3.   Arendt, Hannah, *Eichmann in Jerusalem*, first published in New York, 1963. Citations here are from the New York: Penguin Books, 1992 edition. Here: p. 26.

> When I speak of the banality of evil, I do so only on the strictly factual level, pointing to a phenomenon which stared one in the face at the trial.... Except for an extraordinary diligence in looking out for his personal advancement, [Eichmann] had no motives at all. And this diligence in itself was in no way criminal; he certainly would never have murdered his superior in order to inherit his post. He *merely*, to put the matter colloquially, *never realized what he was doing*. ... That such remoteness from reality and such thoughtlessness can wreak more havoc than all the evil instincts taken together which, perhaps, are inherent in man – that was, in fact, the lesson one could learn in Jerusalem.[4]

The italics are Arendt's, as is her insistence that she presents facts – and not, say, philosophical constructs.

In the duel of explanations between Hausner's monster and Arendt's nondescript bureaucrat blown by the winds of History, Arendt won hands down. Generations of educators, journalists, preachers, politicians and scholars have adopted as fact that the main difference between most of mankind and Adolf Eichmann is the specific historical situation: Most of us, exposed to the historical winds which pushed Eichmann, would probably have been carried away, as he was. Gone was the ancient, biblical story of Genesis that attributes the knowledge of right and wrong to the essence of being human.

There was an abysmal irony in this turn of events. Hausner's historical greatness, by giving individual voices to the survivors of the Holocaust, had shown that even in conditions of total powerlessness and degradation they had remained thinking creatures able to make moral decisions. They were subjects, not objects. Arendt, on the other hand, took the all-powerful SS officer, the murderer, and stripping him of his freedom of choice, turned him into a mere object.

Modern scholars aware of relations between actions and environment often seek the context of narratives. Yet it is too easy to say that Hausner was bound to see Eichmann through the eyes of a potential victim, while Arendt's greater proximity to German culture preconditioned her to minimize Eichmann's significance; that Hausner's Jewish commitment necessarily led him to conclusions other than those of Arendt, the archetypal universalist. For all the significance of nurture, it is the historian's task to scrutinize the facts as coolly as possible. This

---

4.   Arendt, *Eichmann*, pp. 287–8. Italics in the original.

method lacks the dramatic flair of a brilliant woman asserting her truths with the authority of her undoubted erudition, yet has the advantage of being open to empirical evaluation.

This study is not a biography of Eichmann. The focus will be on Eichmann and the bureaucrats he worked with, mainly his subordinates in Berlin, and his counterparts in several of the more significant Gestapo offices in Western Europe. Not all of them knew each other, but all knew Eichmann, and all held similar jobs: They were the desktop murderers.

The first group were the officers and NCOs of the SD (*Sicherheitsdienst*) who sat in Berlin in the 1930s and studied German and World Jewry, whom they saw as Germany's arch-enemies. Five of them will appear repeatedly in our story. Dieter Wislicency was born in East Prussia in 1911. He had once studied theology and had intended to be a minister, until he changed his mind and joined the SA (*Sturmabteilung*) in 1931.[5] In 1936–7 he was Eichmann's commander, but Eichmann was more ambitious, and throughout most of the war he was the commanding officer of Wislicency. When Wislicency left, his successor was Herbert Hagen, who was born in 1913. He will re-appear in our story as the personal assistant to the top SS commander in France.[6] Two additional colleagues of Eichmann, NCOs in the 1930s and officers in the 1940s, were Theodor Dannecker and Richard Hartmann. Dannecker was born in 1913, Hartmann was three years older. Both had failed to complete their secondary education, and both had been members of Nazi formations prior to the takeover of power – Hartmann as early as 1930.[7]

During the war Eichmann was the commander of department IV B 4 of the Security Police, with a main office in Berlin and a branch in Prague. Hartmann, now his subordinate, was there with him, as were dozens of others. Among them we will repeatedly meet his deputy, Major Rolf Günther, a scarred veteran of many street battles fought between the Nazis and their adversaries prior to 1933. He had joined the SA in 1929, when he was 16, even before he completed his high-school studies.[8]

5. Bauer, Yehuda, *Jews for Sale? Nazi–Jewish Negotiations 1933–1945*, New Haven, CT: Yale University Press, 1994, p. 65.
6. Klarsfeld, Serge, *Vichy-Auschwitz: Die Zusammenarbeit der deutschen und französischen Behörden bei der 'Endlösung der Judenfrage' in Frankreich*, Nördlingen: Delphi Politik, 1989, p. 593.
7. BDC, YVA O.68, Richard Hartmann, Theodor Dannecker.
8. BDC, YVA O.68, Rolf Günther; Eichmann, Adolf, *Ich, Adolf Eichmann: Ein historischer Zeugenbericht*, Hrsg. von Rudolph Aschenauer, Leoni: Druffel Verlag, 1980, p. 409.

Captain Franz Novak was the same age, and had joined the Nazis at the same time. He had no secondary education, and was Austrian.[9] Slightly unusual in this group, Captain Friedrich Bosshammer was 36 years old at the peak of activity in 1942. He had joined the party in May 1933 and the SS in November 1937, for professional reasons – as a young and not very successful attorney, he had not found employment in the civil sector.[10]

A third group were the SS officers stationed in The Netherlands. One of them, Lieutenant Dr Erich Rajakowitz befriended Eichmann in Vienna in 1938, and was then sent by him to Amsterdam. He was a lawyer who had not been a member of any Nazi organization before Austria's annexation to the Reich, but, according to his confession after the war, he had supported them, and his decision to join the party in the spring of 1938 had been a natural one.[11] The chief of the Security Police was *Oberführer* (Senior Colonel) Dr Wilhelm Harster, a police attorney by profession, 39 years old at the peak of his activity. He had joined the party and the SS only in the spring of 1933, but should not be seen as a mere opportunist, because from his youth onward he had belonged to a series of nationalist organizations, including the *Freikorps*.[12] Major Wilhelm Zöpf, 32 years old, had been his friend for years. He was also a lawyer, and had been equally politically active.[13]

Yet another group was stationed in France: SS-Colonel Dr Helmut Knochen, an economist, was born in 1910. He had been a member of the *Freikorps*, the right-wing, ultra-nationalist paramilitary militias led by First World War veterans that engaged in partisan military campaigns in the 1920s, and had been a member of the party and the SA since 1932. During his university years he had been active in the Nazi student organization.[14] First Lieutenant Heinz Röthke, a lawyer born in 1912, had studied theology in his youth.[15] Knochen's deputy, Lieutenant-Colonel Kurt Lischka, was one year older and also a lawyer. He had not been a

9. TR.10-515, pp. 9–13.
10. BDC, YVA O.68, Fritz Bosshammer; TR.10-767a, pp. 14–19.
11. Anklageschrift, 15 St 25696/61, YVA TR.10-623.
12. BDC,YVA O.68, Wilhelm Harster; Anklageschrift 14 b Js 48/59, YVA TR.10-978, pp. 16–17.
13. TR.10-978, pp. 19–20.
14. BDC, YVA O.68, Helmut Knochen.
15. Klarsfeld, *Vichy*, p. 594.

member of the party organization before the Nazis came to power, but had joined the SS in June 1933.[16]

Eichmann himself was born in Solingen, but grew up in Austria, and never completed his secondary studies. He joined the Austrian SS in 1932, having previously been a member of a right-wing youth group. He rose swiftly to the rank of lieutenant-colonel, and then got stuck, to his great chagrin.[17]

Although their social backgrounds and education varied, they were all young, male, Christian, and nationalist-minded Germans; they had all voluntarily joined the SS. Isn't this, from the start, too narrow a group to be indicative of all humanity?[18]

At this point it is important to clarify: mass murder by the state is not a Nazi invention. The American scholar Rudolf Rummel has published a series of studies on governments each responsible for the murder of a million or more human beings in the twentieth century. The Chinese and the Soviets spilled more blood than the Nazis, and each of the three regimes murdered more than ten million people; Rummel awards them the name of deca-mega-murderers. In total, he finds that some 170 million people have been murdered by governments, among them 151 million by

16. BDC, YVA O.68, Kurt Lischka; Klarsfeld, *Vichy*, p. 593.
17. Eichmann, Adolf, *Ich, Adolf Eichmann: Ein historischer Zeugenbericht*, ed. by Rudolph Aschenauer, Leoni: Druffel Verlag, 1980, pp. 65–6. Leni Yahil has analyzed this book, and comes to the conclusion that it is basically the interviews given by Eichmann to the Dutch journalist Sassen in the late 1950s. Leni Yahil, " 'Memoirs' of Adolf Eichmann," YVS, XVIII, 1987.
18. Hilberg, who is in a position to know, has pointed out that the bureaucrats who dealt with the Final Solution were fundamentally no different from the rest of their society, that there was no specific training needed in order to do so, and that individuals could be recruited into the heart of the operation at random. Hilberg, Raul, *The Destruction of the European Jews*, New York: Holmes & Meier, p. 1011. While this is undoubtedly true, and significant, it seems nonetheless also to be true that the specific group here dealt with, the SS officers in the middle ranks, had often been involved with the political right for years. Although former members of the leftist SPD could be drafted into reserve police units and sent to murder Jews, there do not seem to have been many of them in this group.
    Interestingly, Henry Friedlander's research into the socio-economic profile of the operators in the T4 program of murdering the German handicapped, found very similar results, especially that they had joined the Nazi party or some ideologically related formation long before this was the obvious way to promote one's career. However, Friedlander's reading of this differs considerably from the thesis suggested here. Friedlander, Henry, *The Origins of Nazi Genocide: From Euthanasia to the Final Solution*, Chapel Hill, NC: The University of North Carolina Press, 1995, p. 191.

15 regimes that murdered a million or more. Governments that try to solve their problems by mass murder are a minority, but unfortunately not a rare phenomenon. Yet the previous sentence contains an important distinction: the potential ability of certain regimes to conduct a policy of murder does not necessarily imply a similar potential at all times, or in all places, or by all regimes. Rummel found, for example, that democratic regimes do not commit genocide.[19] Arendt and her followers blur this distinction. Having identified universal traits in the Nazis, they wish us to accept that in spirit we are all potential accomplices: there, but for the grace of circumstance, go we.

Two events should be mentioned that took place during the years when I carried out this study. First, my colleague and friend Hans Safrian of Vienna preceded me with his book *Die Eichmann Männer*.[20] It contains a fine description of Eichmann as the man who sent his forces across the continent, and of their work there. I saw no need to imitate him, or to engage him on one or another marginal point. Second, I myself became a bureaucrat, one who receives and answers letters, sits in meetings, writes memos, and tries to change something in the world by pushing paper.

Relieved of the need to show Eichmann at work in every corner, I delved into what Safrian had not addressed: the bureaucracy. As I dug deeper, I grew more and more uncomfortable with Arendt's explanations. *The more I came to know these bureaucrats, the less familiar they became.* I realized that this was a group of people completely aware of what they were doing, people with high ideological motivation, people of initiative and dexterity who contributed far beyond what was necessary. And there could be no doubt about it: they clearly understood that their deeds were *not* positive except in the value system of the Third Reich. They hated Jews and thought that getting rid of them would be to Germany's good. They knew that not everyone thought this way, and they deliberately hid information that might have deterred others from cooperating. While most of them sat behind desks rather than behind machine guns, from

19. Rummel, Rudolf J., *Death by Government*, New Brunswick, NJ: Transaction Publishers, 1994, pp. 3–4. Great Britain and the United States *do* appear at the bottom of the list of delinquents, because of their bombing of German and Japanese cities during WWII, and in the British case, because of the blockade of the Central Powers in WWI. Even these cases, however, were in the context of wars against non-democratic powers. Rummel, *Death*, p. 6, and especially pp. 16 ff.
20. Safrian, Hans, *Die Eichmann Männer*, Wien: Europaverlag, 1993.

time to time some were called on to face flesh and blood Jews and decide their fate, and this they did, ferociously, without batting an eyelid.

The facts that stare one in the face, it seems to me, indicate the opposite of Arendt's thesis: There was nothing banal about the evil of Eichmann and his comrades.

From the testimony at the Eichmann trial

Abba Kovner

[Upon the liberation, in Vilna] I saw a desert of walls and empty streets. When I came to a certain street, a woman suddenly ran towards us, and the woman held a little girl in her arms. ... She ran forward towards us and began, in a hysterical voice, to tell her story. What I understood from her was that she and the child, who looked like a three-year-old but who was certainly four or older, had been hiding in an alcove for more than 11 months. How they were able to exist in that alcove and to live for 11 months — I couldn't understand. She poured out her story. She burst out crying, bitterly. At that moment, the child in her arms, who had seemed to be dumb, opened her mouth and said: *"Mama, men darf shein weinen?"* (mother, are we allowed to cry already?). ... This question by the little girl says more than enough. However, I don't know whether the innocent question of a baby is evidence at a trial.

(*The Trial of Adolf Eichmann*, vol. I, pp. 455–6)

Chapter 1

From Theory to Practice: 1933–8

Political police are neither a German nor a Nazi invention. In fact, there seems to have been a connection between the rise of the nation state and of political police forces, even if the linkage is not always direct, and even if the police organizations took different forms in different places.[1] The authority of political police forces grew as the power of the central government increased. Imperial Germany, for example, trained special policemen to keep watch on public organizations and prominent figures. By the end of the First World War, the records of the political police in Hamburg alone filled thousands of volumes, and included many reports on the Social Democratic party. The surveillance of this party did not cease even when one of its members was president of the Republic and another was prime minister.

The founders of the Weimar Republic had wanted to establish a more liberal regime. Political policemen were to have no place in it, and the force – which was called Division V – was duly disbanded in Prussia in 1919. But the new democracy found its stability threatened by extremists at both ends of the political spectrum and soon sacrificed ideological purity on the altar of survival. To make it sound better, however, the new unit was given a different designation; in the Berlin police force it was called Division 1A. A similar process took place in other German states.[2]

This should not, however, be misinterpreted. On the eve of the Nazis' rise to power, police surveillance of political activity was far more benign than what the police commanders of the Third Reich aspired to and achieved. The substantial differences are much more numerous than the similarities and continuities. The Nazi political police was largely a new creature. Was the new form it took an inevitable outgrowth of the regime's ideology, or was it the men who set up the new political

1. R. Gellately, *The Gestapo and German Society: Enforcing Racial Policy, 1933–1945*, Oxford: Clarendon Press, 1990, pp. 22–3. He quotes Foucault, *Discipline and Punish*, pp. 218, 273.
2. Gellately, *Gestapo*, pp. 24–6; Buchheim, in Krausnik *et al.*, *Anatomy*, London: Collins, 1968, pp. 144–5.

watchdog force – Heinrich Himmler, the Commandant of the SS (the Reichsführer SS or RFSS) and his right-hand man, Reinhard Heydrich – who molded and fashioned it?

The SS was set up within the SA in 1923, and was reestablished after a hiatus in 1925, to provide protection for party speakers from the disturbances that were a routine part of Weimar political culture and a notable feature of Nazi rallies in particular. When Himmler was appointed Commandant of the SS in 1929 it had 280 men. When the Nazis came to power less than four years later it had 50,000. While support for the party greatly increased during these years and its membership swelled, the staggering growth of the SS was due mostly to the talent of Himmler, who was expert at getting a large variety of missions assigned to his organization. One of these growth measures was the establishment, in 1931, of an internal security service called the *Sicherheitsdienst*, or SD, whose job it was to gather intelligence about enemies of the party, both external and internal. In setting up the SD, Himmler enlisted a young officer who had recently joined the SS, after being cashiered from the navy for unbecoming conduct. This was 28-year-old Reinhard Heydrich.[3]

The SS was an organ of the party. Theoretically, at least, the Nazi rise to power was not supposed to change this. Citizens owe allegiance to the state and its government, not to a political party, even if that party is in power. The government can enforce its policies and require all citizens to obey its laws, but a party can impose its will only on those who voluntarily join it. Nazi party leaders could use political terror to enforce their party's policies, but if they wanted to act in the name of the state, they had to hold an official state office in addition to their party position. So, on March 1, 1933 Himmler received the relatively junior post of Chief of Police in Munich, and he appointed Heydrich to be commander of the political police there.[4]

Himmler and Heydrich established and broadened their power through a series of intrigues.[5] In doing so, they succeeded in bringing

3.   For a detailed description of the political violence of the times, see Charles B. Flood, *Hitler, the Path to Power*, Boston: Houghton Mifflin, 1989; for the development of the SS and police formations: Heinrich Höhne, *The Order of the Death's Head*, London: Secker & Warburg, 1969; Hans Buchheim, "The SS – Instrument of Domination", in Krausnik *et al., Anatomy*; Shlomo Aronson, *Heydrich und die Anfaenge des SD und der Gestapo*, Stuttgart: Freie Universität, 1971.

4.   Aronson, *Heydrich*, p. 98.

5.   Aronson, *Heydrich*; George C. Browder, *Foundations of the Nazi Police State: The Formation of Sipo and SD*, Lexington, KY: University Press of Kentucky, 1989.

about fundamental changes in the nature of the police force as a whole and in the political police in particular. First, they united the police forces in the different states into a single national organization. Second, they were able to obtain for the political police terrifying operational tools, such as "protective custody" and the connection with the concentration camps. These demonstrate the profound discontinuity between the national civil ideology of the Weimar Republic and that of the Third Reich. On the basis of these two changes, Himmler and Heydrich were able to bring about a growing integration of the different branches of the police force, which was a government agency, and the SS, which was a Nazi party body that pursued ideological goals.

During the first stage, they set up political police units that were independent of the regular police. On March 15, 1933, Himmler was appointed Chief of the Political Police for the entire state of Bavaria, a post that had not existed until then. He would hold this new position in addition to continuing to serve as police chief of Munich. Heydrich's job was to organize an efficient body that would advance Nazi interests from within the political police of Munich. In parallel, in Prussia, Goering created a headquarters for a political police force independent of the general police – the *Geheime Staatspolizeiamt*, or Gestapo. This head-quarters was established in stages until April 16, 1933, and was located on 6 Prinz Albrechstrasse, in the same building that housed the security police headquarters. At the head of the organization stood Rudolf Diels, a public servant from the interior ministry who had been in charge of surveillance of the Communist party even before the Nazis came to power.

During the second stage, Himmler and Heydrich took control of the political police forces in all the rest of the German states, with the exception of Prussia, by planting their own men in key positions throughout the country. Werner Best recalled that Himmler was prepared to engage in shameless flattery of the state governors in order to get the appointments he wanted; it may well be that Hitler made it clear that he supported Himmler in this matter.[6] On April 20, 1934 Goering appointed

---

6.   The best description of this process is to be found in Browder, *Foundations*, chap. 9. Also, Aronson, *Heydrich*, p. 169. Ulrich Herbert, in his magnificent biography of Best (*Best: Biographische Studien über Radikalismus, Weltanschauung und Vernunft, 1903–1989*, Bonn: Dietz, 1996) has shown how untrustworthy the postwar statements of Werner Best really were, and how too many important historians, including Aronson, allowed him to unduly influence their understanding of the

Himmler his deputy in the Prussian political police. From this point onward, for the first time in German history, the barriers to coordinated work by all the political police forces in all of Germany were removed. Legally the forces of each state were independent, but in practice Heinrich Himmler was the commander of all of them.

The third stage was reached only in 1936. On June 17 of that year, Hitler signed an order appointing Himmler Chief of German Police in the Ministry of the Interior. This was significant in two ways. First, all the police forces throughout Germany were now united into a central police force. Second, and even more important, the police force was tied to the SS. "A process was thus initiated which first diluted and then gradually obliterated governmental authority over the police – the process of integrating the police into the sphere of authority of the *Reichsführer-SS.*"[7] All the police forces in Germany were united now under a single common command. The national chief of police was also the commandant of the SS forces, who was under the Führer's direct command. In practice, the German police force now operated at Hitler's will, without being under control of the civil aparatus. Or, to put it another way: if, starting in 1933, the SS had drawn closer to the police and encroached on its prerogatives, from this time onward the police force drew close to the SS and took on more and more of its traits and roles.

This was a historic milestone, the beginning of a new era. About a week after Himmler's great victory and his appointment as police commandant, he issued an order about the police force's new organizational structure. It established the *Ordnungspolizei* (Order Police), or Orpo, and placed Kurt Daluege at its head. It also established the *Sicherheitspolizei* (Security Police) or Sipo, which included two sub-branches: the *Kriminalpolizei* (Criminal Police) or Kripo and the *Geheime Staatspolizei* (Political Police) or Gestapo. Heydrich was commander of the Security Police.[8] Significantly, the two new forces, Orpo and Sipo, were termed "head offices" – and head offices existed only in the SS and not in the civil system. In this way, Himmler made it absolutely clear that the

cont.

period. Nevertheless, this particular statement seems correctly to reflect the characters involved, and is not of central importance to Best's project of rewriting history.

7. Buchheim, in *Anatomy*, p. 157.
8. Order of Himmler, 26.6.1936, quoted in Browder, *Foundations*, p. 231.

police had been integrated into the SS. At the same time, he separated the political police from the rest of the police force and attached the criminal police to it. He brought the police force close to the SS, but distanced from it the most ideological units. Point and counterpoint, for the advancement of his goals.

Himmler, Daluege, and Heydrich now stood at the head of the new national police hierarchy; they also stood at the head of the SS. This duplication created a wide opening for camouflage and and bureaucratic evasion. They gave orders and carried out actions under different titles, with their places in the chain of authority left vague. To give a concrete illustration, Police Chief Himmler was subordinate to Minister of the Interior Wilhelm Frick, but SS Commandant Himmler was subordinate to no one but Hitler.

This blurring of the boundaries between party and state was evident not only in the chain of command but also in the way the police worked. A prime example of this was the institution of *Schutzhaft*, or "protective custody."

Orginally, protective custody was meant to protect the detainee from danger to his own well-being. But as early as the First World War an entirely different understanding of the term became firmly rooted – detention meant to protect the state from a possible future crime against it. In an attempt to balance the state's security needs with the rights of the detainee, the police were required to obtain court approval, and the detainee was given the right to appeal. Even then, the government was uncomfortable with this arrangement, and in 1932 the police lost the power to impose this sort of protective custody. Limited use of protective custody was reinstated a short time later, during the maelstrom of the final days of the Weimar Republic. But the real turning point was the state of emergency promulgated the day after the Reichstag fire.[9] While protective custody was not mentioned in the state of emergency declaration, the suspension of the fundamental right of personal liberty meant in practical terms that the police would be allowed to arrest people for unlimited periods, without any external review of the reasons for the detention. Such freedom of action was unprecedented in Germany, and the Security Police would make broad use of it.

---

9. Signed by Hindenburg, by advice of the cabinet, 28.2.1933. Klaus, *The Third Reich*, London: George Allen & Unwin, 1984, p. 5. In addition to Aronson, *Heydrich*, valuable information on "protective custody" is to be found in Gellately, *Gestapo*.

Even before the Nazis came to power there were officials who were considering bringing back protective custody on a large scale; it was clear that prison facilities would have to be erected for this purpose.[10] Before a decision was made on the idea, and certainly before it was carried out, the government changed. The Nazis moved quickly to implement the program. The first camps were established largely by SA units; their subordination to any official bodies was loose, and in Prussia police commanders were forced to bargain and compromise in order to obtain control over them. Himmler was more successful in Bavaria. He was able to establish a three-way system in which he headed the SS and the police and Heydrich ran the political police, as a state organ, while the prison camps (Dachau, to begin with) were run by the SS (Heydrich's counterpart was Theodor Eicke, the commandant of Dachau). In doing this, Himmler copied the model established by Hitler, who made a practice of dividing tasks between rival organizations, thus strengthening his position as the only arbitrator between them. Eicke was not in the police force, and he had no right to arrest people or to impose protective custody; on the other hand, Heydrich had nowhere to house his detainees except in the camps. Himmler alone controlled the entire system, as part of his double authority as SS commandant on the one hand and police commandant on the other. This model of separation between the police and the camps was preserved, in its general outlines, until 1945.

One of the leading figures in shaping the role of the camps in the new regime was Werner Best, a talented attorney and Heydrich's deputy. He was able to phrase the intentions of his commanders in legal language and impose their goals on the existing authorities. The cornerstone of his outlook was that the role of the government was to protect the state and society from their enemies, and that in the battle against the most dangerous enemies it was forbidden to tie the state's hands in any way. The Security Police fought this battle for the government, and in the struggle it was above the law. Its actions, it was claimed, should not be subject to any supervision whatsoever: lawyers should not act on behalf of detainees, government offices should not make regulations, and courts should not intervene, because the enemies of the state would know how to take advantage of these limitations. Nor should any restrictions be allowed on the use of force against enemies while they were being interrogated or kept in the camps (although in the summer of 1937 Best

10. Aronson, *Heydrich*, p. 90.

gave his consent to mild restrictions demanded by the Ministry of Justice, because he realized that they amounted to nothing). Of course, the definition of individuals or groups as enemies of the state was purely ideological and required absolutely no basis in fact. The ideology and its servants were above any law, even Nazi law.[11]

Himmler made no secret that these were his intentions. He recorded his expectations from the police in the Third Reich in a collection of articles prepared in honor of the 60th birthday of Minister of the Interior Frick, in March 1937.

> The leadership roles [of the Reich] are the preservation and development of all the forces of the nation. The personal well-being of the individual will be set aside in the face of these tasks, because the significance of the individual and the expression of his existence is in the framework of the people and not the individual. ... The National Socialist police fulfills the will of the leadership for the security of the people and the state not through individual laws, but through the reality of the National Socialist leadership regime, and from within the missions assigned it [the police] by the leadership. For this reason it is not to be held back by formal constraints, because these [legal] limitations will then restrain the leadership itself.[12]

In plain language: the police will do what the leader tells it to, without legal restrictions, and without considering the needs of the individual, because the leader knows what is really required for the nation's welfare.[13] Heydrich made a similar distinction between a "defensive" and an "offensive" police force. Traditionally, Heydrich argued, police forces protect the existing order, but the National Socialist police force had to be on the offensive and act to assist in the establishment of a National Socialist society and regime.[14] They all understood precisely how different the police force under their command was from any traditional police force.

11. For a detailed discussion of these twin issues, "protective custody" and torture by the security police, see Herbert, *Best*, pp. 150–60.
12. Quoted from Ruth Bettina Birn, *Die Höheren SS- und Polizeiführer: Himmlers Vertreter im Reich und in den besetzten Gebieten*, Düsseldorf: Droste, 1968, p. 8.
13. For a brilliant analysis of this train of thought see Hannah Arendt, *The Origins of Totalitarianism*, 2nd edn, New York: Meridian Books, 1958, chap. 11 ("Totalitarian Propaganda"), pp. 341 ff.
14. Birn, *HSSPF*, p. 8.

On January 25, 1938, Frick issued a directive authorizing the Gestapo to place under protective custody any person representing a danger to the people, the state, or to security. The directive, which remained in force until the collapse of the Third Reich, also forbade the use of protective custody as a punitive measure,[15] but that probably got a smile out of Himmler and Heydrich. When you could put someone in jail by saying he was dangerous, who needed punitive powers?

There were plenty of men under their command who liked that kind of talk. George L. Browder called them "radical enforcers," men with no patience for legal niceties. They wanted to get their job done, and their job was to protect society. Humanitarian considerations and legal requirements were considered hindrances. He notes that many such policemen in Germany came from right-wing anti-Communist, but not necessarily Nazi, backgrounds. The most prominent of these was Heinrich Müller, chief of the Gestapo during the war,[16] but he was not unusual. Most Gestapo men had worked in the police force before the Nazi rise to power. Only a few of them had had ties to the Nazis or the SS prior to 1933, and these few were found among the new recruits. That they had no earlier links with the SS does not, however, mean they were indifferent to its goals.

> It would be less than accurate to suggest that these men remained the "apolitical experts" they are alleged to have been. Many of them had, or at least developed, definite political views, and they found the powers of the police over suspects much more palatable than the far more restricted ones of the old Weimar democracy. They were every bit as interested in "cleaning up the country" as their masters, and certainly needed little prodding to move with brutality and violence against the ever-increasing numbers of people who were declared opponents and criminals.[17]

"When it came to enforcing racial policies designed to isolate the Jews, there can be no doubt that the wrath of the Gestapo knew no bounds, often dispensing with even the semblance of legal procedures."[18]

Policemen in many countries secretly, and perhaps not so secretly,

15. ZSL AR 518/59 Bd.II, p. 291.
16. Browder, "The SD: The Image and Significance of Organization," in George L. Mosse (ed.), *Police Forces in History*, London: Sage, 1975.
17. Gellately, *Gestapo*, p. 255; see also pp. 50–7.
18. Gellately, *Gestapo*, pp. 186–7.

long to battle their enemies without legal constraints. What demands explanation is not this utopian yearning, but the actual willingness to act without restraint.[19] A policeman might have such wishes, and even expresses them verbally, but this need not mean that he will act accordingly when the restrictions are removed. It may well be that the strength of the wish is a product of the inability to act on it (this is something like someone saying "Hold me back or I'll kill him" when what he really means is "Because you are holding me back, I can say that I want to kill him").[20] In the meantime, the question is an open one: will the average policeman act up to the boundary of what is permitted him, and if he is allowed to act without restraint will he do so? Or do the constraints perhaps reflect a fundamental recognition, both by the policeman and by the society in which he lives, that not every goal sanctifies every means – and perhaps even that there are means which cannot be sanctified by any goal? There is also a larger question: were German policemen ordinary policemen? Or were their actions determined more by their cultural conditioning and other local factors than by the fact that they were policemen?

To understand the organizational context of the Security Police during the war years, it is necessary to examine another important stage in its evolution. The prewar Political Police was largely a professional force with a certain ideological identification, or at least a professional willingness to support an ideological policy for the solution of society's ills. On the way to the creation of the Nazi Security Police of the war years, it was merged with its mirror image, an ideological organization that gained, over time, professional expertise – the SD. By SD, I mean the active SD – those parts within the Head Office of Reich Security which

19. My thanks to Dr Dierk Jülich of Hamburg for his insights on this point. And see Dierk Jülich, "Erlebtes und Ererbtes Trauma," Lecture given at Akademie Frankenwarte, Würzburg, 15.5.1993; also Dierk Jülich, "Die Wiederkehr des Verdrängten – Sozialpsychologische Aspekte zur Identität der Deutschen nach Auschwitz," in H. Schreier and M. Heyl, *Das Echo des Holocaust*, Hamburg: Verlag Dr R. Kramer, 1992.
20. This scene, so familiar to anyone who has ever seen a Mediterranean brawl, would be totally foreign in some other cultures. Anyone who speaks more than one language and has lived in more than one society will be aware of the fact that different cultures supply their members with different modes of articulating – and controlling – emotions and impulses.

during the war carried out the original SD missions: information collection within the state and from overseas.[21]

The SD was established in 1931 as the intelligence organization of the SS. Heydrich was appointed its commander in 1932. In the summer of 1934, when Himmler and Heydrich emerged as the powers in the Security Police throughout the Reich, Heydrich succeeded in grounding the status of the SD as well. An order from Deputy Führer Rudolf Hess on June 9, 1934 established that the SD was to be the only intelligence organization in the party. Another order, from July 4, 1934, immediately after the liquidation of the leaders of the SA in the Night of the Long Knives, set out the division of labor between the SD and the Security Police – the police would fight the enemies of the National Socialist state, while the SD would fight the enemies of the National Socialist idea. In keeping with this, the police would carry out operations that were forbidden the SD and the SD would concentrate on gathering intelligence and transferring it to the Political Police when operational action was needed; SD and police stations would work in coordination with each other.[22] The logic of this division of labor was twofold: when operational activity – that is, arrests – were required, they were carried out by the Political Police, since the SD, which was solely a party organization, had no legal authority to make arrests. There were other cases, however, when the criminal evidence was not sufficient for police action, especially ideological enemies, whose actions were defined as negative not because of what they did but because of the Nazi interpretation of what they did. In such cases the SD acted, because this was an area that was beyond the law where the police were not permitted to act.[23]

The SD was a very small organization. In the fall of 1933 it had no more than 300 men; at the end of 1935, perhaps a thousand, and about 3000 at the beginning of 1937. Heydrich drew a whole range of characters into the organization. About a quarter of them were veterans of front-line combat units of the First World War, and of the *Freikorps*; the

21. The term SD is also used in two other ways. Sometimes it refers to the entire Security Police, *SD und Sipo*, including the *Einsatzgruppen*. This is the common, but imprecise, use. At other times it is used to mean what would be better termed the "total SD" – that is, the SS officers in the Security Police, as well as the new recruits to the police force who were not holdovers from the previous regime. These were considered the most loyal foundations of the regime within the system. See Browder, "SD," in Mosse, *Police Forces*.

22. Quoted from Aronson, *Heydrich*, p. 196.

23. Aronson, *Heydrich*, pp. 196–7. The interpretation is mine – Y.L.

rest were younger. Many had been members of the party and the SS even before they reached the SD. Some historians have identified in many of them problems of dysfunctional self-assurance and inability to integrate into normal society – problems that were solved by joining a framework that defined itself as elitist.[24] Others have devoted their attention to a secondary group among the enlistees, men who had an educational profile much higher than that found in most Nazi frameworks, holding law or other types of academic degrees. It was this group of some 300 young men who afterwards became the spearhead of Nazi ideological policy, the hard-core Nazi criminals.[25]

The SD's work was divided among three branches (called *Ämter*). Amt I dealt with administration, Amt II dealt with information from within the Reich, and Amt III collected information from outside the Reich. Within Amt II, divisions II 1 and II 3 handled "enemies of the world-view" (*Weltanschauliche Gegner*), subdivision II 11 dealt with enemies: the church, Judaism; according to the division within this subdivision, II 112 dealt with Jews. The numbering system went on to lower levels: Eichmann was in charge of information on the Zionists, and he was called II 1123.[26] The commanders of II 112 were Leopold von Mildenstein, who was replaced by Kuno Schröder. When Schröder left in the summer of 1936, Wislicency, his commander, took his place until Hagen was appointed to the post at the end of the year.[27]

At the head of the sister unit, the Department of Jewish Affairs in the Security Police, stood Dr Karl Haselbacher, a lawyer by training. From 1934 to 1937 his department dealt with the legal aspects of restricting Jewish freedom. When the policy changed and the center of gravity switched to forced mass emigration, in 1938, his department was pushed out of the center of the picture and he was transferred to another post, in

24. Browder, "SD," in Mosse, *Police Forces*.
25. Aronson, *Heydrich*, pp. 160–5; Herbert, *Best*, pp. 13 ff., 228 ff. Michael Wildt is currently writing a "group biography" of these men.
26. Aronson, *Heydrich*, pp. 202–3. This organizational structure was completed in January 1936, following a period of repeated changes; this time it remained stable until the begining of the war. For a full description, see Michael Wildt, *Die Judenpolitik des SD 1935 bis 1938: Eine Dokumentation, Schriftenreihe der Vierteljahrshefte für Zeitgeschichte*, München: Oldenbourg, 1995.
27. Aronson, *Heydrich*, p. 203. US National Archives T–175 roll 410 frame 2934963–69: Mildenstein replaced, 17.2.37, by Schröder. Frame 2934977–82: report from 5.7.37 that Schröder is leaving, and Wislicency, commander of II/1 took direct command of the department.

Vienna. He was killed in France in 1940, which may have saved him from the eternal disgrace that some of his colleagues later endured for their actions.[28]

While the Gestapo's Department of Jewish Affairs persecuted those who had violated the anti-Jewish laws, such as the Purity of Race Law, II 112 tried to follow the form and activity of "World Jewry". This was in keeping with Himmler's order of July 1, 1936, according to which the department was responsible for all Jewish issues that were not directly under the purview of the Security Police.[29]

*

The portrait up to this point is not that of a typical police force. In generalizing from the deeds of its men to the possibilities latent in every human being, or in every bureaucrat as part of a system, or in every policeman as one who must grapple with enemies of society, this must be kept in mind. The bureaucrats on which this study focuses acted in the framework of a bureaucratic system, or more precisely, a police system, which was not only different from a typical police force, but which was also unprecedented in Germany. For the first time there was a united police force in all of Germany; for the first time it had commanders who openly declared goals of a new kind, goals unfettered by legal constraints, or by the restrictions that characterize democratic societies; for the first time the police force was called on to make routine use of ideological protective custody; for the first time it was tied to extra-governmental forces – concentration camps as an operational tool and the SD as an ideological beacon – which pushed it in entirely new directions.

None of this can decide the issue. Did these new systems turn normal men into monsters, or did men with monstrous tendencies take advantage of an opportunity to act on their base urges? Perhaps both possibilities are no more than inverse expressions of a third explanation, which is that the normal contains within it a potential for monstrousness – that monstrousness, under certain conditions, is itself normal? What is clear from this description is that there was no fortuitousness here. Those who designed the system, and those who remained within it and acted according to its rules, knew what they were doing, and they knew that the situation was a new one, perhaps unprecedented.

28. Aronson, *Heydrich*, pp. 177–8; Wildt, *Die Judenpolitik*, p. 14.
29. NA T–175 r.410 fr.2934988–90. JM.4711.

If we are to believe their stories, in the 1930s they were certainly still innocent bureaucrats, even with positive personality traits. In recalling his activities during this period, Eichmann described himself as a convinced Zionist and an inquisitive student of the Jewish world.[30]

The picture outlined in the documents of the period is different.

On August 28, 1936, Schröder (then an *Oberscharführer*, or sergeant) wrote a summary of the activities of his department. He acknowledged that up until the end of 1935 they had not done enough in the battle against Judaism, because the department's men were too busy learning the subject. Now charts had been prepared with tables, updated as needed, describing the various Jewish organizations. The charts also served as teaching aids. At the beginning of May 1936 a week-long course was held for experts on Jewish affairs in the local SD stations. The problem was that some of those who attended were transferred afterwards to other departments, where there was no demand for their knowledge. The regional departments submitted monthly reports. The staff of II 112 was now preparing information files on the different organizations, and these would be sent afterwards to C (Heydrich's code name). The department staff, together with the staff of the parallel department in the Security Police of Berlin, were visiting Jewish gatherings for both surveillance and research purposes. The hope was that there would soon be approval for dividing the department into subunits, each one of which would keep track of a different arm of Judaism – assimilationists, religious Jews, Zionists. The report concludes with a statement of principle: The Jew as a human being, is, by his race and nationality, an absolute enemy of National Socialism. He influences other nations with his hostile ideologies, such as liberalism, and especially with his tools: Freemasonry, Marxism, and Christianity. But this understanding was to be based on facts, and the presentation of these matters in an unfounded or fantastic way, as is done "by those termed antisemites" (the reference is apparently to Julius Streicher and his like) should be avoided. Guidelines in this spirit were given to the regional experts in the various courses they attended.[31]

During 1936 reports on different Jewish organizations were written in the department. Schröder wrote about ORT, the Jewish vocational training and educational organization. The report described its

30. Eichmann, *Interrogation*, vol. 1, p. 139.
31. NA T–175 r.410 fr.2934344–46. YVA JM.4711.

organizational structure and prominent figures, and included a diagram, as well as a map of the Reich showing the organization's deployment and a list of activists and their addresses – a total of 36 pages. The author was especially impressed with how this farflung network was spread throughout the Reich, enabling the Jews to send secret information through clandestine channels. This was especially dangerous because ORT was extremely hostile to the Reich. It was aided by Wall Street economic barons on the one hand, and by Marxist workers on the other. "This is an organization worthy of special attention," he concluded.[32]

On July 27, 1936 Eichmann finished writing a short report on Agudat Yisrael, an organization of the ultra-orthodox Jewish community. He stated that Agudat Yisrael hardly engaged in any political activity, although it had strong ties to organizations outside the country that were inciting against the Reich. He attached a map of the deployment of the organization's officials throughout the Reich, including their names and addresses, and called on the regional stations to keep an eye on them.[33]

He devoted the following three months to composing a report on the Zionist movement (completed on October 20, 1936). It combines in a fascinating way a reasonably historically accurate survey with the drivel of Nazi racial conspiracy theory. Chaim Weizmann, for example, invented "several types of poison gas" in the First World War – a prophetic slip of the pen? The major part of the misrepresentation (or misunderstanding) touched on the role and importance of the Haganah, the Zionist self-defense force in Palestine. According to Eichmann, the word Haganah means "secret" (it actually means "defense"). He was very impressed with the wide network of spies with which the Haganah, and especially its intelligence service, had infiltrated all the other important intelligence organizations, including those of the British and French. The sense of conspiracy was heightened by the "fact" that the center of this network was in Paris, where the Jew Léon Blum was prime minister. The report included surveys of various Zionist organizations, but the space devoted to the Haganah was inflated out of all proportion. When Eichmann describes the Zionists of Germany, he asserts that, while they are absolutely hostile to National Socialism, and while all policemen in the local stations should keep watch on them, their actions should not be

32. NA T–175 r.411 fr. 29355378–414, and especially 2935311. YVA JM.4712. 20 May 1936.
33. NA T–175 r.411 fr.2935454–499. YVA JM.4712.

overly restricted so as not to interfere with their efforts to encourage Jewish emigration.[34] While Eichmann's claim during his interrogation that he and the Zionists were allies is not devoid of an element of truth, it does not reflect the historical reality.

In the middle of December 1936 the department staff submitted a work plan for the coming year. They identified two tasks: ejecting the Jews from all areas of life, including the economy; and encouraging emigration. In order to advance both these goals they asked to be allowed to train further personnel. For this purpose, they would make use of their existing files on the aims of World Jewry, and of additional ones they wished to prepare. They also proposed improving work procedures against the Jews.[35] The report provides an understanding of the world view of the department staff: in order to conduct a struggle against the Jews there would have to be well-developed networks of informers who would supply information to local offices of the SD. To process this information, the stations would need people with expertise in the Jewish organizational structure. They would be trained in II 112, where the surveys were prepared and courses held. The II 112 staff considered themselves to be at the forefront of the struggle against organized Jewry, which pervaded the Reich. Jewry, they believed, had clear goals and knew how to achieve them. To fight them, the Reich needed the same.

This world view was to a certain extent unique to the men of the SD. The reality of a complex Jewish conspiracy was accepted by many Nazis; the attempt to penetrate this system by studying it deeply was, in contrast, exceptional in the Nazi landscape. It would seem to derive – at least partially – from the SD's nature as an organization that gathered "ideological" information, but which had no operational authority. On the other hand, the collection of ideological information was always intended for practical purposes, such as supervision of Jewish organizations, and for the purpose of advancing policy. The successful integration of information gathering, knowledge acquisition, and policy planning could explain how the men of this small organization later came to have such pervasive influence.[36]

When department commanders wrote reports summarizing their work, they again and again repeated the fact that up until the end of 1935

34. NA T–175 r.411 fr. 2935416–451. YVA JM.4712.
35. NA T–175 r.411 fr. 2934950–55. YVA JM.4711.
36. Wildt, *Judenpolitik*, p. 63.

they had dealt almost exclusively with training – that is, studying the Jews.[37] Such study continued after 1935. In June 1937 Heydrich instructed the department's staff to meet with a party member named Dr Arlt, from Silesia. Dr Arlt made an excellent impression on his interlocutors – he was fluent in modern Hebrew, seemed to possess great knowledge of Jewish subjects, and offered to give crash courses in Hebrew so that the officials could cope with documents.[38] In December 1937 an order was given in the department that all the workers had to read, within ten days, Josef Kastein's book *History of the Jews*; it was determined that each week there would be an evening of discussion on a Jewish historical issue, making use of literature that would be distributed.[39]

These people devoted many long months to studying Jewry, but this certainly gave them no empathy for the Jews. Their conviction that covert Jewish networks were conspiring to rule the world only grew stronger. Jerusalem historian David Bankier has gone over the raw material that was available to Eichmann's colleagues in their "studies," and especially the reports of Jewish informers. He uses this documentation to illustrate some of the complexity of Jewish life in Germany in those days, and to depict how the Jews attempted to cope with this hostile regime.[40] It would be difficult to find any points of agreement between his conclusions and theirs.

Despite these months of study, they understood nothing. Obviously, there is no contradiction between their great knowledge of the Jews and their antisemitism. The salient point is, however, that they were antisemites. Just as a polygon with three sides is always a triangle, a person who sees a Jewish conspiracy everywhere and who hates the Jews for this is an antisemite, though he might, years later, try to put things in a different light. Some of the central figures in this study were proven antisemites years before the beginning of the extermination policy. Not only were they indoctrinated; they were active indoctrinators themselves.

At the beginning of 1937 members of the department initiated the establishment of a card file on German Jewry. This would have

37. NA 28 August 1936, Schröder, NA T–175 r.410 fr. 2934944–46, YVA JM.4711; 7 December 1937, Hagen, TR.3-1185. Eichmann described this period in detail, *Interrogation*, vol. 1, pp. 327–30.
38. NA T–175 r.410 fr.2934956–57, YVA JM.4711, 2 July 1937.
39. TR.3-1510.
40. David Bankier, "Jewish Society through Nazi Eyes, 1933–1936", *Holocaust and Genocide Studies*, vol. 6, no. 2, 1991.

enabled them to monitor all Jews, both to "defend" German society from them and more efficiently to enforce anti-Jewish measures. Lacking practical experience and funding, they did not succeed in bringing the idea to fruition, and in July Heydrich halted the project, even though he agreed with the concept.[41] However, he brought the department staff closer to practical activity by putting them together with police from Gestapo department II B 4 when the latter interrogated Jews with senior positions in the community, and on visits to Jewish offices. After the attempt to establish their own card file failed, SD men Dr Franz Six, Wislicency, Eichmann, and Hagen met with Gestapo representatives and asked for access to its card files. Werner Best, then Heydrich's deputy and commander of the Gestapo administration, ordered the transfer of all the card files, including the active ones, to the SD. The practical significance of the decision was that from that time on it was not possible to shape policy or legislation against the Jews without involving II 112. Officially, they remained a research group on the periphery of events; in practical terms they had already moved towards center stage, and were trying to advance their preferred policy, emigration.[42]

The men of Eichmann's department also traveled outside of Germany in order to pursue their studies. In August 1937 Wislicency went to observe the Zionist Congress in Zurich.[43] In October of that same year Hagen and Eichmann went to the Middle East, their major object being to tour Palestine. The trip lasted for a month, but the visit to Palestine did not work out because the British authorities refused to allow them to enter the country, and they had no choice but to conduct some of their meetings in Cairo.[44] On their return they composed a 58-page report.[45] They saw what they saw through the prism of their world view. The difficult economic situation in Palestine, for example, was in their analysis due to the absence of Aryans; lacking Aryan influence, the Jews cheated each other. A concrete example of this inability to manage an

41. Wildt, *Judenpolitik*, pp. 36–7.
42. NA T–175 r.410 fr.2934963–69, 17 Feb. 1937, and fr.2934988–90, 7 Dec. 1937 (JM.4711); Wildt, *Judenpolitik*, pp. 38–9.
43. NA T–175 r.410 fr.2934983–87, JM.4711.
44. The case has been described in detail in: Heinrich Höhne, *The Order of the Death's Head*, London: Secker & Warburg, 1969, pp. 336–7; Wildt, *Judenpolitik*, pp. 40 ff.; Friedlaender, *Nazi Germany*, p. 201. Prior to the journey, Eichmann had had talks with a representative of the Haganah in Berlin, Feivel Polkes, who invited him to Palestine. Wildt, ibid., p. 43.
45. NA T–175, r.411 fr.2936013–71, JM.7412.

organized economy was the fact that in Jerusalem there were forty Jewish banks, each making money by cheating the others.[46]

Thus antisemites travel the world. After all, we are not talking about views of rational needs, economic for example, because the (imaginary) economic behavior of the Jews of Jerusalem had no effect on the Reich's economy. Eichmann and Hagen were also aware of this when they discovered, to their obvious disappointment, that the position of the Arabs in Egypt was fundamentally different from their own. Their ideological hatred of the Jews was not deep-seated; their problem was rather specific conflict and friction and, if those specific circumstances vanished, so would the hatred.[47] Wislicency had written a very similar report on the situation in Palestine back in March 1937, without even setting foot there. The Jews, he wrote, lived by exploiting the non-Jewish population, or from mutual fraud. He counted 58 bank branches in Tel Aviv, and also added a moral to his story. The Jews are parasites, he declared, and are not able to maintain an organized economy. The goal of Zionism was to establish a state from which the Jews could exploit other countries.[48]

This also has importance for the discussion of the universality of the bureaucrats. These were bureaucrats with a very exceptional kind of hatred, a hatred that led people to break through boundaries. It was not the hatred of the stranger among them, or of the other nearby. Hatred is apparently a natural and common human emotion; hatred devoid of any rational basis, whose only justification is ideological, is a less common phenomenon. To be precise, the initiative for the trip came from above, from the superiors; the distorted view of reality came from below, from the people who wrote the report; the acceptance of the report and the advancement of its authors came again from above. A bureaucratic system imposes on its members a common will, but it is also built on the assumption that the bureaucrats accept this will. The bureaucrat must accept the system's fundamental assumptions as a condition of survival, not to mention advancement. But the reverse is also true. The bureaucrats' acquiescence and their willingness to take an initiative determines the operational capacity of the bureaucratic system. These SD men, of all ranks, were of the initiating type.

Their interest in proceeding from theory to practice received

---

46. NA T–175 r.411 fr.2936043, JM.7412.
47. NA T–175 r.411 fr.2936031, JM.7412.
48. NA T–175 r.410 fr.2934821–29, JM.7411.

expression in the first attempt to integrate the two at the beginning of the summer of 1937. At the time, Eichmann proposed new procedures for surveillance of the Jews of Upper Silesia. The proposal received the blessing of Six and Heydrich, and Eichmann was sent to Breslau. This was a kind of first practical test for Eichmann, and its success can perhaps explain his promotion to officer rank even before his transfer to Vienna a year later.[49]

Among the millions of documents that lay in sealed boxes in archives in the Soviet Union, until recently out of reach of scholars, is an interesting collection that can help us understand the state of mind of the department's staff. It records a gathering of experts on Jewish affairs from the SD districts, a kind of professional training course attended by some 50 SD men, most of them NCOs. The seminar began on November 1, 1937 at 9:30 in the morning and went on almost without a break until after 7:30 in the evening. The initiative was Heydrich's. Opening remarks were made by Dr Six, then an SS major, and by SS Brigadier Dr Wilhelm Albert; it was sponsored by the senior officers.[50]

SS Sergeant Helmut Hagelmann lectured on "The Current State of the Identification of Jews in Germany by the Various Authorities, and an Evaluation of Their Contribution to the Compilation of a General Jewish Card File." The underlying assumption of his talk was that there was a need to record in a card file (or database, in modern terminology) all Jews and descendants of Jews living in Germany. Only then would it be possible to know how many of them there were, and to identify their influence on the German nation's cultural, community, and economic life. In other words, it would be possible to uncover the dimensions and character of the Jewish conspiracy, and this would make it easier to fight it.

He enumerated a number of bodies that could contribute important information: regional party offices; teachers' associations (especially in the rural areas, where teachers would be an excellent source for identifying children from mixed families); local census rolls; and

---

49. Wildt, *Judenpolitik*, p. 35.
50. OSSOBI 500–4–302, copy in YVA O.51(OSSOBI)–11. Since the discovery of the documentation of this conference, it has drawn considerable interest. Saul Friedländer notes that it was the largest gathering of its type (*Nazi Germany and the Jews*, Vol. I: *The Years of Persecution, 1933–1939*, New York: HarperCollins, 1997, p. 199); Wildt describes it in detail and published sizeable segments of the proceedings: Wildt, *Judenpolitik*, pp. 45ff.

also the Nazi labor organization (DAF), statistical offices and Gestapo bureaus, all of which could provide information on the Jewish community. The record would be made on the local level with information on more important Jews being recorded at the district level, or even at the level of the Security Police headquarters, according to their importance. Jews would be considered a threat to the Reich if they were active in nationwide organizations, or if their influence on culture, community, or economics was large, or if they were suspected of having ties with foreign intelligence organizations, or if they engaged in anti-state activities. The second category would include Jews whose influence was local and not national, but who were nevertheless in a position to cause harm – for example, providers of essential supplies to the military.

Dannecker presented a lecture on "Anti-Jewish Legislation Since 1933." He outlined the major points of the legislation and explained that, according to new instructions on cooperation between the Gestapo and the SD, it was no longer sufficient to notify the police that "a given Jew would be sent to a concentration camp because of his activity against the state," but that it was necessary to be precise and note what the specific charge was. He promised that the department would issue an updated list of all regulations to all Gestapo and SD stations.

Dannecker gave a second lecture after the lunch break, entitled "German Jewry: Organization, Changes, Spiritual Life, and their Treatment." He distinguished between three types of Jewish organizations: assimilationist, religious and Zionist. The most problematic were the assimilationist organizations, because they maintained that Jews could be an integral part of German society. He devoted most of his attention to the Jewish war veterans' league. This group tried to justify the continued presence of Jews in Germany by publicizing statistical data about the number of German Jewish soldiers who had fallen in battle in the world war. Because of this, Himmler had forbidden them (on November 7, 1936) to engage in any activity other than supporting wounded veterans. A number of assimilationist groups were disbanded, among them the *Verband Nationaldeutscher Juden* of Max Neumann. This organization was so extreme in its adherence to the nationalist line that its members came close to being Jewish antisemites. It was dissolved at the end of 1935 in order to prevent ordinary citizens from being confused about the National Socialist position on race.

Dannecker attributed only minor importance to Jewish religious and welfare organizations because their political activity was limited and without direction. The most important organizations, in his opinion, were the Zionists, who promoted emigration. Among these, he preferred the Revisionists because of their uncompromising line on mass Jewish migration to Palestine. The members of Herzliya, the Revisionist youth movement, were even given the right to wear uniforms — behind closed doors. The SD considered wearing a uniform to be a coveted privilege, and hoped thus to encourage young Jews to join this radical Zionist organization.

Afterwards, Dannecker addressed the role of the SD. "The SS's principal mission has been and remains to completely push the assimilationists out of Jewish political activity, in order to bring the Jewish problem to a complete solution." To achieve this, he proposed action on three fronts. First, he said, it was necessary to pinpoint the orientations of Jewish community activists, including those who did not hold official positions. Second, the same should be done with Jewish teachers. Teachers with patriotic German sentiments should be removed and replaced with teachers with a Zionist outlook. Third, all Jewish educational institutions should be closely monitored in order to verify that the Zionist approach was the leading one.

Dannecker, who would later be responsible for preparing French and Bulgarian Jewry for deportation, summed up with a general declaration that is worth quoting in full:

> We should reach a state of affairs in which German Jewry will always be facing the recognition that all their activity is always under close National Socialist scrutiny, that their organizations and actions are always monitored by the police, and that in the end any Jewish attempt to remain in Germany is entirely without prospect.
>
> This will be the Security Police's method of dealing with the Jews: never to give them a moment's peace, always to keep the leading Jews in suspense with the help of repeated interrogations, always to respond in the sharpest way to any infraction — even the smallest — of the instructions given by us, accompanied by full penetration of Jewish life, and especially of internal Jewish activity.

Dannecker knew how, on the day of reckoning, he would demolish both collective and individual Jewish resistance. It is worth noting that, among all the speakers that day, he stood out in that, even at this early date, his attitude towards violence was documented and clear: he was for it. Between December 1934 and May 1935 he had been stationed as a guard at the Columbia Haus prison in Berlin and at the

Oranienburg camp. A friend from those days recalled afterwards how much enjoyment he had gotten out of torturing prisoners. Dannecker, the friend said, would recall with great mirth the guards' practice of throwing a prisoner's hat on grass it was forbidden to walk on, and then ordering him to retrieve it, so that they could beat him for disobeying orders. An acquaintance from that period remembered that Dannecker was a "fanatical Jew-hater," something which could not have been invisible to the men of II 112 who in March 1937 asked that he be transferred to them from Stuttgart, where he served as the official in charge of Jewish affairs in the local SD.[51] When such a man proposed keeping Jewish leaders in constant tension, or responding severely to any violation, he did not have in mind administrative measures – he meant torture and terror. It is reasonable to assume that his colleagues in the audience believed the same.

Hagen explained to the seminar the significance of the proposal for the partition of Palestine as presented in the Peel Report. He briefly related the series of events that led to the report and the positions of each side. Then he focused on the danger it presented. If a national Jewish entity were to come into being, the Jews of Germany would certainly demand the rights of a national minority, which would make it very difficult for the National Socialists to carry out their policy. His operational conclusion was, however, surprising. In anticipation of this danger – which was in any case not immediate, since the partition plan was not going to be accepted – German Jewish immigration to Palestine, including covert immigration, should be accelerated. Apparently, his position may be understood as follows: he saw no danger to the Reich from a small Jewish state in Palestine, but he feared that the Jewish community in Germany would benefit from the political protection provided by such a state. For this reason, it was necessary to get all the Jews out of Germany as quickly as possible, even if this would contribute to the establishment of a Jewish national entity in Palestine.

Eichmann gave a fairly long lecture called "World Jewry: Its Political Activity, and the Implications of the Activity on the Jews Residing in Germany." The importance of this talk lies largely in its fundamental assumptions. It was absolutely clear to him that there was a worldwide Jewish conspiracy, and the more facts he learned about the

51. Claudia Steur, *Theodor Dannecker. Ein Funktionär der "Endlösung"*, Tübingen: Klartext, 1997, pp. 17–21, 153.

Jews, the more he was convinced of this. Like his colleagues, he divided the Jews into three groups: the orthodox, the assimilationists and the Zionists. The orthodox Jews did not interest him in particular, and he referred his audience to an information sheet he had distributed. In summing up the nature of assimilationist Judaism he stated that: "The achievement of equal rights has, since the French Revolution, been the way to penetrate all areas of the German people's lives, and we have witnessed how in a small number of decades the enemy has managed to upset the nation's life in art, in science, in law, and in education; how it has taken over all areas of molding public opinion such as literature, theater, and film. … This activity has brought in reaction the rise of the antisemites, and to the acme of National Socialism. Jewry has recognized its great enemy, and has taken defensive measures."

If the presentation is typically ideological, the details that appear afterwards are not typical. Eichmann went into great detail about an imaginary conspiracy by the welfare arm of the Alliance Israélite Universelle to liquidate Nazi leaders – Konrad Henlein in Czechoslovakia and Julius Streicher in Nuremberg had already been targeted. The organization, said Eichman, was connected to the Unilever margarine factory that had Dutch and British Jews among its owners; the president of the concern was a Czech Jew named Schicht who had five sons, each one with a different nationality. The description, covering four pages, came in that part of the lecture in which he was describing assimilationist Jewry.

It was, then, only consistent that, when he turned his attention to the Zionist movement, he devoted almost all his time to its covert – and menacing – tentacle: the Haganah. "The influence and areas of activity of the Haganah reach out to all parts of the world."[52] He described a huge, global organization equipped with modern weapons, including artillery and aircraft. The Haganah also had a well-developed intelligence service, with agents planted in the British and French intelligence agencies and also, of course, throughout the Reich. He called on his listeners to uncover this and to keep an eye on the intelligence agency representatives in their districts. Historiography on the SD–Haganah connection of the 1930s has focused largely on the "positive" side of the link: the common interest in advancing Jewish emigration.[53] In reality, it would seem that Eichmann

52. Ibid., p. 199. Conceivably, Eichmann felt himself vindicated when Israeli agents abducted him in Argentina many years later.
53. Hoehne, *Death's Head*, pp. 336–7.

and his colleagues were more interested in tracing the activities of what they saw as a hostile spy network that was pulling strings all over Europe – an organization that existed, perhaps unfortunately for the Jews themselves, only in the Nazi mind.

Eichmann made use in his lecture of a diagram showing the interconnection of the agencies of World Jewry. Even though the diagram included only major organizations, it was, Eichmann himself admitted, an incomprehensible tangle of connecting lines. But, he insisted, the chaos was but a Jewish ruse, an attempt to conceal the conspiracy's true purpose and the roles played by the different institutions. This deception was so sophisticated, he said, that there was ostensibly no coherence among the different organizations; there was coordination only at the highest levels, or when it was necessary to confront a serious opponent, like National Socialist Germany. Then, he maintained, they united and acted in concert.[54] He called on the members of his audience to trace the lines connecting the organizations in their districts; Jews with foreign citizenship should be removed from key positions in organizations, because their being there was not coincidental – they were part of the conspiracy. Foreign Jews could remain in their posts only if removing them would clearly prevent the advancement of emigration.

This, then, was the situation in November 1937, at an internal conference whose discussions were confidential (they in fact remained unknown for 50 years). The men of the department spoke as antisemites, and viewed the world from an antisemitic point of view. They taught others to do the same, and developed in them sensitivity to the fine points of their outlook, while granting them a motive ("the Jewish conspiracy threatening Germany") and giving instructions on how to hurt the Jews.The different shading of each talk gives a sense of how each of the speakers thought and processed his data; the result was a unified picture in its broad outline, but complex in its details. It goes beyond slogans and abstract formulas – here, an entire range of data is plugged into the formulas. Beyond this, and most importantly, there is original development of a policy according to which the leadership of Jewish organizations would be exploited for the advancement of Nazi goals. Dannecker said this in the clearest possible way, but his colleagues

54. Ibid., p. 201. For a discussion of the ability to invent connections, chains of command, and secret networks which existed only in the minds of these antisemites, and to create detailed charts to reflect them, see Friedländer, *Nazi Germany*, p. 200.

thought the same – the Jews should be harmed and, simultaneously, their organizations should be used to advance emigration. This line does not appear in Hitler's speeches, in the Nazi press, or in other places, and it would seem to be an original contribution made by the SD.

The men in the department were not disinterested officials carrying out orders, but full partners in the enterprise. Since they believed that their personal initiative would contribute to victory, they invested considerable effort and thought in this direction. While they were still low-ranking bureaucrats in an organization lacking operational authority, they were brimming with proposals for furthering anti-Jewish policy. Some of the lines of action that would be taken in the future were already clearly formulated.

Over time, the bureaucrats of II 112, and after them the bureaucrats of IV B 4, ceased to be "rank and file" bureaucrats on the Jewish issue. By 1937 they were already the "experts": information booklets they wrote were distributed in SD offices throughout the Reich;[55] a series of SS officers, including senior ones, attended courses they taught;[56] and Himmler's headquarters even asked them to give him their opinion on a book that discussed the struggle against German Jewry. Wislicency replied that the book was a good one, but too detailed to be of interest to the average party member.[57] A historian of the SD has stated that the members of the organization were sincere in doing their duty and acted out of ideological conviction; they should not be seen as cynical utilitarians looking out for promotion – at the very least, not the educated among them.[58] Another historian, writing on the *Einsatzgruppen*, noted that the commanders of the murder units in the fall of 1939 were taken mostly from the SD because this organization's upper staff was of a generally high educational level, and of great ideological commitment. Alongside this, they felt no legal or bureaucratic inhibitions.[59] In his opinion, the SD was exceptional in displaying these characteristics.

What happened to the ideology when the bureaucrats received operational authority? As we shall see, during the war years Eichmann

---

55. NA T–175 r.411 fr.2935415, YVA JM.4712.
56. NA T–175 r.410 fr.2934963–69, YVA JM.4711.
57. NA T–175 r.411 fr.2935750–51, YVA JM.4712: Graf Ernst Reventlov, *Judas Kampf und Niederlage in Deutschland*.
58. Browder, "SD," in Mosse, *Police Forces*.
59. Krausnick and Wilhelm, *Truppe des Weltanschauungskrieges*, Stuttgart: DVA, 1981, p. 35.

and his colleagues rarely devoted time to philosophical discussions about an imaginary "Jewish conspiracy." They were too busy sending Jews to their deaths, and the documentation they created reflected the confrontation with operational issues rather than ideological ones. How are we to understand this documentational opaqueness? Does the lack of verbal preoccupation with ideology reflect a lack of identification, or simply a lack of time? To put it another way, did their preoccuaption with ideology in the 1930s derive from the frustration of people whose activity was confined by the bounds of "intelligence gathering" and who could not engage in operational activity? Did they, from the moment they were given operational authority (almost unlimited, it should be noted), abandon ideology, or did they act consistently under its influence?

*

Eichmann was among the first SS men to arrive in Austria after the *Anschluss*, on March 16, 1938.[60] Hagen came with him, but returned shortly thereafter to Berlin. Within two months Eichmann had opened the Central Emigration Bureau, which was actually a building containing representatives of all the official bodies from whom a potential Jewish émigré needed documents. The bureau functioned like a conveyor belt of dispossession – a Jew would enter the building as a man of means and come out with nothing but an emigration permit.[61] Faithful to the policy he had helped develop, Eichmann was assisted considerably by the Jewish leadership in Vienna. He was quick to take advantage of the atmosphere of terror that pervaded Vienna from the time of the Nazi entry into Austria, when Jews were chased through the streets and tortured by their non-Jewish neighbors. Eichmann estimated that about 50,000 Jews had left Austria by the fall.[62]

The successful transition from ideological-intelligence activity to operational activity took place here, in Vienna. Theory became practice.

The department's semiannual report for the second half of 1937, signed by Wislicency on January 15, 1938, reflects the aspiration, though

60. NA T–175 r.410 fr.2935006–21, JM.4711. The best description of Eichmann's activities in Vienna at this period, used extensively in the following pages, is in the first chapter of Hans Safrian, *Die Eichmann Männer*, Vienna: Europaverlag, 1993.

61. Herbert Rosenkranz, *Verfolgung und Selbstbehauptung: Die Juden in Österreich, 1938– 1945*, Vienna: Herold, 1978; also Leni Yahil, *The Holocaust: The Fate of European Jewry, 1932–1945*, New York: Oxford University Press, 1990, pp. 104–6.

62. Safrian, *Männer*, pp. 45–6. However, Safrian also cautions: no more than one quarter of these Jews would have left through the channels of the Zentrale Stelle.

still a cautious one, to become operational. In anticipation of the Führer's visit to Rome, for example, the department collected information on the Jewish community there and sent it to the Security Police (it again echoed the line that the Jews were a vast network and dangerous to the Nazis). The report also included recommendations for streamlining the work of the bodies promoting Jewish emigration, and it asked that the department be given additional manpower to achieve this. Significantly, the report also stated that the increasing pressure of day-to-day activity did not leave much time for ideological training. Wislicency regretted this, and wrote that an attempt would be made to devote two evenings a month to it.[63] This implied that the decreasing attention to ideology was caused by the workload, not by apathy.

The bureaucrats, for their part, were not aware at the time that this transition was underway. As far as they were concerned, Eichmann was sent as the department's representative in order to pursue its work in the field. He was chosen, apparently, because of his Austrian background. A letter from Eichmann to Hagen, dated April 30, 1938, shows to what extent Eichmann saw himself as still part of the team. He asked Hagen to save him a particular newspaper article that interested him, and he sent Hagen an interesting article from a Viennese newspaper. In addition, he informed Hagen that the president of the Jewish community of Vienna had been transferred from Dachau to the Vienna Gestapo, and that he could now be interrogated.[64] That same day, in Berlin, Hagen wrote to the Ministry of Propaganda that an article in the Zionist newspaper *Jüdische Rundschau* noted that since the Germans overran Austria many Austrian Jews were writing letters to the editor; Hagen wanted to confiscate the letters and hand them over to II 112.[65] In May dozens of boxes of documents confiscated from Jewish organizations in Vienna reached the department in Berlin, which began processing them.[66]

A letter from Hagen to Eichmann dated May 23, 1938, containing recommendations on how to encourage Jewish emigration from Vienna (for example, encouraging commercial ties with Palestine) shows II 112's attraction to the practical.[67] A series of reports by them on discussions — both in Berlin and in Vienna — with one Wolf, a senior official of the

63. NA T–175 r.410 fr.2934993–5003, JM.4711.
64. TR.3–1516.
65. NA T–175 r.411 fr.2935613, JM.4712.
66. NA T–175 r410 fr.2935044–46 (20.5.38); fr. 2935047–48 (17.6.38). JM.4711.
67. NA T–175 r.411 fr.2935617, JM.4712.

central bank, clearly indicate an entry into operational activity. In Berlin, it was agreed with Wolf that there was a need for changes in the way foreign currency was transferred in order to speed up emigration;[68] when Wolf reached Vienna he was not willing to approve large sums of money being taken out of the Reich, but he spoke with Eichmann about the establishment of a large fund of foreign currency to be provided by foreign Jews in order to finance the emigration of poor Jews.[69] A week later Wolf was willing for Eichmann to allow the removal of foreign currency from the country in certain cases.[70] The author (apparently Hagen) of an internal memo from the end of August was ecstatic about the appointment of Franz Walter Stahlecker to head the emigration office, since it gave the SD a central operational mission. Eichmann should be sent additional manpower to carry out the task, he wrote.[71] In spite of all this, when Hagen wrote the activity report for the second half of 1938, he proved clearly how little he understood that times had changed. He detailed a plan, as yet unapproved, to establish a subdepartment, II 1124, that would deal with Austria, and which would itself be divided into smaller units: II 11241 would deal with central Jewish organizations, II 11242 would deal with assimilationist organizations, and so forth.[72]

Hans Safrian's description completes this finding. He traced Eichmann's doings not in the previous bureaucratic context, but rather in the context of events in Vienna after the *Anschluss*. His clear conclusion is that Eichmann was carried along by a wave of local antisemitic activity. More than a month after his arrival in Vienna, Eichmann was still writing to Hagen that his mission would soon be completed, his replacement would arrive, and he could continue with his career. But the pressure from many Viennese elements was so violent, comprehensive and resolute that the Jews were frantically looking for a way to get out of Austria at any price. Eichmann took advantage of the Jewish plight. Safrian sums up his work with the representatives of the Jewish organizations in one word: "tyrannical". His and his men's treatment of the Jews who went through the Emigration Office was consistently characterized, so Safrian maintains, by primitive brutality.[73]

68. NA T–175 r.411 fr.2935760–63, JM.4712.
69. TR.3-1151, 15 June 1938.
70. TR.3-1171, 20 June 1938.
71. TR.3-1571, 26 Aug. 1938.
72. NA T–175 r.413 fr.2938476, JM.4714.
73. Safrian, *Männer*, pp. 38–44.

In summary, 1938 displayed two new trends: the transition to operational activity, and dwindling active preoccupation with theory. The transition into an operational mode was already evidenced in Berlin, but most of it took place under Eichmann in Vienna. From the point of view of the officials in Berlin, Eichmann was the Vienna representative of II 112,[74] and his principal tasks had not changed: surveillance of Jewish organizations, study of the enemy, and training other Nazi bodies in the correct understanding of the Jews. During the time that Eichmann was managing to chase tens of thousands of Jews out of Vienna, his colleagues in Berlin hosted a senior official from the Ministry of Propaganda for a seminar.[75] While the SD was looking for channels of operational activity, Eichmann found one, or perhaps, took advantage of the situation and created one. In the framework of a given direction of policy set by his superiors, he acted not as a drab bureaucrat carrying out orders, but rather as a very diligent, very violent bureaucrat who was very successfully taking advantage of a fortuitious moment. His personal initiative was on such a scale that, even months later, his erstwhile colleagues in Berlin still did not understand how much he had changed. The importance of this point for our discussion cannot be exaggerated: what put Eichmann at center stage, and won him rapid promotion, was precisely his ability to perform on a plane higher than that of a drab bureaucrat.

Yet Eichmann's colleagues were not typical bureaucrats either. They succeeded, as a group, in insinuating themselves from the margins of the new regime, as a small party research group, into the heart of activity in one of the Third Reich's most central enterprises. The story of the murder of the Jews of Germany, France, Slovakia, Bulgaria, Greece, and of course Hungary cannot be told without running into Hagen, Dannecker or Wislicency, even if Eichmann was above them all. Historian Michael Wildt challenges the claim by one of the most important German historians of the Holocaust, Hans Mommsen, that antisemitism was not a motive for these men's deeds: "Their antisemitism, in rational, scientific, and pragmatic guise, was the foundation of their activity."[76] The secret of their success, he adds, was their similarity to Hitler: like him, they aspired

74. NA T–175 r.410 fr.2935006–21, 2 July 1938. JM.4711.
75. NA T–175 r.411 fr.2935649, JM.4712. The visit took place on 28 September 1938. The preparations were lengthy, and left a trail of dozens of documents. The expenses generated were RM 208.80, and included RM 5.90 for a bottle of Cognac and RM 2.90 for cigarettes.
76. Wildt, *Judenpolitik*, p. 48.

from an early stage to get all the Jews out of Germany. They never compromised on this goal; they aspired to change reality, not to change their ideology; and every time they encountered difficulties, they chose to overcome them by becoming more extreme. On the basis of an examination of their deeds in the 1930s alone, he reached the conclusion that "Arendt, in seeing in them men frightening in their normality, erred."[77]

As the workload grew greater, so the time devoted to shaping the world view of the members of the department declined. This also reduces the historian's ability to find pure expressions of their view of the world. At the time of the transition to operational activity, in Vienna in 1938, new SS men were brought into the circle of activists in the department, and these men did not devote years to careful study of the Jewish question. Safrian considers them "typical Austrian National Socialists" who were expert at exploiting the situation to aggrandize their personal egos, their social status and their economic well-being at the expense of frightened and humiliated Jews. He makes it clear, however, that there was no need to teach them the fundamentals of Nazi and antisemitic philosophy. This they brought with them from home.[78]

There is no indication of a weakening of ideological commitment at the time of the transition to operational activity and the addition of new men to the staff. On the contrary, when a careful search of the documents confiscated from the mansion of Alfonse Rothschild in Vienna did not turn up information on links between Jewish industrialists and Marxists, all they concluded was that they had to search the offices of Louis Rothschild at the bank.[79] It may also have been that they had no great need to write down their antisemitic thoughts when it was simpler and more enjoyable to beat Jews. Of course, it remained an ideological position diluted with a great deal of pragmatism. A report from July complained of the damage, primarily to foreign relations, being caused by the unbridled slurs of *Der Sturmer*.[80] The motives were ideological; the behavior patterns were pragmatic.

77. Wildt, *Judenpolitik*, p. 63.
78. Safrian, *Männer*, p. 56.
79. NA T–175 r.411 fr.293552, 30 June 1938. JM.4712.
80. NA T–175 r.410 fr.2935006, JM.4712.

From the testimony at the Eichmann trial

Benno Cohn

Q.   Can you tell the court about a meeting with a man called Eichmann, or about meetings with Eichmann, if there were any?

A.   Yes. I myself had only very few meetings. The first meeting was, as far as I remember, in 1937. Before that we had already heard from some German officials that there was a new man who stood out by his toughness, much tougher than the others who looked after these matters, a very agile person. They were somewhat afraid of him, of his expert knowledge, of his personality. But we had not come to know him. Then one day there was a public meeting. We held a valedictory meeting to take leave of Rabbi Dr Joachim Prinz who was leaving the country. ... The hall was packed full. The public thronged to the meeting. Suddenly I, as chairman of the meeting, was called to the door, and my clerk from my office, told me: "Mr Eichmann is here." I saw a man, for the first time, in civilian clothing, and he shouted at me: "Are you responsible for order here? This is disorder of the first degree!" There was much pressure from people trying to get in. And he threatened to take measures himself if I did not to put some order into it all. He complained that he had received a blow in the belly from a Jew who did not know him, who did not know he was from the Gestapo ...

...

[In March 1939] I received a telephone call stating that the Gestapo was calling the representatives of the Jewish institutions to a meeting. ... I went there with some misgivings, as I already had my immigration papers in my pocket. ... Others at the meeting were Heinrich Stahl, the Chairman of the Jewish Community in Berlin, Dr Lilienfeld, Dr Kotzover and Dr Eppstein. ... We went in, there was a rope, and behind that rope there sat or stood Eichmann. ... He had papers in front of him. A French emigrant newspaper, the *Pariser Tageblatt*, if I am not mistaken. It was a newspaper which we had not seen before in Germany, as it was banned. He was very upset that we had published something about him in that paper – he read out to us excerpts: That he was *"Der Bluthund Eichmann"* (bloodhound Eichmann) – I am using the language used at the time – *"blutunterlaufene Augen"* (bloodshot eyes), *"ein neuer Feind,"* *"Judenfeind"* (a new enemy, an enemy of the Jews). I don't remember all the expressions, but they were all very trenchant. He accused us that one of us had supplied this false and misleading information about him. And then he said that Dr Landau, the director of the JTA (Jewish Telegraphic Agency) whom I knew very well, had been in Berlin for a few days and that it was undoubtedly to him that we had supplied the information. Who had given this out for publication – that was his first question. He was very tense, shouting at us and threatening us with all the measures he was able to take. None of us admitted to having supplied the information. That was obvious. Anything else would have been suicidal.

That was the first point. Then he went on to the second point of the meeting. He put a question to us with regard to our visit to Vienna. I must mention here ... that Eichmann had invited representatives of German Jewish institutions to Vienna to become acquainted there with the Central Office for Jewish Emigration. The others all had been in Vienna. He shouted at them and turned to them beratingly: "Why did you act against my explicit instructions forbidding you to get in touch with the Jews, with the Jewish leaders in Vienna? That had been strictly forbidden and yet you did it!" He resorted to rude language, barrack language (*Kasernenstil*), quite a different style from what we were used to. He attacked us and accused us that we had breached the ban on any contact with the representatives of the Jews of Vienna. Whereupon somebody got up, I believe it was Stahl or Dr Epstein. They stood up and said: "After all that happened when we were visiting Vienna, we are entitled – and it is only human – to get in touch with our friends in distress there in order to comfort them. This fate has overcome them only recently, whereas we have for some time now been living under this rule. It is only human and natural for us to get in touch with them, and you must understand this." Eichmann wound up with the following words, more or less: If such a thing occurs once more, you will go to a *Konzert-Lager* (concert camp). That was a vulgar term for *Konzentrationslager* (concentration camp).... Eichmann replied very rudely and used foul language. I am ashamed to utter such awful words. But then, awful things have happened since then. I could in German ...

Q. You don't have to put it in Hebrew. Actually, if you can still recollect the very words Eichmann used, please quote him in his own words.

A. There was just one expression that I remember. I have not heard it again since. I learned this expression from Eichmann's vocabulary. He said: *"Sie elender Geselle, Sie alter Scheissack"* (you miserable rascal, you old shitbag).

(*The Trial of Adolf Eichmann*, vol. I, pp. 220–1, 227–8)

Chapter 2

Documents in the Bureaucratic System

Documents are the historian's main source of information. They are the tool he uses to test the statements of his colleagues, both those with whom he agrees and those with whom he does not. Documents must, however, be perused with care, for they cannot always be trusted. The fact that something appears in writing does not ensure that it is correct. The writer may have been mistaken, or misled, or he may have wanted to mislead others, or he may simply have been lying. Furthermore, not only the document's contents may be suspect – its identifying details may be untrustworthy as well.

Take dates. Albert Speer, the Nazi minister of armaments and war production, describes a document created by his office approximately in the middle of July 1944, discussing a proposal to change the Reich's governmental structure. The date on the document is not the date it was written. It was postdated to the day the document was supposed to be laid before Hitler – July 20, 1944. Another example: Hitler's directive on the commencement of the so-called "euthanasia" program was not issued on the date it bears (September 1, 1939) but rather several weeks later. Hitler issued an order setting up a single central intelligence organization late in the war, but signed it on a date other than that which appears on the document. There were also many instances in which orders were issued after the fact, in order to provide cover for the perpetrators.[1]

Or the addressee. Because of an established bureaucratic policy, tens of thousands of envelopes were addressed to persons other than the

---

1. Speer, Albert, *Inside the Third Reich*, New York: Macmillan, 1970; "Euthanasia": Hilberg, *Destruction*, p. 872; and for a detailed discussion see Friedlander, Henry, *The Origins of Nazi Genocide: From Euthanasia to the Final Solution*, Chapel Hill, NC: The University of North Carolina Press, 1995; intelligence service: Black, *Kaltenbrunner*, Princeton, NJ: Princeton University Press, 1984; post-dating: see for example Eichmann's description of Himmler's order to Globocnick to kill Jews in Poland, after they had already been killed. *Interrogation*, vol. 1, p. 240.

name that appears in the salutation. The policy was that, in communicating with an official in a different agency, the writer should address it "To office X, for Y."[2] If the writer did not know who in the office would handle the matter, he addressed the letter to the office alone. Even when he addressed the letter to a specific person, the matter was frequently taken care of not by that person but by one of his assistants.

Also the signature. The signer of a document generally was not the person who wrote it, and often the writer was not the person who initiated it. In many cases, there is great doubt today as to the identity of the document's creator, which is to say the person who determined what its content would be. This is a major stumbling block for historians, because the tendency is to conflate these processes and attribute them all to the person who signed the document.[3] The signer was indeed responsible for what the document says, but the question is whether he was the only one responsible.

The more senior an official, the greater the number of subordinates who will carry out his orders. But his ability to give specific instructions will be dissipated, because his expertise in the details of execution is limited. At the highest ranks, this lack of familiarity with particulars is a real weakness – the senior official cannot know how to instruct his subordinates so that they will accomplish the mission in the most efficient way, nor is he even aware of new possibilities being created in the field that can advance or delay the execution of his orders. As Eichmann remarked cynically of his local commander in Vienna: "He was in no way burdened by acquaintance with the facts."[4]

The head of the system expresses his will, at the middle levels it is translated into detailed instructions,[5] and at the junior levels it is carried out. When underlings run into a problem or into new possibilities, they notify their superiors at the middle level, who in turn draft new proposals for action, and present them to the top man. He approves, and the proposals return to the working level in the form of instructions. The

2. Eichmann, *Interrogation*, vol. 2, p. 631.
3. For example: "In March 1938 Heydrich instructed Eichmann to examine the matter [of removing the Jews to Madagascar]." Leni Yahil, *The Holocaust*, p. 254 – although Yahil often *is* careful on this point.
4. Eichmann, *Memoirs*, p. 88.
5. Eichmann, *Interrogation*, vol. 1, pp. 47–8: "Himmler would say one sentence, and an army of clerks would be affected. Dozens of letters, orders, between all sorts of offices; a struggle of signatures and commands."

assumption is that this method integrates in a maximal way the broad outlook of the senior official with the lower officials' view of reality in the field. The mid-level officials must be an efficient pipeline in both directions – they must transfer principles of policy from above to below, and report the difficulties or opportunities for action from below to above.[6]

Some bureaucrats have senior officials sign instructions in order to make sure that other units cooperate. A department head in office A cannot demand compliance of a department head in office B, so he will address his colleague in the name of a more senior authority. Later, then, the historian is liable to attribute to the senior official a document that was merely placed on his desk for signature.

The structure of government ministries in Germany remained stable from the First World War throughout the Third Reich period. The ministries were generally fairly small, each headed by a minister who was a political figure. Under him was a director-general, sometimes two. The director-general was the top career official in the ministry. Each ministry was divided into branches headed by deputy directors-general. Each branch had departments, topped by department heads, or *Referents*. The senior officials were assisted by junior office workers, and in many cases that was the entire ministry. There was no need for an inflated staff in the central offices in the capital, since under their control, although not under their direct management, there were other government offices handling routine work in the cities and districts. These field offices were headed by a president. For example, each region had a financial president, who was in charge of the office that collected taxes. The ministry in the capital was largely a kind of head office, dealing with supervision, budgetary matters and personnel, as well as drafting legislation. The presidents of the regional offices were more senior in rank than the referents, but in practice the latter were the presidents' counterparts in the central office.[7]

Some ministries grew and added an intermediate level between the deputy director-general and the referent, because of a large number of

---

6. And see: Simon, Herbert, "Decision Making and Administrative Organisation," in Merton, *Reader in Bureaucracy*, New York: Free Press, 1952, pp. 190–3.

7. Brecht, Arnold and Glaser, Comstock, *The Art and Technique of Administration in German Ministries*, Boston: Harvard University Press, 1940, pp. 10–12. As a bureaucrat in the German Ministry of the Interior in the 1920s, the author had chaired an inter-departmental commission that determined the procedures used henceforth by all governmental departments.

departments. At the beginning of the war, in September 1939, Himmler reorganized the police and set up a Reich Security Head Office (*Reich Sicherheit Hauptamt*, or RSHA). Its first commander was Heydrich. The RSHA can be seen as the Third Reich's "Ministry of Police Affairs" (although the Order Police was not part of its portfolio). Himmler played the role of minister, Heydrich that of director-general; Gestapo chief Heinrich Müller, Criminal Police (Kripo) chief Arthur Nebe, Otto Ohlendorf and the rest of the branch commanders were deputy directors-general, and the heads of the divisions were the intermediate rank between them and the referents. For our purposes, it is important to understand that Eichmann was, by all accounts, a referent; this is how he labeled himself over and over again in his interrogation and his memoirs, and others knew him as such. The referents were, in many ways, the foundation stones of the government ministries. No other position is described at such length by Arnold Brecht in his definitive book on the German bureaucracy:

> The *Referent* is the chief technical adviser and aide of the Minister, Secretary, and Division Director, in charge of a particular field of work. His functions, relating to legislation as well as administration, are basically but not exclusively staff functions. The [Referent] is normally one of the foremost experts in his field,[8] at least regarding its governmental sides. ...
>
> The term *Referent* means literally "reporter," which maintains the fiction that he merely reports to his superiors regarding actions to be taken. Although such reports are a fundamental part of his duties, he is actually in control of most current business, once policies have been approved by his superiors.[9]

Eichmann was not just a bureaucrat who climbed up the ladder to the rank of lieutenant-colonel. He was a referent and enjoyed all the authority and status that went with the position. He was not, however, an ordinary department head. Perhaps because of the subject under his direction, or perhaps because bureaucratic traditions were less strong in the Security Police, he was not merely the principal expert in his field, heading a typical staff of five. Rather, he headed an office with a staff of

8. Elsewhere Brecht writes that the referent was expected to be *the* expert on his subject: p. 25.
9. Brecht, *Administration*, pp. 179–80.

dozens, divided into smaller teams with their own areas of expertise.[10] He was the only department commander whose letters went straight to Müller or Heydrich, rather than passing through his direct commanders, Albert Hartl and Roth, the commanders of IV B. Bureaucrats at each rank in the RSHA had their own special signature color. Eichmann signed in orange, the color used by division heads rather than department heads. Eichmann's was the only department in the branch that had its own independent file system. Apparently, this was because of the exceptionally large percentage of its documents that was classified as "secret" and "top secret" (more than half the documents that survived from the period after the spring of 1941).[11]

This was the situation in the main office in Berlin. A similar bureaucratic structure, but with more junior officials, existed in German provincial cities and in the foreign capitals under Germany's sway during the war, only with more junior ranks. So, for example, Röthke was Referent for Jewish Affairs at the Security Police station in Paris.

The source for this structure is early in the Weimar period, in a "General Order for Administrative Procedures in the Offices of the German Reich," issued on September 2, 1926, by the German government after two years of intensive inter-ministerial effort. With it, Germany became the first and only country in which all members of the government service worked according to a single set of regulations. These regulations, and the management of the government apparatus, did not change in any significant way during the Third Reich.[12] Perhaps this was because of the great efficiency achieved through the order, or it may reflect the fact that most of the Weimar bureaucrats continued to work under the Nazis.

On June 1, 1940, a directive signed by Bruno Streckenbach was sent out to all the branches of the RSHA; it contained precise guidelines

10. Hilberg, *Destruction*, p. 996, describing the changing conditions under the Nazi regime: "In essence, then, there was an atrophy of laws and a corresponding multiplication of measures for which the sources of authority were more and more ethereal. Valves were being opened for a decision flow. The experienced functionary was coming into his own. A middle-ranking bureaucrat, no less than his highest superior, was aware of currents and possibilities. In small ways as well as large, he recognized what was ripe for the time. Most often it was he who initiated action."

11. TR. 10-754, pp. 79–80.

12. Brecht, *Administration*, pp. 4, 45; and compare the description of the Nazi Foreign Office (Browning) and Innenministerium (Lösener).

for creating documents. The document was similar to the order of 1926, and apparently was inspired by it. Some guidelines seem to have been taken from school lessons: "Long, complicated sentences should be avoided, and margins should be left for comments." Later in the directive the rules for identifying and signing documents are described: "The agency title is to appear in the upper left hand corner and under it the department title." The agency title could be "The Reichsführer in the Ministry of the Interior," or "RSHA," or "The Commander of the Security Police and the SD." Department IV B 4 was subordinate to all these, and each of these headings was used on different occasions. The line beneath the agency title was the filing code. It contained the referent's symbol, the filing data for the document, and the level of its classification. So, for example, the documents from the Wannsee Conference were marked

IV B 4 1456/41 gRs (1344)

which means Department IV B 4, File 1456 (1344) which was opened in 1941 and classified as *geheime Reichsache*, or top secret. The series of files whose numbers were in the 1400s dealt with the "evacuation activities" in the East.[13] Another example:

IV B 4a–2 2093/42g (391)

means Franz Novak (a–2) within the Department, File 2093 (391) from 1942, classified secret (*geheim*).[14]

Streckenbach's instructions (which, of course, may only have been signed by him) also specify how men of different ranks were to sign documents: "The head of the institution signs with his own name, those of one rank below him sign iV – *in Vertretung*, and those of other ranks sign iA – *im Auftrag*. If the institutional symbol was the Minister of the Interior, only the Reichsführer [Himmler] was to sign iV. If the heading was RSHA or "Commander of the Security Police and the SD," the branch chiefs [such as Müller] would sign iV." This difference is very significant – a person signing iV, "as the representative of," was in fact signing at his

13. TR. 10-767, p. 952. And see document 500–4–302 from "The Special Archive" (OSSOBI) in Moscow (captured German documents): a list of the files of Referat IV B 4. The list is incomplete, and is undated, but was created some months prior to the Wannsee Conference, as the Räumungsaktion series only reaches 1416: *Nahplan 3*. YVA O51.OSOBI.11.

14. A detailed breakdown of the codes and their respective "owners" throughout the whole period may be found in TR. 10-767, pp. 248–54.

own discretion, under the authority that his commander had granted him. A person signing iA, "at the direction of," was not signing at his own discretion, but rather by order of his commander, who did not want to be bothered signing himself. The source of authority for the signature is not the rank of the signer but the rank of the person who gave the order to sign. Since there was no institutional symbol called Division B, or even Branch IV, Eichmann never had the authority to sign iV. This does not mean that each time he signed iA he went to his commander for permission. If he was acting in accordance with the written instructions he had been given, he would have signed without bothering his commander, knowing that, were he to ask, the answer would be in the affirmative.[15]

At the end of Streckenbach's instructions is a color code. Each rank was assigned a special pencil color. Officers using it were to write comments or certify that they had read a given document by making a mark with the appropriate colored pencil.[16]

Different departments dealt with shaping policy, but not always in coordination with one another. This may be seen in an order signed by Heydrich on September 27, 1939 and again on December 2, 1940. Instructions appearing in a document on RSHA letterhead were on no account to be allowed to contradict instructions that appear in another document with the same letterhead.[17] One way officials tried to prevent this was by cooperating in the preparation of regulations and memoranda. Eichmann describes this:

> Sometimes one of my men in some place would point out unclear regulations, or local difficulties in carrying them out. In such a case I would call in my expert on the subject and we would analyze the situation. I would assign him to look into the matter and submit a proposed solution, and to determine whether this required a new regulation or whether a police directive would be sufficient. If we were not sure, we handed it over to the discretion of the commanders. Afterwards, the expert prepared the directive, which was marked with his office's symbol, and I would mark that I had seen it. It was handed over to the commanders, sometimes to the Reichsführer himself. When it returned to us we prepared the final copy. The expert's mark was in the upper corner; the signature – in accordance with the importance – I,

15. Eichmann, *Interrogation*, vol. 1, pp. 600–5.
16. TR. 10-767a, pp. 95–9. And compare with Brecht, *Administration*, to see the similarities to the regulations of 1926.
17. TR. 10-767a, pp. 89, 94.

Müller, or even Heydrich. I never put out a directive at my own discretion, without receiving approval from above.[18]

This account illustrates how a junior official would approach a mid-ranking superior with a proposal. He would in turn submit it to a senior official. The mid-ranking official then would receive approval to draft an appropriate regulation or directive, whereupon he would return to the lower-ranking official with a signed order explaining how the junior official had to operate. The latter would then carry on in the way he had wanted to in the first place – but now on the authority of an order, not at his own discretion. In any case, it is clear that the referent's competence to formulate legislation was not impaired by the transition from a democratic to a totalitarian regime. On the contrary, every move was made within the four walls of the institution, without any interference from parliamentary committees or the press.

It was not only junior officials who needed orders to cover them. The Security Police engaged in radical missions, and no one there was prepared to act at his own discretion – not even Heinrich Müller, the Gestapo chief. Eichmann assumed that even Heydrich and his successor as chief of the RSHA, Ernst Kaltenbrunner, did the same.[19] But the fact that Heydrich expressed his wishes did not grant "bureaucratic existence" to the wishes. That required legal authority, supplied by promulgating regulations and marking them with the numbers of specific offices. From here on out Eichmann could demand cooperation from other offices without involving Himmler and Heydrich, by noting, for example, that he was acting in accordance with regulation IV B 4b 3031/42g (1319) of August 14, 1942.

His colleagues would know what this referred to, provided that the department distributor (the *Verteiler*) did his job. Each office had such an official, whose task was to direct incoming and outgoing mail. In IV B 4 this was Lieutenant Rudolf Jänisch. One of the men in Branch II did this for all RSHA systems: every piece of mail directed to the Security Police reached him, and he sorted it and distributed it to the departments.[20] When letters reached Jänisch, he examined his files to see whether they belonged to an existing file, and numbered them; if the subject was a new one he opened a new file. Afterwards, he placed the documents before the

18. Eichmann, *Memoirs*, pp. 134–6.
19. Eichmann, *Interrogation*, vol. 1, pp. 157–8; TR. 3-29, p. 9.
20. TR. 10-652, p. 113.

appropriate official.[21] This official was termed the "first reader" — that is, the first person to relate to a piece of incoming mail. He could take care of it himself, or pass it on with his comments or proposals.[22]

Jänisch was also responsible for distributing directives and regulations. He had a list of addresses of all the Security Police bodies on the entire continent (the list was also called the *Verteiler*), and he had to be familiar enough with the work of each department to know who should receive a copy of any given regulation he was distributing.[23] The distribution list also noted how each writer addressed everyone else — Himmler, for example, addressed the Foreign Minister as "My Dear Ribbentrop," using the intimate *Du*.[24] With the help of this list, junior officials in the department could write letters from senior officials in their organization to those in other agencies.

This system was created originally in order to take some of the load off senior officials. Heydrich, for example, generally assigned Eichmann to write his letters for him, while he did no more than read and approve them before signing them himself.[25] A famous example is the letters of invitation for the Wannsee Conference, scheduled for December 9, 1941. The invitation sent to Luther in the Foreign Ministry was marked "personal!" and was sent to "Dear party Member Luther," but the code on the letter is IV B 4 3076/41g (1180), because it was prepared in IV B 4.[26] This ability to draft letters for higher-ups carried with it another potential, however — that of directing policy. A mid-level official like Eichmann, if he won the confidence of his commanders, could function at a much higher level than his nominal rank without anyone knowing about it. All he needed was his commanders' willingness to sign documents. He could not, of course, act without their knowledge, but under these circumstances the boundary between one who carries out orders and one who initiates and shapes policy becomes very blurred.

An important example of this may be found in Goering's letter to

---

21. TR. 10-652, pp. 129–30.
22. TR. 10-754, p. 201.
23. TR. 10-767a, p. 233.
24. TR. 10-767b, pp. 329–30.
25. Eichmann, *Interrogation*, vol. 1 p. 432. And see Heydrich to Ribbentrop, 24.6.1940, requesting to be invited to any future meetings on the solution to the "Jewish question." The code of this invitation was IV D 4. TR. 10-464.
26. TR. 3-946, Eichmann, *Memoirs*, p. 480. The wording was identical to all recipients, except for the name. See TR. 3-890, invitation to Hoffmann.

Heydrich, dated July 31, 1941,[27] in which Goering orders Heydrich to prepare "a final solution to the Jewish question." Eichmann noted in his memoirs that he wrote the letter, which was placed on Goering's desk for his signature.[28] At the time of his interrogation in Israel he no longer remembered. Either way, the letter was brought by Heydrich to Goering, because Heydrich saw a need for an authorizing document according to which he could demand cooperation from other offices.[29] The initiative came from below, not from Goering.

There is a somewhat strange example in directive IV B 4(RZ) (neu) 2494/41g (250), which was distributed to all the police stations. It ordered that all attempts by Belgian and French Jews to emigrate be thwarted. The subject and the code show that the directive was prepared by Hartmann, the expert on emigration, but it was signed by Walter Schellenberg, the RSHA's chief of counterintelligence, who was Eichmann's superior but not his direct commander. There is no way of knowing why he in particular signed the directive, but it is clear that it cannot be attributed to him.[30]

In 1943 the Italians hindered the German plan to deport the Jews of southern France. A series of urgent letters was sent from Paris alerting Berlin to the situation and seeking a solution. Some of these were written by Röthke, who was a lieutenant, but were signed by Knochen, who was a colonel, and were sent not, as usual, to Eichmann, according to accepted practice, but to Müller – an attempt to emphasize the serious nature of the issue not only in words, but also in form.

Under Kaltenbrunner, Eichmann wrote periodic activity reports intended for Himmler. The signature was always "your faithful Kaltenbrunner" – indicating that, even within the system, where there was ostensibly no need to make an impression with the rank of the signer, this kind of camouflage was still used.[31] It may well be that Kaltenbrunner was too busy, but it is more reasonable to believe that he knew that Eichmann was much better acquainted with the subject than he was.

This camouflaging of the true author occurs on a regular basis within Eichmann's department. Most of the letters that emerged from it were not written by him, but until the end of 1941 he – or his

27. Nuremberg document PS–710.
28. Eichmann, *Memoirs*, p. 479.
29. Browning, *Fateful Months*, pp. 21–2 and note 47 there.
30. TR. 3-441.
31. TR. 3-856, p. 4.

commanding officers – signed them all. The earliest surviving document signed by one of the department officers was written on December 3, 1941. It bore the signature of Friedrich Suhr, then the third-ranking official there.[32] After the spring of 1942 Günther's signature appears with a frequency similar to Eichmann's; the practice in the department was that Eichmann *or* Günther would sign.[33] On November 10, 1942 Günther signed a letter to the Foreign Ministry about an Italian Jewish woman named Jenni Cozzi,[34] and on March 15, 1943, Eichmann signed a second letter on this subject. Eichmann's letter states: "as I already wrote to you in November" – but of course it had been Günther, not he, who had signed that previous letter. In fact, both letters had been written by the same third man, one of the department officers, and in neither case did that man himself sign.[35]

There are a number of ways to determine who actually wrote a given letter – even if this does not solve the question of its gestation. First, when the code of a section within the office appears, the letter was not written by anyone more senior (although there were rare cases of typographical errors). In his interrogation, Eichmann claimed that all documents marked IV B 4a were prepared by Günther (or his men), and that he, Eichmann, simply signed them.[36] Not a single case is known in which a senior official wrote a letter and used the code of an official of lower rank. On the other hand, the lack of a section code does not rule out the possibility that an officer of lower rank wrote the letter and for whatever reason did not mark it with his code. This lack of clarity derives apparently from a certain nebulousness in Streckenbach's instructions, which did not state explicitly whether it was required to include this code or not.[37] If the subject of a document and the code at its head indicate a given section, there can be no doubt that that is indeed its source.

Second, there were a few cases, especially after 1942, in which a junior officer signed a letter himself. If this officer had no subordinates, then he was the author of the document. A third method of identification is based on the fact that every typist had a personal code. In principle each typist worked regularly with a single officer, and the prosecutors

32. TR. 3-1283.
33. TR. 10-767c, pp. 912–13, referring to a signature dated 31.3.1941.
34. TR. 3-744.
35. TR. 3-745.
36. Eichmann, *Interrogation*, vol. 2, pp. 630, 638, 1154.
37. Eichmann, *Interrogation*, vol. 1, p. 592; TR. 10-767a, pp. 212–13.

who prepared the indictments in West Germany's proceedings against Eichmann's subordinates were even able to prepare a chart showing all the dates on which secretaries worked on a temporary basis with an officer other than their own.[38] In the field stations this method of identification was similar, since there were fewer people working there, and fewer typists. Knochen's signature on a letter from Röthke's typist came from the latter's desk; when Knochen really wrote a letter on a Jewish issue, his own secretary would type it.[39] In Holland, letters written by the commander of IV B 4, Wilhelm Zöpf, were marked with the letter L; his assistant, Gertrude Slottke, marked letters she wrote with the code "e."[40]

The last and best way is to obtain the admission of the responsible person during interrogation. Of course, this was done with only a minority of the officers.[41]

*

Kaltenbrunner was appointed commander of the RSHA at the end of January 1943. A few days later he sent Himmler a message on the transfer of Jews from Theresienstadt. He divided the camp's residents into age groups and ability or inability to work. Thousands of the Jews were laboring on the upkeep of the ghetto, among them 4800 alone caring for the elderly. Conditions were crowded, making epidemics inevitable. Kaltenbrunner held that the population should be thinned (*Auflockerung*). He asked permission to send 5000 elderly Jews to Auschwitz. Jews with connections would not be sent.[42] On February 10, 1943 he received an answer from Lieutenant-Colonel Rudolf Brandt, a member of Himmler's personal staff: the Reichsführer was not interested in removing Jews from Theresienstadt, because this would violate the policy of letting the Jews there die peacefully.[43]

Peter Black, in his excellent biography of Kaltenbrunner, interprets this correspondence thus: Kaltenbrunner, new in his position, was testing his strength. He wanted to prove his willingness to contribute to the Final Solution. After his initiative was rejected (and in a fairly

38. TR. 10-767a, pp. 143–53. This identification was done only in relation to the officers against whom trials were being prepared.
39. TR. 3-815.
40. ZSL AR 518/59 Bd.III, pp. 541, 553.
41. TR. 10-767a, p. 153.
42. Undated, however, early February 1943. TR. 3-1181.
43. Adler, Hans G., *Verheimlichte Wahrheit*, Tübingen: Mohn, 1958, p. 299.

humiliating way, since the answer came from an officer of far lower rank), he refrained from additional initiatives, satisfying himself with exerting his strength and authority in cases where there were malfunctions or slowdowns in the speed of his work.[44]

Black's error was that he focused on an individual, Kaltenbrunner, rather than on the system. He must have read everything Kaltenbrunner ever wrote and, after arranging it all chronologically, he tried to discover the logic behind it. Except that Kaltenbrunner did not write this particular document – Günther did. Or perhaps Novak. Or another mid-level officer, such as Fritz Wöhrn, or Ernst Mös, or Werner Kryschak. The code (IV B 4a) is not precise enough for us to be able to determine the author with certainty. In any case, some junior official wrote it and Kaltenbrunner only signed it; therefore, the reply from the junior officer was not meant to insult him, and Kaltenbrunner was in fact not insulted and did not change direction. Nor did he decide to abstain from policy changes, and Black's explanation is incorrect. Perhaps.

This story drives home the central historiographical problem for historians of bureaucracies: how seriously should signatures be taken? Beyond that, is it at all possible to identify the "parent" of a measure resulting from a policy designed by a bureaucratic system? Maybe it is impossible to do more than point to a group of officials and say "they, together, designed the policy"?

But there are two ways to try to advance this inquiry, and I will demonstrate them in Kaltenbrunner's case.

1   Follow the file. Each subject was given its own number, and every document was filed by subject. If Kaltenbrunner's letter was exceptional, it is reasonable to conclude that this was because Kaltenbrunner, new in the system, in fact initiated it. If the letter was a continuation of the existing series of documents, apparently a lower official wrote it and asked Kaltenbrunner to sign. In the case before us, however, this method does not help much, since file 2093/42g (391) contained all the instructions for the deportation of German Jewry, and many members of the department's staff wrote letters that were filed there. It was a huge and varied file.

2   Follow the policy. Did Kaltenbrunner's proposal to Himmler constitute a change in policy regarding Theresienstadt? It would

44. Black, Peter, *Kaltenbrunner*, Princeton, NJ: Princeton University Press, 1984, pp. 152, 153, 159.

seem that it did, for from the time of the Wannsee Conference, at the latest, this camp was meant to be a place to which elderly, war-decorated, or well-connected Jews were sent, Jews about whom someone was likely to ask questions. Their transfer to this old people's ghetto was meant to quash the voices of meddlers in advance. During most of 1942 no Jews were deported from Theresienstadt, and Kaltenbrunner's idea was in fact an attempt to change direction, and for this reason it was rejected by Himmler.[45] Yet this does not answer our question, either, since it may well be that officials such as Günther, who had been aware for months of the exhaustion of the pool of Jews available for deportation from the Reich, hoped to exploit a window of opportunity with the arrival of a new commander in order to realize a change in policy that was beyond their own personal power to implement.

The existing documentation is insufficient for us to determine what happened. The discovery of a large number of similar documents would not improve the situation, since a low-ranking official could have written a letter for his commander, or could have written the letter at his own initiative, explaining to his commander why the letter was needed. In either case, the letters would bear the same code. The greater our sensitivity to these author codes, the greater our accuracy in describing the shaping of policy – and, when the issue is the creation of policy within a bureaucratic system, there is no objective testimony. This is even more true with regard to the testimony of the bureaucrats of murder, who later had no reason to recapitulate events with precision.

On the face of it, this conclusion would seem to support Arendt's claim. Not only is the bureaucrat drab and banal – he is also invisible. Decisions were not made by a specific person, but rather sprouted from within an undergrowth of senior officers who could make decisions and subordinates who knew what to propose. The coming chapters will show that there need be no contradiction between this conclusion and the claim that they all understood their mission clearly and pursued it out of choice. When they faced groups of officials with other intentions, they reacted in a way that was meant to advance, as best they could, the policy that they had chosen.

45. Black, *Kaltenbrunner*, p. 152. Although 5000 Jews, not specifically elderly, had been deported in January 1943. Hilberg, *Destruction* (1985 edn), p. 438.

Chapter 3

Toward the Final Solution

In May of 1943, Yisroel Friedman, 8 years old and totally alone in the world, was wandering through the Polish countryside, trying to cross the Vistula, because he had heard that one could hide with the partisans on the other side.

As I walked, a Gentile with a cart loaded with sacks of wheat stopped next to me. I climbed aboard and fell asleep, and the wagoner continued to drive — straight to the Gestapo. I don't know how he knew I was Jewish, but he must certainly have imagined that only a Jew would be wandering around with torn clothing, neglected, with all kinds of sores and boils on his body. I'm sure he was paid for this. Then the German police began to ask me questions. A tall German faced me and began to ask me all kinds of questions in Polish. I told him that my father had been killed in the war, my mother was very sick, and I had a little brother whom I had to feed. I lived in a certain place and had come here to get food. Then he asked me, are you Jewish? I said — No! He asked me to cross myself and I did this with no difficulty. I knew all the prayers by heart. But this did not convince him, and he ordered me to undress. So I undressed and stood before him stark naked, cupping my hands over my genitals. He ordered me to put down my hands. He saw that I'd been circumcised and I began to make things up. I told him that I'd had an injury and they'd done some surgery on me. I tried to sell him this story and I don't know if he bought it or not. In any event, he told me to get dressed and we went outside.

I knew that behind the house there was a path leading to the forest. He walked around the yard with me and offered me a cigarette. I was about eight years old then, and I told him that I did not smoke. Then I saw him open the holster of his handgun and I ran. I bumped into a fence and jumped over it. He fired several shots; one of them grazed the skin of my leg. I managed to get past the fence. They began to chase and search for me. I didn't know the area well, but I knew about a quicksand marsh nearby. I went into it and managed to grab a branch and lie on it with my whole body. After I heard the voices fading away, I left and went even deeper into the forest. For two weeks I did not dare come out. I drank from creeks, I ate the fruit that grew in the forest, and I'd even make little bonfires and try to catch birds. Sometimes I succeeded.[1]

Not a story we can easily fit into any familiar context. An eight-year-old expert at survival. A Polish farmer, selling him to his death for bounty. And above all, a German policeman, stationed in some remote village at the edge of a Polish forest, who interrogates the child, disbelieves his tale, invites him to take a walk in the yard so as not to make a mess in the office, offers him a cigarette, and then cold-bloodedly shoots to kill. Upon missing, he then organizes a posse, and goes after the "delinquent." A policeman unlike any we have ever met.

It is precisely this bizarreness, this surreality which was all too real, that we have yet to explain satisfactorily. For many years, historians trying to do so seemed to feel that, if only they could unravel the decision-making process leading to the policy of murder, they might gain an insight – or at least an inkling of one – into the phenomenon itself. This led, in the 1980s, to a tremendous squabble between two groups of interpreters of the historical documentation – the intentionalists and the functionalists. The former claimed that Hitler knew where he was leading his anti-Jewish policy, hence there was intention. The latter saw no Nazi blueprint, and instead read from the documents a cumulative development, defined by the structure of the Nazi form of government and the way it worked.[2]

In the middle of the decade there were those who claimed that the debate had ended – not because one camp had persuaded the other to give in, but because it was understood that there could be no resolution

---

1. YVA, 03.6948.
2. See, for example, Karl Schleunes, *The Twisted Road to Auschwitz*, London: Deutsch, 1972; Uwe D. Adam, *Judenpolitik im Dritten Reich*, Düsseldorf: Droste, 1972; Martin Broszat, "The Genesis of the Final Solution," *Yad Vashem Studies*, XIII, 1979; and Hans Mommsen, "Die Realisierung des Utopischen: Die 'Endlösung' der Judenfrage im Dritten Reich," *Geschichte und Gesellschaft* 9, no. 3, 1983. A summary of the discussion in the mid-1980s, mildly supportive of this camp, may be found in Christopher Browning, *Fateful Months: Essays on the Emergence of the Final Solution*, New York: Holmes & Meier, 1985. The terms identifying the two camps were coined by the British historian Tim Mason, in "Intention and Explanation: A Current Controversy about the Interpretation of National Socialism," in Gerhard Hirschfeld and Lothar Kettenacker, *Der Führerstaat: Mythos und Realität*, Stuttgart: DVA, 1981.

of the issue.[3] The state of the documentation is such that neither side can be proved correct. In fact, each side cites the same documents in its favor, but reads them differently. Some of those who declared the ceasefire tried to achieve a synthesis between the positions of the two sides, and to find a middle way that would learn something from each of them.[4]

That effort was not particularly successful; the contenders stood their ground, although they did draw somewhat closer to each other. The extreme positions on each side were abandoned, but in the 1990s there were still respectable historians publishing serious studies that bolstered one party or the other.[5] While, to a certain extent, the lines of the debate have changed and progressed over time, the question of the cause of the Final Solution continues to preoccupy historians,[6] and will apparently continue to do so for a long time to come.

In the spring of 1996 Daniel Jonah Goldhagen stormed into the arena. His book, *Hitler's Willing Executioners: Ordinary Germans and the Holocaust*[7] sold in quantities, and attracted media attention, of a kind generally reserved for doubtful biographies of members of the British royal family. It became an international media event, and the author's tour of Germany at the end of that summer was apparently the most tumultuous event there since reunification. Goldhagen's thesis was simple – simplistic, actually. He said that Hitler was able to lead the Germans in the mass murder of European Jewry because this is what the Germans had really wanted to do all along. From the end of the nineteenth century, Goldhagen argues, an eliminationist antisemitism pervaded German society, and its principal aim was to rid that society of Jews.

It is no coincidence that Goldhagen, unlike both the intentionalists and functionalists, refrained from dealing with the first two years of

3. For example, Yehuda Bauer, "Auschwitz," in Eberhard Jäckel and Jürgen Rohwer, *Der Mord an den Juden im zweiten Weltkrieg*, Stuttgart: DVA, 1985.

4. Christopher Browning, *Fateful Months: Essays on the Emergence of the Final Solution*, New York: Holmes & Meier, 1985. He calls himself a "moderate functionalist," yet is actually trying to synthesize the diverse positions.

5. For the intentionalists: Richard Breitman, *The Architect of Genocide: Himmler and the Final Solution*, New York: Knopf, 1991. For the functionalists (and not even particularly moderately so): Hans Safrian, *Die Eichmann Männer*, Wien: Europaverlag, 1993.

6. See the controversy about the recent thesis of Aly and Heim: *YVS*, XXIV, 1994, contributions of Götz Aly and Sussane Heim, Dan Diner, David Bankier, Ulrich Herbert.

7. Daniel Jonah Goldhagen, *Hitler's Willing Executioners: Ordinary Germans and the Holocaust*, New York: Knopf, 1996.

the war. He was not seeking to explain how murder appeared in the process of policy development; instead, he saw the policy as a reflection of what a society of latent murderers wanted to do. In his claim that the policy derived from a conscious will to murder, he is more extreme than any intentionalist. On the other hand, in projecting this will onto all the actors, he steals the thunder from the functionalists, because if the impetus for genocide came from rank-and-file Germans, then it was from the intentions of the public, rather than those specific to the Nazi leadership, that the policy emerged. Yet the huge uproar he created obscured the fact that in recent years there is a growing group of mostly younger scholars who in one form or another support a new thesis, neither intentionalist nor functionalist. They argue that a very large number of Germans were predisposed to carry out a policy (or policies) built on killing those who obstructed the Aryan progress towards its glorious destiny. And it is interesting that many of these scholars are Germans.

At the beginning of the 1980s, Benno Müller-Hill was already drawing attention to the sizeable contribution made by senior, respected physicians to the Nazi policy of murdering the handicapped. A group of psychiatrists in Berlin tried to uncover the dark past of the institution where they worked, and found themselves criticizing even the great scholar after whom the institution had been named after the war. Karl Bonhoeffer, who was by all accounts a liberal and progressive figure in his field, was nevertheless willing to ignore the interests and feelings of individual patients in the pursual of research that he thought would advance knowledge. He was certainly no Nazi murderer, but he bore much responsibility for the development of the anti-humanist attitudes that became ensconced in German medicine between the wars. Henry Friedlander has described the policy of murdering institutionalized handicapped patients, most of whom were Germans, as the first stone on the road to the policy of murder that was turned afterwards against the Jews.[8]

8. Benno Müller-Hill, *Murderous Science: Elimination by Scientific Selection of Jews, Gypsies, and Others, Germany, 1933–1945*, Oxford: Oxford University Press, 1988; *Totgeschwiegen 1933–1945: Zur Geschichte der Wittenauer Heilstätten, seit 1957 Karl-Bonhoeffer-Nervenklinik*. Herausgeber: Arbeitsgruppe zur Erforschung der Geschichte der Karl-Bonhoeffer-Nervenklinik. Wissenschaftliche Beratung: Götz Aly, Berlin: Edition Hentrich, 1989; Henry Friedlander, *The Origins of Nazi Genocide: From Euthanasia to the Final Solution*, Chapel Hill, NC: The University of North Carolina Press, 1995. And see also, in English, Götz Aly, Peter Chroust and Christian Pross, *Cleansing the Fatherland. Nazi Medicine and Racial Hygiene*, Baltimore: Johns Hopkins University Press, 1994.

Götz Aly and Susanne Heim have examined the positions and actions of economists, sociologists, and space planners (*Grossraumpläner* – a German profession that combined urban and rural planning), first in the 1930s but especially in the occupied areas in Eastern Europe. They found a group of young and educated men, not necessarily Nazis, who believed that the main problem in Eastern Europe was overpopulation. These men proposed solving the problem by getting rid of millions, beginning with the Jews.[9] Ulrich Herbert focused on a group that was similar in its age and education – the mainstream intellectuals of the political right, and especially lawyers. He found among them a coherent and cogent outlook of German nationalism (*Völkism*) and antisemitism. They held these views long before the appearance of Hitler, to whom they adhered with a certain reluctance only after it became clear to them that he was about to take power.[10] Hannes Heer and Klaus Naumann have edited a collection of studies that address the crimes of the German army in wartime. The army was the only large organization in which there were Germans from all walks of life. Their findings were also presented in an exhibition called "The Crimes of the Wehrmacht." Hannes Heer's article in the book, called "Killing Fields," concludes with this sentence: "The decision to deal with the crimes of the Wehrmacht means turning from the writing of the history of the war to the writing of the social history of the war."[11]

An international conference of historians at Yad Vashem in Jerusalem on the subject *German Society's Response to Nazi Anti-Jewish Policy, 1939–1941*, the proceedings of which were published in 1998,[12] demonstrated that this tendency may be developing into a broad school of interpretation, as a majority of the historians present – again, most of them Germans – presented well-researched and balanced findings the common denominator of which was, however, that the participation of German society in the Nazi persecution of the Jews in the 1930s clearly exceeded the confines of the party, not to mention the leadership. Perhaps this interpretation might be summed up in the words of Saul Friedländer,

9. Götz Aly and Susanne Heim, *Vordenker der Vernichtung: Auschwitz und die deutschen Pläne für eine neue europäische Ordnung*, Frankfurt/M: Fischer, 1993; Deborah Dwork and Robert van der Pelt, *Auschwitz, 1270 to the Present*, New York: Norton, 1996.

10. Ulrich Herbert, *Best: Biographische Studien über Radikalismus, Weltanschauung und Vernunft, 1903–1989*, Bonn: Dietz, 1996.

11. Hannes Heer and Klaus Naumann (eds), *Vernichtungskrieg: Verbrechen der Wehrmacht 1941 bis 1944*, Hamburg: Hamburger Edition, 1995, p. 75.

12. German Society's Responses to Nazi Anti-Jewish Policy, 1933–1941, conference at Yad Vashem.

"Through a process of interpretation and innovation, party, state, and society gradually filled in the remaining blanks of the ever harsher code regulating all relations with Jews. What party agencies and the state bureaucracy left open was dealt with by the courts, and what the courts did not rule on remained for the German people to figure out."[13] The motivating force behind this phenomenon, suggests Friedländer, was what he calls "redemptive antisemitism": the *Weltanschauung* whereby getting rid of the Jews was regarded as a central and essential component in a political program that would redeem the world. Unlike Goldhagen's eliminationist antisemitism, the very existence of which remains doubtful, redemptive antisemitism is a far more convincing phenomenon.

The concept of redemptive antisemitism is not enough to explain the Holocaust, or even the actions of the low-ranking policeman from whom we fled at the beginning of this chapter. The reason is that it begs prior questions, such as the roots of this "faith," the reasons why it was accepted by large numbers of people, and the ways in which it was translated from world view into action. If, however, we agree that the concept is historically relevant, and that there is good reason to focus on it, we will be able to progress along a new channel of inquiry, one that will help us understand the Nazi murderers from the point where the discussion of the way decisions were made is no longer fruitful.

So, for instance, Michael Wildt, historian of the SD, found that the principal characteristic of the SD's work was extremism. In any given situation they proposed solving the ideological problems at hand (such as the presence of Jews) by making conditions worse; when this did not solve the problem, they used even harsher measures.[14]

One study that entirely confirms Wildt's thesis, even if it is not based on it, is Götz Aly's important work, *The Final Solution: The Transferring of Nations and the Murder of the European Jews*.[15] After finding, in his previous book, that the personnel of the occupation administrations were brimming with ideas about how to remold the population of Eastern Europe, he directed his attention to the bureaucrats who were involved in

---

13. Saul Friedländer, *Nazi Germany and the Jews*. vol. I: *The Years of Persecution, 1933–1939*, New York: HarperCollins, 1997, p. 306.

14. Michael Wildt, *Die Judenpolitik des SD 1935 bis 1938: Eine Dokumentation*, München: Oldenbourg, 1995.

15. Götz Aly, *"Endlösung": Völkerverschiebung und den Mord an den europäischen Juden*, Frankfurt/M: Fischer, 1995. The framework of the description of events as portrayed from this point on, and particularly the discussion of the plans for transfer of populations, borrows heavily from Aly.

the attempt to carry out these ideas in the field. This means, first and foremost, Himmler, who acquired yet another title for himself for the purpose: that of Reich Commissioner for the Strengthening of Germandom, or RKFDV. One of the primary new findings of Aly's study is the somehow overlooked fact that among the major figures involved in implementing Himmler's ideas were Heydrich and Eichmann. Another is that, from the point of view of these executives, the population transfer policy was a web of ever-increasing failure.

If, at the end of the 1930s, the major Nazi effort was aimed at the forced emigration of the Jews, and Eichmann stood at the center of the execution of this policy, very soon after the beginning of the war Heydrich expressed a new position. This was that, during the war, it would not be possible to continue emigration, and since in any case there were now many more Jews under German rule, the Jews should be moved as far away as possible, to the edges of the area under German control. At a meeting of his senior officers on September 9, 1939, he spoke about German plans for Poland. Part of the country would be annexed to the Reich, and what remained would be turned into a non-German *Gau*, or administrative region (what was later called the Generalgouvernement). Within a year all Jews were to be transferred into ghettos in the Polish area. The Polish population would be divided into several categories, according to the degree of resemblance to Nordic Aryans. The lowest categories would be treated the most harshly. Eichmann was the most junior participant in the meeting, but the fact that he was invited shows that Heydrich saw him as a natural candidate to make the transition to the new policy.[16]

On October 10, 1939, Eichmann was instructed by his commander, Heinrich Müller, to prepare the deportation of 80,000 Jews from the area of Katowicz. But that very day no other than Hitler intervened, producing uncertainty for Eichmann and Müller. The Führer made a speech about policy in the East. Ethnic Germans, he announced, would be brought from distant parts of Eastern Europe to the Reich; a new eastern border would be drawn for Germany; Poland would be dismantled; and an "arrangement" would be made for the Jewish problem. The next day Hitler assigned implementation to Himmler. But for many

16. TR.3-983; Aly, *Endlösung*, p. 29.

weeks thereafter the borders kept shifting. This made it impossible to plan, since it was not clear who had to be moved where.[17]

At this time, Eichmann tried his hand at deporting Jews by sending more than 3000 of them from Ostrava and Vienna to Nisko, where he thought a Jewish ghetto would be established. The action was halted a few days later. Seev Goshen sees this as an attempt by Eichmann to act on his own initiative, an attempt that was stymied by Müller for precisely this reason. Aly describes the incident less dramatically, and implies that the plan was halted because conditions were not yet ripe, since it was necessary to deal with more urgent matters, such as the absorption of German immigrants.[18]

Over the following two years or so, planners of the population transfers promulgated a series of short and long-term plans. The first short-term plan, called *Nahplan* 1, had originally been to deport all Jews from the newly annexed territories, as well as all Congress Poles from Posen, East and South Prussia, as well as an additional, yet to be determined number of Poles that the Germans defined as hostile.[19] These deportations were to start immediately, in November, but were put off until December. It turned out that most Poles could not be deported for economic reasons, and anyway, being very poor, their homes were not deemed suitable for the incoming Baltic Germans, who needed larger apartments, in the cities. Therefore, the plan was changed, and the new intention was to deport 80,000 Jews and Poles.[20]

In reality, 87,883 Poles and Jews were deported, between December 1 and 16, 1939. This deportation did not, however, go smoothly. The deportees were shunted from place to place in freight cars. In many cases they froze to death along the way or reached their destinations mad from thirst and hunger. Despite instructions from Berlin to the contrary, they were not allowed to take food, coats, or blankets. SS officers in the Generalgouvernement complained about trains reaching them without coordination. There were cases in which sealed cars full of deportees stood at stations for as long as eight days, until a solution for them was found.[21]

17. Aly, *Endlösung*, pp. 35–46, 61.
18. Seev Goshen, "Eichmann und die Nisko-Aktion im Oktober 1939. Eine Fallstudie zur NS–Judenpolitik in der letzten Etappe vor der 'Endlösung'," *VJHfZG*, 1981, vol. 1, pp. 74–96; Aly, *Endlösung*, pp. 62–4, 127.
19. Himmler to the HSSPF in the East, 30.10.1939. TR.3-1397.
20. Heydrich to the HSSPF in the East, November 28, 1939. TR.3-1459, 1469.
21. Adler, *Verwalteter Mensch*, pp. 114–15; TR.3-1399, pp. 1–2.

Of course, it was not the deportees' tribulations that disturbed the SS officers – it was the logistical chaos. Heydrich appointed Eichmann to coordinate the matter on December 19, 1939.[22]

After the completion of *Nahplan* 1, planning began for the second phase, *Nahplan* 2. On December 21, 1939, Heydrich approved a plan for deporting to the Generalgouvernement the 600,000 Jews from the Polish districts that had been annexed to the Reich. They were not, however, to be sent to the Lublin area, because the army opposed having a large concentration of Jews close to the German-Soviet border.[23] The more they worked on the plan, the more it changed, since removal of the Jews would not in itself provide homes for the ethnic Germans who had been brought west from Polish areas annexed by the Soviet Union.

The changes were spelled out when Eichmann presented the plan, updated to the date of its presentation (January 8, 1940) at an interministerial meeting to determine future work procedures. The plan now called for the deportation of 350,000 Jews and *Poles*. In January 12,000 people, 2000 of them Jews, would be expelled from Danzig. A precise date had not yet been set, mostly because of coordination problems with the absorption authorities in the Generalgouvernement. When the time came, the RSHA would hold a meeting with the Ministry of Transportation in order to set a timetable for the trains. Then this would be conveyed to representatives in the east. At the meeting were representatives of the Security Police, the economic ministries, the transportation ministry, the finance ministry, and the trusteeship office, which dealt with the seizure of property.

The police representatives from the East stated their grievances resulting from the first deportation attempts. Later in the meeting, the participants discussed how to achieve maximal efficiency. It was decided that each train would carry 1000 deportees. An attempt would be made to deport women and children in passenger cars, in order to prevent them from freezing. The deportees could take with them up to 100 zlotys, but it was important to make sure that they did not take any Reichsmarks. They could also take food. Notification was to be made to the trusteeship office about each deportation, so that it could seize the abandoned property. Regular reports would be sent to Krakow and to Eichmann.[24]

22. TR.10-767a, pp. 53–4; Adler, *Verwalteter Mensch*, p. 15; Aly, *Endlösung*, p. 103.
23. Aly, *Endlösung*, p. 110.
24. TR.3-1399: notes taken by Abromeit during the meeting, January 8, 1940.

There were no further deportations during January. On January 30, 1940, Heydrich called a meeting of senior officials: four top SS regional commanders, four of their deputies, and senior commanders from the RSHA, including Streckenbach, Müller, and Ohlendorf. Among the lower-ranking participants were Eichmann, Günther, Dannecker, and Rajakowitz. Heydrich announced the establishment of department IV D 4, which would coordinate the "evacuation" campaigns. Afterwards he spoke at length about the population transfer plans. Artur Seyss-Inquart, the acting governor of the Generalgouvernement, and Friedrich Wilhelm Krieger, the top regional SS commander in Cracow, agreed in principle with the policy, but had reservations about many technical details, some of which touched on matters of principle, such as the lack of jobs for the deportees. Heydrich did not change his position. The meeting lasted for two hours, and after it some of the participants remained to speak with Eichmann and his men on professional matters.[25]

In the meantime, constraints in the field continued to cause problems. Quarters still had not been found for many of the 40,000 urban ethnic Germans from the Baltic countries, so on very short notice an interim plan was put into effect. Between February 10 and March 15, 40,128 people were deported. Among them were about 1000 Jews from Stettin, but most were urban Poles. In parallel with the deportations, more than 10,000 patients at mental institutions in western Poland were murdered, with the object of making room to house ethnic Germans temporarily.[26]

By the time they proceeded to implement *Nahplan* 2, they had noticed that the ethnic Germans coming from Vohlyn and from East Galicia were rural farmers. To resettle them, it was necessary to evict Polish farmers rather than urban Jews. Furthermore, the train authorities gave notice that they did not have the capacity to carry hundreds of thousands of Jews. As a result of these constraints, the *Nahplan* 2 (which was given the number 2 even though it was at least the third wave of deportations), carried out between April 1940 and January 1941, affected some 120,000 people, almost all of them Poles, and not Jews. The weakest were deported to the Generalgouvernement, the stronger sent as laborers to the Reich.[27] The identity of the deportees made no difference

25. TR.3-468.
26. Aly, *Endlösung*, pp. 110, 114–16.
27. Aly, *Endlösung*, pp. 111–12.

to Eichmann, who dealt with the problems that came in from the field: coordinating trains, disputes over the amount of food which the deportees were to be provisioned with, complaints about irregularities in the execution of the deportations, and so on.[28]

The delay in the deportations was not to the Jews' benefit, since German authorities in the annexed territories prepared for the deportation by stripping the Jews of their property. When the deportation was late in coming, they opted for another intermediate solution – putting the Jews into ghettoes. So it is not surprising that the first large ghetto was established at the beginning of 1940 in Łódź, on the eastern edge of the Polish territory that had been annexed to the Reich.

On April 24, 1940, a memorandum was sent out from the desk of Richard Hartmann, the member of Eichmann's staff who dealt directly with the Jewish organizations, saying that according to the orders of the Reichsmarshal (Goering), Jewish emigration from the Reich was to be increased, even in time of war. But Jews with defense skills were not to go to enemy countries, and because of foreign policy considerations there was to be no emigration to Palestine.[29] Gideon Rafael, then involved in the clandestine Aliya Bet operation that was smuggling Jews into Palestine, argues that during precisely this period (March–May 1940) he made contact with a representative of Eichmann, Alexander von Höppner, and proposed removing 40,000 Jews from Germany, via Italy and Rhodes, to Palestine. The plan failed because of Italy's entry into the war.[30] On the other hand, a letter from the department signed by Heydrich and sent to the Foreign Minister in June noted that, because of the large number of Jews, it was impossible to solve the problem through emigration. Thus it would be necessary to find a territorial solution.[31]

In the summer, when new political possibilities opened up after the defeat of France, the Germans began to look seriously into the idea of deporting the Jews to Madagascar.[32] Up to this point, they had not managed to get rid of even a few hundred thousand Jews. The

28. TR.3-1402, 10.2.40; TR.3-1401, 27.2.40; TR.3-1485, 8.3.40; TR.3-1486, 30.3.40; TR.3-1487, 11.4.40; TR.3-1403, 18.4.40; TR.3-1404, 5.6.40; TR.3-1405, 5.6.40; TR.3-1406, 7.8.40; TR.3-1488.
29. TR.10-767a, pp. 47–8.
30. *Haaretz*, December 12, 1994 (Hebrew). And see also Yehuda Bauer, *Jews for Sale? Nazi–Jewish Negotiations 1933–1945*, New Haven, CT: Yale University Press, 1994, pp. 49–50.
31. TR.3-464, 24.6.40.
32. Aly, *Endlösung*, pp. 128–35.

Madagascar idea promised, at least on the face of it, a solution for millions – and the Germans had more Jews on their hands than just those in western Poland.

Himmler himself was not certain of Hitler's intentions, and submitted to him a six-page document with proposals for what to do with different ethnic groups in the East, including the Jews.[33] Himmler expected the Jews to disappear, perhaps via emigration to Africa. Hitler agreed with the spirit of the document, although he did not hold a discussion about it.[34] When it became clear that France had been defeated, the Madagascar idea was activated. It had been discussed publicly for some time in Europe, and had also been taken up by diplomats in Poland, Germany, France and Great Britain. In 1937 an investigative mission had even gone from Poland to the island to find out what the prospects were. It may well have been discussed, back in the spring of 1938, within the SD;[35] Goering mentioned it as a realistic option in a meeting he conducted after Kristallnacht.[36] It is not clear, however, who spurred interest in it this time. When Browning focused on the foreign ministry, he arrived at the following description of the chain of events:

> June 3, 1940: Franz Rademacher, Eichmann's counterpart in the foreign ministry, who had just been appointed to this position, applied to his superior, Martin Luther, and suggested looking into the idea of transferring the Jews of Europe to Madagascar.

33. Nrbg.doc. NO–1880, 25.5.1940.
34. Richard Breitman, *Architect*, p. 118. Breitman sees Himmler submitting his memorandum (twice – Hitler didn't respond the first time) as a trial balloon, to determine Hitler's intentions. He rejects the possibility of the physical destruction of whole peoples as un-German – yet the mere mention indicates that the idea was already there. Ibid., pp. 118–22. Breitman's interpretation is interesting, precisely as his overall reading of the documents places the decision to kill all of the Jews in late 1940, i.e. earlier than the date preferred by many historians. Yet even he sees no decision in the spring or summer of 1940. Bauer's reading of this document is similar to that of Breitman: Yehuda Bauer, "Who Was Responsible and When? Some Well-known Documents Revisited," *Holocaust and Genocide Studies*, vol. 6, no. 2, 1991.
35. Adler, *Verwalteter Mensch*, p. 69; Leni Yahil, "Madagascar – Phantom of a Solution for the Jewish Question," in George L. Mosse and Bela Vago, *Jews and Non-Jews in Eastern Europe 1918–1945*, Jerusalem: Israel Universities Press, 1974 – especially p. 321.
36. Nuremberg Document PS–1816; and see Bauer's comments in "Who Was Responsible?" p. 133.

June 4, 1940: Rademacher spoke on the subject with Paul Wurm, the foreign editor of *Der Sturmer*, who thought it an excellent idea. Luther forwarded the proposal to Ribbentrop, who also agreed.

June 16–17, 1940: Hitler and Ribbentrop met in Munich with Mussolini and his foreign minister, Galeazzo Ciano, and raised the idea in their talks. Rademacher received approval and began to work on it (there is no date on the approval document).

June 24, 1940: Heydrich approached Ribbentrop, asserting that he was responsible for the solution to the Jewish problem and demanding that he be made party to Ribbentrop's discussions. During the summer Rademacher collected data, thought, and wrote a draft proposal.

August 15, 1940: Dannecker brought Rademacher the Security Police plan, which became known as the Dannecker plan. It stated that the entire operation would be run by the SS, with the foreign ministry playing only a marginal role. Rademacher continued to work on his plans.

End of August: Rademacher submited a progress report to Luther. He envisioned a joint operation by many arms of the government, including the SS, but under the coordination of the foreign ministry. Furthermore, he suggested calling a meeting of representatives of all the organizations with the foreign ministry hosting (that is, taking the leading role). In September interest in the plan petered out, though Hitler may have discussed it with other high-placed officials in February 1941.[37]

Breitman accepts this reconstruction, and notes that the SS entered the picture only after June 24, 1940, when Heydrich wrote a short and pointed letter requesting that his men be made part of any discussion of the subject. Both Wislicency and Eichmann remembered otherwise – they said they initiated the matter, as early as May (apparently as soon as it was clear that France would be vanquished).[38] It may well be that as far as the SS was concerned, Himmler's letter to Hitler (May 25, 1940) was when the idea began being pursued in a practical way, but without documentation this can be no more than a presumption.[39] The fact that the earliest document that links the Security Police to the subject is

37. Christopher Browning, *The Final Solution and the German Foreign Office*, New York, 1978, pp. 35–43; Hilberg, *Destruction*, p. 398. He quotes the diary of Gerhard Engel, adjutant at Hitler's headquarters, February 2, 1941.
38. Breitman, *Architect*, pp. 123–4; TR.3-773, pp. 4–5; Eichmann, *Interrogation*, vol. 2, p. 812.
39. My thanks to Professor Yehuda Bauer for the suggestion.

Heydrich's letter does not add to or detract from this presumption, since Jänisch knew how to draft letters like these, and there is no way of knowing who actually wrote it.

The question, then, remains open. Did Rademacher initiate the matter, with Eichmann's men being drawn in after him, or did the Security Police initiate it, and Rademacher put it into writing after hearing about it (perhaps because he was not used to an atmosphere of secrecy)? A third possibility is that both parties came up with the notion independently, influenced by their environment, perhaps even by the reverberations of conversations between Hitler and Himmler on the May memorandum? The same question may be asked of Hitler. We know that Ribbentrop briefed Hitler on the proposal shortly before the summit with Mussolini, but did Hitler raise it with Mussolini because of Ribbentrop's initiative? Or did Ribbentrop raise a possibility that Hitler had already thought of, and had planned in any case to raise with Mussolini? Maybe Ribbentrop was trying to signal Hitler that he, too, not just Himmler, was thinking innovatively, in tune with Hitler's intentions? There is no way to answer this question, and it may be seen as a small-scale model of the explanation or lack thereof of the way the really momentous decision on the murder of all the Jews in Europe was made about a year later.

What is clear is that the Security Police moved faster than Rademacher did, perhaps because they had an entire team at their disposal. Eichmann and Rajakowitz drove over to the emigration department in the Ministry of the Interior and got information on Madagascar. Afterwards, they collected more data from a geographic research institute in Hamburg. With this, they drew up a first draft of the plan. There were discussions with the participation of representatives of the foreign ministry, Deputy Führer Hess, the Ministries of the Interior, Propaganda, and the Economy, and other branches of the SS. After going through twelve to fifteen drafts, the plan was ready, as noted earlier, in the middle of August 1940.[40] It was much harsher than the one formulated by Rademacher.

The proposal was to deport the approximately four million Jews who were under Nazi rule. It included the geographical data and pointed up the necessity of preparing the island to absorb millions. These tasks would keep the Jews occupied during the first stage, until the settlement could support itself (or not – Dannecker showed no interest in whether

40. TR.3-172; Eichmann, *Interrogation*, vol. 1, pp. 138–40; vol. 2, pp. 793, 800.

the deported Jews would be able to survive). The supreme government would be German, and air force and naval bases would be built there. With regard to internal affairs, a police state would be established under the commander of the Security Police, but the Jews would have regional and general councils of elders. The emigration would be planned by the regional headquarters of the Security Police, which would control the Jewish leadership groups. The Jews would be allowed to take only 200 kilograms of property, with the rest going to a trusteeship office. The transfer of the Jews, at a rate of two ships carrying 1500 Jews each per day, would continue over a four-year period. An agreement would have to be reached regarding the provision of a fleet and free passage from the French and British. The financing would be Jewish. To carry out the "proposed final solution," it was suggested that a unit of the Security Police be sent to Madagascar, and that SS representatives participate in the formulation of a peace treaty, so that they could see to it that the needs of the plan were taken into account.[41] The general concept – deporting the Jews at their own expense, with most of the work being carried out by their leadership under the supervision of the Security Police – had its origin no later than 1937, when Dannecker was merely a sergeant in the SD.

In October 1940 there was a single attempt to deport Jews from Germany. On the 22nd of that month, 6504 Jews were expelled from Baden and the Palatinate, and more than 500 from the Saarland. All were sent to camps in southern France. Apparently, the initiative came from the local Gauleiters, and it received Hitler's blessing. Eichmann and the RSHA were at the center of the operation, but without this being RSHA policy. This was therefore also one of the few deportation operations to which the Jewish leadership was not made an accessory to preparations. Here the Security Police acted by surprise, not according to their established practice. During his interrogation in Israel, Eichmann remembered his concern that his men might not be able to get the trains into France – he said he sweated a lot until they got over the border. "I only know that it would have been very bad for the Jews and for me, too, had the transports gotten stuck on the border. In that case they [the trains] could not have gone on nor returned" (because he and his organization would not have allowed them to return).[42] Given that the deported Jews stayed

41. TR.3-172, 17 pages.
42. Adler, *Verwalteter Mensch*, pp. 152–3; Hilberg, *Destruction*, p. 397; Leni Yahil, *The Holocaust*, p. 177; Eichmann, *Interrogation*, vol. 1, pp. 144–5.

in the Gurs concentration camp until they were deported once more, to their deaths, it is not clear what could have been worse for them.

The Madagascar plan was already moribund, and in the interim period, before additional dramatic events, an interministerial meeting was held in the Reichsführer's headquarters on October 30, 1940. On the agenda was the possibility that German Jews who were in the Soviet Union might want to return to the Reich. The participants, Eichmann among them, estimated that there were hundreds of such Jews, and that they had no property. There was a consensus that their return to Germany should be prevented. But Eichmann opposed stripping them of their citizenship, which would deprive them of a legal claim to return. In his opinion, other countries would be reluctant to take in refugees if it was clear in advance that they could never be returned to Germany. Better, he said, to prevent the return of the Jews by dragging out the processing of their requests. At this point, Eichmann was still seeing the issue through the eyes of an expert on emigration; likewise, the Madagascar plan did not eliminate his previous interest in regular emigration, when that was possible.[43]

In the last months of 1940, Himmler's men were occupied with planning the continuation of the population transfer program, which was called the Third Immediate Plan, or *Nahplan* 3. In order to put the best face on an unsuccessful program, Himmler brought together senior party officials and the Gauleiters in Berlin on December 10, 1940 at 10 a.m. He appeared in civilian clothes and gave a lecture, using data prepared for him by Eichmann. The data exaggerated the number of Jewish expulsions, as compared with the number of ethnic Germans absorbed, by including all the Jews who had emigrated since 1933, as well as the excess of Jewish deaths over Jewish births. The draft prepared by Eichmann on December 4 stated:

> II. The Final Solution of the Jewish Question. By resettling the Jews out of the European economic area to a yet to be determined territory. In the framework of this project approximately 5.8 million Jews will be affected.

43. TR.3-1059; Bauer points out that some attempts to emigrate Jews continued until autumn 1941, so much so that "The two policies, murder and extrusion, were for a short period in operation at the same time." Bauer, *Jews for Sale?*, p. 53.

A few months previously the SS had planned to deport four million Jews to Madagascar — apparently the number of Jews under German rule. Now it anticipated deporting to a yet-to-be-determined destination almost six million Jews. These were all the Jews on the continent west of the Soviet Union. Some were under direct German rule, others in the planned German sphere of influence.[44]

The plan dealt with Jews only marginally. For the benefit of about a quarter of a million ethnic Germans from Lithuania, Bucovina and Dobrodgea, some 770,000 Polish farmers and 60,000 Jews from Vienna were to be expelled from their homes and sent to the General-gouvernement. The official date for launching the program was January 21, 1941; the deportations began in fact on February 5, 1941. The expulsion of the Jews of Vienna began on February 15, and by mid-March 5000 had been dispossessed. The plan was canceled on March 15, after less than 3 percent of the mission had been accomplished. It encountered the determined opposition of the local German governors in the Generalgouvernement, who foresaw that a significant increase in the populations of their districts without an appropriate infrastructure would lead to a loss of control. Army officers demanded a massive thinning of the local population in order to set up large training areas. In March, when preparations for the invasion of the Soviet Union intensified, the army took control of the train tracks and began carrying out their own population transfers in order to position their forces for the invasion. All these developments increased German pressure to pack the Jews into smaller ghettoes. Yet this provided no solution to the Jewish problem for the Germans — it only intensified it.[45]

A week after the deportations were halted (March 21, 1941), Eichmann met with Leopold Gutterer, Goebbels' director-general, and with a representative of Speer. When Gutterer said that Goebbels (who was Gauleiter of Berlin) wanted to get rid of the remaining Jews in the

---

44. Aly, *Endlösung*, pp. 195–9. Aly points out that the number of close to six million is *not* to be read as an early intention to murder six million Jews, but is rather coincidental, especially given that there did not yet exist a plan to murder all the Jews. To which one might add that the efforts later made were to kill larger numbers, efforts which were partially thwarted only by the Allied victory in the war.

45. Aly, *Endlösung*, pp. 218–25, 232–5, 255–8. Documents from Eichmann's department coordinating the deportations: TR.3-1462, 15.2.41; TR.3-1407, 21.2.41; TR.3-1408, 26.2.41; TR.3-1409, 27.2.41; Müller's order of cessation: TR.3-1395.

city, Eichmann tried to play a trick. He related that Heydrich had presented to Hitler, about two months previously, a plan to evacuate 60,000 Jews from Vienna, and that Hitler had approved it. While the execution of the plan had been delayed in the meantime because of pressure from the Generalgouvernement authorities, there were fewer than 60,000 Jews in Vienna. If the deportations were renewed, it would be possible to make up the difference with about 15,000 Jews from Berlin. Gutterer asked Eichmann to prepare for Goebbels, who was not his commander, a plan for evicting the Jews of Berlin.[46] From this we learn that Eichmann hoped that the cessation of the deportations to Poland was temporary, and would be rescinded. He may even, in this way, have been trying to enlist Goebbels' interest in the matter. It also shows that a successful referent, whose expertise was well known, could have been called on from time to time to contribute his talents even to the heads of other ministries.

But perhaps the most important thing is Eichmann's description of Heydrich: "Party member Heydrich, who has been designated by the Führer to carry out the irrevocable evacuation of the Jews."

What exactly did Eichmann mean, and on what did he base this statement? Dannecker had used similar phrasing in Paris a few months earlier, and the SS commandant in Holland, Hans Rauter, had expressed himself in similar terms in April.[47] Eichmann, Dannecker, and Rauter were not frustrated bureaucrats searching for information on the policy against the Jews. They were SS officers who were preoccupied with this issue on a routine basis, and the SS had been the central body involved in this policy since the end of 1938. Presumably their words were based on information they received. It is reasonable to assume they knew more than what was recorded in the documents — that is, more than historians know now.

A letter of May 20, 1941, prepared by Hartmann, the department's emigration expert, and signed by Walter Schellenberg, commander of Gestapo branch IV E — apparently filling in for Müller —

46. Adler, *Verwalteter Mensch*, pp. 152–3.
47. Klarsfeld, *Vichy*, pp. 363–4. For a detailed description of Dannecker's statements: see the chapter on France, below. On April 18, 1941 Rauter, HSSPF in Holland, wrote a letter to the Reichskommissar Seyss-Inquart, in which he referred to Heydrich as the special commissioner in charge of the solution of the Jewish question. ZSL AR 518/59 Bd.II, pp. 286–7; see also Joseph Michman, "Planning for the Final Solution Against the Background of Developments in Holland in 1941," *Yad Vashem Studies*, XVII, 1986, p. 153.

makes it clear to the Security Police commanders in France and Belgium that, for two reasons, they should prevent Jewish emigration from those countries. First, this would come at the expense of emigration from the Reich. Second, the Final Solution was approaching.[48] Jewish emigration from Germany should continue to be encouraged, as ordered by the Reichsmarshall. Even if they still did not know precisely what the Final Solution would be, they knew that it was coming. As Bauer has shown, there was not necessarily a contradiction between preparations for murder and a willingness to allow limited emigration.[49]

The great amount of experience that the men of the department had gained in the transfer of Jews and Poles prepared them to undertake similar operations in other places later. Between the beginning of July and the end of September 1941, 13,269 persons were deported, almost all of them Slovenes and only five of them Jews, from a Slovenian area annexed to southern Austria. Each time a train left, the Security Police in Lower Styria sent notification to IV B 4. It is interesting to observe how the staffers became more efficient – it took them 172 words to report on the first train, on June 7, 1941, but only 46 words in the final reports in September. This was the last time that Eichmann supervised the deportation of a non-Jewish group.[50]

The transition from a policy of encouraging emigration in the 1930s to murder in the 1940s took place in parallel with the development of the war and as a side effect of it. In practical terms it was impossible to leave the country except in small numbers.[51] The major emigration route for German Jews after October 1939 went via Trieste to Palestine. This path was blocked by the Italians in May 1940, apparently out of fear that Italy's entry into the war against Britain would leave many alien Jews in its territory. Between the fall of France in 1940 and October 1942 thousands, perhaps even a few tens of thousands, of Jews were able to

48. The original wording is *zweifellos kommende Endlösung*.
49. TR.3-441; Bauer, *Jews for Sale?*, especially chapter 4.
50. TR.3-1079; Aly, *Endlösung*, p. 106.
51. A letter written by Hartmann and signed by Eichmann, sent to Rademacher on September 4, 1940, had requested the impossible: that the Hungarians continue to allow Jews to cross Hungary on their way east, yet understand that the Germans would not allow Hungarian Jews to cross Germany on their way to Spain and Portugal. TR.3-123, IV D 4b(Rz) 2237/40. The following year, Schellenberg signed a similar document by Hartmann, attempting to put a stop to Jewish emigration from Western Europe: TR.3-441, IV B 4b(Rz) (neu) 2494/41g (250), 20.5.1941.

escape via Spain; only a minority of these came from Germany.[52] Mass emigration operations along the lines of Vienna in 1938 were impossible.

On July 16, 1941 a crew of SS officers was sitting in the headquarters of the governor (*Reichsstatthalter*) of Warthegau, talking about possible ways of solving the Jewish problem. Among them were men who had already spent many months at failed efforts to push Jews into the Generalgouvernement, and they undoubtedly felt frustrated by what seemed to them to be a hopeless situation. This was at the end of the fourth week of the invasion of the Soviet Union – an operation that at the time still looked like a success. It had been three weeks since the *Einsatzgruppen* began murdering Soviet Jews, and the SS men knew of this as well. One of them, Rolf-Heinz Höppner, sent this summary of the meeting to *Lieber Kamerad Eichmann* – Dear Comrade Eichmann:

> It may well be that some of the attached proposals will seem fantastic to you, but in my opinion they are feasible:
>
> 1. All 300,000 Jews in the district will be put together into a huge work camp and employed in industry.
> 2. It will be possible to take out units of laborers for external work.
> 3. SS Brigadeführer Dr Wilhelm Albert thinks that the number of guards necessary for such a camp is much smaller than the number of Security Police now needed, and the risk of epidemic that now hangs over the population of Litzmannstadt [Lodz] and other cities in which there are ghettoes will be reduced.
> 4. It will be impossible to prevent the death of a part of the Jews from hunger. Serious consideration should be given to whether it would not be more humane to find some swift method to liquidate [*erledigen*] them.
> 5. Jewish women of childbearing age will be sterilized, so that the Jewish question will be solved in the next generation.
> 6. The *Reichstatthalter* himself has still not expressed an opinion. The impression is that Übelhor in Litzmannstadt opposes the liquidation of the ghetto, because he is making good profit there.[53]

Two weeks later Heydrich went to Goering to get his signature on a new operational order on the Jewish matter. The document had been prepared in advance, in Eichmann's department, and Goering was only

52. Browning, *Foreign Office*, p. 43; regarding immigration through Spain, Haim Avni, *Spain, the Jews and Franco*, Philadelphia: Jewish Publication Society, 1982, p. 91. Regarding plans to move Jews through Trieste, prior to the Italian entry into the war, see the interview with Gideon Raphael, *Haaretz*, 2.12.1994.

53. TR.3-1410.

asked to sign it.[54] It authorized Heydrich to take all necessary measures to carry out a comprehensive solution to the Jewish problem in the entire region of German influence across Europe. He was to work in tandem with other bodies as needed. The document also instructed Heydrich to report in the near future on the preparations that were being made towards this object.[55]

Up to this point, each time Heydrich or Eichmann had wanted to enlist the services of an official in a different office to assist on a Jewish-related matter, they had cited Goering's January 1939 directive to Heydrich, which appointed Heydrich to coordinate Jewish emigration. Now that the policy would clearly soon no longer be one of encouraging emigration, they would not be able to refer to Goering's previous directive as a source for their authority to secure the collaboration of officials not under their direct command. Now, with the new order in hand, Heydrich and Eichmann could obtain the cooperation of other officials under force of their mission to prepare a Final Solution.[56] That they chose Goering to sign the order reflected the friction between the party and SS on the one hand and the government bureaucracy on the other. Had the order been given to Heydrich by his SS commandant, Himmler, it would not have been of much use, since the SS commandant was a party and not a government official. Heydrich needed a legal imprimatur for his activities, one that would be accepted by the government bureaucracy. Goering, for his part, was the government official responsible for the four-year plan, and an order from him would be binding on the bureaucracy. Furthermore, he had played a central role in the formulation of anti-Jewish policy, at least since 1938.[57]

54. Adolf Eichmann, *Ich, Adolf Eichmann: Ein historischer Zeugenbericht*, Hrsg. von Rudolf Aschenauer, Leoni: Druffel Verlag, 1980, p. 479.
55. Nuremberg documents, PS–710. No record of Heydrich reporting back to Goering has been found.
56. Browning, *Fateful Months*, pp. 21–2, and Buchheim in Krausnik *et al.*, *Anatomy of the SS State*, p. 176, both believe this was a retroactive order, given to cover activities which were already underway. Other historians doubt that this was *the* order to kill all Jews; see Hillgruber, "Extermination," *YVS*, XVII, 1984, p. 12. Bauer sees it as *precisely* that: the written echo of an oral order from Hitler. Yehuda Bauer, "Who Was Responsible and When? Some Well-known Documents Revisited," *Holocaust and Genocide Studies*, vol. 6, no. 2, 1991.
57. Adler, *Verwalteter Mensch*, p. 85; U. D. Adam, *Judenpolitik im Dritten Reich*, Düsseldorf: Droste, 1972, p. 176. As an example of Goering's centrality and his being the representative of Hitler for decisions on Jewish issues, see his chairing of the large interdepartmental meeting following Kristallnacht (Nbg. Doc. PS–1816).

These facts alone, which have been known, fall short of resolving the question of whether the initiative to murder the Jews came from above or below. What they do demonstrate, however, is that even if the order precipitated from above, after May 1941, it fell on very fertile ground. Low-ranking officials had already advanced ideas for killing on a large scale, and had sent them upward for consideration. The moment they reached Eichmann, he sent them farther up. So senior decision makers knew that the men in the field were willing, and that it was possible to progress towards the Final Solution (an intentionalist explanation); or perhaps the decision makers heard the talk of their subordinates, bought the idea, and handed down appropriate orders (a moderate functionalist explanation).

The most fateful points of decision, such as the routine shaping of policy, are obscured by a bureaucratic thicket that makes it impossible to identify the initiator and motivator. It is possible, however, to spread the bramble apart and bring some light to the scene. Breitman has found evidence indicating that Hitler and Himmler were leaning towards a decision to murder the Jews as early as the end of 1940.[58] The documents surveyed here can neither contradict nor confirm this, since they concern officers of low rank who were not party to the making of decisions. Yet it can be seen that even if the decision in principle was made at the end of 1940, news of it did not reach the men of the middle level, even the most central of them, until the summer of 1941. Even if Hitler had made the decision earlier, he had not yet decided to act on it, except perhaps on Soviet territory.[59]

Perhaps there was no initiator in the narrow, precise sense of the term. It is difficult today to find a serious historian who still claims that the Final Solution could have been carried out without Hitler's knowledge

---

cont.

Adam, pp. 204–12. Yet this interpretation leaves me slightly uneasy. Goering had indeed been an important figure, back in November 1938; the disastrous (for the Germans) Battle of Britain, which he had said they would easily win, *must* have put a dent in his standing by the summer of 1941. Perhaps this was a late case of utilizing his stature while it still lasted.

58. Breitman, *Architect*, pp. 135–44.

59. And see my "Rollbahn Mord: The Early Activities of *Einsatzgruppe C*," *Holocaust and Genocide Studies*, 2/2, 1987. While my interpretation of the role these units played in the evolution of the decision to murder all Jews is not the only possible reading, it is clear that the commanders of EG-C did not regard themselves as being the executors of a final solution, pp. 233ff.

and approval. On the other hand, why must we assume that there was a single, specific moment, clear and well-defined, in which someone, even Hitler, made a decision and handed down an order to begin implementation of the genocide? Is it not at least as reasonable that there was a search for a solution to the Jewish problem, and that the idea of liquidation, which was already floating around, then crystallized? This view would explain why we find documents that seem to be heading toward a decision, followed by actions that would seem to indicate that a decision had not yet been made.

Browning proposes that in the summer of 1941, apparently in July, Heydrich was told by Hitler to carry out a kind of "feasibility study" of the murder of all European Jews; that Heydrich requested the July 31 order soon thereafter; but that the decision to carry out the action was made only in the middle of October.[60] He notes that even if Hitler had already intended in the summer that all the Jews of Europe should be murdered, and had notified Himmler and Heydrich of this, it was still necessary to map out its implementation. The model put into action on Soviet territory was already then proving itself problematic, but the construction of death camps and gas chambers is an obvious alternative only in hindsight. It may be added that the decision could have been made without necessarily determining simultaneously when it would actually begin.

Lack of clarity is not an excuse for not pedantically confronting the documents. Quite the opposite. As Browning has already noted, there is a danger that historians have read the documentation too literally. When reality itself was fluid and amorphous, documents reflecting a clearly delineated reality cannot be created, and scholars should not try to impose clarity through the use of fragments of documentation, especially when there is no doubt that links in the chain of events, perhaps key links, were never committed to paper. Messages may have been passed on orally.[61]

Nevertheless, some inferences may be drawn that are more plausible than others. Hitler did not announce his decision in a national address. Himmler did not issue a directive about it to all of his officers.

60. Browning, *Path*, pp. 113–17.
61. Browning, *Path*, pp. 113–14. Anyone who has seriously attempted to cut through the entanglement of conflicting proofs and refutations, readings and counter-readings, interpretations and hypotheses on the decision and moment of activation of the Final Solution must have felt a twinge of frustration.

The army's commanders – on this all scholars agree – were not party to the discussions. The decision had to be made (or, more accurately, to crystallize) within a tightly restricted circle (according to the intentionalist view) or somewhat restricted circle (according to the functionalist scenario). The circle of those who knew about it had to widen as its implementation progressed. In the critical second half of 1941 there were still many in Germany, among them senior bureaucrats, who knew nothing about it. Since the Jewish issue was so central, they must have continued to write and send out documents that were no longer relevant, even though they did not know this. The historian should not confuse matters by attributing significance to what was written by an official who could not have known what he was talking about.[62]

Eichmann knew exactly what he was talking about. Apparently, his men were among the first to deal with the matter. They carried out the "feasibility study". On this score, the direction taken here can provide very real insight, since the new mission of department IV B 4 in the summer of 1941 brought a change in its status. Unlike the Madagascar proposal, where the department was but one of the elements that cooked up the scheme, or the expulsion from Poland, in which Eichmann was called on to coordinate matters after the dimensions of the chaos became clear, here he and his men stood for the first time at the center of the preparations for a policy whose implementation had not yet begun. The image of Eichmann created after the war, depicting him as having activated the policy of murder, was never correct. But in the summer of 1941 conditions were created that provided a foundation for the myth.

Once it was decided to examine a final solution, the research body was chosen. This group was naturally very much involved in its implementation. This is the procedure in any well-ordered bureaucratic system. An idea can be discussed and ripen for a long time; a decision to appoint a team to "carry out a study" is a turning point, and the beginning of implementation is the watershed. The turning point came in the summer of 1941 – but because of its significance and the horrible innovation it involved, no public announcement was made. The "research team" armed itself with an authorization for its work – Goering's letter – but took care, for the time being, to work quietly.[63]

---

62. This seems to be the major drawback of Safrian's description of this period, to name but one important historian. *Eichmann Männer*, chapters 4, 5.
63. A recent and very important article by Christian Gerlach, "Die Wannsee-Konferenz, das Schicksal der deutschen Juden und Hitlers politische Grundsatzentscheidung, alle

An interesting interpretation of the document of July 31, 1941 and of its use was given by Wislicency in 1946. He claimed that the Madagascar plan was alive until the autumn of 1941, when it was replaced with the liquidation policy. Even if the truth of this seems doubtful, it implies something interesting if this is really what Wislicency thought. For even when Eichmann knew that liquidation was on the agenda, he allowed the men in other departments to continue to believe that the Madagascar plan or some similar alternative in the East was the blueprint.[64] That means that those who were supposed to help with the logistics of this huge operation – in the legal, economic, political or transportation fields – did not have to be told all the details for them to make a full contribution.

Eichmann himself gave several accounts, but what is common to all of them is that he heard about the liquidation plan from Heydrich, approximately at the end of the summer of 1941. When he said that he remembered being surprised, because he would never have thought of such an idea himself,[65] it is clear he was lying. Höppner had outlined a similar plan in the middle of July.

In IV B 4, preparations for the Final Solution began in August 1941 at the latest. As a first step, the department prepared the regulation requiring Jews in the Reich to wear an identifying badge, an important psychological step in disconnecting them from their surroundings and leading them towards the "civil death" that preceded deportation. The badge was effective because of its conspicuousness. The edict won Hitler's approval and was issued by Heydrich on September 15, 1941, over his own signature.[66] It was printed on Ministry of the Interior letterhead, to ensure cooperation from all the civil authorities that had to be involved.

cont.

Juden Europas zu ermorden," *Werkstaatgeschichte* 18 (1997), pp. 7–44, puts the decision of Hitler in December 1941, and even brings a hand-written note of Himmler as substantiation. The method used here, as well as its proposed conclusion, seems to retain its validity even after a careful reading of Gerlach, who can be critiqued by Browning's comment.

64. TR.3-773, p. 5. See Browning's summary of the various interpretations in *Fateful Months*.

65. Browning compares the various versions in *Fateful Months*, pp. 23–6; Eichmann, *Interrogation*, vol. 1, p. 169.

66. Lösener, "Als Rassenreferent im Reichsministerium des Innern," *VjHfZ*, 1961, p. 303; TR.3-1064, Reichsministerium des Innern, Pol S. IV B 4b 940/41–6.

The regulation, which had been prepared by Friedrich Suhr, one of the officers in Eichmann's department, and some of his men, was distributed to Security Police stations, government ministries, the Order Police, senior and regional SS commanders, and others. All were ordered to act in accord with it. It contained instructions on the wearing of the badge, prescribed how it was to be sewn on clothing, told how the badges were to be distributed, and ordered punishment by "protective detention" for Jews who violated the order. The second part of the regulation, longer but less well-known, further restricted Jews' freedom of movement. They were allowed to travel for certain purposes only, even then requiring identifying documents and special temporary permits. The types of transportation were restricted. Flying, for instance, was allowed only with an exceptional permit, and with the Jew segregated from the rest of the passengers. Different rules were made for internal and inter-city travel. Specific consideration was given to the handicapped, especially to wounded veterans, apparently for the sake of public opinion. The permits had to be drafted according to a template created in Berlin, but Suhr did not object to their being reproduced or made by carbon copy. The officials who issued the permits were ordered to maintain follow-up records and to take care to collect the permits when they expired.

The link between the two parts of the regulation is clear: with the Jews publicly branded, the population would help oversee the restrictions on movement. Furthermore, because of the restrictions, Jews would be forced to remain close to home, making it easy to round them up. So, apparently, it was hoped. In practice, though, the restrictions were not fully observed, and half a year later, on March 24, 1942, Heydrich signed a reissue of the orders, which was distributed throughout the Reich. This was also prepared by Suhr and his men. To learn who initiated the March directive, one has to know who took notice that the earlier orders were being carried out only loosely. If it was the men in the field, it would be reasonable to assume that Suhr asked for and received backing from Heydrich; if the complaints came from above, it is more reasonable that Heydrich assigned the task to Eichmann, who in turn passed it on to Suhr. Either way, Heydrich's signature was required in order to impress the order's recipients with the serious nature of the matter. The new directive contained no significant changes from the original order.[67]

67. TR.3-1174, Reichsministerium des Innern, Pol S. IV B 4b (940/41–6-) 1155/41–33-.

A recent study by Peter Witte focuses on September 1941. He does not linger over the events of that summer, and he does not necessarily contradict Browning. Witte searches not for the theoretical decision to murder, but for the decision to commence with deportation. He traces this to the middle of September. At that time several Nazi elements were urging deportation of the Reich's Jews. Among them were the planning officials of *Generalplan Ost*, the project of emptying eastern Europe of its non-German inhabitants in order to make space for the resettlement of Germans. Other advocates were the staff of the German embassy in Paris and the heads of the regional and local authorities who coveted the homes that would be vacated. These voices reached Hitler at a time of renewed successes on the eastern front, when it was still possible to believe in Nazi invincibility. Hitler now handed down an order to begin the deportations, after having delayed until then.[68]

At about the time of the appearance of Witte's article, an interesting piece appeared in a non-scholarly publication, *The New Yorker*, based in part on interviews with important scholars in the field. In it, Hitler's biographer, Allan Bullock, ponders whether Hitler was a cynical player of politics or whether he actually believed in his own doctrine. His appraisal is that Hitler began as a pragmatist for whom ideology came second to acquiring and maintaining power. By the autumn of 1941, however, Hitler became convinced he was unstoppable, and that he need not defer the pursuit of his ideological goals. Before this, Bullock maintains, Hitler was manipulative, crafty, and deliberate; from this point onwards he was drunk with his successes, lost his pragmatism, and was guided only by his desire to achieve goals that he truly believed in.[69]

As Hitler's mouthpiece, Himmler ordered Heydrich to try to empty Germany and the Protectorate of Bohemia and Moravia of Jews, and to deport them to the East. From there they would be moved east

68. Peter Witte, "Two Decisions Concerning the 'Final Solution to the Jewish Question': Deportations to Łódź and Mass Murder in Chelmno," *Holocaust and Genocide Studies*, vol. 9, no. 3, Winter 1995. Interestingly, while Witte is clearly breaking new ground in proving the extent of agreement and complicity of various agencies in the new policy, his description of Hitler's decision resembles that given 20 years earlier by H. G. Adler (*Verwalteter Mensch*, pp. 176–7). For whatever reason, Adler's description was then completely overlooked by all participants in the subsequent discussion until Witte, who seems to have reached his conclusion independently of Adler.

69. Ron Rosenbaum, "Explaining Hitler," *New Yorker*, 1.5.1995.

again in the following spring.[70] The significance of this order for those implementing it was that the Jews were to be evicted from Germany even before the liquidation facilities were ready for them.[71] In the meantime, with the deportation to Łódź, the Security Police gained experience of how to conduct a mass transfer of Jews.

The timing of the first deportations to Łódź, in the middle of October 1941 (involving almost 20,000 Jews) was the result of Hitler's decision, not of the system's readiness. The Security Police had not completed their preparations. The deportations were carried out even before the subject of Jewish property had been dealt with and before general operative instructions had been drafted. Instructions were rushed out to the relevant stations,[72] and on October 15, the first of the trains left.

Immediately upon the commencement of the preparations for the new policy, Eichmann signed a letter by Hartmann to the foreign ministry in which he explained that, in light of the approaching final solution, Jews should be prevented from emigrating, except from Germany.[73] Two weeks later, emigration from Germany was also forbidden. On October 1, Himmler barred all Jewish emigration except for exceptional cases, but for some reason the order remained secret for more than three weeks. When it was decided, on October 23, to issue it, it was done in a directive to all SS commanders in Europe. It was prepared by Hartmann and signed by Müller.[74] According to the guidelines, emigration was to be permitted only if it was likely to benefit the Reich, and only with the approval of the RSHA. In his interrogation in the 1960s, Hartmann said that there were never any cases in which emigration was connected with the Reich's interests, so after October 1941 he did not approve even a single instance

70. TR.10-767b, p. 256.
71. Chelmno, the first death camp, started functioning on December 8, 1941, although its construction began earlier; the other camps opened even later. Only at Auschwitz were there any kind of facilities for mass killings with gas, and the German Jews were not sent there. The single gas chamber might not have been up to the job anyway. And see Bauer, "Auschwitz," in Jaeckel and Rohwer, *Der Mord an den Juden.*
72. TR.10-767, p. 257; the document itself has not been found, only mention of it.
73. TR.3-1178, IV B 4b(Rz) 849/41, August 28, 1941. Schellenberg's order of May 20, 1941, had mentioned the *zweifellos kommende Endlösung*, i.e. one that had not yet arrived. Now, it had.
74. TR.3-1209, IV B 4b(Rz) 2920/41g (984); Adler, *Verwalteter Mensch*, pp. 29–31.

of emigration.[75] For some reason, the foreign ministry was not on the distribution list for the directive of October 23, and it was only on November 19, 1941 that Hartmann/Eichmann notified it – with a request that the information not be passed onward – that Himmler had issued a general prohibition against emigration.[76]

It is interesting to follow Hartmann. At first he was one of the employees of the Reich Center for Jewish emigration, the Berlin counterpart of Eichmann's emigration office in Vienna, and in this capacity he had encouraged emigration. When the possibilities for emigration were reduced, he was left the only official dealing with what remained of the subject. When the policy was reversed, he was still sitting at the same desk, putting out letters with the same reference marks. But now the result for the Jews was the opposite – death instead of life.[77]

On October 10, 1941, Heydrich conducted a meeting in Prague in which he combined his position as chief of the RSHA with his new job of the acting Reich commissioner in Bohemia. Eichmann, Günther, and other SS officers participated. The subject was the expulsion of the Jews of the Protectorate. It was determined that the swiftest solution would be to concentrate them in a camp within the region. This was the first time that Theresienstadt is mentioned in Nazi documents, and with a different emphasis than what actually came to be afterwards – at the Wannsee Conference the camp was already being spoken about in terms of a "model ghetto," not as a transit camp on the way to liquidation. The camp was to be exceptional in the SS landscape because it was run from the RSHA, not from the Head Office for Economics and Management, the WVHA, which ran most of the camps. SS-Captain Dr Siegfried Seidl began setting up the camp at the beginning of November.[78]

The minutes of the meeting provide a glimpse into the style of speech and manner of thinking that was apparently current among Eichmann and his colleagues when they met behind closed doors, with no reason to be afraid of speaking their minds. It was decided that, in order

75. TR.10-767c, pp. 669–70. Hartmann's inability to remember is, in this case, doubly striking, as there actually *were* cases where the RSHA (presumably through Hartmann) *did* authorize emigration. An example would be the case of seven Jewish industrialists whose emigration from Holland was authorized in late 1942, in order to expedite the transferring of ownership of their property to the Germans. TR.3-588, 14.12.43. Additional cases, see ZSL 107 AR 689/66 Bd.II, p. 169.
76. TR.3-179, IV B 4b(Rz) 1097/41.
77. TR.10-767c, pp. 655–6. Cases of obstructing emigration: TR.3-1558, 1559.
78. TR.3-1193; Adler, *Theresienstadt*, pp. 21, 722; TR.3-109.

to make things easier for the Nazis, the Jews themselves should bring enough food for a few weeks. Straw on the floor would serve as bedding because putting in beds would take up too much space. The large apartments would serve the ghetto leadership and the Nazi headquarters. The rest of the Jews could dig themselves holes in the ground. Measures would have to be taken so that epidemics would not escape from the ghetto into the surrounding area, that sewage not flow into the Eger River and thence into German Sudetenland, and that the Jews not be buried in the ground but be cremated instead (in order not to pollute?). Eichmann also mentioned the possibility of transferring Jews from Prague to Nebe and to Rasch, "commanders of camps for communist prisoners in the east." This was an original way of describing two of the commanders of the *Einsatzgruppen*. Everyone present at the meeting knew very well that Nebe and Rasch took care not to hold onto prisoners for more than a few hours before murdering them.[79]

The major deportations of Germany Jewry began, as noted, in October 1941. Between the fourth and the sixteenth of the month, 19,833 Jews were deported to Łódź, half of them from Vienna and Prague, and half from other places in the Reich. Some 5000 Gypsies were also deported. The operation was run by IV B 4. The choice of destination derived from several constraints. The army demanded that railroad tracks in the Baltic area be kept free, and the previous attempt at deportation into the Generalgouvernement had not been successful. Łódź was at the eastern edge of the Reich, and a large ghetto was already in place there. The deportees to Łódź were murdered in Chelmno, starting at the beginning of 1942.[80]

A week after the end of this wave of deportations, on October 23, the referents on Jewish affairs from all the Reich Security Police stations were called together by Eichmann. He and his staff presented the lessons that had been learned from this action and handed out instructions for the continuation of deportations. Each Jew would take 50 Reichsmarks,

---

79. TR.3-1193.
80. Adler, *Vewalteter Mensch*, pp. 172–4. The first German Jews to be mass-murdered were the thousands deported in November to the vicinities of Kovno and Riga. They were shot by members of Einsatzgruppe A between November 25 and 30, 1941. Fleming, *Hitler and the Final Solution*, pp. 78ff.; Broszat, "Genesis of the Final Solution," *YVS*, XIII, 1979, p. 93.

bedding, toiletry, eating utensils, and food for three days.[81] Three weeks' worth of food should be sent along with the shipment. Before leaving, the following things should be searched for and confiscated from the Jews: weapons, jewelry, money, and objects of value except for wedding rings. Food ration cards belonging to the Jews should be sent to the nearest branch of the Ministry of the Economy. Personal documents, with the exception of identification papers or passports, should be confiscated. Identification papers should be stamped "evacuated." The general food and money should be deposited with the commander of the escort. A copy of the list of deportees should be sent to IV B 4. The Jews should be allowed to take personal equipment and medicines. Each referent heard when the Jews of his city were to be deported, and how many. The regulations regarding reporting and escorts were explained. The attendees heard about the prohibition against emigration, which had been issued that same day.[82] Equipped with these instructions, the men returned to their cities in order to prepare the Jews for deportation. They would be cut off entirely from their surroundings, so that their disappearance would cause no unrest. The referents also saw to it that no Jew would remain behind by mistake, because of absence from his residence, for example. They rejected requests by Jews to be exempted from the deportations and, most importantly, they rounded the Jews up and sent them off.[83]

On that same day, October 23, Eichmann (where did he find the time?) and Bernhard Lösener, the Jewish affairs expert in the Ministry of the Interior, also met with representatives of the armaments branch of the Wehrmacht command, the OKW. The army representatives wanted to make sure that the Jews working in their industries would not be deported. Eichmann and Lösener promised that none of these Jews would be deported without the army's consent.[84] Between November 11, 1941

81. It is not clear what the purpose of the 50 RM was. They were not returned to the deportees, nor did they cover the cost of the deportations. Adler, *Verwalteter Mensch*, pp. 547–8.
82. TR.10-767, pp. 258–9, 666–9; Eichmann, *Interrogation*, p. 421. The police station in Würzburg supplied the police escort with rations for ten days, and added: 2 bottles of Schnaps, 3 cans of concentrated milk, 2 packages of cheese, half a kilo of butter, 13 sausages, matches and tobacco. Adler, *Verwalteter Mensch*, p. 452. This had not been specified in the meeting of October 23, 1941.
83. Adler, *Verwalteter Mensch*, pp. 354–79.
84. Hilberg, *Destruction*, p. 441, quoting from the memo of the participants from the Wehrmacht.

and the second half of January more than 25,000 Jews were deported from the cities of the German heartland into the Baltic region.[85]

The principles applying to Jewish property were formulated during the course of the initial deportations. It was only on November 25 that the "Eleventh Regulation of the Reich Citizenship Law" was promulgated, establishing that a Jew who left Germany forfeited his property to the Reich (with a reservation meant to protect non-Jewish creditors).[86] Two days later Heydrich signed a memorandum prepared, apparently, by Suhr, which stated that lists of Jewish property were to be prepared and submitted within a month. Banks and economic institutions were directed to report on the Jewish property they held. In order to reduce the Jews' ability to conceal their property, they were forbidden to have control over it except in special circumstances of urgent need. Jews who held property without a permit would be placed in "protective custody" and their property would be confiscated. Non-Jews who received property from Jews would also be arrested. (On this point, Suhr issued a memorandum three days earlier, but only its number has survived: IV B 4b 1027/41).[87]

Until their deportation, however, the Jews remained property owners, and the RSHA knew how to exploit this. From the moment of deportation and confiscation, the property passed into the hands of the Reich Ministry of Finance, and the RSHA no longer had access to it. Yet the deportation operation received no budget from anywhere. The department funded the deportation from Germany by taking advantage of a lacuna between blocked Jewish property and confiscated Jewish property. On December 3, Suhr signed a memorandum on this subject and sent it to all stations. The funding would come from a special bank account, called *Sonderkonto W* (special account W). The Security Police were to see to it that before deportation, each Jew would contribute at least a quarter of his property to this account. He suggested that it would be well to explain to them that the money would cover the expenses of the Reich Association for the shipments, for the central purchase of food, and so on. The money could be collected when the Jews were notified of the evacuations, or when they filled out their statement of capital before

85. Adler, *Verwalteter Mensch*, p. 87.
86. Hilberg, *Destruction*, p. 301 (1961 edn).
87. TR.3-739, IV B 4a 1146/41–32.

the deportation.[88] The fund was established at the order of IV B 4 in December 1941.[89]

Preparations for the Wannsee Conference began at the end of November. Invitations were sent on November 29, 1941. In Eichmann's opinion, the reason for holding this meeting was that Heydrich wanted to show everyone that he had come into a central position of power.[90] But the explanation given in the body of the invitation was more prosaic – the need for coordination in the wake of Goering's order of July 31, 1941 (which Heydrich had initiated), and the deportations already being carried out from the territory of the Reich. Representatives from the General-gouvernement were invited because of negative experience with them in the past and because of the impression in the RSHA that they were trying to act on their own. The meeting did not take place on the date set because of the American declaration of war; the invitations for the new date, January 20, 1942, were written by someone on Heydrich's staff in Prague and not by IV B 4.[91]

The subject of the Wannsee Conference was the deportation of the Jews of the whole continent to their deaths in the East. The meeting was on the level of directors-general – that is, above the department level.[92] Eichmann prepared the statistical data for Heydrich's lecture, and afterwards edited the transcript (which was taken down by a

88. TR.3-1283, IV B 4a 1033/41–39-. The suggestion that one collect money from the Jews on the eve of their deportation, purportedly to help the Reich Association finance the deportations, was passed from Epstein to Gutwasser (the man in charge of the finances of the Reichsvereinigung in IV B 4b), sometime after November 3, 1941. Gutwasser told Epstein to put his idea in writing. Hilberg, *Destruction* (1985 edn), pp. 467–8.
89. Adler, *Verwalteter Mensch*, pp. 563–4. Other monetary sources at the disposal of the RSHA were VUGESTAP in Vienna, where Gestapo personnel sold Jewish goods; the Emigration Fund in Prague; "contributions" collected by Gestapo staff at the train stations; as well as funds of the Reichsvereinigung. The Jews were paying for their deportation. Adler, p. 630.
90. Yehoshua Büchler, "Document: A Preparatory Document for the Wannsee 'Conference'," *Holocaust and Genocide Studies*, vol. 9, no. 1, Spring 1995; TR.3-890; Eichmann, *Interrogation*, vol. 1, p. 239. See also Eberhard Jäckel's lecture at the 8th International Conference, Yad Vashem, 1991, *50 Years to the Decision on the 'Final Solution'* (unpublished).
91. TR.3-890; TR.3-1101; TR.3-891.
92. Hilberg suggests a more precise title: The First Final Solution Meeting, as this was the first in a series. *Destruction*, p. 417. The protocol is to be found in the Nuremberg documents, NG–2586-G.

stenographer) and distributed it among the participants. Being the lowest-level official there, he remembered with delight drinking cognac with all the higher-ups.[93] To a certain extent, it was a milestone – the decision to murder all the Jews had already been made, and implementation had already begun. Within the Reich, the need for policy makers would decline, while the need for policy implementers would grow. Following Eichmann and his department will reveal more and more activity on lower levels, since the implementation of the policy was carried out on a lower level of the hierarchy than was its formulation. After January 1942, wherever we find Eichmann making friends with men of much higher rank than his, it will generally be outside the Reich, where there was still a need to shape policy. Within Germany, he had fewer and fewer opportunities of this type, but his department held an ever more important position, located as it was at the center of the execution of the policy.

Before applying himself to the daily routine of the liquidation, Eichmann still had a few opportunities to take part in strategic discussions in the Reich, although these were discussions in which the rank of the participants was declining. The second Final Solution meeting was planned for March 6, 1942 at Kurfürstenstrasse 116, Eichmann's own office. The invitations were sent out from IV B 4 over Heydrich's signature much earlier, on January 26.[94] The staff of the foreign ministry knew how to read documents – it was not the addressee, Luther, who responded, but his referent, Rademacher – and he responded to *Lieber Kamerad* Eichmann, not to Heydrich.[95]

On March 6, 1942, there was a meeting of representatives of the Foreign, Propaganda, Justice and Interior Ministries, of Hitler's chancellery, the party bureau, the Ministry of Eastern Territories, the Generalgouvernement, the RSHA and the director of the Four-Year Plan. The meeting is sometimes referred to as the second Final Solution meeting (after Wannsee).[96] The RSHA's representative was an officer from another department named Bilfinger; Eichmann and his men are not

---

93. Eichmann, *Interrogation*, vol. 1, pp. 242, 408, and vol. 2, p. 871. Dr Lange, representing SIPO Ostland, was one rank lower than Eichmann (Sturmbannf.), but he was there as a proxy, and not on his own account.
94. TR.3-841. The file number was that of the Wannsee documents.
95. TR.3-842, 2.3.42.
96. For a description of the entire series of 'Final Solution' conferences, see Hilberg *Destruction* (1985 edn), pp. 416–30.

mentioned. The reason for this is apparently that another meeting was taking place at the same time, in the same building – a meeting of Security Police from throughout the Reich. Eichmann spoke with Rademacher from the foreign ministry, but he apparently did not participate in the inter-ministerial meeting sufficiently to justify his appearance in the minutes.[97]

The major subject of discussion at the interministerial meeting was the implementation difficulties deriving from Hitler's decision to solve the problem of the *Mischlinge*, or half-Jews, by sterilization. Towards the end, the participants discussed the possibility of imposing divorce on mixed Jewish–Aryan couples. The data on the Jewishness of the spouse would be supplied by the Security Police, and there would be no possibility of appeal.[98]

Between May and September 1942, Jews from Germany, Vienna and Theresienstadt were deported to Minsk, where they were shot.[99] The focus of the deportation operations left Germany for the rest of the continent, yet despite this the deportations from Germany continued. In July and August 39,000 Jews were deported to the Maly-Trostinets camp near Minsk, where they were murdered. Those deported in September and October reached Treblinka. In the absence of survivors and documents, there is almost no numerical data.[100]

The third Final Solution meeting took place on October 27, 1942 in the department's building and was chaired by Eichmann. Participating were representatives of most of the agencies that took part in the previous meetings, but once again the rank of the participants was lower. The subject of the discussion was still the "mixed-breeds." The assumption was that during the course of the war a method would be found to carry out mass sterilizations, and the proposal was that this should be done to all the *Mischlinge*. Sterilizations would be accomplished by deception – they would be presented with two possibilities, deportation or sterilization. Deportation would be presented as a very severe measure, whereas

97. Kempner, R. M. W., *Eichmann und Komplizen*, Zurich: Europa Verlag, 1961, p. 169.
98. TR.3-446.
99. Adler, *Verwalteter Mensch*, pp. 195–7. Unlike the deportees of late 1941, who were forced into a "German Ghetto" and only later removed and shot, these deportees were shot immediately. And see: Ya'acov Tzur, "The Maly Trostinetz Death Camp," *Yalkut Moreshet*, 59, April 1995 (Hebrew).
100. Adler, *Verwalteter Mensch*, pp. 197–8. *Aktion Reinhardt*, the murder of most of the Jews of Poland, was at its height at this period. However, it was carried out by local forces, SS and other, and IV B 4 was not involved: TR.10-767b, p. 346; Hilberg, *Destruction*, p. 408.

sterilization would be presented as a mitigation of this policy. Presumably, most of the victims would choose the lesser evil, sterilization. Also, if officials tried to intervene on behalf of *Mischlinge* acquaintances who faced deportation, it would be possible to "retreat" to sterilization. The process would look voluntary and not mandatory, and there would be no need for coercive legislation. The number of those trying to evade sterilization would be reduced, because they would appear to have a choice. To increase the success rate, it would be necessary to perform the sterilizations in a quiet and simple way, and to call it by some misleading euphemism. After sterilization, the partial restrictions on the victims would remain in force. If the *Mischlinge* insisted, despite all this, on being sent to the East, measures should be taken to ensure that they would have no contact with the opposite sex, so that they would not produce descendants. *Mischlinge* of the second degree — that is, people with a single Jewish grandparent — would be considered Germans and would not be sterilized, but the legal restrictions applying to them would continue. Marriages between Jews and non-Jews would be dissolved by coercion if the Aryan partner did not do so of his or her own volition.[101]

The meeting lasted for about an hour, like its predecessors. There were no other meetings of this type; the decisions made remained on paper and were never implemented.[102] From this point onward the Final Solution needed no interministerial coordination or policy definitions by senior ranks. The documents demonstrate wide-ranging activity, but on the level of the department and its parallels; the major problems were getting Jews out of one country or another. The shaping of policy was concluded, and what remained on site were now largely technocrats. Two things can symbolize this change. First, the fact that from this time onward German Jews were deported to Auschwitz.[103] And second, the fact that from January 1943, Himmler's statistician, Richard Korherr, who was responsible for collecting data for his boss on getting rid of the Jews, received his figures during visits to IV B 4[104] — from the experts.

101. TR.3-106.
102. TR.10-767c, p. 954; Adler, *Verwalteter Mensch*, pp. 290–1.
103. Adler, *Verwalteter Mensch*, p. 198.
104. TR.10-767b, p. 584. Korherr may have been told to create a document which would take the place of Eichmann's *Taetigkeits- und Lagebericht über die Endlösung der europäischen Judenfrage, 1942*. Eichmann's document no longer exists, but it was filed as IV B 4 490/42gRs (1618), and submitted to Himmler. TR.10-767b, pp. 582–3. Korherr's summary of the situation as it was on 31.12.42 was submitted to Himmler on 19.4.43, and was filed later as Nuremberg document NO-5193.

From the testimony at the Eichmann trial

Abba Kovner

This is the story of a woman named Sara Menkes, who was rescued from the pit, and she told me of the execution of a group of women, in October 1941. She told me about this several weeks later. In this group there was, among others, one who you could say was a pupil of mine. For several months I had taught her in the gymnasium, the daughter of Epstein, a teacher at the gymnasium in Vilna. Her name was Tsherna Morgenstern. I shall describe it briefly. They were taken to Ponary. After they had waited at some point, a group of them was taken and lined up in a row. They were told to undress. They undressed down to their shirts. A line of the men of the Einsatzgruppen stood facing them. An officer came out in front of them, looked at the row of women, and his glance fell on this Tsherna Morgenstern. She had wonderful eyes, a tall, upstanding girl with long plaits. He looked at her for a long time, smiled, and said: "Take one step forward." She was terrified, as all of them were. At that moment nobody spoke, nobody asked anything. She remained where she was, evidently panic-stricken, and did not step forward. He ordered her, asking: "Hey – don't you want to live – you are so beautiful – I say to you: 'take one step forward'." Then she took one step forward. He said to her: "It would be a pity to bury such beauty in the ground. Walk, but don't look backwards. There is a path here, you know this path, walk along it." For a moment she hesitated and then she began walking. The rest of us – Sara Menkes told me – gazed at her with a look in our eyes. I don't know if it was only of fear or also of envy. She walked forward weakly. And then he, the officer, drew his revolver and shot her, as the first, in the back.

Why should I tell more?

(*The Trial of Adolf Eichmann*, vol. I, p. 460)

Chapter 4

Executing the Final Solution in Germany

There were many experts in the department, dozens, each with a special area of expertise. There were so many that just managing them – making sure that all were working efficiently, that none was overloaded and none was idle – was itself a full-time job. Jänisch was responsible for preparing the duty roster, according to instructions given by Eichmann and Günther, dividing up the work between the different sections in the department. The historian can trace the assignments because each section had its own code, generally in the form of a lower-case letter or number that was printed after the department code: IV B 4a, for example.

It was not uncommon for officials to move from one section or assignment to another. In fact, the only people whose jobs did not change throughout the duration were Referent Eichmann, his deputy Rolf Günther, and office manager Jänisch, who, in addition to preparing the duty roster, dealt with personnel matters, the archives and guard duty.[1]

Until March 1941 Eichmann's department was called IV D 4; only at the beginning of that month did it receive the notorious code name IV B 4. The change apparently reflects the already noted direction of Nazi policy. At the beginning of 1940, Eichmann was responsible for matters of deportation, whereas Jewish affairs (largely the supervision of Jews in the Reich) was the work of a different department. The new arrangement was the result of the intention, on the one hand, of treating all Jews in a uniform way and, on the other, of keeping the monitoring of local Jews separate from population transfers.[2]

In March 1941, the department was divided into two branches. The one called IV B 4a dealt with evacuation, whereas IV B 4b dealt with Jewish affairs. The Emigration Center retained its identity as a section

1. TR.10-754, pp. 96–8.
2. And see Aly, *Endlösung*, pp. 103–7.

within the department until the end of 1941. Its code was RZ. When emigration was prohibited, the section was disbanded.

Günther stood at the head of the evacuation (deportation) branch. The section heads under his command were Novak (coordinating trains and timetables), Hartmann (Emigration Center and emigration questions), Herbert Mannel (collector of statistical data on Jewish movements) and Franz Stuschka. Stuschka handled organizational matters in the office — training the staff and supervising the intermarried Jews and *Mischlinge* who were employed in maintenance work in the building. Novak, Mannel and Stuschka all identified themselves with the code IV B 4a; Hartmann was IV B 4b (RZ). The second branch dealt with what was called "Jewish affairs" — matters having to do with the Jews but not directly involved in their deportation. This was headed by Friedrich Suhr, who arrived in the department in July 1941. His section heads were Fritz Wöhrn (who supervised the Reich Association of the Jews of Germany and dealt with exceptional cases of Jews and *Mischlinge*), Ernst Mös (exceptional cases not dealt with by Wöhrn, "protective custody"), and Richard Gutwasser (the property of the Reich Association). Also in this branch was a section that handled the office's internal affairs: Karl Hrosinek dealt with salary payments, travel expenses and supplies.[3] All these officials were identified by the code IV B 4b.

On November 25, 1941, the 11th Regulation of the Reich Citizenship Law was promulgated. It decreed that any Jew who left Germany would forfeit his citizenship, and his property would belong to the Reich. Many of its provisions were intended to protect non-Jewish creditors, to ensure that they would not incur any loss because of the seizure of Jewish property.[4] This activity was largely under the purview of the finance ministry, but matters with implications for the RSHA were assigned by Heydrich to IV B 4. To handle this, Eichmann set up two new sections, which went by the code of IV B 4c. The heads of these sections, Karl Kube and Adolf Franken, worked under Suhr. Hartmann lost his special code, (RZ), and became part of IV B 4a; emigration was forbidden in any case, and it was more important to keep the structure simple and transparent.

At the same time its authority was extended; in December 1941, new officers were brought into the department: Otto Hunsche, Max

---

3.   TR.10-754, pp. 96–117.
4.   Adler, *Verwalteter Mensch*, pp. 503 ff.

Pachow, and Friedrich Bosshammer. The Wannsee Conference was held in January 1942 and Eichmann understood that most of the work would now be carried out in his department, rather than on a higher level. In order to handle the new assignments he reorganized the department and decided that each section would be identified by a unique code. This was achieved by adding a number – a different one for each section – after the existing code.

The division into two branches was preserved, although several officers were transferred from one to the other. Günther's section dealt, as before, with the transfer of Jews, but now also with Theresienstadt (which was the destination of some of the deportations). Wöhrn, whose code was a–1, dealt with *Mischlinge*, the Reich Association and with exceptional cases involving prominent Jews. Novak continued to coordinate the trains and was called a–2. Hartmann joined him, but continued to handle the few emigration cases that remained. Mös's section was a–3, responsible for cases in which agencies or people with authority wished to intervene or receive information on a specific Jew. It also was in charge of "protective custody." In April 1942, Hans Liepelt and Kryschak were brought into a–3, which was given the additional responsibility of Theresienstadt and the transfer of well-connected Jews to that ghetto. Later, when the Bergen-Belsen camp was established, this section was responsible for it as well.

In April 1942, as the start of the mass deportations approached, Stuschka was named to censor Jewish mail; he was directly subordinate to Günther. It is not clear if he had a code of his own, although the West German prosecutors concluded from indirect evidence that he may have been a–4. Aiding him in this was Richard Hartenberger, who brought the mail of the Jews from the camps to be read in the office.

Suhr continued to head the second branch; when he left in November 1942, his deputy, Hunsche, replaced him. Their sections dealt largely with matters of law and property – it was here that the department's lawyers worked. Suhr himself, and Hunsche after him, also handled contacts with foreign governments. Hrosinek continued to manage the office. Gutwasser coordinated the Reich Association and dealt with its finances. Pachow joined him after April 1942. When Hunsche replaced Suhr, Pachow also handled Jews of non-German citizenship. We do not know which of them was b–1 and which b–2. The b–3 section was Bosshammer's, and its job was defined as "political preparation for the Final Solution." This meant preparing plans for collecting Jews from various countries and bringing the plan to fruition. He was also in charge of counter-propaganda, striking back at the so-called "atrocity propaganda" disseminated by enemy countries about Nazi treatment of the Jews. When Hunsche replaced Suhr, Bosshammer was transferred to Günther's branch, but retained the code b–3. The b–4 section handled matters that grew out of the new citizenship law regulation. Its head was Kube, and it included Adolf Franken, Hans Blum, Otto Kolrep and Paul Preuss.

On April 15, 1943, the department was given additional functions that had formerly belonged to department II A 5: "exposing enemies of the *Volk* and the state, seizure of their property and revocation of German citizenship." Two new sections were set up for this purpose. Section c–1, headed by Willy Jeske, and afterwards by Paul Pfeifer, dealt with exposing enemies of the people and the state and with the seizure of their property. Hans Wassenberg, and after him Alexander Mischke and Gustav Hüls handled the revocation of German citizenship; their code was c–2. To maintain the symmetry of the department, c–1 was put under Hunsche and c–2 under Günther.[5]

At the end of June 1943, some of the authority previously vested in department IV D 3 was transferred to IV B 4, specifically that involving surveillance of hostile foreigners, and especially the return of Jews and *Mischlinge* who had emigrated from the Reich.[6] At the end of the summer of 1943, Hunsche's sections were transferred from Berlin to Prague. From the beginning of 1944 there was less need for diplomatic coordination with foreign governments, because of developments at the fronts. In contrast, there was greater need for energetic activity in Italy, so Bosshammer was sent there. In March Eichmann, Novak and Hunsche left for Hungary.

This change of assignments found expression in different organizational patterns, both in the RSHA and in the department itself. Beginning on April 1, 1944, the department was called IV A 4b. Some of the sections remained in Berlin, and these had (I) added to their codes; others were transferred to Prague, with (II) affixed to their codes. Each section was identified by an additional lower-case letter after the Roman numeral. Wöhrn, for example, was (I)a, and he dealt with mixed marriages instead of Hunsche and with propaganda instead of Bosshammer. Novak

5. TR.10-754, pp. 101–18.
6. TR.10-754, pp. 82–3.

and his assistant, Martin, were coded (I)b, Mös was (I)c, and their assignments remained the same. The matter of emigration, which had up until then been part of department IV D 3, was now transferred to Eichmann and received the code (I)d, and the man whose job this was was called Karl Anders. After August 1944, the name was changed for some reason to Einz. 1. The Ministry of the Interior transferred to the SS the processing of requests from *Mischlinge* to change their classification; this was now overseen by a new section in Eichmann's department, with the code (I)e. Hartmann (censorship), Hartenberger (mail) and Hrosinek (management) remained in Berlin, still without any special code.

In Prague, Jeske's and Pfeifer's section, which dealt with uncovering hostility to the *Volk* and the state, was called (II)a, and after August 1944 it was called *Festst*. Mischke's and Brower's section was (II)b, and after August *Aberkennung*. (II)c, the code given to Kube and Preuss, changed after August to 11.VO. The assignments of these sections remained the same; only their codes were changed. Hunsche headed the sections in Prague, except for the time he was in Hungary. Mischke and Brower remained under Günther, but transferred to Prague.[7]

The work in the various sections ended around February 1945.[8]

By following the changes in codes it is possible to identify junior-level authors of documents hiding behind the signatures of senior officials. However, this also leads to an interesting conclusion in another area. Proverbially, a bureaucratic system only grows. Growth results both from objective external needs that require additional manpower, and from the needs of the system. When the external need disappears, the systems that addressed it are not dismantled, lest the need appear again, and because of the loss of power for senior officials that this would involve.[9] As expected of a bureaucratic system, IV B 4 grew. But, unexpectedly, when the external circumstances changed and the need for a subunit ceased to exist, the subunit was eliminated. The system may have grown, but it did not add unnecessary fat.

*

The staff of the department participated in the implementation of the Final Solution by drafting directives that instructed the men in the field

7.   TR.10-754, pp. 110–16.
8.   TR.10-754, p. 116.
9.   C. N. Parkinson, *Parkinson's Law* Boston: 1957; Blau and Meyer, *Bureaucracy*, pp. 145–50; R. B. Ripley and G. A. Franklin, *Bureaucracy and Policy Implementation*, Homewood, IL: Dorsey Press, 1982, pp. 40–2.

how to eliminate the Jews. Specified were the types of Jews against whom action should be taken, and how they were to be caught and their property confiscated. The department officials oversaw the rounding up and the transport of the Jews to the death camps, and also saw to it that the truth remained hidden – from the Jews, from foreign governments who inquired about the fate of their citizens, and even from other German government agencies. In the early stages, the department also dealt with emigration, then with preventing it.

An almost perfect example can be found in a directive dated June 4, 1942, containing technical instructions for the evacuation of the Jews to the East (to Izbica, near Lublin).[10] The first paragraph names the executive branch (the Security Police stations). The second paragraph specifies which Jews may be deported and which not (by age, occupation). Paragraph three deals with rounding up Jews and their individual preparation for deportation – what they were permitted and not permitted to take. Paragraph four identifies the train escorts, paragraph five who will receive the shipments, paragraph six the requirement that both dispatchers and receivers report to IV B 4 so that it will be kept up to date. The two final paragraphs address the funding of the operation and the confiscation of Jewish property. After receiving these instructions, each station waited for notification of the date trains would embark from the area under its jurisdiction. Implementation was in the hands of the local authorities, but complications and obstacles were referred to Berlin for instructions.

The document demonstrates the problem of identifying the creators of documents in the department. The signature is Eichmann's, but most of the topics required cooperation and input from several experts. The expert who knew which items Jews were permitted to take was not the same one who dealt with the requirement to report on trains and on how those reports should be worded. Finance was the responsibility of a third expert, and so on. With documents of this type, we can at the most determine who wrote them, but even then it has to be remembered that the author went around the department and collected the contributions of each expert.

The following pages will try to trace the activity of department officials in advancing the Final Solution, and to identify them. The charts on pages xvii–xx depict the measures taken to employ the Security Police

---

10. TR.3-1663, IV B 4a 2093/42g.

in the deportation of the Jews. In general, their role may be summarized as follows: in the autumn of 1941 the Security Police cut Jews of the Reich off from their surroundings, deprived them of their property, closed off all avenues of escape by halting emigration, and began the deportations. At the beginning of 1942 they honed their methods, and in 1943 they took those Jews who had up until then enjoyed immunity.

In parallel with the headquarters work of planning the Final Solution, as described in the previous chapter, the deportation of the Jews of Germany was renewed in February. Trains began to set out eastward, from Theresienstadt as well.[11] At the end of February 1942 Suhr signed an additional directive on property. Its code, IV B 4a 164/42 points to Günther as the source, but Suhr, head of IV B 4b, signed it. West German prosecutors in the postwar anti-Nazi trials determined that Hunsche, then Suhr's assistant, was the author of the document; it may well be that his secretary simply erred in typing the code.[12] In any case, the directive's purpose was to ensure, once again, that all Jewish property be seized before deportation. Every Jew was to fill out, carefully and precisely, standard declarations of property, which would not include the little property that he took with him. Before deportation, the declarations had to be verified. Every Jew was to take fifty Reichsmarks, no more, no less. If a Jew didn't have this sum, he had to take it from a better-off deportee. According to regulation 11, Jews lost their citizenship as soon as they crossed the border, and their property was forfeited to the Reich. If, by chance, a Jew died after receiving notice of deportation but before leaving Germany, his property was to be confiscated in accordance with the rules applying to enemies of the state. The directive authorized involving in the deportation process representatives of the court system, who would come to the assembly points for Jews and carry out the transfer of ownership on land to the state. One copy of the property transfer form could remain with the Jews, but was to be taken upon their arrival in Poland. Blank forms, lists of the Jews dealt with, and questions were all to be sent to Suhr and Hunsche, telephone 259251, Berlin.[13]

Eleven days after the Wannsee Conference, Eichmann issued a directive to the stations in which he announced that "the deportations are the Final Solution." He attached to his operational orders on the deportations instructions for something without which the work could

11. TR.3-109; Adler, *Verwalteter Mensch*, p. 193.
12. TR.10-767a, p. 178.
13. TR.3-1265. The precise date is unclear – at any rate, before March 1, 1942.

not be completed: data collection. By February 9, 1942 each station was to provide the department with a breakdown of Jews in various categories (regular; foreign, by country; workers in war industries, etc.). The numbers were to be precise and up to date because they would determine the assignment of cars and trains for the deportations. Until further instructions were received, no other action was to be taken.[14]

At a second meeting of representatives of the Security Police from all over the Reich (held simultaneously, and in the same building, with the second Final Solution meeting), Eichmann gave oral instructions. He spoke of deporting 55,000 Jews in the near future — 20,000 from Prague, 18,000 from Vienna, the rest from other German cities. Düsseldorf, for example, was to receive one train. An agreement had been reached with army headquarters, the OKH, under which the freight trains bringing Russian prisoners into Germany would take Jews back on the return trip. Local Security Police stations would receive six days' advance notice about trains leaving from their areas. Each train had a capacity of 700, but 1000 Jews would be crammed in. Under no circumstances were Jews to be told in advance. Care was to be taken to collect money from the Jews to pay for their deportation. Commanders of Security Police stations were not to dispatch categories of Jews who were not specified in the instructions (the elderly, for example) because the absorption authorities in the East would refuse to accept them; furthermore, there were already plans in the works to send the elderly to Theresienstadt. At the end of the meeting, representatives who had already taken part in previous deportations shared their experiences.[15]

In the middle of May, Müller signed orders to carry out the transfer of elderly and well-connected Jews to Theresienstadt. The delay apparently stemmed from the fact that the department had been focusing on the other Jews. Another reason was the authorities' desire to accustom the German population to the disappearance of the Jews. For instance, once this became routine, the relatively sensitive taking of Jews who had been wounded in the First World War would be more likely to escape notice. The instructions differed on several points from those relating to the main deportations. First, because of the relatively small number of deportees, they would be transported in special railroad cars and not in entire trains. The cars would be hitched onto regular trains, in

14. TR.3-1278, IV B 4 2093/42g (391), 31 January 1942.
15. TR.3-119.

coordination with the regional train management. Fifty Jews would be put in each car. They would not come into contact with other passengers. Each Gestapo station would receive, each week, notification from Berlin about how many Jews were to be deported. Each car would be escorted by a Security Policeman, and others could be sent to assist him. The policeman would have two copies of the list of deportees. They would be received under the responsibility of the commander of the Security Police in Prague. Reports on the embarkation of each shipment would be sent to him, and of course also to IV B 4. (Up to this point, the instructions were prepared, almost certainly, by Novak. From here on, they were apparently by Suhr or Hunsche.) The baggage the Jews could take was the same as allowed in the general deportations. Even though most of the people involved were elderly, the Gestapo was to frisk them for valuables and weapons. Each shipment would contain a Jewish medical professional. The major obstacle was that regulation 11 did not apply to deportations to Theresienstadt, which was within the boundaries of the Reich. The solution was to act under the force of the regulations of March 2, 1942, pertaining to confiscation of property belonging to enemies of the state.[16] In other words, the older a Jew was, or the more likely that he could be classified as a wounded war veteran, the greater his or her chances were to be considered an enemy of the state. Such cynicism is certainly not mere bureaucratic indifference. It is the attitude of officials unable to think in moral terms.

On May 21, 1942, Günther (or Novak?) prepared for Müller's signature a supplementary order on the collection of data on the Jews. Gestapo stations were directed to send as quickly as possible, within a week, the numbers of Jews remaining in their districts, "in order to exploit to the fullest the possibilities for absorption in the East, after the deportations that have already been carried out." The number of Jews appropriate for Theresienstadt were to be listed separately.[17]

On June 4, 1942, Eichmann signed a directive prepared by Günther's staff. The range of topics indicates that the man who prepared it consulted with the experts, or that Günther knew everything. It stated that the mission of Gestapo stations was to arrest, assemble, and transfer Jews to the East in accordance with a timetable coordinated in Berlin, and to process Jewish property. It was recommended that the Jews be

16. TR.10-767b, pp. 279–83.
17. TR.3-1280, IV B 4a 2093/42g (391).

rounded up before the deportation. Trains would carry 1000, no more. Each Jew would take RM 50 or 100 zlotys, a suitcase with no lock containing shoes and clothing; bedding; food for two weeks; and eating utensils. Valuables, financial instruments, pets, and food ration cards could not be taken. Luggage would be checked. It was desirable to balance the ages of the deportees in each shipment. Jewish organizations could be involved in the preparations. In each group, Jewish "transport chiefs" would be appointed, and each car would have a warden with an armband who would be responsible for order and cleanliness. A Jewish doctor or orderly would be attached, with his equipment, to each shipment. The words "emigrated" or "unknown" would be entered on the police residence registration forms. For each train there would be an escort of an officer and fifteen Order Policemen. Notifications of train departure and arrival times would be sent expeditiously to IV B 4. Such reporting was vital for implementation, which required a great amount of planning and coordination.[18]

Why were such instructions necessary, following the ones given at the beginning of the year? We may suppose that their purpose was mainly psychological. Until the spring of 1942, German Jews were sent to the East, but still not directly to their deaths. Many of them remained in the ghettoes. The death camps were still not fully operational, so news of them could not reach either the Jews or the local bureaucrats in the cities of Germany. By summer, the camps were working at full capacity, and German Jews were being sent straight to them. At this time the men of IV B 4 issued extremely detailed instructions about the eating utensils that the Jews were to bring with them, and about the balance of ages in the shipments of deportees, so that shipments would not arrive without people fit for work. The instructions were meant to protect somebody (their authors? their readers? the Jews?) from the truth.

In this context, it is worth noting the language they used. When they discussed the shipment of Jews to the East, they used euphemisms deriving from the concept "remove" – *Abschieben* (disposal), *Abtransport* (transport), *Evakuierung* (evacuation).[19] Jews who went to Theresienstadt, and they only, underwent *Wohnsitzverlegung*, or "change of address." This indicates that there was a need for one euphemism for the Jews sent to their deaths and a different one for those sent to the ghetto.

18. TR.3-1663, IV B 4a 2093/42g (391).
19. File TR.3-177 contains an unusually large collection of such terms.

Theresienstadt was for many of them only a station along the way to their deaths, but there were no murder facilities there.[20]

By the spring of 1942, the methods used for the deportations from Germany were solidified and improved, and implementation, based on this experience, was initiated in other countries. An essential requirement for keeping the rate of deportations steady was the coordination of trains. At first Günther and Novak worked on this together, but as time went on Günther became more and more occupied with the rest of the department's work and did not find time for the trains. He was able to excuse himself from this responsibility because Novak did the job well. Furthermore, the growing complexity of the subject required a great amount of expertise, which Novak gained and Günther did not. At the beginning of 1942 Hartmann, whose work on emigration was diminishing rapidly, became Novak's assistant.[21]

Until the beginning of the war, the national train company, the *Reichsbahn*, functioned as a commercial enterprise. During the war it continued to operate in exchange for payment, except that priorities were set not according to profitability but according to the needs of the war. To simplify matters, it was decided that the Ministry of Transportation would work with only a single representative of each office or organization. Department IV B 4 filled this function for the Security Police. Train coordination was done on different levels, and Novak dealt only with the highest level, when the train had to pass along its route through the jurisdiction of more than one *Reichsbahn* management authority. Representatives of the department in other regions worked in Paris, Salonika and Bratislava, and in other places as well. IV B 4 did not coordinate trains in the Generalgouvernement or on Soviet territory, but the Security Police forces operated there in the name of the department.[22]

During preparation for the major deportations, Novak inquired of the WVHA where it wanted the trains to go; only afterwards did he consult the train company. Approximate timetables were set at special coordination meetings that took place at the Ministry of Transportation. Further coordination was achieved via contacts between Novak and Otto Stange. Stange was a veteran official at the train company, about sixty

20. TR.3-541; Adler, *Verwalteter Mensch*, p. 381.
21. Novak: TR.10-515, pp. 35–6; Hartmann: TR.10-767c, p. 705.
22. Eichmann, *Interrogation*, vol. 1, pp. 142–3; TR.10-515, p. 36; Raul Hilberg, "The Reichsbahn and Its Role in the Destruction of the Jews," *Yalkut Moreshet*, 24, 1977 (Hebrew).

years old, who, according to his job description, was "responsible for special trains." He sat alone in a room, and spent most of his day in noisy telephone conversations that disturbed those sitting in all the nearby rooms. He was an introverted man who was convinced of the importance of what he was doing.[23] Clearly, he was right – his work was important, and it made him into a mass murderer. He was never brought to trial.

The problem of train coordination had two components. It was necessary to find free time on the appropriate tracks, a problem that was solved by the timetables. It was also necessary to find appropriate railroad cars. Since Novak had in hand a general schedule, he had to assign the cars available to him to stations, to set departure times and to report to the stations about this.[24] This was more complicated within Germany – where the Jews were sent from a large number of stations, sometimes not in large numbers – than it was in other countries, where the Jews were assembled at a few stations. (Hungary in 1944 was in this sense more like the Reich, with the Jews being sent from a large number of stations – and Eichmann and his men were on the scene and supervised directly.)

Novak oversaw the complete implementation and made sure it ran smoothly. For this purpose he prepared standard report forms for the stations of departure and arrival, and these were communicated in urgent cables, so that at any moment he had a fairly clear and up-to-date picture of where the deportations stood. If there were problems in one part of the system that were about to upset the conduct of the deportations, he knew about them and reported to all affected so they could make the appropriate arrangements. He was the man who put out the instructions in the general directives on how to carry out the deportations.[25] The stages described here were carried out in the proper sequence in each case, but all these steps were happening in different places at the same time, because the trains were in constant motion. Years later Jänisch recalled that "anyone who went through the department knew about the deportation of the Jews and their destinations, if only because of the huge and detailed chart on the wall of Günther's room, which noted among

23. TR.10-515, p. 37; *Ich, Adolf Eichmann,* p. 142; Eichmann, *Interrogation,* vol. 1, p. 143; Hilberg, *Trains* (Hebrew), pp. 38–9.
24. TR.10-515, p. 36. For an example, where Novak's assistant Hartmann notified Düsseldorf by telephone, then sent a cable signed by Eichmann, see TR.10-767c, pp. 705–6, IV B 4a–2 2093/42g (391), 18 April 1942.
25. TR.10-515, pp. 25, 39.

other things the destinations of the deportations and the number being sent to each destination."[26]

The preparation of a shipment lasted several days. From time to time something would go wrong, and an accusing finger was pointed at the department, as Eichmann would still remember in his interrogation seventeen years later – when his memory was generally so horribly weak.[27]

How the department functioned when there were unexpected developments may be gleaned from two cables signed by Günther , dated November 25 and 26, 1942. The navy put at the disposal of the RSHA a ship to take Jews south from Norway. In the first cable, to Oslo, Günther gave notice of this sudden possibility and warned that the opportunity should be seized no matter what. He repeated the categories of Jews that it was permitted and forbidden to deport, and went over the details of the regular technical preparations, because the Security Police there had no experience of this sort of action. The next day he was able to tell them that a train was available, and that it would leave from Stettin four days hence.[28] Three months later an additional shipment of Norwegian Jews arrived via Stettin, but this time the local Security Police had to arrange for a train themselves, perhaps because it involved only 160 Jews.[29] Two months later, when Günther was asked about the fate of Norwegian Jewry, he wrote: *"zur Zeit lagermässig untergebracht"* – "as of this time camp accommodations have been found for all of them."[30]

Another phrase that reveals the cynical mind-set of these bureaucrats appears in a letter signed by Eichmann. In November 1942 he wanted to encourage the Bulgarian government to hand Jews over to the Nazis: please remind them that there is *"ausreichende Aufnahmemö-glichkeiten für Unterbringung der Juden"* – "sufficient absorption capacity for settling the Jews."[31]

According to a directive signed by Günther and dated February 20, 1943, the department coordinated special trains for groups of (only!) 100 Jews being sent to Theresienstadt. Smaller groups would be sent in

26. TR.10-767b, p. 390.
27. Eichmann, *Interrogation*, vol. 1, pp. 191–2, 605–6.
28. TR.3-1622, TR.10-767b, pp. 319–20. Both documents were originally filed under IV B4a 3771/42g (1546).
29. TR.3-1621, IV B 4a 3771/42g (1546), 25 February 1943.
30. TR.3-492.
31. TR.3-127.

special cars, which would be coordinated by the local Gestapo station, but after notifying Berlin. Another directive of the same day warned, among other things, of the frequent attempts by Jews to escape from the deportation cars, and instructed that the police escorts be briefed accordingly.[32]

The same file code that was at the top of the directives to the Gestapo stations also appeared at the top of requests or suggestions directed to Himmler, because it was the subject, not the addressee, that determined where the directive was filed. On December 16, 1942 Günther prepared (in cooperation with Novak) a message to Himmler, which Müller signed. It began with a report that, from the middle of December 1942 and for a month thereafter, it would not be possible to carry out deportations because of a lack of trains. There was heavy passenger traffic during that time because of soldiers coming home for the Christmas season. In the second half of January 45,000 Jews would be deported. Ten thousand of them would be from Theresienstadt, half of them non-workers. This would relieve overcrowding in the ghetto. Günther/Müller asked for approval of the operation (apparently the exceptional deportation of elderly Jews from Theresienstadt).[33] The principal importance of this letter, for our purposes, was the type of information sent from Günther (or, actually, from Novak) to Himmler. It reported a halt to deportations because of a lack of trains. Concerning one of the most important elements in determining the rate of the deportation of the Jews to their deaths, it was not Himmler who dictated to his subordinates, but rather his subordinates who notified him of a fact that was not even open for discussion.

On February 20, 1943 Günther himself signed instructions "for the technical implementation of the evacuation of the Jews to the East (Auschwitz camp)," which was sent to the usual recipients.[34] There were no major changes here, and it may well be that the instructions were dictated and distributed in order to rally once again the men of the local stations. They may have needed this after the rate of deportations had slowed because of the declining number of Jews, and then stopped for a time during the battle of Stalingrad. This, apparently, is also the way to understand the directive that was issued on May 21, 1943 over

32. TR.3-541; TR.3-1282.
33. TR.3-192, IV B 4a 2093/42g (391).
34. TR.3-1282, IV B 4a 2093/42g (391).

Kaltenbrunner's signature, dealing with the capture of those Jews still remaining in Germany. By order of the Reichsführer these Jews were to be deported by June 30, 1943, including some of those who had until now enjoyed immunity. The deportations of fewer than 400 of them would be carried out in special carriages on a regular train, during the second half of June. The locals would coordinate and notify Berlin at least eight days in advance. The larger transports were to be ordered via IV B 4 (but the initiative was now local, with the department hearing in advance but not planning and notifying outlying cities). Before the end of June a report was to be sent on the number of remaining Jews, categorized according to the provision under which they had not been sent. Starting in July an updated report was to be prepared each month. It was to follow a model that reported the following for each Jew: 1. serial number; 2. first and family name; 3. date and place of birth; 4. current address; 5. type of exemption; 6. identity of the person who issued the exemption, date and reference code; 7. comments, if any.[35] The directive constituted a late stage in carrying out the deportation; and it brings us to a different issue: protected Jews.

Defining the victims: who gets immunity?

The Nuremberg Laws defined who was a Jew, and the SS did not seek to change this. But there were differences of opinion about the fate of marginal groups, who did not entirely belong to any camp – such as people of mixed ancestry, the Jewish spouse in mixed couples, and Jews with foreign citizenship. Changes in policy regarding them affected tens of thousands of people, and were a product of the general pace at which the deportations progressed, of the state of war and its effect on foreign governments, and of the technical ability to obtain trains. Defining the victims therefore determined to whom the policy would apply, in keeping with the legal definition that had existed since 1935.

At the beginning, no one expected problems in defining the victims. At the large interministerial meeting of January 15, 1941, RSHA representatives Rajakowitz and Neufeld advocated a hard line. The question was how to implement the Nuremberg Laws pertaining to Reich citizenship in newly annexed areas. Both of them favored unqualified

35. TR.10-767b, pp. 564–7, IV B 4a 2093/42g (391).

denial of citizenship to Jews, with the exception of the Jews of the Generalgouvernement, who would retain their current (worthless) citizenship. They proposed, further, that the same rule apply to Jewish partners in mixed marriages.[36] When Eichmann spoke to Rademacher on the telephone at the end of February, he told him that if the Security Police should act against Jews, only citizens of the Soviet Union and the United States would be protected.[37] Eichmann signed the letter to Rademacher giving notice of the intention to transport a Jewish resident of Prague for labor, even though he had American citizenship.[38] A directive from the same file states that, with regard to the restrictions on Jews that were imposed at the beginning of the war, such as the prohibition against listening to the radio or going to the theater, Jews with foreign citizenship would have the same status as German Jews.[39]

When, however, preparations began for the murder of all the Jews, obstacles appeared. While the regulations requiring that Jews wear a star were under preparation, the foreign minister asked Martin Luther to clarify to Heydrich that, because of diplomatic considerations, the law should not apply to Jews with foreign citizenship residing in Germany.[40] A week after the regulation was issued, a soothing letter was sent to the foreign minister. It said foreign Jews would be exempt, but only for the time being, and asked for notice of any changes on the diplomatic front. Perhaps, it asked, it was already possible to include Jews of Romanian, Croatian and Serbian citizenship, because those countries had already instituted the practice in their own territories? Heydrich signed the letter, but Wöhrn prepared it – perhaps because he was responsible for the Reich Association, which distributed the badges.[41] The exemption for foreign Jews appeared in the regulations themselves,[42] which had been prepared by Suhr. There is no way of knowing who originated this solution to the

36. TR.3-728.
37. TR.3-910. Hartmann prepared a summary of the meeting and sent it to Rademacher to be initialed, 12 December 1941. IV B 4(neu) IV D 4(Rz) 288/41g (56).
38. TR.3-911, IV B 4b 675/41–2, 2 July 1941. The letter was probably written either by Wöhrn or by Mös.
39. TR.10-652, p. 75, IV B 4b 675.41, 4 August 1941.
40. TR.3-948, 31 August 1941. At the outbreak of the war there were in Germany some 5200 Jews whose nationality might have protected them. The largest group were Hungarian nationals (1746), followed by Romanians (*c.* 1100). Hilberg, *Destruction*, p. 448.
41. TR.3-949; TR.10-767a, p. 197.
42. TR.3-1064.

problem raised by Ribbentrop, and it is a good example of a contribution to *policy* whose source cannot be identified.

The next group of Jews with immunity were those with Aryan German family connections. The officers of the RSHA sensed that this would be a problem. But its complexity only became apparent when, at their meeting on October 10, 1941 in Prague, they decided that Jews married to Aryans would be sent to Theresienstadt. If the wife was Aryan, she would have to divorce her husband or accompany him to the camp.[43]

In the briefing for local Security Police representatives that took place on October 23, 1941, practical instructions were given. Unlike the declarations that had preceded them, these were very cautious. Foreign citizens, family members of Jews working in war industries, those over the age of sixty, and the German spouses of Jews were not to be deported.[44] Eichmann and his colleagues, recognizing that there was a problem here, decided in the meantime to concentrate on those Jews whose status was not in dispute.

At the Wannsee Conference, Heydrich tried to impose the view of the RSHA. He demanded that Jews from the age of 65, the severely handicapped, those who had been wounded in the First World War, and those holding high service medals (Iron Cross class 1) be sent to Theresienstadt. *Mischlinge* of the first degree (those with two Jewish grandparents) would be considered Jews, unless they were married to Aryans and the couple had children, or they already enjoyed special protection (which should be reexamined). People in these categories would be sterilized if they wished to remain in the Reich. *Mischlinge* of the second degree (those with one Jewish grandparent) would be considered Germans unless circumstances indicated that they were closely associated with Judaism. As to mixed marriages, each case would be discussed individually. Whether to deport them or evacuate them to Theresienstadt would depend on the effect this would have on the Aryan family members. During the meeting, however, it became clear that the issue was not a simple one, and that further discussion was required.[45]

A directive sent to the local stations, dated January 31, 1942,

43. TR.3-1193.
44. TR.10-767b, pp. 258–9.
45. Nuremberg document NG–2586-G. In 1939 there were in greater Germany 64,000 *Mischlinge* of the first degree and 43,000 of the second degree. Hilberg, *Destruction*, p. 418.

recognized the de facto limitations on the use of force. It stated that the following would not be deported: Jewish members of mixed couples, foreign Jews (with the exception of those with Polish and Luxembourgian citizenship and those with no citizenship), Jews working in war industries if their employers were unwilling to release them, Jews over 65 and infirm Jews over 55. If one spouse was over 65 but younger than 68 and was capable of working, both spouses would be deported. Enough lawyers had to be left in Germany to serve the Jews who remained. Couples should not be separated, nor should children up to the age of 14 be separated from their parents.[46]

During the months that followed, the department's staff was occupied with minor revisions and exceptions. Suhr complained to Rademacher about the good life being enjoyed by the Jews of Lichtenstein, who were protected from the Nazis.[47] Either he or Hunsche gave in to pressure from the foreign ministry and instructed the Security Police not to trouble an Italian noblewoman who was Jewish according to the German definition, but not according to Italian Law.[48] Suhr or one of his men proposed that Jewish homes be marked with a white star.[49]

From time to time the policy evolved with no fuss being made. On April 9, 1942 Wöhrn prepared a directive ordering the arrest of *Mischlinge* of the first degree who were having extramarital sexual relations with Aryan women, had been warned, and who were nevertheless continuing to do so. This was not in keeping with the Nuremberg Laws, so Wöhrn added a justification, which was that this behavior was hurting the morale of soldiers at the front.[50] On April 17, 1942 Eichmann signed a directive to Gestapo stations according to which Jews with the medal given to wounded soldiers should not be evacuated to Minsk; they would later be transferred to a special ghetto within the Reich.[51] On April 19, 1942 Novak said in a telephone conversation with the Security Police in Düsseldorf that Jews working in war industries could be deported if they had replacements.[52] On April 22, 1942

46. TR.3-1278, 31 January 1942. Eichmann signed; it is impossible to determine who wrote the letter.
47. TR.3-1188, 17 February 1942, IV B 4a 2162/42 (373/42). Suhr himself signed.
48. TR.3-1190, 13 March 1942, IV B 4b 354/42–4-. Eichmann signed.
49. TR.10-652, p. 80, 17 March 1942, IV B 4b 1025/41–60-. Unidentified signature.
50. TR.10-652, p. 80, IV B 4a–1 190/40–19-. One assumes Wöhrn prepared the circular, as the officer in charge of protective custody.
51. TR.3-1288, IV B 4 2093/42g (391).
52. TR.10-515, p. 40.

Eichmann signed a directive sent to all Security Police stations in which he reprimanded them for employing too many Jews in the local offices of the Reich Association. They too should be deported, in proportion to the size of the community.[53]

On May 15, 1942, an order was issued regarding the transfer of Jews to Theresienstadt. Elderly Jews and those with war medals for heroism and for having been wounded would be sent there. The principal difference between the projected policy and the order as it was finally issued had to do with mixed couples: they would not be sent, unless the Aryan spouse was no longer alive and there were no small children.[54] The intention of the RSHA, as expressed in the fall of 1941, was to include as many Jews as possible in the deportations. The practical instructions given in October 1941 and at the beginning of 1942 were much more cautious. The first step towards closing the gap came in a directive signed by Müller on May 21, 1942, which was sent to all Security Police stations. Jews who had in the past been married to non-Jews, as well as those of mixed parentage who had been defined by the Nuremberg Laws as Jews despite their having a non-Jewish parent (November 14, 1935[55]) were now to be deported. The directive was prepared by Günther, or perhaps by Novak.[56] This small revision could not change the situation as a whole. During all of 1942 there were no significant changes in the immunity of protected Jews.

In September 1942 several Gestapo officers (not from the department) conducted a discussion with representatives of Berlin Jewry on "the problem that the material for deportations is running out."[57] The SS said it could no longer allow itself the luxury of not deporting

53. TR.10-767c, pp. 968–9, IV B 4 2093/42g (391).
54. TR.10-767b, pp. 276–9, IV B 4 2537/42.
55. *Documents on the Holocaust*, Jerusalem: Yad Vashem, 1981, p. 80.
56. TR.3-1280, IV B 4a 2093/42g (391).
57. Hilberg, *Destruction*, p. 463. One might point out that this episode underscores another point: that the deportation of the Jews of Berlin (with the exception of the communal workers) was not carried out by IV B 4, but by the Berlin Gestapo. This would also explain why the non-Jewish wives of Jewish men earmarked for deportation, 28 February 1943, demonstrated against this in front of the Gestapo building on Rosenstrasse, not before Eichmann's headquarters on Kurfürstenstrasse 115/116. See Ball-Kadouri, Kurt J., "Berlin Is 'Purged' of Jews," *Yad Vashem Studies*, V, 1963, pp. 279–80. See also Kempner, R. M. W, "Der Mord an 35,000 Berliner Juden," in *Gegenwart in Reuckblick: Festgabe für die jüdische Gemeinde zu Berlin*, 1970, pp. 181, 189, and also the film by Daniela Schmidt, *Rosenstrasse – wo Frauen widerstanden*, 1990. Copy in Yad Vashem Film Archive, V–1038.

protected Jews. In another conversation, which took place before November 26, 1942, RSHA representatives proposed to the Plenipotentiary for Labor Allocation, Fritz Sauckel, that Poles deported from the Lublin area – if they were of the higher categories – replace the Jews working in the war industries in Germany. Then it would be possible to deport these Jews. Sauckel accepted the idea, and ordered his office to begin preparations.[58] During 1943 the noose began to tighten. Parallel with local actions (such as the deportation of the Jews of Berlin in February 1943), IV B 4 worked on the national level. At the end of April Günther or one of his men sent a letter to the chief of the Security Police in Nuremberg and asked that he confirm the removal of Jews from the war industries. This was in accordance with an agreement with Sauckel and the Minister of Armaments and the Plenipotentiary for Labor Allocation, Speer. Eichmann signed.[59] Günther prepared a general directive on the subject, issued over Kaltenbrunner's signature on May 21, 1943 to all the Security Police stations: the sick and handicapped would be deported. Jews working in the war industries, except those in labor camps, would be deported regardless of their contribution to the industries. Employees of the Reich Association would be deported, and the organization and its branches would be disbanded. It would be replaced by an organization of Jewish members of mixed couples. There would be no change in the status of persons of mixed parentage, nor in the status of Jews married to Aryans. In fact, such Jews who had been arrested thus far for other than security reasons would be gradually released.[60]

On December 18, 1943 Müller signed a directive prepared by Günther decreeing that the Jewish member of mixed couples whose spouses were "not present" and who were not exempt from wearing the badge would be sent to Theresienstadt.[61] (The intention was apparently Jews whose non-Jewish spouse had died and who had *Mischlinge* children.) As late as January 1945, still trying to grab those who had been protected so far, Kaltenbrunner signed a directive ordering the deportation to Theresienstadt of Jewish spouses in mixed marriages, providing they were fit for work, as well as *Mischlinge* who were considered Jews. Jews in this category were called *Geltungsjuden* and

58. Hilberg, *Destruction*, p. 442.
59. Kempner, pp. 121–2.
60. TR.10-767b, pp. 564–7, IV B 4a 3093/42g (391).
61. TR.10-767b, p. 297, IV B 4a 2018/42g (908).

included, for example, those who were members of the Jewish community.[62]

Within Germany the department enjoyed a clear legal status. When it defined who was Jewish, it was working largely with a matter of law (or, in a word more appropriate for a totalitarian regime, of regulation). Outside the Reich the situation was different. There it was necessary to take into account the local authorities or bureaucratic systems. The task of defining Jews in other countries was much more political than it was legal, and generally it was not done within the RSHA but rather in collaboration with the foreign ministry. Another matter: throughout Europe, including the Reich, there were Jews whose citizenship was not that of the country in which they lived. These Jews were under the protection of their governments until such time as protection was denied, and the SS needed the help of the foreign ministry in handling them.

Jews under the protection of foreign governments enjoyed this privilege both in Germany and in other countries – even in Warsaw. At the beginning of 1942 Jews with foreign citizenship residing in the Warsaw ghetto were notified that they had to leave. In April Eichmann attended a meeting at the foreign ministry that discussed the issue. He proposed that the German authorities operate under the assumption that all the foreign citizens had left. If in the future a Jew from the ghetto presented documents proving that he had foreign citizenship, they would be considered forged. If foreign governments interceded they would be told that their citizens had had almost three months to leave, or the foreign ministry could provide vague information (so the documents state explicitly!).[63] Two weeks later the foreign ministry withdrew its consent and requested that Jews who were British subjects or citizens of North and South American countries be separated from the other Jews in the ghetto.[64]

The department had not yet appreciated how great a problem it would have carrying out the Final Solution on foreign Jews, and it was not enthusiastic about devoting time to this. On March 30, 1942, Wöhrn prepared for Eichmann's signature a letter replying to the foreign ministry's pressure about Slovakian Jews wishing to pass through Reich

62. TR.10-767b, p. 297, IV B 4b 3066/40g (159), 19 January 1945.
63. TR.3-941, 21 April 1942.
64. TR.3-942, 5 May 1942.

territory for the purpose of emigration. The department's position was that such passage should not be allowed, but that the issue was in any case irrelevant because preparations for the deportation of tens of thousands of Slovakian Jews were already in full swing.[65] In contrast, at this stage Jews in Germany with foreign citizenship were still exempt from deportation, even from wearing the badge.

Early in the summer of 1942 intensive preparations were made for the deportation of the Jews of Western Europe. On June 9, 1942 Eichmann asked Rademacher for the foreign ministry's position on Jews with foreign citizenship. It is interesting that the letter was prepared on Günther 's side (IV B 4a 2686/42), because the matter would be handled in the future principally by Suhr, and after his departure, by Hunsche.[66] Suhr cabled Dannecker in Paris the next day, advising that the regulation regarding the badge applied only to those foreign citizens in whose home countries the Jews were required to wear such a badge. He was waiting, he said, for permission from the foreign ministry to include the rest of the foreign Jews as well, and would send urgent notification if this was obtained.[67] At the end of July, apparently, directive IV B 4 2644/42 was issued, stating that Jews who were citizens of the United States, Britain and Latin American countries – both neutral and Allied – would not be deported.[68]

A few months of deportations persuaded the department staff that the problem was a serious one. Günther cabled Auschwitz on August 14, 1942 that a train containing 1200 Croatian Jews was on its way to the camp. By mistake a number of Italian and Hungarian Jews had been loaded on as well, he said, and requested that they be separated from the rest. Günther admonished Abromeit in Croatia that this should not be repeated. Logic dictates that Novak prepared the cable, since his office was the address for all the reports on the subject of trains.[69]

The department was still clarifying the policy when, on August 18, 1942, Suhr asked the foreign ministry what Hungary's position was regarding its Jews who were living in Romania. Could they be restricted as German Jews were? Could they be deported to the East? What about their property? Were the Hungarians prepared to accept the territorial

65. TR.3-1234. The identification of Wöhrn: TR.10-767a, p. 198.
66. TR.3-147; TR.10-767c, pp. 858, 877.
67. TR.3-1360, IV B 4a 2248/42, 10 June 1942.
68. Description of this document, see TR.3-1622.
69. TR.10-767b, p. 315, IV B 4a 3013/42g (1319).

principle, according to which Jewish property belonged to the country from which it was taken, without regard to the Jews' citizenship?[70] On September 3, 1942 Rademacher sent Suhr a reply to a telephone conversation they had conducted. Generally, Rademacher said, foreign Jews in the Generalgouvernement would be considered to be like local Jews.[71] The next day Suhr gave Müller a directive saying that Bulgarian Jews in Germany would wear the badge just as German Jews did. Müller signed.[72]

August 27, 1942: Klingenfuss from the foreign ministry to Suhr. Request to refrain for the present from the deportation of Hungarian Jews from Germany, in light of Hungarian objections.[73] November 17, 1942: Eichmann complains to the foreign ministry that Bulgarian Jews are escaping to Spain via Italy, with the help of the Spanish delegation in Bulgaria.[74] December 8, 1942: Hunsche or Bosshammer, over Eichmann's signature, to the foreign ministry: the attempt to argue that Iranian Jews living in France are not racially Jews is "a typical Jewish attempt at misrepresentation and dissimulation." The Jewish problem in Iran is in fact an ancient one, as the book of Esther testifies. (Whoever composed this letter devoted no small amount of time to it, because he provided a lengthy account of the history of Persian Jewry.[75])

On February 18, 1943 von Hann of the foreign ministry asked Hunsche to put into writing the agreement they had reached. This was that Jewish citizens of enemy countries who were living in Germany would be registered with the Reich Association, but would not be subject to the measures being taken against the other Jews.[76]

If these last few paragraphs sound confused, disordered and inconsistent, this simply reflects the reality of the issue of foreign Jews from the beginning of deportations from the rest of the continent through spring 1943. In general, each time the Germans decided to prepare a country to hand over its Jews, it first made the country surrender its right to protect its Jewish citizens in Germany. Afterwards it was asked to agree to their deportation to the East. When this consent was given, the

70. TR.3-929, IV B 4b 2586/42.
71. TR.3-1086.
72. TR.3-1027, Ministerium des Innens Pol.S IV B 4b 940/41–6, 4 September 1942.
73. TR.3-930.
74. TR.3-127, IV B 4 3565/42g (1484). Author unidentified.
75. TR.3-321, IV B 4b 2023/42.
76. TR.10-767c, p. 877.

state was already an accessory to the Final Solution, and it was difficult for it to defend the Jews on its territory.[77] The foreign ministry handled these contacts, in coordination with the RSHA.

On March 5, 1943 an attempt was made to bring some order to the picture. Kaltenbrunner signed a directive prepared by Hunsche,[78] which appears in two versions. One was issued by the Ministry of the Interior, Pol. S IV B 4b 2314/43g (82); the second comes from the same file, but is printed on the letterhead of the Commander of the Security Police and the SD. The first version was sent to the Security Police stations in the Reich, and the second to the forces in the East, perhaps because they were the senior German agencies in their regions, and there was no need to equip them with instructions on the authority of a government ministry because other ministries did not interfere with them there. The directive stated that Jewish citizens of the following countries would be included in the general measures against the Jews, including deportation: Poland, Luxembourg, Slovakia, Croatia, Serbia, Romania, Bulgaria, Greece, Holland, Belgium, France, Norway, the Baltic states, and stateless Jews. A Jew not residing in his country of citizenship would henceforth be without the protection of his government. Because the issue of property had not yet been resolved, the property of deported Jews should be collected and transferred to the appropriate officials. Jews with other citizenships should not be harmed, nor should Jews with dual citizenships, one of which was American or British. Any Jew, whatever his citizenship, who was demanded by another government in exchange for German citizens in its territory, should be detained, with information on him being sent to the RSHA.[79]

A separate directive concerned Jews who were citizens of other European countries. It was issued the same day, with the same code, also from Hunsche's desk — but with "only" Müller's signature, perhaps because its contents were more problematic for a bureaucracy that wanted to kill all Jews. Until March 31, 1943, it permitted citizens of the following countries to return to their homelands: Italy, Switzerland, Spain, Portugal, Denmark, Sweden, Finland, Hungary and Turkey.[80]

77. Hilberg, *Destruction*, p. 553.
78. The identification: TR.10-767a, p. 184.
79. TR.3-535, p. 788.
80. TR.3-230, IV B 4b 2314/43g (82). For the identification of Hunsche: TR.10-767a, p. 184. There exists an additional document, very similar in content, prepared by Hunsche and Eichmann in January 1943. It seems to have been a draft of the

At whose initiative were these regulations crafted? Three conjectures can be made. First, it could have been that the fresh new commander of the RSHA, Kaltenbrunner, was trying to put some order into the hazy situation he had inherited. If this were so, Hunsche merely prepared the regulations, and Müller signed the third directive because Kaltenbrunner did not want to be identified with so moderate a regulation. A second possibility is that the people in the field noticed that after the large wave of deportations of the summer of 1942 they were running into difficulties, and that more and more of their potential victims were protected. They might have then applied to Berlin, with Hunsche at the center of the efforts to shape policy. When the preparatory work was completed, the regulations would then have been submitted to Kaltenbrunner for approval, and he and Müller signed them. The third conjecture is somewhat like the second. The department staff recognized the need for new instructions, and with the arrival of a new commander they prepared a proposal and laid it before him. They assumed that he would accept the opinion of the experts, or that his old ties with Eichmann from their days together in Linz would incline him favorably towards the proposal. In other words, it could be that the proposal came from above, from below, or from the middle.

Possibly even at the time this question could not be answered. A bureaucratic system, by its nature, divides large tasks into small jobs. In shaping the policy of the murder of European Jewry there were many cases – maybe they were even the norm – in which things worked in such a way that a given decision was the result of small actions performed by many officials, without any of them having to take personal responsibility. The German language distinguishes between two situations, both of which are translatable into the word "responsible" – but with distinctly different connotations. The first is *zuständig* – being charged with the performance of some duty. The second is *verantwortlich* – being accountable for one's actions in a certain capacity. In other words, a person carries out actions in an area for which he is *zuständig*, but he may not necessarily be held accountable, *verantwortlich*.

During the rest of 1943 the major part of the handling of foreign

cont.

documents later submitted for the signatures of high-ranking Kaltenbrunner and Müller. Thus we can show that the issue had been discussed in IV B 4 at least two months prior to Kaltenbrunner's signing of the document – which would not, therefore, have been his own brainchild. TR.3-9.

Jews had to do with these regulations. The first problem was that of Romanian Jewry, who could, according to the directives, be deported. On March 25, 1943, some thirty Jews with Romanian citizenship entered the Romanian consulate in Vienna and asked to be protected against the Security Police, who had begun to arrest Romanian Jews. The secretary of the consulate granted them his protection, explaining that he had not heard of his government's consent to a change of policy. Hunsche justified himself at the beginning of April to the foreign ministry by saying that the arrest of the Jews had been accomplished in accordance with the said instructions.[81] The foreign ministry urged that the matter be left alone, and on April 15, 1943 Hunsche notified Eberhard von Thadden at the foreign ministry by telephone that Himmler had permitted the release of Romanian Jews who had already been arrested.[82] The SS continued its retreat a week later when Hunsche prepared a corrected directive for all the original recipients. In the wake of consultations with the foreign ministry, Romanian Jews were not to be deported, but those already arrested would not be released for the time being.[83] The backdown became complete on May 18, 1943, when Hunsche prepared still another directive in which he stated that Romanian Jews would be allowed to return to their country without the approval of the RSHA being required (this was emigration, which had been forbidden for almost two years) so long as they left by June 30. Romanian Jews already detained would be released.[84] If this retreat depressed Hunsche, he could take comfort at home, where his wife had just given birth to his first son.[85]

Some loose ends of this affair remained. The Romanian consulate in Brussels was concerned about nineteen of its Jewish citizens in the city. One of them, Hildegard Schwamenthal, had been born in Germany, but lost her German citizenship and became Romanian through marriage. This was in accordance with the laws of both countries. At the beginning of August Hunsche and Bosshammer met and decided that she could be treated as a German, a decision which raised some eyebrows in the foreign ministry. In the end she was not deported.[86] In another case,

81. TR.10-767c, pp. 881–2, IV B 4 2314/43g (82), signed by Hunsche, 2 April 1943.
82. TR.10-767c, pp. 883–4.
83. TR.10-767c, p. 930, IV B 4b 2314/43g (82), 23 April 1943.
84. TR.10-767c, p. 931, IV B 4b 2314/43g (82).
85. TR.10-767a, pp. 20–5.
86. TR.10-767c, pp. 934–9.

Eichmann signed in September 1943 a letter from Wöhrn to the foreign ministry, asking it to urge the Romanians to verify the return of the Jew Rosenthal from Paris to that country.[87]

The regulations of March 5, 1943 were meant to bring some clarity to an amorphous situation, but in doing so they placed restrictions on the Security Police. Von Thadden telephoned Hunsche on May 26, asking for an explanation of the deportation of the Soviet Jew Max Gurwitsch from Brussels. Hunsche took half a year to reply, then explained that Gurevitz had been deported in August 1942, before there were instructions forbidding this.[88] The minute the Security Police demanded of neutral countries that they take their Jews back, it denied itself the possibility of deporting them. But the main problem was that the Security Police were not able to tell foreign governments what to do. The foreign ministry objected, in their name, to the target date for the return of the Jews, which was set for March 31, 1943, now less than a month away. On April 7 the date was put off.[89] Eichmann signed, on July 5, an impatient letter from Hunsche to von Thadden in which he complained of the need to reject again and again the final date for the return of the Jews. He asserted that the last and final date would be July 31, making it clear that after August 3 all foreign Jews would be treated as if they were German Jews. In order to achieve the Final Solution, he asked the foreign ministry not to add any reservations.[90]

The ministry nevertheless had reservations. It said this was a step with significant implications, and it could not be completed in two days. Furthermore, it added, by the time word reached the governments in question, only a few days would remain until the deadline, and this was no way to work. The governments had to be given at least four weeks, the ministry concluded.[91] What is interesting is that Hunsche was aware of the sensitivity of the issue. In a personal conversation with SS Lieutenant Werner of the Security Police station at The Hague, at the beginning of July, he admitted that even after the deadline had run out, foreign Jews would be deported only in coordination with the foreign

87. TR.3-132, IV B 4a 3211/43, 10 September 1943. Identification of Wöhrn: TR.10-767a, p. 204.
88. TR.3-552. Identification of Hunsche: TR.10-767a, p. 189.
89. TR.3-302, IV B 4b 2314/43g (82). Hunsche prepared, Günther signed: see TR.10-767a, p. 185.
90. TR.3-107, IV B 4 2314/43g (82). Identification of Hunsche: TR.10-767c, p. 932.
91. TR.3-906.

ministry.[92] Only foreign Jews could benefit from this display of moderation; if the Security Police learned that a given Jew was about to receive such citizenship, he was to be deported immediately.[93]

Müller signed, on September 23, 1943, a directive by Hunsche addressed to all Security Police stations. According to an understanding with the foreign ministry, Jewish citizens of Italy, Switzerland, Spain, Denmark, Sweden, Finland, Hungary, Romania and Turkey could be deported. In the first stage men over the age of 24 would be sent to Buchenwald and women and children to Ravensbrück (that is, not to certain death in a liquidation camp). Italians would be arrested immediately, Turks by October 20 and the rest by October 10. There was no need for arrest warrants, but it should be made clear to the camp commands that this was in fact a deportation operation. The deportees' property would be handled as had been prescribed in March. Jews married to Germans, or other such cases, should not be deported.[94]

For some reason, the position taken in this directive was also not final. Almost two months later Eichmann signed a message with the same code to the foreign ministry on the matter of foreign Jews in Greece and Italy. In his opinion, he said, they should be included in the deportations, but if this was impossible, they should at least be returned to their own countries, en masse and under supervision.[95] At the end of February Günther signed a letter by Hunsche to the foreign ministry, again about foreign Jews in Greece — they hadn't been told to return to their countries. The order of the commanders of the Security Police in Greece was to send them to Bergen Belsen for examination. Those who required it would be sent to their countries of origin from there.[96] About 10 messages went out from the department after the end of 1943 dealing with Jews of one country who were in a different country, and in need of one kind of treatment or another. The only major innovation was that after Hunsche left Berlin for Hungary in March 1944, Wöhrn became responsible for file 2314/43g (82). He handled, among others, French and

92. TR.10-767a, pp. 177–8.
93. TR.3-600, Eichmann to Zoepf, IV B 4 4435/43, 26 June 1943, prepared by Hunsche: TR.10-767a, p. 187.
94. TR.3-537, IV B 4b 2314/43g (82). Identification of Hunsche: TR.10-767a, p. 189.
95. TR.3-105, 15 November 1943. Hunsche presumably prepared the document.
96. TR.3-520, IV B 4b 2314/43g (82), 29 February 1944. Identification of Hunsche: TR.10-767a, p. 191.

Argentinian Jews in Hungary, Spanish Jews returning to their homeland via Switzerland, and Turkish and French Jews.[97]

Individual cases

The men of the central department for coordinating the deportation of Jews to their deaths did not work only on setting policy and preparing general directives. They also handled individual cases. We have already seen Hartmann in action, as he switched in the fall of 1941 from assisting Jews who wanted to emigrate to preventing their emigration. A few more requests reached him at the end of 1941, which he rejected in keeping with his orders. On January 23, 1942 he explained to the Security Police command in France that this was currently the policy. There were attempts by Jews to avoid the deportations in Germany by entering France, and Hartmann asked that attention be paid to this.[98] Eichmann signed, on March 12, 1942, a telegram by Mös or Kryschak, who were responsible for "individual cases," to the Gestapo stations in the west. Recently, it said, there had been many cases of attempts by Jews to get into Belgium, sometimes with the use of forged papers. Not long ago such a group had been caught with an escort. If such incidents were repeated, the Jews involved should be sent to the Gestapo station at their last place of residence, and the escorts should be brought to trial. When they finished serving their sentences they should be transferred to "protective custody." Each case must be reported to the department.[99]

After Hartmann became Novak's assistant, he again found himself frustrating Jewish attempts to evade deportation. On April 21, 1942, an Aryan woman in Düsseldorf complained that her children were about to be deported, even though they were only *Mischlinge*. The police in Dusseldorf telephoned Hartmann, who said he knew of two other such complaints. He ruled that the complaints should be checked to see if they were justified. Care should be taken that additional complaints not be sent to other agencies, and to threaten "security police action" if this happened. He should be notified of the results of the inquiry, but *not* by

97. TR.10-767c, pp. 1043–4; TR.3-957.
98. Examples: TR.10-767c, pp. 670–1, 28 October 1941; TR.10-767c, pp. 677–8, 12 December 1941; TR.3-735, IV B 4a 50/42. Identification of Hartmann: TR.10-767a, p. 163.
99. TR.3-707, IV B 4a–3 2264/42g (1008).

urgent telegram. A deportation train carrying 941 Jews, including those of mixed parentage, left the next day for the East; they did not return.[100] Mös or Kryschak refused to allow a Jewish professor, E. M. Meyers, and his family to emigrate in December 1942.[101]

From time to time Hunsche sent the foreign ministry letters requesting information on Jews who had left Germany before the Nazis came to power, and who had left behind property. The point of the inquiry was to find out whether the property could be confiscated. According to their code, these letters were prepared by Kube. We have only two documents with this code, and their numbering methods are unique.[102] Mös and Kryschak dealt with a Hungarian family resident in Heidelberg who, they argued, had disguised their true identity: their name was Romhanyi, not Reich, and the father of the family was a Jew, meaning that his two sons were *Mischlinge*. Their residence permit in Germany was about to run out, and the department was not willing to extend it. They also had a complaint against one of the family members, who "with his astounding behavior grossly violated German hospitality."[103] A man who, in February 1943, could write about "German hospitality" has to be credited with a great deal of cynicism. On April 14, 1943, one of Günther's men notified the foreign ministry that the department opposed removing the brothers Heinz and Alexander Bondy from Theresienstadt and sending them to Sweden, but did not oppose sending three Dutch sisters there, if they produced the appropriate documents (from the wording of the letter it may well be that they were not Jewish).[104]

Working out the fate of individual Jews was not restricted to Germany; it spread to all the countries in which German rule was indirect, where the department's status was less formal. The most famous example was that of 49-year-old Jenni Cozzi, born in Lithuania, who was evacuated with the rest of the Jews of that region to the Riga ghetto. What made her special was that her late husband had been an Italian citizen, and through him she had gained Italian citizenship. As such, the

100. TR.10-767c, pp. 713, 717–18.
101. TR.3-1484, IV B 4a (1597/42g), 1 December 1942, signed by Günther; TR.3-223, IV B 4 1597/42g (1484), 11 December 1942, signed by Eichmann.
102. TR.3-968, IV B 4b–4 L.16105, 26 January 1943; TR.3-1060, IV B 4b–4 F.5864, 8 July 1943.
103. TR.3-135, IV B 4a–3 1354/42, 2 February 1943; signed by Eichmann, addressed to the Foreign Office.
104. TR.3-1238,IV B 4a 4108/43, signed by Eichmann. The case is described in detail by Browning, *Foreign Office*, pp. 156–8.

Italian consul-general in Danzig demanded that she be repatriated to Italy. The correspondence on her case began on December 12, 1942, when Günther described the case to Klingenfuss in the foreign ministry. "She doesn't even speak Italian," he thundered, and sulkily demanded that the foreign ministry arrange for her to be stripped of her Italian citizenship. Günther was also prepared to contend that, as a resident of the ghetto, she had seen too much, and that when she reached Italy she was liable to disseminate atrocity propaganda[105] (an argument reminiscent of Orwell's doublethink: if she really saw it, how could it be horror propaganda?). The correspondence about the woman continued for a year, with contributions from various branches of the German foreign ministry, the Italian foreign ministry, the Fascist party, and an unidentified senior Nazi party official in Berlin. The matter came to an end, as far as the bureaucrats were concerned, after Mussolini's downfall. On September 29, 1943, Eichmann signed a letter by Günther, or by one of Günther 's men who handled the matter, announcing that in light of the change in Italy's status, he saw no reason to pursue the matter, and that the woman would remain in the ghetto.[106]

Wöhrn prepared a letter for Eichmann's signature according to which the owner of a lumber company in Croatia named Viktor Guttman had been arrested and was to be sent with his family to Theresienstadt if the foreign ministry had no objection.[107] On June 12, 1944, Wöhrn had Günther sign a message to the Security Police command at The Hague. It said the foreign ministry had determined that the Turkish citizenship of several Jews (names attached) should not be recognized. They should be included in the impending deportation.[108]

Mös and Kryschak prepared letters for Günther 's and Eichmann's signatures rejecting emigration requests by Jews of various nationalities. When Sweden intervened in favor of a group of Norwegian Jews, the department saw this as a transparent ruse to grant them foreign citizenship, not worthy of attention.[109] It notified the foreign ministry of its decision to deport a Dutch Jewish woman to the East.[110] An interesting

105. TR.3-744, IV B 4a 3208/42, 10 November 1941. The letter would have been prepared by Günther, Wöhrn, Mös or Kryschak.
106. TR.3-746, 754, 748; TR.3-750, IV B 4a 3208/42.
107. TR.3-1048, IV B 4a 4508/43, 2 July 1943. Identification of Wöhrn, TR.10-767a, p. 204.
108. TR.10-767c, pp. 1041–2, IV A 4b (I)a 2314g (82).
109. TR.3-306, IV B 4a–3 3771/42g (1546), 23 July 1943.
110. TR.3-332, IV B 4a–3 4626/43, 27 September 1943.

case was recorded in the department on December 17, 1943: Röthke, the department's man in Paris, asked what he should do with a Jewish inventor he had in custody. The inventor possessed documents about a discovery with military potential. Eichmann signed the reply: the invention had already been patented, so the man was no longer of any value. Deport him.[111] Eichmann signed, on February 11, 1944, an inquiry to the foreign ministry: we have a Hungarian under arrest who adamantly denies that he is a Jew; we are certain that he is; please check up on his parents.[112] (Because if they were to release him, and it were to turn out that he had fooled them, the Final Solution would not be final.)

Drafting directives was a central part of staff work, largely disconnected from the victims. The special cases in Germany and the rest of Nazi-controlled Europe were more closely involved with the reality of victims who had names and personal histories. The issue of "protective custody" was one step closer, because this measure resulted directly in the arrest of a human being.

There was a separate RSHA department that dealt with "protective custody" – IV C 2. The principal functions of this department were to order detentions and to ensure that they were accomplished according to proper procedures (as opposed to the law, the procedures themselves were not necessarily legal). IV B 4 dealt with "protective custody" of Jews, and worked together with IV C 2. The decisions were made in Eichmann's office, then passed on to IV C 2 for implementation. After the end of 1940, Mös and Wöhrn handled the cases that reached the department. Mös was responsible for people whose last names began with the letters A through K, Wöhrn for L through Z. After April or May 1942 most of Wöhrn's work was done by Kryschak, while Wöhrn continued to handle the arrests of prominent Jews. They had to check to ensure that "protective custody" was carried out in accordance with the department's standing orders, so that there would be no claims of groundless arrest. When cases were completed, the decisions were submitted for the signature of Eichmann or Günther.[113]

Eichmann's department also issued orders for "protective custody." September 15, 1941: "protective custody" for Jews without stars. November 13, 1941: Jews must hand over typewriters, bicycles,

111. TR.3-1589, IV B 4a–3 (390/43g).
112. TR.3-566, IV B 4a–3.
113. TR.10-652, pp. 131–6.

cameras, and binoculars in their possession. "Protective custody" for those who refuse. January 5, 1942: Jews must hand over their ski gear. "Protective custody" for dodgers. March 24, 1942: "Protective custody" for Jews who violate the orders restricting their use of public transportation. May 12, 1942: Jews are forbidden to get an Aryan haircut (there is no definition of what this might mean"). "Protective custody" for those who persist in doing so. June 3, 1942: a reminder that Jews are to hand over heaters, vacuum cleaners, irons, record players, and records. "Protective custody" for those who refrain. There were further injunctions of this type that have not survived, but about which information was gathered by the German prosecution after the war. Also forbidden were visits to health spas and parks, art shows, sports events, and restaurants; employing an Aryan maid, smoking in a prohibited place, leaving one's place of residence without a permit, absence without permission from one's place of work, obtaining prohibited food, and dealing on the black market; failing to identify oneself as "Sarah" or "Israel," the names the Nazi regime required all Jews to add to their given names; leaving one's home after 8 p.m., keeping pets, and entering central Berlin boulevards such as Unter-den-Linden. All the orders were issued by IV B 4, generally by IV B 4b, perhaps by Wöhrn. So that their implementation could be monitored, they were sent to the Reich Association for distribution to all Jews, to Security Police stations, to a long list of government agencies, and to most of the senior officials in the RSHA.

Minister of Justice Otto Thierack ordered, on August 6, 1943, that a Jew who committed a violation would be handed over to the Gestapo after legal procedures were completed. This led to a sharp rise in the number of cases of "protective custody" of Jews who had so far enjoyed immunity, especially of Jews married to Germans. "Protective custody" thus became another tool in the hands of those, including IV B 4, who were trying to complete the Final Solution. "Protective custody" was also used in Holland, where cases were referred to Berlin for approval.[114]

Another job handled by Wöhrn, Mös and Kryschak, who were responsible for special cases, was the preparation of instructions for "special treatment." In such cases, a report would come from one of the camps (not the death camps) that the behavior of a particular Jewish

114. TR.10-652, pp. 76–91; ZSL AR 518/59 Bd.III, p. 503.

prisoner justified "special treatment." Wöhrn and his colleagues would prepare a request to Himmler and attach the information in their possession. When approval arrived, they would notify the camp. The camp would then report that the sentence had been carried out, adding a cover explanation whereby death resulted from natural causes. The department would file the report.[115]

The bureaucrats did not see the results of their work, but they nevertheless employed euphemisms. It was not only in IV B 4 that candor was lacking. Adler has shown how Nazi propaganda language succeeded in blurring its own message. Before the war, the language warning about the Jews was so extreme that people did not attribute to the words their literal meaning. A person who called the Jews a nation of murderers was presumed not to mean what he was saying. After creating a situation in which people did not take words seriously, those involved in the murders made great efforts to conceal the truth from the world, and all that got out was rumors. Rumors are treated skeptically, all the more so rumors using language that people had long since learned not to take seriously.[116] In other words, after the language had been corrupted, it could be used as a kind of camouflage.

The RSHA's cover-up of reality did not begin with the genocide of the Jews. From the time of the cruel mass deportations of Jews and Poles in the autumn of 1939, the RSHA was calling this *Aussiedlung*, or "external settlement." The parallel transfer of ethnic Germans was called *Unsiedlung*, or "change of place of residence." The term "Final Solution" appeared in connection with the Madagascar plan. Eichmann used it to mislead his colleagues in other offices, long after he himself knew about the change in policy.[117]

The power of a euphemism derives from its having more than one meaning. The person who uses it can delude his audience, and himself, into thinking that he does not mean what he means — especially if the alternative use is an accepted one, and the real one is not routine. The word *Sonderbehandlung* (special treatment) precisely meets these criteria,

115. TR.10-767c, pp. 1058–62. For examples, see TR.3-1254, IV B 4a 3205/41g (1111), 14 April 1942; TR.3-1255 IV B 4a 225/42g (1178), 23 May 1942.
116. Adler, *Verwalteter Mensch*, pp. 60–4. Further discussion of Nazi abuse of the German language can be found, for example, in Blumenthal and Nachman "On the Nazi Vocabulary," *YVS*, vol. I, 1957; ibid., "From the Nazi Vocabulary," *YVS*, vol. VI, 1967; Esh, Shaul, "Words and Their Meaning: 25 Examples of Nazi-Idiom," *YVS*, vol. V, 1963.
117. TR.3-856; TR.3-172, p. 13; TR.3-773, p. 5.

as is proved by the story of Kaltenbrunner's interrogation at the Nuremberg trials. The prosecutor, Colonel John H. Amen, presented him with a document with his signature on the *Sonderbehandlung* of prisoners at the Walzertraum and Winzerstube camps. How embarrassed the prosecutor was when Kaltenbrunner explained that these were the names of two famous luxury hotels where well-connected prisoners were in fact given special treatment – by being confined in unusually comfortable accommodations.[118]

The men of IV B 4 used the term *Sonderbehandlung* only in the context of the executions of individuals in the camps, since their work did not require them to deal with the fate of the Jews once they had disembarked from the trains. The term had come into use by May 1942 at the latest, but the department staff preferred not to use it, because frequent use caused it to lose some of its ability to cloak its intent. For this reason, a euphemism for the euphemism was coined: *SB-Fälle* (SB cases).[119] To the extent that may be inferred from existing documentation, there was no other case where the department staff invented an abbreviated form of a term. The need to do so in this particular case would seem to indicate the strength of the instinct to conceal and repress what was happening. This is not consistent with the conjecture that they did not understand that what they were doing was wrong.

Hannah Arendt contended that this language of euphemisms kept these men from being able to compare their actions with the "old" meaning of the term "murder."[120] Thus language was used as a device for preventing communication or understanding.

But in reality it looked different, even to low-ranking people in the department. Secretaries Luise Hering, Marie Knispel, Gudrun Hunke, and Ilse Stephan saw the endless reports of death arriving from the camps, with the cause always being stomach and heart ailments. They understood that the Jews sent to the East were being killed. Stephan recalled that at one point reports stopped coming, and she knew that this was because of the large numbers of dead, not because the killing had stopped – this explanation being the only one that fits with everything else that was happening. Once, in November 1943, the foreign ministry requested information on Jacob Leefmans, who had been born in

118. Black, Peter, *Kaltenbrunner*, Princeton, NJ: Princeton University Press, 1984, p. 263.
119. TR.10-767c, pp. 1060–1.
120. Arendt, *Eichmann*, p. 86.

Amsterdam on August 21, 1902 and who had been deported to the East on February 2, 1943. Mös or Kryschak responded, over Günther's signature, that Jacob Leefsma, born on February 18, 1903 and deported to the East on February 2, 1943, had died at Auschwitz.[121] Having a long list of Jews in front of them, they copied the information about the man on the next line. A person cannot see death lists like these, on which appear such similar names of two men of the same age, deported on the same day, without being surprised. The people who worked in the department were of reasonable intelligence, and they understood what was implied by the list.

The secretary Elisabeth Marks, 18 years old, who arrived in the department in the middle of the war, said afterwards:

> When I came to the department, I didn't know, but I learned that its only mission was to advance the Final Solution. This realization came in stages. [Rudolf] Hanke helped me understand. After my curiosity was sparked, I searched for certainty. I made a habit of peeking at [Friedrich] Martin's documents – although he kept most of them in a locked metal cabinet and only the current ones were on his desk. I found the proof in a long list of death reports from Auschwitz, many of which were from the same cause: heart disease. Hanke would comment: "There goes another one." Once I asked explicitly if this was what was happening, and Hanke and Martin asked me if I was an idiot, if I didn't understand yet. ... Once they took the half-Jewish son from an Aryan woman and killed him. I got so emotional that I went to Eichmann [not to Günther – she thought Eichmann more fatherly. And she went because of a half-Aryan child, not on behalf of Jewish children – YL] and he told me that I had to be hard, and that I had much more to learn. ... Once ten or twelve of the workers, officers among them, were sitting and talking about Auschwitz. They were cracking jokes about the *Leichenflederer* [body robbers] who pulled the Jews' teeth out. I asked whether the Jews were still alive and someone commented, "They don't need the teeth anymore, they're dead."[122]

They were so familiar with the details that they could crack jokes about them. Had Hannah Arendt read this, she could have spared us a great deal of misunderstanding.

Seventeen of those interrogated recalled such conversations in the department.[123] Each worker related to the subject in different ways. Erna

121. TR.10-767b, pp. 599–604.
122. TR.10-754, pp. 488–91.
123. TR.10-754, p. 484.

Fingernagel was once sent to fill in for Wöhrn's regular secretary, who was absent. He began dictating, and suddenly exploded in anger and began cursing the Jews. She was frightened, and asked Günther (Eichmann was in Hungary) to bring in someone to replace her. Günther agreed. The regular secretary, Erna Miethling, recalled that Mös did not like to handle *Sonderbehandlung* cases, and did so slowly, with evident reluctance. Wöhrn, on the other hand, worked quickly, without any signs of conscience. Once she even commented to him on his evident pleasure in his work, and he yelled at her and implied that she herself ought to be in a camp. He expressed his regret that there were not more *Sonderbehandlung* cases. Of course, neither pangs of conscience nor enthusiasm had any effect on the final outcome, since all the orders of this type were of a fairly fixed form.[124] Sixteen of the office's employees admitted in interrogation that they made a connection between their work in the department and the rumors they heard outside, on the street. The secretaries working for Wöhrn, Mös and Kryschak typed out death sentences that were imposed for violations like eating potato peel from garbage cans, laziness at work, or petty theft.[125]

Hunsche's secretary remembered a case where he dictated to her something about a *Sonderbehandlung* of children, and became very emotional. "Whoever has children of his own cannot do this to someone else's children," he said unambiguously. Then he continued to dictate the letter. He did not have children of his own yet, but apparently his wife was pregnant with their oldest son. Perhaps his anticipation of this child gave him some qualms. On other occasions he said to his secretary that the department's staff would have to commit suicide if Germany lost the war — and he didn't want his wife to know what his business was. Towards the end of the war he spoke of the necessity of destroying all his documents.[126]

Although we see Hunsche here in a moment of doubt, he was known in the department as an absolute enemy of the Jews, as a convinced Nazi, and as someone who used language that befitted this. He harassed the Jews who worked on the building's maintenance crew, slapping them from time to time, assigning them difficult and unnecessary

124. TR.10-767c, pp. 1108–10.
125. TR.10-767c, pp. 644–7, 1064.
126. TR.10-767c, pp. 946–8.

work, and demanding that they display elaborate respect for him.[127] He accepted Nazi ideology, lived it, and worked to advance and implement it. Despite this, he did not succeed in immunizing himself from the emotional consequences of his actions, and knew that they would be considered crimes by the non-Nazi world. His continued pursuit of these goals was the result of a conscious decision. His was not a case of absent-mindedness within an anonymous bureaucratic system, or of a person unable to understand what he was doing.

Some of the people in the department came into direct contact with Jews. Telephone operator Johanna Quandt recalled a Jew who tried to speak to Eichmann in the office building. Eichmann berated him: "Pig! Stand with your face to the wall when you speak with me!" Günther always took care that Jews should stand three meters from him.[128] Some of the officers, especially Günther and Wöhrn, supervised the work of the Jewish community in Berlin. On October 20, 1942 they conducted a *Gemeindeaktion*, a selection of those employees of the community institutions who would remain and those who would be sent to their deaths in the East. The officers saw the victims at the moment their doom was pronounced. This was not bureaucratic work. Some Jews who were not chosen and who survived testified about that day.

The day before the action the heads of the community's departments were informed they had to ensure that all their employees would come to work on the next day. Günther arrived accompanied by several other officers and ordered the department heads to point out those workers who would be deported. The head of the housing department, Dr Mosse, agonized and chose. The director of the youth department, Mrs Dora Silberman, refused and collapsed in tears. Günther chose instead. At the central building on Oranienburg Street the workers waited in overwhelming suspense from the early morning. Günther and his party stormed in at 1 p.m. The workers stood in rows in the large auditorium, and Günther took a few of them aside. Afterwards he read a list of names. The rest were told to return to work. He told those he had chosen to report for deportation within a few days, warning that those who did not would be responsible for the death of hostages who would be killed in their place. While Günther and Wöhrn strode through the building's corridors, one of them commented that "the time has come to

127. TR.10-767c, pp. 995, 1097, 1100.
128. TR.10-767c, p. 1082; Eichmann, *Memoirs*, p. 409.

clean out this rat hole." One Jew who was present, Wolffsky, recalled that Günther was tall, fitting the image of an SS officer. Next to him, Wöhrn looked like "a bureaucrat who had gotten fat from sitting too long at a desk."

Five hundred and thirty-three Jews were chosen in this action. They were assembled at the station on Hamburger Street. Eighteen chose to go underground. At least 200 were deported on October 26, 1942, the rest later. The trains went to Riga; there were no survivors.[129]

Additional actions took place in Berlin on November 19, 1942, March 10, 1943, May 7, 1943 and June 10, 1943. Wöhrn headed the action of March 1943. He arrived, accompanied by other SS officers, at the Jewish hospital and demanded that its director, Dr Lustig, prepare for him a list of approximately half the institution's employees. The list numbered 300. These persons were deported to Auschwitz two days later, together with other Jews. Of the 964 Jews in the shipment, only seven survived.[130] Wöhrn was in continual contact with the Jews at the hospital; those who survived remembered him with revulsion. He frequently cursed and insulted them, calling them "filthy Jews" and "pigs." He often beat them, and liked to order the previous hospital director, Neuman, to "slap them in the kisser!" (*"in die Fresse schlagen!"*). There were cases in which he was angered by a Jew or a *Mischlinge*, upon which he would arrest them and have them deported to their deaths. This happened to a *Mischlinge* named Bukofzer when, in a conversation with Wöhrn, he referred to Dr Lustig by his former rank, *Oberregierungsrat*, instead of simply as "Lustig." The *Mischlinge* Ellen Wagner was sent to her death after Wöhrn saw her without her Jewish badge. He stood a Jew with his face to the wall for hours, then sent him to prison for eight days because he brought a letter that was missing some sort of stamp. Demanding that he be treated with the respect he thought he deserved, he ordered Jews to stand at attention from the moment of his appearance. He tried to tear badges off Jews' clothing in order to see whether they were sewn on tightly. His appearance always caused panic. Once, two young *Mischlinge* tried to intervene on behalf of their Jewish mother, who had been arrested. Wöhrn rebuked them and suggested that they should

129. TR.3-1431; TR.10-767c, pp. 970–89.
130. TR.10-767c, pp. 991–8.

be happy that she was being sent to Theresienstadt (a "sanitorium") and that she was not going to be killed.[131]

Wöhrn took pride in his Jew-hatred and declared it openly. He justified everything that was happening to the Jews, and was sorry only that the action being taken against them was not energetic enough. Once one of the secretaries asked why so many Jews were being sent to camps, and his answer was that "there's a lot of room there." In this he was like Günther, who told another secretary that "We don't hate the Jews, we despise them."[132]

So much for the banality of evil.

Relations with foreign governments

After the spring of 1942 most of the activity focused on Jews outside Germany. Bosshammer was one of the leading figures in this. Gustav Richter, the RSHA representative in Bucharest, recalled in his interrogation that Bosshammer was his main liaison in the department, "the expert on Balkan affairs". They wrote directly to each other, and Bosshammer supported Richter and urged him on in his attempts to persuade the Romanians to give up their Jews.[133] From Richter's point of view, the difference between Eichmann and Bosshammer was that Eichmann did not have any special understanding of Richter's difficulties, nor patience, which Bosshammer did have. Richter saw Bosshammer as the person in the department responsible for him. A report by Bosshammer on the status of the Jews in Bulgaria was what served Dannecker when he began his contacts with the authorities there on handing over their Jews. Dannecker had the same kind of relationship with Bosshammer that Richter had.[134]

Bosshammer was a watchdog who blocked escape routes, especially in the Balkans. He spoke with officials at the foreign ministry

---

131. Descriptions culled from TR.10-652, pp. 632–41, TR-10-767, pp. 995, 989–91, 1070, 1105–6.

132. Wöhrn: TR.10-652, p. 641; Günther: TR-10-767c, p. 1083. Another group of "desk murderers," the bureaucrats of the T4 program of murdering the handicapped, were similarly involved, in the most immediate way, in the murder of their victims. Henry Friedlander, *Origins of Nazi Genocide*, p. 194.

133. TR.10-767c, pp. 751, 755–6.

134. Richter: TR.10-754, pp. 160–2, 191–3; Dannecker: TR.10-754, pp. 191–3.

about the possibility of frustrating a Romanian plan for the emigration of tens of thousands of Jews to Palestine. On March 3, 1943, he prepared for Eichmann a letter to the foreign ministry containing a request to thwart the efforts of Romanian Jews to send 1000 children with escorts to Palestine via Bulgaria.[135] On April 2, 1943, Bosshammer reacted to a news broadcast in Bulgaria about that country's willingness to allow the emigration of 8000 Jews, most of them children and old people. He said it had to be stopped. The foreign ministry responded that it was not clear whether the Bulgarians really meant it, and that in the meantime it was necessary to wait.[136] Bosshammer himself had three children, two still in diapers.[137] It was enough for a rumor of some emigration plan to reach him for him to seek to block it. One example was a March 6, 1943 news item on a charity ball in Stockholm to benefit Jewish children who were about to emigrate to Palestine. On May 3 and 4 he sent two letters to the foreign ministry with requests to sabotage three emigration plans from Romania and Bulgaria. Eichmann signed the first, Günther the second.[138]

On May 22, 1943 Bosshammer responded in writing to a telephone inquiry from the foreign ministry (Günther signed). He recommended explaining to Romania that the camps in Transnistria would not solve its problem, but that the German camps were always willing to take in any Jews that Romania might wish to transfer. On May 17 he requested foreign ministry pressure on Bulgaria, which was delaying the delivery of its tens of thousands of Jews. Günther, not Bosshammer, spoke about this by telephone with the foreign ministry. Bosshammer was also involved with German efforts to stiffen the moderate Italian line on the Jews in the Italian occupation zone in France.[139]

Like many of his colleagues, Bosshammer did not relate to the Jews as statistics in a bureaucratic task. According to Margarete Giersch, his secretary, "he at times spoke of the Jews as subhuman. It was clear that he supported the activity of the *Einsatzgruppen*. He considered Jews to be

135. TR.10-767c, pp. 758–9; TR.3-231, IV B 4b–3 89/43g. Identification of Bosshammer, in addition to the code, TR.10-767a, p. 170.
136. TR.3-1037, TR.3-1038.
137. TR.10-767a, pp. 14–19.
138. TR.3-887; TR.3-982. Identification of Bosshammer, TR.10-767a, p. 170; TR.3-1034.
139. Romania: TR.3-1229, IV B 4 4326/43. Identification of Bosshammer: TR.10-767a, p. 170. Bulgaria: TR.3-1039. Identification of Bosshammer: TR.10-767a, p. 171. Italy: TR.3-950, IV B 4 90/43 (81), 31 May 1943. Identification of Bosshammer: TR.10-767a, p. 171.

creatures on an inferior level, and it was clear that he would support similar treatment for the rest of the Jews." During a conversation with von Thadden he said that the attempts of Iranian Jews not to be considered Jews were "a typical Jewish ploy". During the Ardennes offensive at the end of 1944 he was so exuberant that he did cartwheels – real ones, in uniform – and prattled about the coming victory. He was deeply depressed after the offensive was turned back. During his interrogation, in the 1970s, he said he remembered nothing. In the transcript of his interrogation, running to hundreds of pages, one finds an astounding number of variations on the simple sentence "I remember nothing of the kind."[140]

It was not only Bosshammer who was dealing with the Balkan Jews. On July 1, 1942 Suhr signed a cable to Rademacher about the Jews of Greece. He requested that Jewish stores be marked, and that Jews who had emigrated there from Germany be arrested on the grounds that they were inciting anti-Axis and pro-Communist activity. He said there was not enough food in Greece, and Jewish speculators on the black market were making matters worse. Furthermore, unmarked (and therefore unidentified) German Jews had penetrated agencies associated with the Wehrmacht and could supply a great deal of intelligence information to the enemy. There was much Communist provocation among the poorer Jews.[141] Suhr was able to weave entire chapters of his antisemitic theory into a single bureaucratic letter.

That a person's world view filters his view of reality is all the more evident when his ideology explains both events and their opposites. One of Hunsche's men drafted a telegram to von Thadden that Eichmann signed on November 15, 1943. The subject: Jews of foreign nationality in Greece and Italy. They were not to be allowed to return to their countries of origin in the usual way because it could be proven that many of them had assisted the supporters of Pietro Badoglio, who had recently become Italian premier, after Mussolini's ouster. Others had done so as well, even if it was impossible to prove it, because they had taken care to cover their tracks.[142]

140. TR.10-754, pp. 566–70, 581; TR.10-767c, p. 1090; TR.10-1166.
141. TR.3-997.
142. TR.3-105.

Covering up the genocide

The first examples of the cover-up date to the beginning of 1941, when German Jews began applying for permission to send money, food and clothing to relatives deported from Baden and the Palatinate the previous October. Their requests reached the department via the foreign ministry. Eichmann signed a rejection of the requests, and explained that the Jews had been told to take supplies with them at the time of their deportation, and in any case that French Jewish organizations were looking after them. Eichmann explained to Rademacher (not to the Jews) that the German economy could not tolerate the removal of money from the Reich. The letters were put out by IV B 4b, but there is no way of knowing whether they were prepared by Wöhrn, Mös, or Hartmann.[143]

After the beginning of the deportations from Germany in the fall of 1941, there were attempts at intervention on the part of the Uruguayan embassy. Hartmann prepared, in December, two replies to three Uruguayan requests. He said the Jews had been deported to Łódź, adding that in any case there no longer was any Jewish emigration, especially involving Jews who had already been deported, because of defense considerations.[144]

Friedrich of the foreign ministry in February 1941 asked Hartmann for the RSHA's help in locating an anonymous writer who had complained of the way that Jews were being deported from Vienna. The correspondence between Friedrich and Hartmann continued the entire year, and Hartmann could report only that there was no way to locate the person.[145] In February 1942 there was similar correspondence between the two agencies, but this time the rank of the signers was much higher. Someone in the department prepared for Heydrich, on February 28, a letter to "My dear friend Luther," with explanations about the search for an anonymous writer from the Warthgau area. What is interesting about the letter is its code: IV B 4 43/42gRs (1005). This level of classification, gRs or top secret, is exceptional, but what was more important was the number in parentheses. According to the German

---

143. TR.3-1061, 17 February 1941; TR.3-1062, 21 March 1941; TR.3-1177, 9 May 1941. If one may hazard a guess, the fact that these documents were not mentioned in the indictments would seem to indicate that the West German prosecutors didn't think that Hartmann or Wöhrn had any hand in their preparation.
144. TR.10-767c, pp. 695–7, 8 December 1941, 19 December 1941.
145. TR.10-767c, pp. 736–40, 20 February 1941.

prosecutors, this code – which reappears from time to time – was the source of the identification number of the unit established during 1942 to take care of the drastic elimination of all evidence. Paul Blobel's corpse-burning unit was called *Sonderkommando* 1005.[146]

Blobel's unit received more from IV B 4 than just its name. The extent of the links between the two units is not entirely clear, but it is known that 1005 relied logistically on IV B 4. Jänisch remembered during his interrogation that from time to time he was assigned to obtain alcoholic beverages and cigarettes to help the SS men in the unit. He also supplied them with extremely large quantities – tens of thousands of liters – of flammable materials for the burning of the corpses. Blobel sent his reports to the department (or at least via the department). There were apparently also certain personnel links between Blobel's men and the office in Berlin. Whenever the men of 1005 were in Berlin, they slept in the department's building.[147]

The staff of IV B 4 knew what the men of 1005 were doing. Blobel gave a lecture on it at a gathering of experts in November 1942. Among other things, he described the furnaces being used by his men, and claimed to have designed them himself. Everything connected to the unit was classified gRs, but this did not keep even the young secretaries in the department from knowing the fine details of its work, for example the reports sent from 1005 telling of bodies that were "straightened" or "cleaned." Once a *Sonderkommando* bulldozer appeared at the department with pieces of bodies and hairs still on its shovel. This act of irresponsibility continued to infuriate the department staff decades later.[148]

The attempts to cover up the facts were, then, meant to deceive the Jews, foreign embassies, perhaps even other German agencies (although the latter needs to be proven, not assumed). Those engaged in the cover-up knew exactly what the truth was, and the language they chose to use should be read accordingly.

The foreign ministry received tens of thousands of inquiries from foreign legations about the fate of Jewish individuals. During the second half of the war most of the inquiries reached Mös and Kryschak; their task

146. TR.3-1089; TR.10-767b, pp. 573–4. And see Shmuel Spector, "Aktion 1005 – Effacing the Murder of Millions," *Holocaust and Genocide Studies*, vol. 5, no. 2, 1990.
147. TR.10-767b, pp. 575–7; Eichmann, *Interrogation*, vol. 1, pp. 264–5.
148. TR.3-584, p. 12; TR.10-767b, pp. 576–7.

was to fend off the inquirers. Most of the letters were coded IV B 4a–3 (or IV A 4b (I)c after March 1944), others were coded only IV B 4a. Mös and Kryschak invented many different excuses. The commandant of Auschwitz was unable to find the Italian Jewish woman Leah Levi even after a thorough search. Certain Hungarian Jews had engaged in activity hostile to the Reich, and had no citizenship papers. They were evacuated to the East, and their current location was unknown. A Jewish woman named König was transferred from Auschwitz even further east, to an unknown location. A Jewish couple had died, he of liver problems, she of heart disease – but it would be better for the foreign ministry to tell the clergyman who had intervened on their behalf that they could not be returned as a matter of principle. We refuse to search for this Italian Jew – please make it clear to the Italian embassy that there is a war on, and that German authorities have more important tasks than to go chasing after Jews. It is unfortunate that the embassy of the Italian Fascist Republic continues to intervene on behalf of Jews in the old way.[149]

In some cases hypocrisy cried out from the words themselves, and even those who did not know the truth could not have avoided seeing it. A Spanish couple adopted by long distance a Jewish girl in Germany, and the Spanish embassy wanted her sent to them. Günther (?) thundered: this is a Jewish fraudulent trick, because by law the girl was entitled to citizenship only if she were under her father's care, and he did not even know her. In any case, the girl was in what Günther unashamedly called "the family camp" of Birkenau, next to Auschwitz.[150]

Other teams in the department worked on the cover-up as well, if not on individual cases. Hunsche (drafting and signing) asked the foreign ministry to rebuke Denmark to keep it from interfering with the Security Police's search for Jews. Günther signed a telegram to the Security Police stations in Western Europe in which he requested, in the name of the Auschwitz command, that they ensure that the Jews not arrive there with knowledge of what awaited them. It was also forbidden for police escorts

149. TR.3-687, 13 April 1943; TR.3-519, 20 June 1943; TR.3-517, 27 August 1943; TR.3-1187, 15 November 1943; TR.3-331, 21 December 1943. Apparently Wöhrn also prepared such documents, as he worked alongside Mös and Kryschak, but only one case has been documented: TR.3-305, 12 June 1944.
150. TR.3-1591, 19 June 1944.

to scare Jews, because the staff at Auschwitz was busy with urgent work, and orderly and quiet reception of the transports was vital.[151]

Slovakia for a long time took an interest in the fate of its Jews who had been sent to Poland. In 1942, after much hesitation and correspondence, Wislicency accompanied the Slovak fascist journalist Fritz Fiala to a concentration camp in Poland and showed him the kind of scenery appropriate for such a visit. In the middle of 1943 the president of Slovakia asked to send a commission of inquiry to the camps. Bosshammer prepared for Eichmann a letter of refusal that was sent to the foreign ministry. It was not possible for three reasons: 1. The journalist Fiala had already visited and had published his findings along with photographs. 2. The 1000 postcards that had arrived from Slovakian Jews deported that year were sufficient to disprove the myths about the horrible fate awaiting the Jews. 3. Wislicency had copies of Fiala's articles; he would be happy to answer further Slovakian questions if there were any.[152]

On January 8, 1944 Bosshammer/Eichmann told the foreign ministry that Wislicency would be returning to Slovakia to discuss continuation of the deportations. It would also be possible to discuss the Slovakian examination of the camps. But discussion does not mean consent, as one learns from the continuation of the correspondence. On February 7, 1944 Eichmann signed a message to the foreign ministry stating that, inquiries having been made, it was impossible for Slovakian officials to visit Poland, but it was possible to visit Theresienstadt (where there were no Slovakian Jews). Bosshammer had in the meantime left the department and gone to Italy; it is not known who prepared the letter for Eichmann.[153]

Bosshammer was hardly writing with sincerity when he mentioned the postcards. Working next to him in the department were Hartenberger, Stuschka and Hartmann, who had handled these very communications. Hartenberger would go to Auschwitz from time to time with blank postcards, and prisoners used them to write a short and positive message on their living conditions. Back in Berlin, Stuschka, and later Hartmann, would supervise the secretaries who censored the

---

151. TR.3-1584. Identification of Hunsche: TR.10-767a, p. 185; TR.3-1206, IV B 4a 2093/42 (391), 29 April 1943.
152. TR.3-143, IV B 4 2145/42g (1090), 2 June 1943. Identification of Bosshammer: TR.10-767a, p. 173.
153. TR.3-145. Identification of Bosshammer: TR.10-767a, p. 174; TR.3-146.

postcards. They checked to ensure that there were no more than twenty-five words, that the message was positive, and that there were no code words or any other sort of information on the trip to the camp and its location. Once they spotted a postcard with letters marked in such a way as to provide the message "there is great death here." Postcards were placed before Eichmann or Günther when there was some doubt about them. Disqualified postcards were destroyed; the rest were sent, and it was on these that Bosshammer based his "truth."[154]

When the South American legations in Switzerland began sending passports to Jews in Holland, the passports were caught in the censorship station in Munich and confiscated by the Gestapo. The Swiss post office demanded financial compensation for registered letters that had disappeared. Wöhrn prepared a letter for Günther about this. It said that if an inquiry were made, the response should be that the letters were lost because of war activity. In any case, there could under no circumstances be a return of mail or payment of fines. This letter was sent to the Security Police command at The Hague.[155]

In the autumn of 1944 they were still dealing with inquiries from the foreign ministry. Von Thadden, who certainly must have known what was going on in Hungary after his visit there in the summer, passed on to the department a Hungarian request to send back a Jewish engineer who had been sent to "Waldsee" — the fake address Jews at Auschwitz were told to write on their postcards. Günther signed a reply a week later: in the wake of the change of government in Hungary, there was no need to address the matter. Furthermore, we do not, he wrote disingenuously, know where Waldsee is, and anyway it was forbidden for a Jew to work in a defense industry.[156]

Up to this point we have been dealing with the officials in the central office in Berlin, those who knew exactly what was happening and who decided to remain part of it. We now turn to other countries: Holland, France and then Hungary. We will ask who did what there; whether the periphery was pushed from the center, or advanced on its own power; whether ongoing contact with non-Nazis and non-Germans affected the determination to kill all the Jews and, if so, how?

It might be possible to reason that the officers in Berlin were so

154. TR.10-767c, pp. 726–30.
155. TR.3-612, IV A 4b (I)a 4297/44, 15 June 1944 – and also TR.3-611, 613. Identification of Wöhrn: TR.10-767a, p. 206.
156. TR.3-1018, 25 October 1944; TR.3-1019, IV A 4b(I)a 4774/44, 3 November 1944.

immersed in the Nazi world that they were unable to distinguish between good and bad. This, after all, is Arendt's fundamental thesis. In the preceding chapters we have seen that this is not how things were, and that officials clearly understood that their actions could be justified only in the Nazi world. In addition, those living in the Third Reich had to harden themselves psychologically in order to carry out the policy. They demanded this of themselves and of their secretaries because they accepted Nazi ideology with full awareness.

For this reason, it is extremely important to examine the conduct of those officials located outside the Reich. They had to function in an environment that did not live according to Nazi moral criteria. Did this affect the resolve of the killers? And if not, what should we learn from this?

From the testimony at the Eichmann Trial

Liona Neumann

Q. How long did the journey take from Vienna to Riga?

A. Six days.

Q. Did you get any food on the way?

A. No, only what we had taken with us. No water. The wagons were sealed and we couldn't get out. It was very cold. We knocked the ice off the windows and sucked it in order to moisten our mouths.

Q. When you arrived in Riga, what happened to your transport?

A. We got off in Riga. The SS had been waiting for us and immediately started driving us off the train and beating us. Vehicles were ready; they said children and old people would be transported to the ghetto, the others would have to walk.

Q. You walked, correct?

A. Yes.

Q. Did you ever see the children or the old people again?

A.   No.

Q.   Do you know what happened to them?

A.   Yes, we learned later that they starved to death in "Jungfernhof"
near Riga. ... Once we arrived at the ghetto we were put up in the
abandoned houses of Latvian Jews who had been killed. Three to four
families lived in one flat. ... I was assigned to the SS disinfection unit.

Q.   What did you do there?

A.   There was a large Jewish hospital, *Linat Tsedek*. We were ten women
from the ghetto of Jews of the German Reich, and ten men from the
Latvian ghetto. Clothing was brought there after all the "actions" that
took place in Riga. Our fellow Jews had to strip before they were shot to
death and buried in a mass grave. Their clothing was collected and
brought to the Jewish hospital for disinfection, and afterwards sent to the
German clothing store.

Q.   Do you remember one particular horrible instance involving one of
the Latvian Jews who worked with you?

A.   Unfortunately I remember it quite well.

Q.   What happened?

A.   How a man from Latvia began to scream holding up his little
daughter's coat full of bullet holes and covered with blood.

(*The Trial of Adolf Eichmann*, vol. I, pp. 508–9)

Chapter 5

Holland

The story of how the Jews of Holland were isolated, deported and murdered is largely known. Yet this story, as it has been told by historians, has to a significant extent lacked a foundation in a precise understanding of how the German system worked and the division of labor within it. The first historian of the killing of Dutch Jewry, Jakob Presser, wrote a good book on this subject, yet one which is nonetheless unversed in the inner workings of the Nazi bureaucracy. He writes, for example:

> At 4:45 p.m. on April 10, 1941, the Presidents of the Jewish Council were summoned to German police headquarters, where *Hauptscharführer* (master-sergeant) Blohm informed them that no Jews would henceforth be allowed to move from Amsterdam to other parts of the country. ... Not to be outdone by Blohm, SS-Chief Rauther ordered Jews to surrender their radio sets before the month was out. ... In September [1941] the Germans started a fresh round of activities, possibly galvanized by the fact that this was the month of the Jewish High Festivals, or else because many of them had just returned from their annual holidays full of fresh ideas and new vigor. Or again, it may have been pure chance.[1]

Opposing that is Hilberg's account. While he was completely aware of bureaucratic systems in general and of the Nazis' system in particular — an awareness he explicitly declares — and, while at the beginning of his chapter on Holland he even presents a table of the German agencies that operated there,[2] he nevertheless failed to look for the internal dynamic of the activity of these bureaucracies. The impression from his description is that it was a system with many branches that operated uniformly. At one point this agency leads, at another a different

1. Presser, *Destruction*, pp. 65, 80.
2. Hilberg, *Destruction*, revised edition, p. 578. The description in the revised edition is considerably more detailed, an important new source being the documentation from the Eichmann trial (TR.3), and the diary of Philip Mechanicus (*Year of Fear*, New York, 1968), as well as Presser's book.

one, but the differences are technical and not substantial, just as in a living body sometimes one foot leads, sometimes the other. A partial explanation for this rather simplistic description of Nazi activity is that most of the documents created by the Nazis did not survive.[3]

German rule in Holland was direct. The royal family and government fled to Britain at the time of the invasion and established a government in exile there. Hitler appointed Dr Artur Seyss-Inquart, a leading Austrian Nazi, to the post of *Reichskommissar* for the Occupied Dutch Territories. Seyss-Inquart came to Holland from Poland where, as the deputy of Governor Hans Frank, he had been involved in merciless population transfers. It was no innocent, then, whom Hitler sent to Holland. Five *Generalkommissare* were appointed to serve under Seyss-Inquart: Dr Friedrich Wimmer, management and justice; Dr Hans Fischböck, economy and finance; Otto Bene, representative of the German foreign ministry; Fritz Schmidt, representative of the Nazi party; and SS General Hans Alvin Rauter, responsible for security and also HSSPF – the regional commander responsible directly to Himmler. The directors-general of the Dutch government ministries continued to work under the Nazis. At first the directors-general functioned as a kind of "alternative government," holding regular cabinet meetings, but over time the Germans replaced most of them.[4] They did not play a part in shaping or implementing the policy of deporting Jews.

The structure of the Nazi agencies that dealt with the Jewish issue was not clear. On the highest level Rauter, as *Generalkommissar* for security, was subordinate to Seyss-Inquart, but as HSSPF he was subordinate to Himmler. Under him was a BdS – the regional Security Police commander – who was subordinate to Seyss-Inquart when Rauter reported to him, and to Himmler when Rauter was subordinate to Himmler. Furthermore, as BdS he was also subordinate to the commander of the RSHA, and on Jewish matters he received the RSHA's orders via IV B 4, even though by his rank he was not subordinate to that department. From July 1940 to September 1943 the position was manned by *SS-*

3. TR.3-1579. Statement of the Rijksinstitut voor Oorlogsdocumentatie (RIOD) to Department 06 of the Israeli Police, 22 July 1960.
4. *Encyclopedia of the Holocaust*; Joseph Michman, "Planning for the Final Solution against the Background of Developments in Holland in 1941," *YVS*, XVII, 1986, pp. 147–9. Seyss-Inquart, Fischböck, and Wimmer were old friends from Austria, and had been active Nazis for years; Fischböck had been one of the central figures in formulating policies of confiscating Jewish property.

Oberführer Dr Wilhelm Harster. He was replaced by *SS-Brigadeführer* Dr Erich Naumann, one of whose previous jobs had been commander of Einsatzgruppe B, which murdered Jews in the Soviet Union. He left in July 1944, and his replacement was *SS-Brigadeführer* Dr Eberhard Schöngarth, who arrived from Poland.

In the office of the BdS there were regular departments mirroring the RSHA model in Berlin. The department that dealt with Jews was first called Special Referat J, but in February 1942 its name was changed to IV B 4. It was headed by *Sturmbannführer* (SS-Major) Wilhelm Zöpf, an old friend of Harster's. All the central agencies were located in The Hague. There were also field offices in provincial cities, and in some there were suboffices of Jewish affairs. The Westerbork transit camp was also under the supervision of the BdS. The Vught labor camp (which the Dutch called 's-Hertogenbosch) was under the control of the WVHA.[5]

Most of the Jews of Holland lived in Amsterdam, and most of the deportation work was carried out by the local office, which was subordinate to Zöpf. The office was called, as it had been in Vienna, the *Zentralstelle für jüdische Auswanderung*, or Central Office for Jewish Emigration; its commander was SS-Captain Ferdinand aus der Fünten. Under his command were Captain Willi Lages, whose official title was BdS-Amsterdam Station, Jewish Affairs. The Amsterdam office was located at Adema van-Scheltemaplain 1.[6]

Immediately upon his arrival in Holland, Seyss-Inquart initiated anti-Jewish legislation and activity. As he himself testified after the war, in Nuremberg, he did this at his own initiative, without having received any explicit orders. Who was a Jew was defined by a law similar to the Nuremberg laws, in October 1940. Immediately thereafter, actions aimed at dispossessing the Jews of their property were launched. Jews had to report on businesses under their ownership, and their business activity was restricted. Some 10,000 businesses were closed in the months that followed, with Jewish owners removed from some 8000 businesses under joint ownership. About 3000 larger businesses were targeted for German takeovers. In August 1941 all Jewish property was blocked – bank

5.   TR.10-1284, p. 25.
6.   This description has been compiled from ZSL 107 AR 518/59 Bd.I, p. 112, Bd.II, p. 290, 305 (2 charts), YVA TR.10-1259 and TR.10-1243; as well as Hilberg, *Destruction*, p. 578; TR.3-355, p. 6. Lages was promoted to *Sturmbannführer* on 1 September 1940, at the height of the deportations (BDC file, found in YVA O.68). He must have been doing a good job.

accounts, financial papers and valuables. The agency that managed the property, the Lippman-Rosenthal & Co. bank, allocated 250 guilders a month to the owner of each blocked account.[7]

According to Hilberg, this economic dispossession was one tentacle of anti-Jewish policy, which was best completed before more severe measures were instituted. Without disputing this, it should be noted that, from Harster's point of view, economic dispossession was not considered to be serious anti-Jewish activity, except as a preliminary. On October 22, 1940 he wrote that "It can be said that preparatory steps have been taken on the Jewish subject that will make it possible to act against the Jews when the time comes."[8] It may be that he knew about the Madagascar plan, or it may be that he simply understood that the Nazi regime would never be satisfied merely with expropriation and isolation.

A representative of the directors-general applied to *General-kommissar* Wimmer during the early days of the occupation with regard to the restrictions on the employment of Jews. At the time, Wimmer was considered an easygoing man who was willing to listen, but he "did not succeed in understanding why anyone would want to treat the Jews as normal people."[9] On September 13, 1940 a regulation was issued permitting the dismissal of civil servants. Jews were not mentioned, but they were fired under the provisions of the regulation. During the fall of 1940 workers in certain groups (employees of the Amsterdam municipality, members of university faculties) were required to declare whether they were Aryan or Jewish. On January 10, 1941 this requirement was extended to all Jews.[10] A type of action typical of Holland is evident here – Dutch authorities took exception to the German policy and expressed their opposition at the beginning. However, when their objections were of no avail, they ceased. In contrast, the Germans were not infected with such humane considerations, even the "moderates" among them.

The Dutch objections and their ineffectuality reached their climax

7. ZSL 107 AR-Z 12/68 Bd.IV, YVA TR.10-1270, p. 386; Hilberg, *Destruction*, pp. 570–7. In January 1943 the individual payments were suspended, and further payments were made through the Jewish Council, p. 580.
8. *Meldungen aus den Niederlanden*, quoted in ZSL 107 AR 518/59 Bd.II, p. 285.
9. Presser, *Destruction*, p. 17, quoting the *Commission of Enquiry into Government Policy in 1940–1945*, The Hague: Dutton, 1955, p. 589.
10. ZSL 107 AR 518/59 (Raja), p. 26; Presser, *Destruction*, pp. 19–21.

– and end – in February 1941, a month full of events that threatened, for a short time, to halt the escalation of Nazi persecution, but which in the end only promoted it.

Members of the NSB, the Dutch Nazi party, descended on the Amsterdam quarter where many Jews lived, attacking property, buildings and people. They encountered violent opposition from Jews and Dutch workers, and one of the Nazi attackers was killed in the clash. In response, on February 12, the Nazis closed the area, evacuated the non-Jewish population, and created what was for all intents and purposes a Jewish ghetto. A few days later a German police patrol encountered violent opposition at a Jewish business in the area; acid was sprayed on one of the policemen. In response, a raid was conducted in the neighborhood and 400 Jewish men between the ages of 20 and 35 were arrested and sent to Buchenwald, where some of them died, and from there to Mauthausen, where the rest died. Only one member of the entire group survived. In reaction to the arrests, Dutch industrial, transport, and shipyard workers launched a protest strike, shutting down these sectors entirely, and demonstrated in the streets. The number of workers involved was estimated at 18,300. Only on the second day did the Nazis succeed in organizing a response. They imposed military rule and harshly repressed the strike.[11]

Which German agencies played a part in these events? The first attack was carried out by local Nazis, apparently at their own volition. The Jewish quarter was blocked at the order of Dr Hans Böhmker, a subordinate of *Generalkommissar* Wimmer. Before the order was given there was disagreement between Böhmker, who wanted a closed ghetto, and Rauter, who saw no need for this, since the Security Police already knew the addresses of all the Jews.[12] The German policemen who were attacked while on their patrol were from the Security Police. Rauter issued the order to arrest 400 Jewish men as hostages and to deport them to the Reich. Afterwards, he issued an official announcement about this.

11. Presser, *Destruction*, pp. 45–54; Hilberg, *Destruction*, pp. 581–3. For a description of the deaths of the hostages in Buchenwald and Mauthausen, see Eugen Kogon, *Der SS-Staat: Das System der deutschen Konzentrationslager*, Frankfurt/M: Büchergilde Gutenburg, 1959, pp. 213–15.
12. Presser, *Destruction*, p. 47; Joseph Michman, "The Controversial Stand of the *Joodse Raad* in the Netherlands," *Yad Vashem Studies*, X, 1974, p. 15. There is a clear conceptual difference between the two positions: Böhmker sought the good of Amsterdam as he understood it, hence the wish to seal off the Jews; Rauter sought to get rid of the Jews entirely, and for that their addresses sufficed, for the moment.

Normally, he would have given such an order to Harster, but Harster was not in Holland that day. He was summoned back, but in the meantime the order was carried out by his deputy, SS-Lt. Colonel Friedrich Knolle, who brought his large and menacing dog to the raid. Harster and his men had no doubt that the deportation was cleared first with Himmler, and may perhaps have been ordered by him directly. When a public outcry ensued at the news of the mass death of the deportees at Mauthausen, Seyss-Inquart himself ordered that no additional hostages were to be deported.[13]

There was a further development, perhaps the most fateful of all. On February 12, after the clash with the Dutch Nazis and before the incident with the Security Police, Böhmker summoned Abraham Asscher, the chairman of the Jewish community, and two rabbis, and ordered them to set up a Jewish council, or *Joodserad*. The first job assigned to them, by Böhmker, was to collect all the weapons Jews had in their possession.[14] From the moment the council was founded it served as a tool of the Nazis.

The events did not result from Nazi planning, and certainly not from planning by the Security Police.[15] There is here, however, a model familiar from other places, such as the Reich itself and France: after a period of legal organization and economic dispossession came a violent event. In the Reich the SS took advantage of the events of *Kristallnacht* to strengthen its hold on the Jewish issue. In Paris the Security Police initiated the violence. In both places the SS's position was strengthened. In Holland no improvement in the position of the Security Police was evident, because all the German agencies were working along the same lines. But the situation of the Jews worsened. The Dutch public exhausted its capacity for protest (although thousands of individuals were to help in hiding Jews when the deportations began). The Jews of Amsterdam became more vulnerable, geographically, and the Nazis established a Jewish body there that would aid them in their missions.

On April 18, 1941 Harster proposed, via Rauter, to Seyss-Inquart the establishment of a *Zentralstelle*, or Central Office for Jewish Emigration

13. ZSL I 107 AR 557/67 Bd.1, pp. 21, 117–18; ZSL AR-Z 12/68 Bd.II, p. 215; Presser, *Destruction*, p. 51; Hilberg, *Destruction*, p. 581, quotes NG–2285.
14. Michman, "*Joodse Raad*," pp. 15–16.
15. Michman notes that there are no documents telling of preparations to set up a Jewish representative body prior to Böhmker's meeting with the rabbis, and sees this as an indication that it had not been planned in advance. Further, he sees the founding of the council as part of a struggle between the German administration under Seyss-Inquart (Böhmker) and the SS. "Planning," pp. 146, 150–2.

that would serve as "an example of a solution to the problem of the Jews of Europe". He knew that significant measures were pending, and wanted them to be his responsibility. On the other hand, the formulation he used seems to imply that the initiative for his proposal did not come from the RSHA in Berlin, but rather originated with him or with some junior official in Holland. Otherwise how can the aspiration to serve as an example for the rest of Europe be understood? Seyss-Inquart, who probably had no objection to serving as an example for the rest of Europe, did not want such an office to be subordinate to the Security Police, out of fear that property confiscation and the economic power it provided would be removed from his authority. He therefore permitted Harster to establish the office only as a subunit within the bounds of the Security Police.[16]

The summer of 1941 saw a continuation of the measures that restricted Jewish living space and brought them closer to "civil death". The letter J was stamped on their identity cards. Section 45 of order 138 of July 25, 1941 authorized Rauter to promulgate regulations for the preservation of public peace. He issued a "declaration on Jewish movement" containing a series of restrictions and prohibitions against Jewish entry to various places. The restrictions took force on September 15, as did similar regulations in the Reich itself at the same time. Soon after this, travel restrictions were added, as were orders on transferring Jews from the provinces to Amsterdam. About half of Holland's Jews now resided in three special neighborhoods there.[17]

In August *Generalkommissar* Schmidt commented to the effect that the Führer was no longer interested in modifying Jewish life so that it

16. ZSL AR 518/59 Bd.II, pp. 286–7. Michman reads the development differently. He notes that Rauter's letter to Seyss-Inquart of April 18, 1941 names Heydrich as the initiator of the creation of the *Zentralstelle*. He strengthens his claim by noting that Rajakowitz was sent to Holland in April 1941. Finally, he tells of the sending of two Jews from the *Zentralstelle* in Prague, Edelstein and Friedmann, to assist the Jews in the Amsterdam office ("Planning," pp. 150–4). However, the reference to Heydrich proves only that he, and the bureaucrats in Berlin, were informed of the developments, and concurred; it does not prove that they were the initiators. Conversely, it does not explain why Holland was singled out by Heydrich. Furthermore, Harster's suggestion did not originate in the office of the specialists of Jewish affairs, but rather elsewhere: BdS III b.Nr.4783/41. The interpretation offered here would have the initiative coming from Harster's people in Holland, who were actively backed by the RSHA in Berlin.

17. Presser, *Destruction*, p. 83; Hilberg, *Destruction*, p. 583. Relocation seems not to have started before January 1942: Presser, pp. 111–13.

could exist in the Aryan environment. Rather, he was interested in removing the Jews. Schmidt's comment indicates that the leaders of the Nazi regime were at the very least closely following events in the Reich, even if they were not receiving detailed instructions on every matter.[18] At the end of August Gertrud Slottke, a member of Zöpf's staff who was not an SS member but who was very much involved in the deportations, prepared a document for Harster's signature on the matter of "Combating Jewry in its totality." It stated that the goal of the activity was "the final solution of the Jewish question by way of the removal of all Jews."[19]

In the same document Harster ordered the establishment of a department for Jewish affairs within his office, to be called the Special Referat J. The mission of the department was fivefold: 1. to carry out the instructions of the Reichskommissar; 2. to coordinate Security Police activity on all aspects of the Jewish problem; 3. emigration matters; 4. preparation of instructions and lines of action for the *Zentralstelle* (which had been established a few months earlier); 5. collection of Jewish property. The common denominator for all these responsibilities was "processing of the Jews in preparation for their deportation." To head the department he appointed Lt. Dr Erich Rajakowitz, an old acquaintance and colleague of Eichmann from their work together in Vienna in 1938.[20]

The purpose of this appointment is not clear. It could have resulted from a recommendation from Berlin that was difficult to reject, because Eichmann wanted to get his own men into such positions (such as Dannecker in Paris). If this is the way it happened, the appointment was meant to subordinate Amsterdam to Berlin. On the other hand, the structure that Harster established in Holland, that of a central department planning and shaping policy and superior to a local executive department, is strikingly similar to the relation between IV B 4 and the outlying stations in the Reich, and could indicate that Harster intended to be fairly independent. According to this analysis, the establishment of Referat J was a declaration of independence which asserted that planning, not merely execution, would also take place in Holland. The appointment of Rajakowitz may thus have actually been an attempt to appease Eichmann, or to cast wool over his eyes. Clearly, he could not oppose the appointment of his own man. Whatever the motives were, on February 3,

---

18. Presser, *Destruction*, p. 97. Unfortunately, he gives no source for this important statement, purportedly made on 20 August 1941.
19. ZSL 107 AR 518/59 Bd.II, p. 349.
20. ZSL 107 AR 518/59 (Raja), pp. 32–3; Bd.II, p. 288.

1943 Harster again reorganized his forces, eliminating Referent J and Rajakowitz's appointment, and establishing IV B 4, headed by his own man, Zöpf.[21]

Seyss-Inquart did not intend to invest the Security Police with all the responsibility for the deportation of the Jews. On November 25, 1941 he summed up the situation for his senior officials. The legal infrastructure for addressing the Jewish question was ready. Now it was necessary to cut the Jews off from their surroundings. To ensure uniformity, this would be coordinated by Böhmker, Seyss-Inquart's plenipotentiary in Amsterdam. Police activity would be in the hands of the chief of the *Zentralstelle*. The two would work together as needed. Because immediate deportations were not expected, solutions should be sought for the large number of unemployed Jews.[22] In mentioning this, Seyss-Inquart reminded the Security Police that it was serving him, in areas he would determine, and that it was not to pursue an independent policy. Seyss-Inquart's observation that no deportations were to be expected in the near future indicates that he had very good sources of information. While deportations had already begun in the Reich, he knew it would be many more months before it would be possible to deport the Jews of Holland.

Harster did not give in. At the beginning of February he added to his role as referent of Jewish affairs the responsibility for Jews arrested for criminal activity ("individual enemies," an ideologically charged term). The targets were largely Jews charged with violating some anti-Jewish regulation. Among the first of these to be arrested were those who violated the new marriage law (on March 23, 1942, Seyss-Inquart had imposed the Nuremberg laws on this matter in Holland). On April 1 Harster announced that Jews planning to marry non-Jews would be arrested and sent to Mauthausen. Zöpf was more precise – women would be sent to Ravensbrück. Jews would be those defined as such by the Reichskommissar on October 2, 1940.[23]

The initiative to require Jews to wear a badge came from Berlin. It was first discussed at a meeting of referents for Jewish affairs in IV B 4 on March 6, 1942. Apparently there was no representative from Holland present, since Dannecker, who was there, requested on his return to Paris to get together his colleagues from Belgium and Holland for coordination.

21. ZSL AR 518/59 Bd.II, p. 289.
22. ZSL AR-Z 592/67 Bd.I, pp. 140–2. Fünten and Böhmker had a meeting on the subject two days later, November 27, 1941: Presser, *Destruction*, p. 97.
23. ZSL 107 AR 518/59 Bd.II, pp. 293–5.

When no Dutch representative arrived, he updated them.[24] For some reason he chose to send the update message to Lages in Amsterdam – either from unfamiliarity with the Dutch system, or perhaps out of some consideration deriving precisely from his being well-acquainted with it. He expected the regulation to be published simultaneously in the three countries on April 15, 1942. Despite the attempts at coordination, the order was issued in Holland several weeks prior to its publication in France. Rauter signed it on April 29, 1942.[25] The Dutch responses were not much to the Germans' liking, since many of the people of that country identified with the Jews and lent them support. Zöpf (not Lages) reported this to IV B 4 in Berlin, as well as to his colleagues in Brussels and Paris.[26] It may well be that the report to France was a sign of collegiality, or it may be that his intention was to make it clear that The Hague was the address, not Amsterdam.

The atmosphere in the German administration in Holland was ripe for the deportation of the Jews, but there is no evidence of it pressuring Berlin to begin. In the spring of 1942 Eichmann visited Holland and told his colleagues about the deportation plans. He reported on a large conference (Wannsee, apparently) to drive home the point that it was a general and not just an SS policy.[27] On June 9, 1942 he signed a letter to Rademacher of the foreign ministry, according to which the deportation of the Jews of France, Belgium and Holland was about to begin.[28] Two days later representatives of the Security Police in the three countries met with him in Berlin. Holland was represented by Zöpf, as was appropriate given the division of labor there. It was determined that 15,000 Jews between the ages of 16 and 45, fit for labor, would be deported from Holland.[29] Dannecker, Zöpf, and their Belgian colleague, Kurt Asche, met with Eichmann, not with the experts on his staff. On June 20, 1942 Eichmann spoke by telephone with Rademacher and gave him revised numbers: 40,000 Jews would be deported from France, the same number from Holland, and 10,000 from Belgium. Two days later a document was sent to Rademacher, signed by Eichmann, repeating the announcement in writing, and assuming that the foreign ministry would

24. TR.3-457, 10 March 1942; TR.3-1259, 16 March 1942.
25. Presser, *Destruction*, p. 120.
26. TR.3-1359, 8 June 1942.
27. ZSL RSHA 413 AR 1310/63 E5, p. 5.
28. TR.3-147.
29. TR.3-585, Dannecker's report on the meeting, 15 June 1942.

not object.[30] The ministry did not in fact object. It asked only that foreign Jews be deported first.[31]

On Friday night, June 26, 1942, at 10 p.m., Fünten and his deputy, Captain Wörlein, notified the leaders of the Jewish council of the intention to begin deporting Jews for labor in the East. David Cohen, co-president of the council, was stupefied: "But that violates international law!" To this, Fünten replied with all sincerity that whoever won the war would decide that. The Judenrat was told to supply hundreds of Jews each day. The intention was to begin the deportations on July 15, 1942, and every week to send two trains carrying 1000 Jews each. Bene reported to the foreign ministry in Berlin that at first 25,000 non-Dutch Jews would be sent.[32]

One more thing had to be arranged before the deportations began – the takeover of Westerbork. The Westerbork camp had been established by the Dutch in the fall of 1939 to house Jewish refugees from Germany. After the German occupation, the Germans merely replaced its Dutch commander with a different Dutch commander. At the end of 1941 they began to incarcerate hundreds of Jewish prisoners there, and in the spring of 1942 they enlarged the camp, bringing its capacity, at the end of June, to 10,000. On July 1, 1942 command of the camp was transferred to the Security Police. Erich Deppner, and then Josef Dischner, commanded it for short periods, followed in October 1942 by Albert Gemmeker. Unlike his two predecessors, Gemmeker was right for the job, and he remained there until the eve of the camp's liberation in the spring of 1945. Working under him were his secretary and no more than twelve other Germans; Dutch policemen guarded outside, Dutch administrative officials worked inside. Jewish prisoners held many administrative posts themselves.[33]

During his interrogation, Zöpf recalled that at the time of the transfer of the command of Westerbork to the Nazis there was rivalry between Berlin and the locals. He said that Eichmann sent several men and secretaries to run the camp. Deppner, who had been appointed by

30. TR.3-82, June 20, 1942. The document is marked IV B 4a, hence it was written by Günther or one of his subordinates. Even when Eichmann was actively involved in something, he didn't necessarily write his own letters.

31. TR.3-98. The document is undated. Hilberg (*Destruction*, p. 584) assumes it was written in July; office 06 of the Israeli Police dated it as late as July 27, 1942, more than a month after the original question. If this is the case, the deportations were in full swing before the response from the foreign ministry came in.

32. ZSL AR 518/59 Bd.II, p. 312; Presser, *Destruction*, pp. 136–8.

33. ZSL AR-Z 12/68 Bd.IV, pp. 400–3.

Harster, succeeded in getting rid of them and the camp remained under Harster's control. There is no confirmation of this story from other sources. In practice, the camp received logistical support from department I/II of the BdS, and was operationally subordinate to Zöpf. Orders reached it also through the *Zentralstelle* in Amsterdam. Gemmeker would be told, for example, how many Jews were to be deported and when, and he would determine which of the camp's residents would be deported. Over time, the tables turned. Gemmeker would notify The Hague that his supply of Jews was running out. Then his superiors at The Hague would have to find additional Jews, or decide on the deportation of Jews who had until then enjoyed immunity of some kind.[34]

On July 5, 1942 the first summonses were sent out to 4000 Jews, who were told they were being deported to a labor camp. On July 14 the Security Police arrested 700 Amsterdam Jews and held them as hostages. The leadership of the Jewish council published an announcement that, if the 4000 Jews did not report for work, the 700 hostages would be dispatched to a concentration camp. In addition, the council sent messages to the personal addresses of the 4000 candidates for deportation containing a direct plea: "The fate of 700 people depends on you."[35] Lages was among the commanders of this operation; the Jews were held in the courtyard of the Security Police building in Amsterdam. Unlike other places, where the bureaucrats of the murder operation had to make a special effort to see Jews with their own eyes, to make a special trip to Jewish institutions or to a camp outside the city, in Amsterdam the Nazis' own office building served as a detention and concentration camp.

> They stood the Jewish women in the center of the yard and forced the men to march around them. German secretaries leaned out of their windows and took souvenir photographs. To judge from their cheers, they apparently really enjoyed the scene. One of the officers joined in the gaiety, which reached its climax when a young Jewish mother was separated from her baby daughter, who was lying in a carriage, and broke out in an attack of hysteria. It wasn't that the Germans were cruel or sadistic, it was just that the incident appealed to their peculiar sense of humor.[36]

34. ZSL AR-Z 12/68 Bd.II, pp. 213–14, 227, Bd.III, p. 35.
35. Presser, *Destruction*, pp. 140–5; facsimile of the announcement: Presser, *Destruction*, p. 145. See also ZSL AR 518/59 Bd.II, p. 313.
36. Presser, *Destruction*, p. 144. Although he does not say so explicitly, it appears that Presser himself was among those detained.

Probably, if we had more such testimony, we would not so easily be taken in by theses about neutral bureaucrats carrying out, with soulless efficiency, any job that rolled onto their desks.

There is no way of knowing which of the Security Police officers thought up this exercise. There is no documentation to indicate that the idea came from Berlin. On the contrary, since this was not the practice elsewhere, it appears that the initiative came from someone who was familiar with the special conditions in Holland, where there was the intention of exploiting the obedience of the Jewish council in order to persuade the Jews to report on their own. Nevertheless, during the course of July fewer and fewer Jews reported for deportation. In the week of August 3–10, Lages, Fünten and Wörlein met eleven times with the council leadership in an attempt to solve the problem.[37]

The Nazis then handled the problem in their own way. On August 6 they carried out a large "action," or roundup, in which they arrested 2000 Jews, who were brought to police headquarters in Amsterdam. Fünten, who ran the operation, chose 600 of the detainees the next day and sent them to Westerbork.[38] The rest of the 2000 were released. Some Jews who worked at close quarters with Fünten received the impression that he did all this very reluctantly. The president of the council, Cohen, remembered after the war that Fünten had been on the verge of tears; a young Jew named Leo de Wolff told Jakob Presser a few days later that Fünten complained about his commanders giving him such difficult jobs instead of doing the work themselves.[39] Such testimony is generally accepted with alacrity by scholars who want to see the murder bureaucrats as normal people functioning in difficult times, people like you and me, drab officials who may have failed in a place where we would have overcome, but who should serve as a warning signal, because who knows? Perhaps we would act the same way they did, had we not learned from them about the potential weakness of bureaucrats around the world?

For this reason it is important to read another piece of testimony, of a Jew who was among the detainees, and who received the impression that Fünten was enjoying his omnipotence over 2000 terror-stricken Jews. He made fun of them, tortured them psychologically, and during the long

37. Presser, *Destruction*, p. 151.
38. ZSL 107 AR 518/59 Bd.II, p. 322.
39. Presser, *Destruction*, pp. 152–3.

hours in which he determined who would be sent to Westerbork and who released, he evinced no signs of being merely a bureaucrat carrying out distasteful work. He demanded – and received – absolute silence. He chose people for life or death with perfect cynicism, separated husband and wife, and from time to time halted the sorting operation for many long minutes to relish the effect.[40] A person whose world view does not sit well with this testimony will ask, of course, "What can you expect from testimony given by a victim?" The proper response is, "And what can you expect from testimony given by a perpetrator whose conscience is not clear?"[41]

The day after the action, the Security Police published a warning in the Jewish newsletter. It said that 1 whoever fails to report for deportation as required would be arrested and sent to Mauthausen; and 2 any Jew who does not wear a badge will also be sent there, as will anyone who changes his place of residence. The last provision was directed against those planning to hide. Still only a small number reported, so there was another raid, this time in a better-off area in southern Amsterdam, on August 9. The method worked, and from then on the Security Police depended on raids. Bene reported to the foreign ministry in Berlin on August 12: the Jews of Holland have realized what happens to deportees and are not reporting, as they did at first. It will be necessary to use harsher means to catch the Jews.[42]

The Nazis had to cope with a number of issues relating to defining the categories of deportees. The first was citizenship. After the two initial trains were dispatched, someone in the Security Police suggested stripping deportees of their citizenship, to prevent interventions by outside forces. It is not clear precisely who had this idea, but it was vetted by Harster and Rauter, and was discussed by Seyss-Inquart. Not only did Seyss-Inquart not object, but he asked for the foreign ministry's position on a more radical decision – stripping all Dutch Jews of their citizenship, on the grounds that they were enemies of Germany.

40. Presser, *Destruction*, pp. 153–5. Here Presser is openly recounting his own experiences and impressions.
41. An additional testimony comes from Harster, relating to his friend and subordinate, Zöpf: One of his hobbies was photography; he even used to take films of the raids. ZSL 107 AR 518/59 Bd.II, p. 279. A charming hobby.
42. Presser, *Destruction*, pp. 155 ff., ZSL 107 AR 518/59 Bd.II, pp. 321–3. Bene also noted that 8500 Jews had already been deported, to be followed by 1500 within the week.

Bene asked where Berlin stood on this. He himself was of the opinion that the gambit was too broad, and that it was preferable to act as in the Reich, where, according to regulation 11 of the Reich citizenship law, Jews lost their citizenship upon leaving the country.[43]

In the meantime there was progress on an auxiliary issue. On July 30 Eichmann spoke on the phone with an officer named Burger, who was in Brussels. Burger told him that, according to existing orders, he was allowed to deport only non-local Jews, and that most of the non-Belgians in the country were Dutch and French. A letter from IV B 4a, signed by Eichmann, to the Security Police stations in these three countries asked them to agree on procedures on this point.[44] Two weeks later Rajakowitz, in his capacity as acting deputy to the chief of IV B 4 in The Hague (Zöpf), signed a letter to the BdS in Paris and in Brussels. He stated that since Jewish citizens of Holland were being deported from that country, it did not matter that the regulation stripping Dutch Jews of their citizenship had not yet been promulgated and would not be in the near future. There was no reason not to deport Dutch Jews from France and Belgium as well. Rajakowitz signed iA, meaning that the decision had been made by Harster or someone above him.[45] When experts explained that the German authorities could not revoke the citizenship of Dutch citizens — only the Dutch themselves could do that — it was decided to shelve the idea. Rademacher recommended that the police should not provide any information on the fate of the deportees, so as not to provide any opening for third parties (such as Sweden, which was acting as a liaison between the Dutch government-in-exile and Germany) to seek visits to the camps.[46]

There were also doubts about deporting a second category of Jews — the converts to Christianity. On July 10, 1942 the Ecumenical Council wrote to Seyss-Inquart, Schmidt and Rauter to protest the persecution of the Jews. On July 14, they received an answer from Seyss-

---

43. TR.3-1428, 17 July 1942. ZSL 107 AR 689/66 YVA TR.10-1284 Bd.II, p. 166.
44. TR.3-710, IV B 4a 3233/41g (1085), 1 August 1942.
45. TR.3-1243, 12 August 1942, BdS den Haag IV B 4 4942/42. The recipients of the letter regarded it as an order, and 83 Dutch Jews were deported from Drancy, among them seven children without parents, including Ruth Leiner, born 7 May 1939. Only one of these deportees, Arthur Salomons, survived. ZSL AR 518/59 (Raja), pp. 37–9.
46. Hilberg, *Destruction*, p. 584, cites NG–2632, Memorandum by Rademacher, 10 August 1942.

Inquart stating that Jews who had become Christians before January 1, 1941 would not be deported.[47] On July 17, 1942 there was a Generalkommissars' meeting with Seyss-Inquart. Rauter raised the subject of the non-deportation of Christianized Jews. Schmidt spoke at length and Rauter understood that Schmidt had promised the representatives of the churches that the approximately 2000 converted Jews would be allowed to leave for Brazil — a promise that Rauter was not prepared to honor. Seyss-Inquart himself defended the decision not to deport converted Jews (though he apparently did not speak about letting them go to Brazil). He, Seyss-Inquart, did not have to provide explanations. The converts should not be deported for the time being, and if this would silence church circles he would consider that an achievement. He also reassured Rauter that it would be possible to deport the converts after all the other Jews had been taken care of.

Rauter wrote up his impressions of the meeting and sent them to Harster, his subordinate. It may be that he wanted to update him on what was permitted and what forbidden for his forces to do, and it may be that he wanted, via Harster, to inform the center in Berlin and let his subordinate have it out with them. If Berlin got angry, it would be angry at Harster; if Berlin changed its decision, that would be good, too. Harster (actually Zöpf, over Harster's signature) in due course reported to Eichmann. He blamed Schmidt for making promises before clearing them. No reply from Eichmann is known, and there was certainly no challenge from Berlin to Seyss-Inquart's decision. Bene reported to the foreign ministry in Berlin noncommittally: according to a decision by Seyss-Inquart, Christianized Jews would not be deported from Holland so long as the church did not oppose the deportation of the rest of the Jews.[48]

On July 26 Harster reported on continued opposition from Catholic circles. He and Rauter discussed the matter with Seyss-Inquart on July 27. As a response to the behavior of the Catholic bishops (and because the attempt to silence them had in any case not succeeded) it was decided to deport immediately those Jews who had joined the Catholic church.[49]

The orders to arrest the Catholic Jews were issued by Harster on

47. ZSL I 107 AR 557/67 Bd.I, pp. 179ff.
48. Rauter: TR.3-615, 18 July 1942. Harster: TR.3-616, 20 July 1942. Bene: ZSL 107 AR 518/59 Bd.II, p. 314 (the report was sent on 17 July 1942).
49. ZSL 107 AR 518/59 Bd.II, pp. 316–17, Bene to Foreign Office, 31 July 1942, pp. 317–18, Harster to IV B 4 (Haag), 30 July 1942.

August 2. Six hundred people were arrested and were sent to Auschwitz five days later. Of the 987 deportees on that train, only two survived. Of the others, 522 were murdered immediately upon arrival – among them the Catholic convert Edith Stein, who was later canonized by the Vatican. The route taken by the orders is not clear. The instructions were given by Seyss-Inquart himself on July 27. Harster recalled that he himself had written a memorandum that reached IV B 4 in The Hague and was then sent to the *Zentralstelle* in Amsterdam and to other outlying stations. He was apparently not present at the operation itself, though his deputy Knolle was. It is not clear, however, what Knolle contributed to the operation. In his interrogation, Rajakowitz recalled that he was the duty officer for the Security Police on August 3, and in that capacity he received a telephone call from Rauter, who told him that the operation had already been carried out by Security and Dutch Police forces, and that the people arrested were now to be sent to Westerbork. Rajakowitz supervised the loading of the prisoners on trucks, comparing their names with names on a list that had been given to him in advance.[50] In any case, all the signs are that the entire operation was conducted by Nazi elements in Holland, without intervention from Berlin.

The Protestant Jews were rounded up over a period of time and sent to Westerbork, not to Auschwitz. About 350 of them were shipped in September 1944 to Theresienstadt; most of them survived.[51]

The progress of the deportations in Holland differed from that in France. The deportations in France began at a rapid pace, but within a few months the Nazis began to encounter increasing difficulties. Not so in Holland. Most Jews there were rounded up in lightning arrest operations at the beginning of September, generally in the evening, when Jews were confined by order to their homes. This was because fewer and fewer Jews obeyed the personal summonses they were receiving.[52] But, unlike in France, the documents of the Security Police in Holland do not reflect any growing concern about their inability to carry out the mission on time; instead, the Nazis in Holland were worried about how much effort they would have to exert to complete the task. At a time when the Security Police in France were carrying out large-scale arrests in order to assemble

50. Deportation: ZSL 107 AR 518/59 Bd.II, pp. 318–20. Includes a quotation from Harster's report of 31 December 1942; Chain of command: ZSL I 107 AR 557/67 Bd.I, pp. 21, 117–18; ZSL AR 518/59 (Raja), pp. 1942–4.

51. ZSL I 107 AR 557/67 Bd.I, pp. 179 ff.

52. Presser, *Destruction*, pp. 158 ff.

Jews for deportation, their colleagues in Holland came to rely on this method only in the autumn. In September they still were not expecting problems.

Rauter sent a letter to Himmler on September 10, 1942. It may well be that he himself drafted it, or at least dictated its contents: "Catching the Jews gives us all a big headache. I am not prepared in any case to cancel a deportation train, because whatever we deport is that much more of the job done." He described plans to prevent the cancellation of trains. The relocation of protected Jews – the intermarried and workers in the defense and diamond industries – would be completed in the middle of October. By that time, Westerbork and Vught, another camp in Holland, should be able to take in 40,000 Jews between them, which would make it possible to carry out large-scale arrest operations. The big mop-up of Holland had yet to begin, Rauter concluded. This was no secret in the SS, and the next day Bene wrote to the foreign ministry that up to that point there had been no shortage of Jews to fill the deportation trains, and that measures were being taken to ensure that this would be the case in the future as well. There was, apparently, also an order from Seyss-Inquart from that same time, according to which the deportation of Dutch Jewry would be completed before May 1, 1943.[53]

Rauter reported again to Himmler a week later. Up to that point about 20,000 Jews had been deported (including those who had been sent to Mauthausen), and 120,000 remained. Seyss-Inquart had already agreed to the deportation of intermarried Jews who had no children by their non-Jewish spouses. So there were only 14,000 Jews who could not at that point be deported. Further on in his report, Rauter told about the Dutch employment service, the *Werkverruiming*, which was sending Jews to special labor camps. The Nazis had up to this point refrained from harming these Jews, in order to give the impression that they were immune. There were already about 7000 Jews in these camps, and the hope was that their number would soon reach 8000, with 22,000 family members outside the camps. On October 1 all of them would be taken at once to Westerbork and Vught. In mid-October all of Dutch Jewry would be declared *vogelfrei*, "without any legal protection." It would be forbidden for any Jew to be outside a camp without a special permit. Deterrent and disciplinary measures would be taken against Dutch people

53. ZSL AR 518/59 Bd.II, pp. 324–5. Sent: 11 September 1942; Seyss-Inquart: ZSL AR 689/66 Bd.II, p. 167. However, *their* source is not clear.

who helped Jews hide. Rauter hoped that he would be able to increase the deportation rate to three trains a week instead of two, and to complete the deportation of the 30,000 prisoners by Christmas. In addition to Security Policemen, party, NSB and Wehrmacht personnel would also be employed in the operation. The deportation of 50,000 Jews would be completed before the end of 1942. Himmler commented in the margins: *sehr gut* – very good.[54]

The deportation of Holland's Jews was run from the senior levels – by Rauter, with the knowledge of Seyss-Inquart and Bene. This work does not presume to determine what precisely the working relationship was between Rauter and Seyss-Inquart, because their rank lies outside the focus of the study. It is clear, however, that they directed the policy, without requiring frequent orders from Berlin. In the fall of 1942 this had an unexpected result. When Novak and Günther notified Himmler that from September there would be no trains for deporting Jews, the news reached Paris from Berlin, but the Germans in Holland remained ignorant of it. Since they did not wait for instructions from Berlin, they did not know about the delays originating there.

The next large action came on October 2, 1942. It was commanded by Harster, together with his subordinates Lages and Fünten. The orders were prepared in Lages's office. At six in the evening – Friday night, the Sabbath – large numbers of German and Dutch police began arresting Jews in and outside Amsterdam. At least 13,000 were detained, and thousands of others were sent from the labor camps to Westerbork. A total of 25,000 reached that camp. The number would have been larger, but many of the Dutch policemen gave the Jews advance warning or refrained from arresting a lot of them. Seyss-Inquart received a report on the operation on October 5, and Himmler received a report (from Rauter) on October 7. After the operation no more large actions were carried out; those arrested in small operations were no longer sent to the courtyard of the Security Police building, but rather to the large theater, the Hollandse Schouwburg.[55]

On November 11 Lages commanded a raid on a Dutch factory whose workers had thus far enjoyed immunity. Hundreds of workers were arrested, and on November 30 they were deported from Westerbork to Auschwitz together with their families. Eight hundred and twenty-five

54. TR.3-1496, 24 September 1942; Hilberg, *Destruction*, p. 587.
55. ZSl 107 AR 518/59 Bd.II, p. 326; Presser, *Destruction*, pp. 163, 171–3.

Jews, of whom only eight men returned after the war. The excuse for revoking immunity was, apparently, that one of the Jewish workers was suspected of having committed sabotage.[56] But the Security Police had intended in any case to reduce the number of Jews enjoying the protection of the defense industry. On November 20 Rauter received notification from the official responsible for the clothing industry that 800 Jews had been laid off by factories in this sector, and that their names had been handed over to Fünten. "Additional lists are on the way," it said.[57] A representative of the body supervising the armaments industry, a naval officer, wrote on December 2 to Rauter, with a copy to Zöpf. He confirmed the release of 1500 workers from various industries. He sent the list of their names to the *Zentralstelle* so that they could be arrested, adding that further lists would be sent in the coming weeks.[58] Notification of the policy was sent to Seyss-Inquart and to Rauter; the lists of names went to Fünten.

Lages apparently wrote the chapter on the deportation of the Jews in the Security Police 1942 annual report. Retrospectively, he surveyed the transfer of the command on the Westerbork camp to the Security Police, the deportation of 28,606 Jews in forty-two trains, the difficulties growing out of the unwillingness of the Dutch to cooperate, and the isolation from their surroundings of the Jews who had not yet been deported. Looking ahead, he wrote of the need to reduce the numbers enjoying immunity. He intended, at the beginning of 1943, to deport 8000 invalid Jews along with the medical staff treating them.[59]

When he spoke of deporting invalids, he was thinking, among others, of the patients at Apeldoorn. Apeldoorn is a town to the east of Amsterdam, about a third of the way to Westerbork. Outside the town, in a quiet rural area, was a large Jewish hospital for the mentally ill. At the end of 1942 the institution had about 1100 patients and at least 400 staff members. Up to this point the residents had enjoyed a tranquillity that was absent in the rest of the country. There was no curfew, and the people there could move with relative freedom outside the institution as well. The Germans seemed far away.[60]

The initial inquiry came from a senior official in the Reich health

56. TR.3-599; Presser, *Destruction*, p. 175.
57. TR.3-598.
58. TR.3-599.
59. ZSL 107 AR 518/59 Bd.II, pp. 330–1.
60. Presser, *Destruction*, pp. 178–9.

system, Reich Health Führer Dr Leonardo Conti. He wrote to Seyss-Inquart on December 22, 1942 with copies to Rauter, Wimmer and Harster, asking to look into the possibility of evacuating the Apeldoorn hospital so that it could serve Germans wounded by Allied bombardments in the western part of the Reich.[61] Dr Conti did not indicate who the source of his information on the hospital was. After the Christmas and New Year celebrations Rauter or Seyss-Inquart or both of them ordered Harster to look into the place's potential. When the results of the inquiry came in, they ordered the evacuation of the facility. In less polite words, they ordered the deportation of Jewish psychiatric patients to their deaths in the East.

Harster received the order, and told Zöpf to assign the examination to Fünten, who came back with a carefully written report, including a map or diagram, which Harster passed on to his superiors. After they ordered him to proceed with the evacuation, several technical problems arose, and Eichmann was brought into the picture. Eichmann's men solved the problems, and sent the solution in the form of an operational order to Harster, who passed it on to Zöpf. In addition, they supplied a 25-car train, together with an escort squad, from the Reich. At some stage there was even a conversation between Eichmann and Seyss-Inquart on the matter.

Zöpf received the orders from Harster and assigned them to Fünten. Zöpf apparently participated in writing the report on the visit to the institution, and was the man who served as liaison between Eichmann and Harster. When the orders to evacuate the hospital arrived, he ordered Fünten to carry them out, and Gemmeker to provide security. Someone – Harster or Zöpf – also sent a Security Police unit.

Fünten was sent to look into the situation at Apeldoorn. He made his visit on January 11, 1943, receiving a guided tour from the hospital director, the Jewish Dr Jacques Lobstein. Fünten said that he was looking for a place to house homeless Jews. Nine days later, on January 20, 1943, Gemmeker showed up at the institution with Jewish order police from Westerbork. Many members of the hospital staff and some of the patients took advantage of this last auspicious moment to slip away. On the night of January 21, 1943 Gemmeker's men, under Fünten's command, loaded the inmates onto the waiting train, some of them with their hands bound. There they waited until morning, when Fünten asked for staff volunteers

61. ZSL AR-Z 12/68 Bd.IV, p. 398; Presser, *Destruction,* p. 179.

to escort the train, promising that after the train arrived at its destination they could return home. About twenty volunteered, and Fünten chose an additional thirty.

The train reached Auschwitz on January 24, 1943. It held 869 patients, 36 female staff members, and 16 male staff members. There were no survivors.[62]

There is nothing surprising about the ability of callous bureaucrats, or those cut off from reality – anywhere in the world – to decide on a policy that may cause suffering, even to defenseless mental patients. But can we therefore conclude that every such bureaucrat is capable of planning the murder of 1200 inmates and their nursing staff in order to make room for ill people he likes better? Is a typical bureaucrat capable of personally overseeing the forcible evacuation of schizophrenics and children into freight cars that will take them to their deaths? Does every official have the potential ability to stand before a frightened medical staff and ask for volunteers for a task that means death, while falsely promising a swift return home? Does the fact that this happened in one particular place indicate that the potential always exists, in the same degree?

In this context it is worth recalling Gemmeker at Westerbork. There are no testimonies describing him as an especially fanatical Nazi. Zöpf, his commander, described him as having "balanced" political opinions. The representative of the German Ministry of Justice, Dr Hans Georg Calmeyer, who tried to save Jews from deportation by issuing certificates of their Aryan race, remembered that Gemmeker always accepted his certificates even though his superiors did not like it. Jewish survivors also later testified that Gemmeker's treatment of Jewish prisoners was tolerable, and in their opinion deviant behavior and mistreatment had their source in the blind hatred of his secretary, a German named Elisabeth Hassel.[63]

These testimonies have to be placed against several facts. First, Gemmeker, who determined who would be sent to death and who would remain in the camp, was capable of adding to a deportation train prisoners who had taken cover from the rain under a forbidden roof, or Jews who had not greeted him properly as he walked through the camp.

62. This description is based on TR.3-1351, ZSL 107 AR 518/59 Bd.II, pp. 331–2, 107 AR-Z 592/67 Bd.VI, pp. 1040–3, Presser, *Destruction*, pp. 179–83, De Jong, Lois, *Het Koninkrijk der Nederlanden in de Tweede Werldoorlog*, Amsterdam: RIOD, 1975, vol. 6a, pp. 319–25.
63. ZSL AR-Z 12/68 Bd.I, pp. 41–9, Bd.II, pp. 222–3, 293, Bd.IV, pp. 423 ff.

Second, in Gemmeker's case there is a story similar to that of the deportation from Apeldoorn. Once a female prisoner in the camp gave birth to a premature baby. Gemmeker himself came to the hospital each day to inquire about the baby's health and to follow its fight for life. Six weeks later he announced with satisfaction that the boy was strong enough to be sent to the East. The next day mother and son were deported to their deaths.[64]

The decision to deport the inmates of Apeldoorn was made in the framework of attempts to keep up an accelerated rate of deportation, even as the number of Jews in easily deported categories began to run low. In addition to the ill and the hospitalized there was a second group, much larger but presenting a somewhat more complex problem: those with immunity. The immunity policy in Holland was different from that in other places. At first, several groups were broadly defined as being protected from deportation. This included perhaps a third of the Jews. Over time, this number grew or shrank. In August 1942 there were 26,700 protected Jews, while in September their number rose to 46,000. In the middle of November the number declined to 43,000. In July 1944 there were 12,000 protected Jews remaining in Holland.[65]

With the help of the immunity-granting policy the Security Police was able to minimize potential opposition of some of the Jews to deportation. The immunity that most of the Jews of the community institutions enjoyed, and which they were afraid of losing, effectively paralyzed them. From the point of view of the Security Police, the need to deport those with immunity became more pressing as the number of deportable Jews dwindled. Prior to this the immunity papers had been issued under Zöpf's direction, with Slottke taking care of the actual work. When the policy changed and Jews with immunity began to be deported, she generally made the decisions in individual cases, not always waiting for orders from above. When Dr Calmeyer began issuing numerous certificates of the non-Jewish origins of people who had previously been considered Jewish, she complained to Zöpf; the day after the action of May 26, 1943 she complained to Zöpf that some of those freed by Calmeyer were *"exceptionally* typical Galician Jews."[66]

On October 5, 1942 Zöpf wrote out a message for Slottke.

64. ZSL AR-Z 12/68 Bd.IV, pp. 429, 434–5.
65. ZSL AR 518/59 Bd.II, pp. 350–1.
66. ZSL AR 518/59 Bd. II, pp. 348–53, 475.

Eichmann had told Zöpf that Jews who were too old or too important to be sent to Auschwitz should be sent to the "propaganda camp" of Theresienstadt. This could be done from time to time in a special train, and Zöpf asked Slottke to handle the matter.[67] It could be that she was busy with other things; in any case, she spoke about the matter by telephone with Günther in Berlin only on January 25. She inquired about precisely which Jews were to get preferred treatment (*Verdienstjuden*). Günther explained: war veterans with medals from the level of Iron Cross class 1, or black medals for having been wounded. This included women (nurses) with medals. Austrian Jews would be handled like Germans, but not Hungarians: they had their own country and would be taken care of separately (so this was a political rather than a moral distinction). Children up to the age of 14 would be deported with their parents to Theresienstadt. Those over this age were old enough to be deported on their own to Auschwitz. In cases of doubt, it was preferable to be lenient and to deport to Theresienstadt (Günther knew about the pressure to increase the deportation of Jews from there to Auschwitz). Günther added that he would speak personally about the matter with Second Lt. Alfonse Werner from the Dutch office, who was in Berlin that day.[68]

Slottke (who may not have known about the intention to deport Jews from Theresienstadt to the death camps) interpreted this in the harshest way possible, and considered it her job to ensure that there be no doubtful cases. On March 22, 1943, she submitted to Zöpf a list of 179 war veterans who were not privileged to be sent to Theresienstadt. The list was passed on to Fünten and to Westerbork with the request to send them to the East. A week later she sent a second list containing the names of 150 war veterans and 91 war widows who were to be deported to the East. One of the widows was 92 years old (a widow of the war of 1871, perhaps?) and five others were over the age of 80.[69]

In order to get the most propaganda effect out of the special deportation to Theresienstadt, it was suggested that the people be sent in regular passenger cars. The train personnel supported this because it was

67. TR.3-619.
68. TR.3-623. Years later, during her interrogation, Slottke had an interesting explanation for her involvement: Günther made the call, it was late at night, Zöpf was no longer in his office, and the operator simply directed the call to her. She noted his directives, and forwarded them to Zöpf. ZSL 107 AR 518/59 Bd.III, p. 528.
69. ZSL 107 AR 518/59 Bd.II, pp. 355–7.

simpler to route regular passenger trains. Seyss-Inquart, who had apparently spoken with Eichmann, wished to present the deportation as a "change of residence," and believed that it would be possible to send them directly from Amsterdam.[70]

From spring 1943 Zöpf and Slottke worked, together with IV B 4 in Berlin, to prevent the granting of protected status. They took care to prevent South American passports from reaching the Jews to whom they were addressed. Eichmann even proposed sending these Jews posthaste to the East, before anyone had a chance to get the protective documents to them.[71]

The deportation efforts won clear, almost public support, from the leaders of the Nazi regime in Holland. On March 23, 1933 Rauter gave a speech to party and SS personnel. On the deportation of the Jews, he said that it was necessary to solve the Jewish problem in such a way that no Jew would remain in all of Europe, and to do this one had to be tough and compassionless. He mocked the Dutch church: "If they say they can't take responsibility before God [for standing aside when the Jews were deported], why don't they hand the responsibility over to me? I am willing to atone with my soul for the sins I am committing against the Jews! Whoever recognizes the significance of Jewry as a nation and as a race cannot act differently than we do." In this context he cited Hitler's speech of January 1939. Rauter's choice of language is interesting: *"Ich will mit meiner Seele büssen für das was ich hier gegen die Juden verbrochen habe"* ("I am willing to atone with my soul for the sins I am committing against the Jews"). He used religious terms quite cynically, both to express his scorn for the Jews, and to scoff at religion and the morality it teaches. As was common with these men, he was fully aware of his decision to disregard the morality he had been raised on. The audience, so the stenographer noted, applauded at this point.[72] Bene made a weekly report to his superiors in the foreign ministry in Berlin, a report that included much information on the deportation of the Jews. Among his sources for preparing the report was the weekly report signed by Harster and given to Seyss-Inquart, a report written by Zöpf or his staff.[73]

On April 27, 1943 Zöpf sent a report to IV B 4 in Berlin. Of 140,000 Jews who had been registered in Holland, 58,000 had been

70. TR.3-624, 15 April 1943.
71. ZSL AR 518/59 Bd.II, p. 355.
72. De Jong, *Koninkrijk*, vol. 7a, p. 331.
73. ZSL AR 518/59 Bd.II, pp. 335–7.

deported in 60 trains to the East, 4000 had been sent to camps in the Reich, 300 to Theresienstadt, and 6000 had emigrated or fled from the country, for a total of 68,000. Some 71,700 still remained like a cancer in the body of the *Volk*. Of these, 9300 were in Westerbork, 8800 in Vught, and 528 at Barneveld. Some 35,000 Jews were residing legally in Amsterdam, 5900 in the provinces, and 10–15,000 Jews were hiding illegally throughout the country. Rapid deportation was not possible. There were 8500 intermarried Jews who could not be deported; the Jews in Barneveld were protected by Seyss-Inquart. The 13,000 members of the Jewish administration and their families, like the 5500 employees of the defense industries, 1600 Jews who had converted to the Evangelical church, 1000 whose racial background was not clear, and 2000 workers at the camps, all had permits to remain in the country. It was possible, of course, to transfer more members of the first two groups to Vught, but since there were plans to establish a large ammunition factory there those Jews would be needed to work and could not be deported. The Jews in hiding could be uncovered only at a slow pace. The report's conclusion: very possibly in the coming year it would not be possible to fill all the planned trains.[74]

The reaction from Berlin was immediate. Within days (perhaps only two days, even[75]) there was a meeting headed by Rauter in which Harster, Zöpf, and an unidentified representative of the RSHA participated. In its wake Harster signed a series of new orders, dated May 5, 1943, which were prepared by Zöpf's staff and sent to Fünten, to the outlying stations, and to the commanders of the Westerbork and Vught camps:

1 The RFSS wishes that during 1943 everyone possible will be deported.
2 A new Buna — synthetic rubber — factory was being built at Auschwitz, outside the range of the West's bombers. There would be a need for a large number of laborers in the months of May and June. (Was this prologue meant for those who would otherwise have objected on the grounds that the workers were needed for the Vught factory?) The pace of the deportations would be increased. The goal was to deport 8000 Jews in May. The trains would be coordinated between Harster's office and the RSHA.
3 The RSHA wanted 15,000 deportees in June. Arrangements should

74. TR.3-589.
75. ZSL 107 AR 518/59 Bd.II, p. 337.

thus quickly be made for the deportation of the Jews in the Vught camp.

4 It was Rauter's intention to empty Amsterdam of its Jews. After removing the current political opposition, the implementation would be in two stages. First, Jews would be prevailed upon to move to Vught of their own volition. Fünten was to decide what was preferable — according to neighborhoods, or in alphabetical order. *Jooserad* workers would also be transferred, and no consideration should be given to the Jewish role in the economy.

5 It should be ascertained that the supervisory authority of the weapons industry knew that by May it had to give up its Jews. Jews who were not transferred to Vught (apparently to continue to work there in the meantime) would be transferred together with their families directly to Westerbork.

6 All the Portuguese Jews would be transferred to a special facility within Westerbork. Rauter and an RSHA representative would check into their origins.

7 Barneveld: the lists would be reexamined. The intention was to transfer everyone there to Westerbork in the near future.

8 The RFSS intended to establish, in Germany, a camp for about 10,000 Jewish citizens of France, Belgium and Holland who, thanks to their overseas connections, could be used to apply pressure on foreign governments. They might well be exchanged for returning Germans.

9 Intermarriages:

A. Jewish women from the age of 45 would be freed of the obligation to wear the yellow badge. This would prove to others that Jewish spouses in mixed marriages could get rid of the badge if they were sterilized.

B. In contrast, childless intermarried Jews would be transferred to Westerbork.

C. Others would be sterilized voluntarily in Amsterdam, or forcibly at Vught.

D. A report would be prepared for Seyss-Inquart detailing the men's places of employment.

E. All would be transferred to a special location, apparently on the country's frontier. Rauter was not prepared to have any Jews of any type in Amsterdam.

10 In order to encourage people to inform on Jews in hiding consideration should be given to offering to release Dutch prisoners from prison camps.

11 Abandoned orphans would be transferred to an institution to be

determined. There they would be under observation and their inherited traits examined to see if any of them were Jewish.

At the end of the document Harster again emphasized the importance of the matter: despite the political situation (meaning, apparently, the bad turn the war was taking) the above preparations were not to be taken lightly.[76]

In his interrogation in the 1960s Harster testified that the inspiration about abandoned children was "a typical Rauter idea".[77] The Nazis had already deported most of the available Jews. Difficulties were to be expected, of course, but they were solvable by a change of the Nazis' own policy. There was no need to take the Dutch authorities into account, except in the matter of the Jews in hiding, and there it was unknown citizens who were hiding the Jews, not the Dutch authorities.

The new instructions put the field officers in a dither. This reflected not only the new and severe instructions, but apparently also the fact that the men in the field had not initiated the change, and that carrying out the mission was not easy for them. This being the case, it is apparently correct to say that even though the document was prepared by Zöpf, its contents were determined by the more senior participants in the meeting with the RSHA representative, and Zöpf only recorded and worded the orders.

This is notably evidenced in Zöpf's letter to Westerbork, five days after the issuing of the orders (May 10). At the beginning of the letter he explained the RSHA's demand that in May no fewer than 8000 Jews be deported. A shipment of 1200 had already gone out on May 4 (in other words, before the new orders). There were 1450 sick and elderly Jews at Vught who would be sent on the second train. The third train, an especially packed one, would take 1630 Jews from Westerbork. The deportation of prisoners and redoubled efforts to uncover Jews in hiding would allow the deportation of 1500 more at most, for a total of 5780 Jews. He was weighing several possible actions to obtain the 2200 Jews still needed. 1 Deportation of the Jews from Vught. 2 An additional roundup in Amsterdam, but there were insufficient Orpo police for this. 3 A general evacuation of Amsterdam, but this would be hard to accomplish and would also be psychologically difficult. First, it would be necessary to transfer them via Vught, and it was hard to believe that

76. TR.3-1356.
77. ZSL 107 AR 518.59 Bd.III, p. 542.

they would reach Westerbork in time. Second, it would alarm the Jews who did not receive orders in the first wave. 4 Demanding of the war industries to speed up their handing over of 800 Jewish workers with their families. In this case, the Jews would have to reach Westerbork eight days before the end of the month. This solution also seemed problematic to Zöpf, because the war-industry Jews knew that they were designated for Vught and not for Westerbork and deportation, and sending them to the latter would cause disturbances among those that remained.[78] Zöpf did not state his preference.

Slottke and a junior official, SS-Sergeant Fischer, were sent the next day to Barneveld to reexamine the Jews imprisoned there. They found many lawyers, former officers in the Dutch army, and senior government officials, together with their families and relatives. They recommended vetting each and every case, carefully, and were convinced that many could be deported.[79] This action would not, however, significantly effect the deportation figures, given the small number of Jews in the camp. Someone, it is not clear who, decided among the different options, and received Rauter's blessing. On May 20 Rauter signed an order stating that all Jews without work permits had within the week to leave Amsterdam and to report to Vught.[80] The next day, when it became clear that the response was minimal, action was taken against the Jewish council.

On Friday morning, May 21, Fünten notified the leaders of the Judenrat that they must hand over 7000 of their employees for deportation. When they objected he referred them to Lages, who said that there was nothing to be done and that they had to obey orders. The council discussed the matter at two in the afternoon, and the two presidents were assigned to choose the 7000 people. This process went on until Sunday, when orders to report for deportation were printed and sent. On Monday, May 24, some of the people reported and others went into hiding. All were to report by May 25. That evening, after many failed to report, the presidents were summoned. The Germans, apparently

78. TR.3-590. At about this period — according to Lages during his 1949 interrogation in Amsterdam — the decision was made to begin paying informants for uncovering Jews. One of Lages's subordinates, Hassel, was in charge of these activities. ZSL 107 AR-Z 592/67 Bd.VI, pp. 1078–9.

79. ZSL 107 AR 518/59 Bd.II, p. 369. The issue was not resolved, and months later Eichmann was still trying to have them removed from Holland. TR.3-603, 28 August 1943.

80. ZSL 107 AR 689/66 Bd.II, p. 174, or TR.3-592, 20 September 1943.

Fünten, announced that because of the failure to deliver the required number there would be a roundup. On May 26 the old Jewish quarter of Amsterdam was surrounded, blocked and sealed, and there was a house-to-house search conducted by German Orpo police. Three thousand Jews were arrested. Among them were council workers who were considered indispensable, but Fünten and Lages refused the presidents' request to release them.[81]

The chain of command for the action would have begun with Harster, who apparently received approval from above for his decision. Harster or Zöpf would have notified Lages of this by phone. They would also have notified him which categories of Jews could be deported. Fünten would have prepared the appropriate lists of Jews marked for deportation, and Lages would have coordinated the activity with the Security and Order Police units, with the Dutch police, and with the *Hausraterfassung*, the German government unit that dealt with the confiscation of Jewish homes and their contents. The command in the field would have been Lages's, unless otherwise decided.[82]

No-nonsense Slottke also took part in the action of May 26, and wrote of it the next day that the validity of Jewish immunity documents should be checked again. She, for example, had the previous day encountered Jews whose documents indicated that they were protected because of their large property, even though their clothing showed that they were poor. Otherwise, the action proceeded quietly, with the exception of a few women who went into hysterics. Harster and Zöpf also wrote reports on the action. They interpreted the lack of Jewish response to the orders to report for deportation as a Jewish attempt to test the seriousness of the Security Police. The Jews who had been arrested, so they wrote, were "ready to go."[83]

On June 20, 1943 there was an additional action, in east and south Amsterdam. Harster and Zöpf decided on this, and it was carried out by Order and Security Policemen, who again conducted house-to-house searches. All the Jews rounded up — 5500 of them — were deported to Westerbork. The surprise factor — all preparations had been kept secret — apparently contributed to the success of the operation. It may well have been that conducting it on a Sunday added to the surprise. Harster and Zöpf noted in their report to the Reichskommissar that the arrested

81. Presser, *Destruction*, pp. 202–6; ZSL 107 AR 518/59 Bd.II, pp. 340–1.
82. ZSL AR-Z 592/67 Bd.VI, pp. 1081–3.
83. ZSL 107 AR 518/59 Bd.II, pp. 341, 364–5.

Jewish Council workers had been greeted by the other prisoners in Westerbork with a great deal of *schadenfreude*.[84]

Bene read the report, and reported on its contents to the foreign ministry in Berlin. There had been 140,000 registered Jews in Holland, and 102,000 had already been removed. Of these, 72,000 had been deported to the East, 10,000 had been sent to other camps in Germany, had emigrated or had fled. About 20,000 were prisoners in camps in Holland. In eleven months three-quarters of the country's Jews had been taken care of.[85]

The center in Berlin was much more involved in the final stages of the deportation; the first stages had been largely the initiative of the local SS. Slottke later recalled that Mös visited them fairly frequently, and in her opinion he was the official "responsible" for them in Berlin.[86] A document of Zöpf's, prepared by Slottke on June 22, indicates that Zöpf had recently been in Berlin to be briefed. In the days that followed (June 24–25) there were discussions in which Rauter, Harster and Zöpf participated, dealing with the possibility of presenting the relatively new camp of Bergen-Belsen as a "good" camp. The Jews would be told that the camp was meant for Jews who would be exchanged for Germans. Jews with some sort of protection would be sent there, and this would perhaps make it possible to tempt Jews in hiding to come out into the open.[87] Another advantage: Jews whose deportation the RSHA would not allow could nevertheless be gotten out of Holland.[88] In the meantime, 9000 Jews had to be found to fill the four trains assigned by the RSHA, and to find these Zöpf issued orders for additional roundups.[89] At the beginning of July Alfonse Werner, a junior officer under Zöpf's command, spent an entire week in the IV B 4 offices in Berlin, where he received a briefing from each expert on his field.[90]

84. ZSL 107 AR 518/59 Bd.II, pp. 341–2, 367; Presser, *Destruction*, pp. 207–8. The secrecy was ensured by a scheme: Lages convened all the policemen together the evening before the action and they watched a film. Afterwards, they were all taken to headquarters, and kept there until the next morning. ZSL 107 AR-Z 592/67, pp. 1083–5.
85. ZSL 107 AR 518/59 Bd.II, p. 341.
86. ZSL 413 RSHA 1310/63 E5, p. 10.
87. ZSL 107 AR 518/59 Bd.II, pp. 359, 362–3.
88. ZSL AR 518/59 Bd.III, pp. 545–6. This rather self-incriminating interpretation, whereby the SS in Holland tried to circumvent a policy line laid down in Berlin, was made by Zöpf during his interrogation.
89. ZSL 107 AR 518/59 Bd.II, p. 342.
90. TR.10-767c, pp. 897–8.

On August 27, 1943 Eichmann participated in a meeting in the WVHA offices, and the next day he telegraphed Harster that it had been decided to deport 2400 Jews working in the Vught camp. The deportation would be carried out in stages, in order not to slow production. Eichmann asked also – again – if it was not possible to deport the Jews of Barneveld, at least to Bergen-Belsen.[91] That same day Harster announced to Bene of the foreign ministry an agreement between Seyss-Inquart and Himmler according to which intermarried Jews would be freed of the requirement of wearing the badge, and from some of the other restrictions applying to Jews.[92] It would seem that this was an attempt to render invisible to the public those Jews whom it was already clear would not be deported at all. As regards the Jews of Vught and Barneveld, there was no response from Holland for several weeks. Werner visited IV B 4 on September 16 and 17 and heard once more about the need to deport them. On September 20 Zöpf cabled Eichmann that the position of Rauter and the new BdS, Naumann, was that the Jews of the two camps should not be deported, since they were an essential workforce.[93]

On the night of September 28 the last big action took place. Between 3000 and 5000 Jewish council workers – pretty much everyone who remained – were arrested. Remaining in Amsterdam were the Portuguese Jews, the "Calmeyer Jews," whose supposed status as Aryans had to be checked, and those who were in hiding. There were no others.[94] It was two days before Rosh Hashanah.

Eichmann apparently understood that the considerations of the SS commanders in Holland took precedence over his own, and that it was not possible to deport the protected Jews from that country. This was true in particular with regard to the intermarried Jews and those in the diamond industry, two categories that Seyss-Inquart asked be taken care of by his own men. On November 5 a cable signed by Eichmann went out to Naumann, containing a request at least to worsen the conditions of the prisoners, out of pure spite. It also said to make sure that the Jews did not receive visas that would allow them to emigrate.[95] A week later he

91. TR.3-603. Weeks later Zöpf answered: only some of the Barneveld Jews can be deported. ZSL AR 689/66 Bd.II, p. 178, 20 September 1943.
92. TR.3-463, 28 August 1943. Harster's letter was addressed to Bene.
93. Werner: TR.3-592; Zoepf: TR.3-593.
94. Presser, *Destruction*, pp. 212–13.
95. ZSL AR 518/59 Bd.II, pp. 359–60; TR.3-606.

arrived in Holland himself and had several meetings with Naumann, his men and industry representatives. They identified groups of Jews that could be deported, such as 600 criminal (sic) detainees and 400 who had been designated for exchanges with Palestine. These would be deported to Auschwitz. They also decided to deport 1300 residents of Westerbork to Theresienstadt. In contrast, Eichmann agreed that diamond polishers would not be deported, and that some of them would even remain free.[96] The train to Theresienstadt, containing 870 Jews, departed on January 18, 1944. Notably, it was only after the train had left that Naumann signed a letter by Slottke to Seyss-Inquart containing a retroactive request to approve the deportation. Seyss-Inquart gave his approval some weeks later,[97] but it would seem that everyone involved considered this merely a formality. Everyone knew that if Naumann and his men had decided to deport Jews, Seyss-Inquart would not stop them.

On January 21, 1944 Zöpf received notification from Eichmann's office (IV B 4a) that Jews who were still free should be arrested. He passed this on to Fünten.[98] At the beginning of February Eichmann enlisted Kaltenbrunner, who signed a letter to Naumann: from the routine reports it could be understood that Sephardic Jews were not to be deported, perhaps because Seyss-Inquart was not convinced that they were Jews. If this was the reason, there should be no doubts, he said. These were the descendants of immigrants from Spain in the fourteenth and fifteenth centuries. They should be included in the deportations.[99] This level of expertise did not come from Kaltenbrunner; there was apparently a great need to convince Seyss-Inquart that he had no reason for concern.

Mös arrived from Berlin on February 8 to discuss the advancement of the deportations.[100] That same week Gemmeker requested Zöpf's permission to change the policy in Westerbork. Up

---

96. TR.3-602, 1352. In an internal note, Naumann wrote to Zöpf: "*Heben Sie mir ja die Diamantspalter gut auf, der Obergruppenf.* [Seyss-Inquart] *hängt mich sonst auf.*" ZSL AR 518/59 Bd.II, p. 360; *c.* October 11.43. By keeping in Seyss-Inquart's good graces where it was important to *him*, one assured his cooperation everywhere else.

97. Train to Theresienstadt: TR.3-335, see also TR.3-336. Seyss-Inquart: TR.3-337, 9 February 1944.

98. ZSL AR 689/66 Bd.II, p. 182.

99. TR.3-614, 3 February 1944.

100. TR.3-609. During his visit Mös forbade delivering foreign passports that arrived by mail to Jews. This caused unforeseen problems: In April, the Swiss authorities asked where the mail was disappearing to (TR.3-611, 8 April 1944). Wöhrn and Günther suggested saying it had been destroyed in air raids. Under no circumstances were fines to be paid (TR.3-612, 15 June 1944).

until this point Jews had not been deported while sick; now he asked to deport to Auschwitz 400–500 of the patients in the camp hospital. Patients expected to die within a few hours anyway would not be deported.[101]

At the end of February Seyss-Inquart wrote to Bormann (knowing, we may assume, that what he wrote would reach Hitler). He boasted about the deportation of the Jews as accomplished in Holland, but disputed the demands arriving from Berlin to deport the intermarried Jews — unless the intention was to deport them with their families.[102]

On July 5, 1944, when the American and British forces were already advancing towards Holland, orders arrived from the RSHA to deport all the Jews who still remained in the country. An SS captain Dr Ulrich Grotefend was sent from the RuSHA to clarify problematic cases of origins; he did not have time to do much.[103]

Bene summed it up on July 20, 1944: the Jewish problem in Holland could be considered solved. There had been 140,000 Jews. Of these, 2500 had been declared "Aryan" or *Mischlinge*. Another 4000 had died. Some 8000 had fled. A full 105,000 had been deported. In total, 119,500 Jews had left. Remaining were about 8600 intermarried Jews and 11 Argentinian citizens, all of them free. In the camps there were 475 Protestant Jews, 826 protected Jews in Barneveld, and 2300 Jewish prisoners in Westerbork. About 9000 were in hiding. All in all, 21,212 Jews remained, bringing the total to 140,712.[104] The Nazis could retreat from Holland with their minds at ease.

This survey has shown that there was no significant difference between Eichmann and his officers in Berlin and the SS officers in Holland. The major concern of both groups was the deportation of Jews to their deaths. All of them happily contributed to the murder of Jews and if there is a lesson to be learned from the events in Holland, it is that the reservoir of officials willing to be involved in the project was large. A second point is that their diligence was not reduced in the least by their distance from the center. Leni Yahil, in summing up the story of the rescue of the Jews of Denmark, argues that the massive opposition of the Danes to the

101. ZSL 107 AR-Z 12/68 Bd.IV, pp. 19427–8.
102. TR.3-1439, 28 February 1944.
103. ZSL AR 689/66 Bd.II, p. 183.
104. ZSL AR 518/59 Bd.II, pp. 346–7.

"abnormal" behavior of the Nazis moderated even the Nazis.[105] Arendt would interpret this as meaning that the Nazis in Denmark were forced to recognize the evil of their actions, and therefore tried to avoid it. The story of the deportation of the Jews of Holland is problematic for this thesis, because in Holland there was also opposition to the Nazis (although less determined than that of the Danes) and it made no impression on them. They were so similar to their colleagues in Berlin that Eichmann and his men had almost no need to interfere.

From the testimony at the Eichmann trial

Joseph Melkman

Q. Please tell the court in what manner the deportations [from Westerbork] to the East were organized.

A. The commandant advised the Jewish administration of Westerbork that on the following day – this was always a Tuesday – a certain number had to be sent, 1000 or 2000 or 3000, and the Jewish administration was required to provide lists, the names of those who were to be sent, slightly more than the quota, for there was the obvious possibility that some of them would die en route, and the number reaching Auschwitz always had to be exact. If they had to supply 1000 they used to send 1020. They started dealing with these lists already on Friday and Saturday. Sometimes people were included in the lists who were in possession of documents which provided them with so-called protection against being deported and, if there was a lack of human material, this immunity was canceled. This was already known by Saturday. And then, the closer it was to Tuesday, the greater the tension. And on the night between Monday and Tuesday, at three in the morning they closed the hut in which we were staying, they sealed it hermetically, it was forbidden to leave or come in. And then the hut leader read out the names of the people who were condemned to deportation – an alphabetical list. And I must say that all the terrible things that I saw afterwards, in the camps, or

105. Leni Yahil, *The Rescue of Danish Jewry: Test of a Democracy*, Philadephia: Jewish Publication Society of America, 1969, pp. 385 ff.

murderous beatings and more than that, the most powerful impression that remained with me, and also with others, was of that night, three o'clock on Tuesday morning, when there was absolute silence and darkness, and they called out as if they were pronouncing a death sentence every night on those about to be deported. Sometimes you yourself could have been among them, and if not you yourself – then relatives, friends, acquaintances. But every single week there would be a certain number of death sentences at that hour. This made such a horrifying impression on us, on all of us, on all those who also wrote about it, that we still feel some trepidation about Tuesday, which was the day of the death sentence for the Jews of Holland. ...

The conditions in a hide-out are somewhat known to the world through the diary of Anne Frank. But perhaps, in order to give some impression of what it means to be in a hide-out, I shall describe one child whom I saw. My wife and I worked in the children's home in Westerbork. They always brought to this place children who were seized by the Germans, children who did not have parents, or whose parents had hidden themselves [separately] or who had already been deported. In practice they were orphans, and we attended to them, but of course for a very short time, for they had no protection and accordingly were deported, almost invariably, straight away. I remember one case of a child whose name was van Dam – his first name I do not recall. He was ten years old. He had been cooped up for a whole year in a narrow room, he was not allowed to talk in a normal voice – and I do not mean talking loudly. He was not allowed to walk as a child would walk, lest the neighbors hear him. When he came to Westerbork, he came to the children's home and also began speaking in whispers. When we told him that there was no need to do so and he understood that everything was permitted here, he began running round the grounds of the children's home all the time, he could not stop himself, and he shouted very loudly, for he had been forbidden for a whole year to speak and to walk.

Q. What happened to him?

A. He was sent three days later to Auschwitz.

(*The Trial of Adolf Eichmann*, vol. II, pp. 615–17)

Chapter 6

France

Germany invaded France on May 10, 1940; France surrendered six weeks later. The defeated country was divided into four zones. Alsace and Lorraine were annexed to the Reich, and two northern departments were attached to the German military government in Belgium. This chapter does not deal with these two relatively small areas. It will look at the two larger zones. The largest of these covered France's north and west, and was put under German military rule. The southeastern third of the country remained relatively independent and was known as Vichy France, because its seat of government was the city of that name. Its head of state was Marshal Philippe Pétain. The Germans called this area the "unoccupied zone"; the French called it the "free zone" or "the unconquered zone."

The zone under direct German rule was headed by a military governor called the *Militärbefehlshaber Frankreich* or MBF. The first man to occupy the post, beginning on October 25, 1940, was General Otto von Stulpnagel. He and his men were headquartered in Paris.

The German government maintained an embassy in Paris alongside the military government. The ambassador was Otto Abetz; his expert on Jewish affairs was Karl-Theo Zeitschel, a former naval officer and a member of the Nazi party since 1923.[1]

To the disappointment of Heydrich and Daluege, Himmler did not appoint an HSSPF for France. Heydrich had to be satisfied with sending Dr Max Thomas as his representative in Belgium and France; at the head of the small Security Police force sent to Paris stood *SS Sturmbannführer* (Major) Dr Helmut Knochen. Under him was Major Karl Bomelburg, chief of branch IV, and the man responsible for

1. John P. Fox, "German Bureaucrat or Nazified Ideologue? Ambassador Otto Abetz and Hitler's Anti-Jewish Policies, 1940–1944," in Michael G. Fry (ed.), *Power, Personalities and Policies: Essays in Honour of Donald Cameron Watt*, University of Southern California Press, 1992; Serge Klarsfeld, *Vichy-Auschwitz: Die Zusammenarbeit der deutschen und französischen Behörden bei der 'Endlösung der Judenfrage' in Frankreich*, Nördlingen: Delphi Politik, 1989, p. 592.

Gestapo affairs. Kurt Lischka arrived in Paris in November 1940 and was appointed Knochen's deputy.[2]

From the moment of their arrival in Paris, the Security Police men sought to expand their authority and enhance their power. At first they were not even allowed to maintain direct radio contact with their headquarters in Berlin. On August 24, 1940, Dr Thomas was appointed Commissioner of the Sipo and SD in France and Belgium, and he worked out of Paris. His forces were part of the Security Police and were subordinate to the RSHA in Berlin. All contact with them ran, however, through the military government, and they had no operative authority. On January 2, 1941 it was decided that in "urgent cases" they would be allowed to act alone, making arrests, searching houses and confiscating property. On March 25, 1941 they received authority to arrest suspects at their own discretion for a period of up to seven days, and to maintain independent contacts with the French police — but they had to make report of "substantive contacts" to the military headquarters. Along with this, the Paris office established three outlying offices — in Bordeaux, Rouen, and Dijon. The Dijon office itself had branches in Nancy, Besançon, and Orléans.

Liberation from subordination to the military headquarters received a significant impetus in the final months of 1941. At the beginning of October Knochen initiated an attack of French collaborators and Security Policemen on Parisian synagogues. Not only did he fail to coordinate this with military headquarters — he even refrained from making a true report after the fact. A power struggle ensued between the military headquarters and the OKH on the one side and Heydrich on the other. Thomas was transferred from Paris to Einsatzgruppe C in the Ukraine; after a period of ambiguity, it was decided that Knochen would remain in Paris. In principle he was made subordinate to the IDS (the Sipo Inspector) in Düsseldorf, but in practice he emerged from the affair strengthened and independent, now being the senior representative of the Security Police in France. The affair was one of the reasons for von Stulpnagel's decision to relinquish his post on February 5, 1942.

Otto von Stulpnagel was replaced on February 17 by his cousin,

2.   *Zur Geschichte der 'Endlösung der Judenfrage' in Frankreich unter besonderer Berücksichtigung der Aufgaben der Sicherheitspolizei und des SD. 1940–1944. Historisches Gutachten von Dr Wolgang Scheffler.* Prepared for 130(24) JS 1/66(z), Staatsanwalt Köln. YVA, P. 26–43 – this is the Bestand and file, in which the relevant pages are 16–17; Klarsfeld, *Vichy*, p. 593.

General Karl-Heinrich von Stulpnagel. Himmler took advantage of the switch to shore up the status of his units in France, which was made easier for him by the fact that von Stulpnagel himself demanded, as a condition of accepting the job, a separation between military and political issues. On March 3 Himmler appointed an HSSPF for France, Karl Oberg, who until then had been SSPF in Radom, Poland. The appointment was made with the approval of Hitler, who issued a personal order on the matter. Heydrich brought Oberg to Paris himself, while making a visit there at the beginning of May, and the new HSSPF took up his job on June 1. On May 20, Knochen's title and job changed in an important way. He was now no longer just a commissioner, but commander of the Security Police. He was also promoted to the rank of colonel, one rank above Eichmann.[3]

Notably, HSSPF Oberg and MBF von Stulpnagel had served together in the same battalion during the First World War — a common memory that united them and set them apart from the other senior Nazis in France.

Oberg had no headquarters of his own, only secretaries, an adjutant and a personal assistant, Herbert Hagen. This was the same Hagen who in 1937 had been Eichmann's commander in the SD; since 1940 he had held other positions in the Security Police in France.[4] Another of his subordinates from his days in SD headquarters, Dannecker, had also been stationed in France since the summer of 1940. He was now Knochen's expert on Jewish affairs.

Also working in the Security Police building in Paris were secretaries who had been brought for this purpose from Germany. One of them, a young woman named Ilse Warneke, caught Dannecker's eye, and during a series of walks together through Paris, they fell in love. When Ilse got pregnant they married; the ceremony was held in Berlin, but their colleagues in Paris gave a party for them also. On the assumption that they spoke, at least at times, about their work, wouldn't they also have spoken about the persecution of French Jewry? And when Ilse went back to live in Berlin and Dannecker came to visit her as often as he could, did he not update her about his work in their office? As we follow Dannecker's efforts to murder the Jews of France, some thought might well be given to this young family and to what extent their love story is banal.[5]

3. Scheffler, *Geschichte*, pp. 11, 16–24, 26, 42; Klarsfeld, *Vichy*, p. 35.
4. Scheffler, *Geschichte*, pp. 30–1.
5. Claudia Steur, *Theodor Dannecker: Ein Funktionär der "Endlösung"*, Tübingen: Klartext, 1997, p. 92.

The Security Police did not act resolutely against French Jewry until the end of 1941. The Vichy government did so fairly independently,[6] and there had been several prior attempts by other German elements. Ambassador Abetz conferred with Hitler on August 3, 1940 about possible lines of action against the French Jews. Abetz proposed some ideas at a meeting with the MBF two weeks later: prohibiting the entry of additional Jews to the occupied zone, making preparations for removing the Jews who were there already, and looking into the possibility of confiscating Jewish property. A military staff member named Mahnke prepared a reply, dated August 22, 1940, explaining that if the measures were of too general a nature, they would have negative results, because they would create the impression that the area had been annexed to the Reich. It would be better instead, he suggested, to act against individuals. In any case, he had no compassion for the Jews, and it was clear to him that it was necessary to fight them because they were endangering the Reich. Abetz's response: the French would have to understand that by the end of the war no Jews could remain.[7]

No one waited for the representatives of the Security Police, and certainly not for Eichmann, in order to launch the measures against the Jews of France. The entry of the Security Police, and especially the appearance of Dannecker, did, however, add a new dimension to anti-Jewish policy. As early as 1937 Dannecker had had clear ideas about what measures to take against the Jews; from the time he began working in France he seems to have known, in one way or another, about the real policy goal, as he wrote in a memorandum on 21 January, 1941:

Central Office of Jewish Affairs in Paris

By the wish of the Führer, the Jewish Question is to be resolved in a final way after the war[8] in the German-controlled and German-influenced territories of Europe.

The Chief of the Sipo and SD has received from the Führer, through the RFSS [Himmler] and through the Reichsmarshal [Goering] the task of

6. See Michael Marrus and Robert O. Paxton, *Vichy France and the Jews,* New York: Basic Books, 1981. Their central thesis, now accepted by all mainstream historians, is that the Vichy government acted against its Jews of its own volition.
7. TR. 10-878, p. 61 (indictment against Lischka); Klarsfeld, *Vichy,* pp. 356–9; ZSL 104 AR-Z 1670/61 Bd. IV, p. 71.
8. The assumption at the time would have been that the war would soon be over.

preparing the project of the Final Solution. Based on the substantial experience of dealing with the Jewish question that has accumulated in the departments of the Sipo and the SD, and building upon the preparatory work which has been carried out over a long period, the outlines of the project have been developed and submitted to the Führer and the Reichsmarshal.

It is clear that this is to be a gigantic project, and its success will depend on painstaking preparation. This will need to encompass the preparations for a complete removal of the Jews, as well as the detailed planning of their resettlement in an as yet to be determined territory.[9]

The rest of the document discusses in detail and at great length the measures to be taken so that on the appointed day it would be possible to carry out the mission. All Jews would be identified, isolated from the rest of the population, and they and their property supervised until deportation. Management and supervision must be carried out by a central office. It should not be entrusted to the French authorities, who had already shown themselves incapable of such a mission. Dannecker cited the partial implementation of their own anti-Jewish laws of October 4, 1940 as concrete proof of the French inability to take serious action.[10] A central office for Jewish affairs should be established to handle the entire range of issues, such as the preparation of a card file with information on all Jews, registration and management of Jewish property, internment of non-French Jews in concentration camps, direction of anti-Jewish propaganda, and other such tasks. The office would be French, but would be subordinate to the German Security Police. Dannecker sent his proposal to the ambassador. Two weeks later, on February 3, 1941, he submitted it also to Werner Best in the military government. Abetz supported him.[11]

It is hard to know what importance to assign this document. Were it clear that Dannecker had been connected with reliable and central

9. Klarsfeld, *Vichy*, pp. 361–2.
10. This does not contradict the findings of Marrus and Paxton, whereby Vichy was running ahead of the Germans in its anti-Jewish policies; it does, however, highlight the fact that for SS officers in the know, the French policy was not convincing, even at this early stage.
11. Klarsfeld, *Vichy*, pp. 364–5, 14 February 1941. Werner Best had left the RSHA early in 1940, after falling out with Heydrich. In France he belonged to the staff of the military governor, where he was in charge of overseeing the French administration, and especially the police and legal system. Herbert, *Best*, pp. 254 ff.

sources of information, we would have to place the document along with others that describe the development of the genocide policy. After all, he is speaking here of Hitler's will that all Jews be deported in the framework of the Final Solution project that Himmler and Goering assigned to Heydrich – and this prior to the first preparations for the murder of the Soviet Union's Jews. There do not, however, seem to be any appropriate responses from the senior members of the system who received the document, and it does not seem that it caused any reversal of their conception. They may have seen it merely as an awkward attempt by Dannecker to gain more power. In retrospect, Dannecker was correct, but it seems likely that he was simply prescient in seeing which way the wind was blowing. Even he, in any case, was still not talking about murder.[12]

In keeping with his position, Dannecker strove incessantly to create a Jewish representative body. To this purpose he met in September 1940 with Chief Rabbi Julian Weill; his unrelenting pressure produced some results when, at the end of January 1941, the Jews established the *Comité de Coordination*.[13] The day after writing the document quoted above, he signed Knochen on a proposal to concentrate the non-French Jews in camps. Knochen submitted the proposal to the military commander on January 28, explaining that the Jews supported the English and De Gaulle, and that in any case the French would be glad of the opportunity to take over Jewish property. According to Dannecker, there were 100,000 Jews who were not French citizens in the Paris area. He spoke of this with the embassy staff a month later, on February 28, and expected to have no problem persuading the French to establish camps in the occupied zone.[14]

In preparation for the first meeting between von Stulpnagel and French Prime Minister Pierre Laval, on April 4, 1941, Best briefed the military governor on the goals of the Jewish policy. It should be made

---

12. But what *did* he mean by *"endgültige Lösung"*? And if he *did* know about a decision to murder the Jews, he wouldn't have written it in a letter to the Embassy, would he? We seem to be at the limit of what historians can know; clearly, we don't know it all.

13. Richard I. Cohen, *The Burden of Conscience: French Jewish Leadership during the Holocaust*, Bloomington, IN: Indiana University Press, 1985, pp. 26–9. And see Jacques Adler, *The Jews of Paris and the Final Solution: Communal Response and Internal Conflicts, 1940–1944*, New York: Oxford University Press, 1987, pp. 55–63, who shows how Dannecker in his actions preceded the other German agencies in France.

14. TR.3-1071; TR.3-442.

clear to the prime minister of France, he said, that Germany's goal was the "dejewification" of Europe; the first stage was to make preparations for the deportation of all the Jews who were not French.[15] In the months and years that followed, the Germans and French would tussle and bargain over more limited goals, but even at this early stage everyone knew that the Germans aspired to remove all the Jews from France.

Beginning in the middle of June 1941 there were coordination meetings each Tuesday in Dannecker's office for the purpose of standardizing German policy and ensuring its implementation. Representatives of all the German bodies in Paris participated. Dannecker explained to Lischka that the meetings were necessary because experience had proven that not all figures in the military government were sufficiently tough on the Jews, and this tendency was more than likely to grow stronger in light of the French position,[16] which he did not expect would be rigid enough for his needs. Rudolf Schleier, the consul-general in the embassy, discussed the French position with Dannecker on July 1, 1941. It was clear to both of them that they could not expect full cooperation from the French, and therefore they should start with foreign Jews. After the French became accustomed to this, they would themselves want to continue with the deportation of the French Jews.[17] Schleier was significantly more senior than Dannecker, and meetings between them were not a matter of routine. Apparently anyone who really wanted to know the score must meet with the men from the SS.

In Berlin, Eichmann and his men knew about the coming "Final Solution for the Jews of Europe," and the Paris station knew something as well. Dannecker wrote on July 1, 1941 that "Everything should be prepared so that, when the mission of solving the Jewish problem is assigned to the commander of the Security Police, we will be able to serve as an outlying station of the European Jewish commissariat."[18] In other German ministries there was also an atmosphere of growing extremism regarding the Jews. Zeitschel proposed to Abetz that in his upcoming meeting with Hitler he should recommend the sterilization of all Jews in Europe. A day later he changed his position — it would be better to discuss in Berlin their deportation to a special region in the East.[19] There

15. ZSL 104 AR-Z 1670/61 Bd. V, p. 731; Ermittlung.
16. TR.10-878, pp. 69–70.
17. United Restitution Organisation (Italy). YVA O. 48–32, p. 37.
18. TR.10-878, p. 39.
19. Klarsfeld, *Vichy*, pp. 367–8, 21 August 1941, 22 August 1941.

was pressure from below to take more strenuous measures against the Jews, in parallel with the even more extreme decision that had already been made by Hitler, and which the Security Police was preparing to carry out. As it happens, Abetz met with Himmler rather than Hitler on the deportation idea, and Himmler confirmed that it would be carried out when trains could be found.[20] Two months before the beginning of the deportations from France not only the Security Police knew about it, but also the German ambassador.

The mass arrests began on May 15, 1941, when the French arrested 3733 Jews, most of them of Polish citizenship. On August 20, an additional 3477 Jewish men were arrested in Paris, without regard to citizenship (Americans excepted). They were sent to the camp at Drancy. A few days later several hundred more Jews were arrested. On October 20 Dannecker reported to the embassy in Paris on 7443 Jews in three camps − Drancy, Pithiviers and Beaune-la-Rolande. On December 12, another 743 French Jews were arrested and sent to the Compiègne camp as military retribution for underground activity against Wehrmacht soldiers. It was carried out by the Field Gendarmerie and the Security Police, in cooperation with French policemen.[21]

All these actions were initiated by the military government, rather than the Security Police. Werner Best, formerly a top Security Police commander but now the man who oversaw the French police in the military government, ordered the first arrests after his hopes were dashed that the French commissar for Jewish affairs, Xavier Vallat, would do so himself. The August arrests came in response to the beginning of anti-German activity by the French Communist underground. Again, it was Best who gave the orders to the French police. Now the camps were full, and in keeping with the accepted Nazi practice of making conditions worse in order to make the policy more severe, it was clear that the arrested Jews had to be deported to the East in order to make room for more. The main advocate of taking more extreme measures against the Jews in 1941 was the army, not the SS, and its considerations were largely political. As the activity of the French underground grew, so did the pressure from Hitler to respond forcefully and to execute French hostages. The leaders of the military government feared the escalation this would cause, and preferred to respond by arresting Jews, and afterwards by

20. Klarsfeld, *Vichy*, p. 33, 8 October 1941.
21. TR.10-878, pp. 71–2, Lischka; Klarsfeld, *Vichy*, p. 34; Herbert, *Best*, pp. 308–12.

deporting them to the East.[22] It would seem that the understanding at the base of this policy was that the French would be bothered less by the arrest and deportation of Jews than by the killing of hostages. On the other hand, the arrest of Jews, and especially of Jewish citizens of France, was in any case meant to cow the French and put a halt to the activity of the underground.

The power of the military government was not, however, sufficient to deport the Jews from France. True, von Stulpnagel tried to deport them in an order he issued on December 14, 1941, but the RSHA slowed the pace. A letter signed by Müller notified Knochen that the growing pressure on the trains in the Christmas season made it impossible to deport Jews and Communists from France for the time being.[23]

At the end of February 1942 it was decided in Paris to try again, this time from within the Security Police. Lischka signed a letter of Dannecker's to Eichmann, in which he argued that the German prestige with the French had been damaged because of the delay in the deportations, and that there were growing pressures to free the Jews. He asked for special approval to take action. Berlin responded to Knochen that there was actually a plan to deport a thousand Jews; further details would be given to Dannecker during his upcoming visit to Berlin.[24] On March 6, Dannecker was in Berlin, where he took part in the conference of experts called by Eichmann. He took advantage of the opportunity to pressure Eichmann personally, but this time he presented his request in a different way: in the light of recent problems with the French government, it was desirable to do something positive, for example to deport several thousand Jews.[25] Eichmann confirmed that Heydrich was expected to decide on the issue, and then it would be possible to discuss with the French the deportation of about 5000 Jews.[26]

Dannecker knew on March 10, 1942 at the latest that the deportation of 1000 Jews had been approved, and that it was scheduled

22. Herbert, *Best*, pp. 308–14.
23. Stulpnagel: ZSL 104 AR-Z 1670/61 Bd.4, p. 4; Müller: TR.3-333, 24 December 1941.
24. TR.10-878, p. 94, 26 February 1942; TR.3-694.
25. Dannecker's reasoning seems to have been the opposite of that in the MBF – that the deportation of the Jews would be welcomed by the French. No matter who was reading the French mood more accurately, the practical result was the same – that the Jews must be deported.
26. TR.3-113. Dannecker wrote that the meeting took place on 4 March, which was perhaps the date of his arrival in Berlin. The meeting took place on 6 March.

for March 23. It was not clear who would bear the costs, and who would be responsible for escorting the trains, but it had already been determined that the deportees would take up to fifty kilograms of personal equipment, including a blanket and work shoes, as well as food for three weeks. The commander of the escort would be supplied with a list of the deportees, and a copy of the list would be sent to IV B 4. The next day Eichmann announced that there was authorization to deport 5000 Jews in addition to the first thousand. The deportees would be citizens of Germany, France and Poland, not including Jews in mixed marriages. Likewise, Dannecker was to update IV B 4 on an ongoing basis about the camps from which the Jews were being taken and who was funding it. When he thought it necessary, Dannecker knew how to respond quickly, and he cabled a reply to Eichmann that same day. There were 1115 candidates for the first deportation; costs would be born by the OKH, which had ordered the reprisal activity of the previous December 12. The military government would supply the police escort. He asked Berlin that the trains carry freight cars, because it was easier to guard them. The departure station would be Paris North, and the deportees would arrive there from Compiègne and Drancy. Finally, he requested that the deportation take place as agreed, on March 23.[27]

Eichmann notified Rademacher about the deportation of the first thousand on March 9. Luther, Rademacher's boss, asked on March 11 for the position of the embassy in Paris. That same day Eichmann notified Rademacher that in fact an additional 5000 would also be deported. The embassy replied on March 14 that it had no reservations about the deportation of the first thousand, and two days later that it also did not oppose the deportation of the additional 5000. Rademacher notified Eichmann that there was no opposition to the deportation of 6000 Jews on March 20 – that is, eight days after Eichmann had already given Dannecker the go-ahead.[28] Dannecker knew of the embassy's consent, and mentioned it to Eichmann on March 17. Both agreed there was no reason to wait.[29]

That same day Dannecker notified the military government, basing himself on the previous decision, that their role in the operation would be to choose the Jews and to transport them to the train station.

27. TR.3-54; TR.3-693; Klarsfeld, *Vichy*, p. 376.
28. TR.3-177.
29. Klarsfeld, Serge (ed.), *Die Endlösung der Judenfrage in Frankreich*, 1977, p. 50. Signed by Lischka.

On March 20 Novak called Dannecker from Berlin and announced that the first train would depart only on March 28, and that it would be made up of passenger cars rather than the freight cars Dannecker had requested. Dannecker applied to the military government in an attempt to change the decision.[30]

In the final days before the deportation Dannecker held meetings with French police Captain André Tulard, and with Jacques Schweblin from the special Jewish Affairs police. He told them how to prepare the Jews for deportation. For example, the deportees were forbidden to carry metal items of any kind except spoons.[31]

The first deportation train, carrying 1112 Jewish men, departed from Compiègne on March 27, 1942. When it arrived at Auschwitz none of the men was sent directly to death, but despite this not one survived the war.[32]

There were many participants in this first death deportation. The Security Police began the preparations when they were still vaguely subordinate to the military government. By the time the first train left, everyone was already waiting for the new appointments and the reorganization of the forces. Hitler had already appointed Oberg, and Knochen and Dannecker knew that they were on the verge of being given much broader freedom of action. It was against this background that Dannecker and Knochen submitted a memorandum (on February 22) laying out plans for the future. It noted the success in the establishment of the Jewish council, the UGIF (a mandatory Jewish umbrella organization that succeeded the *Comite de Coordination*), and reviewed at length the establishment of a Jewish card file. The card file had been put together by the French police, and contained much data on the Jewish population. Dannecker saw the cooperation with the French police as important in carrying out the deportations – as they were in carrying out the three initial rounds of arrests.[33]

*

The activity of the Security Police in France is not a new story, and has been recounted elsewhere.[34] It can be summed up in two paragraphs.

---

30. TR.3-587, 1210, 1211.
31. TR.3-1213.
32. Klarsfeld, *Vichy*, p. 330.
33. TR.3-316.
34. Marrus and Paxton, op. cit.; Klarsfeld, op. cit.

With the approach of the beginning of the mass deportations it was necessary to impose a Jewish star; this was done with the change in the German administrative structure in France. In parallel, various preparations were made: trains, operational orders, preparation of absorption camps. In summer 1942 began the mass arrests and deportations to the East. They soon faced the problems of determining the extent of deportations; in other words, deciding what sectors of the Jewish community could be sent immediately. For example, it needed to be specified whether children could be deported, and under what conditions Jews with French citizenship could be included. When they were unable to meet the predetermined pace of deportations, ever-increasing endeavors were made to speed things up.

In 1943 they tried to return to the previous summer's accelerated pace, but without success. A huge effort was invested in attempts to broaden the circle of deportees, largely by changing the French law on the granting of citizenship, and by improving French cooperation. The Italian administration in southeastern France created great complications by granting protection to the Jews there. From the end of 1943, in a race against time, most of the German effort was focused on capturing individual Jews. In summer 1944, as the Allied forces advanced through France, the Germans actually succeeded in speeding up the deportations.

The purpose of this description is to focus how and why decisions were made and policy implemented. Who initiated what and when? Was policy directed centrally from Berlin or by experts in the field, i.e. the Security Police officers in Paris? What obstacles had to be overcome to send Jews to their deaths, and what may be learned from this about the Nazis?

The decision to impose an identifying Jewish badge reached Western Europe from Berlin. The RSHA considered this a necessary condition for the beginning of deportations, making it more difficult for Jews to evade arrest. In Germany the badge was instituted about two months before deportations began; in the west it was done a bit earlier. Dannecker heard about it when he visited Berlin in March 1942. The badge under discussion was a Jewish star, which would be instituted in Belgium and Holland as well. Two weeks later he notified IV B 4 that no problems were expected in Holland and France, but that the head of the military government in Belgium, General Roder, refused to require Jews to wear a star unless he received an explicit order from his superiors.[35]

35. TR.3-1344, 20 March 1942.

Roder controlled two French districts, and Dannecker wanted the badge to be instituted in all of France simultaneously.

Dannecker wrote the document, but Knochen signed it. This procedure would become entirely routine at the French Security Police station, but in parallel there were many messages that Dannecker or his replacement, Röthke, signed themselves. The explanation in this case may be found at the end of the document, where Dannecker/Knochen emphasized the importance of unity in this matter in all countries of Western Europe, and asked Eichmann to arrange that Roder receive appropriate orders. In order to get such senior officials to act, it was necessary to have the signature of the senior officer, Knochen.

In France the decision ran into difficulties as well. In mid-April Dannecker and members of the embassy staff discussed the possibility that the French would pass a law requiring marking of Jews. Those present were doubtful.[36] At the beginning of May Knochen discussed the issue with Abetz, who was convinced that the measure was essential. The next day Zeitschel, Abetz's subordinate, wrote to Dannecker, Knochen's subordinate, and spurred him to mark the Jews as soon as possible. Unusually, Dannecker was not carried away with enthusiasm, and commented that it would be better to wait until the technical preparations were completed.[37] A week later Dannecker and Knochen notified Berlin and the outlying stations in France of their intention to use a set of regulations to label Jews. As in the previous year in the Reich, it was decided that exemptions would be given to Jews from foreign countries after the issuing of the regulations, but not as part of them.[38]

The last two weeks of May saw a lively correspondence on the subject. Exchanges within the military administration spoke of the need to prepare the French population through appropriate propaganda. Dannecker, this time without Knochen's cover, sent to Berlin and the outlying stations the detailed wording of the regulations awaiting publication. The regulations themselves were issued over the signature of the military governor on May 28, to take force on June 7.[39]

France is not Germany, and the reactions to the star were different, as Knochen reported when he signed a letter by Heinz Röthke (who would later replace Dannecker). Most of the French populace was

36. TR.3-444, 17 April 1942.
37. Klarsfeld, *Frankreich*, p. 55, 3 and 4 May 1942.
38. TR.3-1357, 9 May 1942.
39. Klarsfeld, *Frankreich*, pp. 60–1; TR.3-1358, 14 May 1942; Klarsfeld, *Vichy*, p. 378.

apathetic, the letter stated, and many opposed it – some openly, for example by wearing badges in identification with the Jews. Only the antisemitic camp was cheering. Knochen concluded his report by reiterating additional restrictions expected in the future.[40] Paris was notifying Berlin, rather than the opposite.

While it is difficult to find ideology in the messages of busy bureaucrats, it is not impossible. In the spring of 1942, during the preparations for the large death deportations, Lischka signed a letter of Dannecker's to Zeitschel. They refused to free a certain Jew who had been arrested, and stated that in future there would be no exceptions which might be interpreted as German weakness. "An impression is liable to be given that there are among the Germans no enemies of the Jews except Hitler."[41] The tone of the document is clear: most of us hate Jews; it is important for the French to understand this, so that they know how to work with us.

In the middle of May Dannecker scored an impressive success, a real coup – he was received for a conversation with the military commander for rail affairs, Lieutenant-General Kohl. Captain Dannecker spent an hour and a quarter with the general, briefing him extensively on the new policy against the Jews, and was pleased to discover that the general was a sworn antisemite. Kohl wholeheartedly supported the plan to deport all Jews to their deaths (so it says explicitly in German: *restlose Vernichtung*), and promised to supply as many trains as needed. That same day Dannecker/Lischka cabled to IV B 4 about their impatience; the general's generosity should be exploited at once. While the capacity of the camps was not large and it would be necessary to conduct additional raids, 5000 Jews should be taken now.[42] General policy was dictated from Berlin, but the men in the field needed no prodding. If they needed anything from Berlin, it was precise instructions for implementation, not general guidelines. Failure of deportation trains to run at this time was because of lack of capacity in the camps or other considerations in Berlin, not because of foot-dragging in France.

On June 11, 1942 there was a meeting in Paris of Security Police

40. Klarsfeld, *Vichy*, pp. 382–3, 17 June 1942; and see also ibid., p. 384, Röthke to Knochen on the large number of Jews who refrained completely from equipping themselves with stars.
41. Klarsfeld, *Frankreich*, p. 53, 3 April 1942.
42. TR.10-878, pp. 147–8. The meeting with Kohl took place on 13 May 1942, and Dannecker reported on it on 15 May 1942.

representatives there with colleagues from Brussels and The Hague, with Eichmann participating. Eichmann informed them that, for technical reasons, it would not be possible to deport Jews from the Reich during the summer, and therefore Himmler had ordered the deportation of Jews from Romania and Western Europe for labor in Auschwitz. The deportees must be fit for work, between the ages of 16 and 45. It was decided to deport 15,000 Jews from Holland, 10,000 from Belgium, and 100,000 from France.[43] Dannecker had long been readying himself for this moment, and even asked that the process be expedited. This is an example of an initiative from below drafted in the form of an order from above.

The next day Dannecker realized that his great coup with General Kohl was not so great. Unexpected problems prevented the general from supplying trains.[44] But the cat was already out of the bag, and now that a decision had been made they did not allow contingencies to interfere with it. If the men in Paris could not supply the trains themselves, the central office in Berlin would take responsibility. The day after Dannecker's notification (and confession) of his inability to obtain trains without help from Berlin, he prodded Novak. Three thousand Jews were "ready to march," he said, as if they were setting off on a military operation – when a bureaucrat like Dannecker felt contempt or repugnance, it was evident in cables that ostensibly dealt only with business matters. His pressure paid off when Eichmann replied the next day (June 18) in a cable to Knochen (more accurately, Novak wrote to Dannecker, using Eichmann's and Knochen's signatures) with the dates of three deportation trains that would set out during the next ten days.[45]

At the beginning of June Dannecker wrote of the necessity of having the French pass a law like Germany's regulation 11, revoking the citizenship of Jews who left France.[46] I have not, however, found any evidence that the subject was raised with the French. In any case the plans at this stage were to deport only Jews without French citizenship. On the other hand, preparations for deportation were made, of course, in

43. TR.3-585, Dannecker's summary of the meeting, written 15 June 1942.
44. TR.3-52, 16 June 1942.
45. TR.3-57. A second version, a note by Dannecker from the same day, cites the trains as coming from the French branch of the train company. Klarsfeld, *Vichy*, p. 383. One gets the impression that in both cities there were near-frantic attempts to find trains, and that the bureaucrats themselves were not always clear as to who was procuring, and who merely authorizing them.
46. TR.3-585.

coordination with the French. Many thousands of the Jews marked for deportation in the first wave resided in the Vichy, French-ruled zone. The Germans wanted the French Police to arrest them and send them to the German zone. In mid-June Knochen met on this matter with the French chief of police, René Bousquet. Dannecker, the expert, briefed his commander on points to be covered in the discussion – for example, he stressed making it clear to Bousquet that the detention camps established in the French zone should be concentration camps, not spas.[47] The meeting was not a great success, and Knochen recorded his impressions in the margins of Dannecker's recommendations: "Bousquet still has reservations. We pressured him."

The state of affairs during the second half of June 1942 was as follows: The officers of the Security Police were occupied with preparations for the mass deportation of the Jews from France – deportations which had not yet begun and whose problematic nature they themselves may not yet have realized. Their French colleagues also knew of the new policy, but had not yet formulated a clear position on implementation. In Berlin, Himmler issued instructions to Müller, and from him to Eichmann, to deport with all due speed all the Jews in France.[48] Nevertheless, the three trains approved at the end of June were assigned to carry to Auschwitz 3000 of the 5000 Jewish men whose deportation had been decided on at the beginning of the year. No practical action had yet been taken to capture additional large numbers of Jews, much less to deport them. The mass arrests and deportations began only in mid-July. In the weeks between the issuing of the orders and the beginning of implementation there was feverish, almost frenzied bureaucratic activity; many of the problems that would later slow the rate of deportation were already clearly noted during this period.

On June 16 Dannecker traced for himself what was to be expected. First the 26,000 Jews residing along the coast would be concentrated ("*konzentriert*"). The intention was to send 15 trains of 1000 Jews each within a few weeks; in parallel, at least 15,000 Jews would be concentrated in Paris. The French could be expected to supply additional thousands of Jews from the southern zone.[49] Ten days later, at a meeting with Bousquet's deputy Jean Leguay, the music was different. Leguay

47. Klarsfeld, *Vichy*, p. 381, 15 June 1942.
48. TR.3-59, 23 June 1942.
49. TR.3-873.

related that Bousquet would be coming to Paris in order to speak with Oberg. Dannecker understood this to mean that the French wanted to find a way to avoid providing Jews, and went on the offensive. There were clear orders to deport the Jews from the occupied zone, he said, and the French police would have to set up to handle this. As for the southern zone, that was another matter. The Germans were willing to take thousands of Jews, the French had to decide whether that interested them. When Leguay said that the whole matter went far beyond the law, Dannecker replied that the anti-Jewish laws should on no account be allowed to remain on paper only.[50]

Dannecker did not discount the difficulties presented by the French position, and asked the embassy to put pressure on the Vichy government. Two days later he notified Leguay that he would conduct a roundup of Jews in France even without French consent, but he asked for 2500 uniformed policemen to assist him. At this point he was informed that Eichmann was about to arrive in Paris.[51]

On June 30, 1942 Dannecker assembled his experts from the field stations for a briefing. Since the first stage would be the deportation of the Jews from the provinces, he told them, they must quickly report on the number of Jews in their regions. Since the French were slowing things down, it was essential that the Security Police take the initiative and make no compromises.[52] After briefing his subordinates, he also briefed his commander, Eichmann. They did not anticipate problems in deporting the Jews in the occupied area, but were concerned that the French government was evincing increasing opposition to taking Jews from the area under its control. The two of them agreed that the foreign ministry should intervene. The embassy staff, which had previously exhibited a certain enthusiasm for deporting the Jews, was of the opinion that it was actually preferable to begin by deporting non-French Jews, implying that Jewish citizens of France should not be deported at all. The transportation directorate, on the other hand, approached Knochen that

---

50. TR.3-1525, 26 June 1942.
51. TR.3-1069s, 27 June 1942, 29 June 1942; TR.3-58.
52. TR.3-59. One can safely assume that, had Dannecker ever been brought to a postwar trial, he would have claimed that he was merely following orders — obviously.

same day and offered its assistance in preparing trains for the deportation of 40,000 Jews.[53]

On July 2, 1942 there was a meeting between Bousquet and senior figures in the German Security Police – Oberg, Knochen, Lischka, Hagen and others. Bousquet related that Pétain and Prime Minister Laval were not interested in having French policemen arrest French Jews in the occupied zone, or any Jews at all in the southern zone. The atmosphere was tense, and Knochen voiced an implied threat that the Führer would not accept such a position. Bousquet beat a partial retreat and agreed to joint action against non-French Jews in both parts of the country.[54] This could be seen as a harbinger of the future: the French had their own ideas on the use of their policemen, and they were not willing to harm Jews who were French citizens. The Germans also compromised, and in exchange for French cooperation in the deportation of foreign Jews, they gave up (only two weeks before the operation began) on deporting French Jews. They would later regret it.

On July 4 Dannecker briefed Knochen in advance of another meeting with Bousquet. The topics were: 1. A complaint against French delays. 2. The French must understand that their policemen in the northern zone were subordinate to the HSSPF, even if he ordered the arrest of French Jews; the Germans for their part were prepared to make do with the arrest of Jews who had become citizens after 1919. 3. The French were to provide detailed information on the number of Jews under arrest in the southern zone. After the meeting, Dannecker summed up what had been accomplished. Bousquet, he wrote, tried to suspend all activity by waiting for future legislation, but the Germans did not consent to this; after being pressured, Bousquet agreed to cooperate in turning over to the Germans non-French Jews arrested in the southern zone. Later in the day Knochen met with Laval himself, and they endorsed the agreement. Dannecker was quick to report the achievement to Eichmann, it was now permitted to deport all stateless Jews from both parts of France. He acknowledged that this was less than satisfactory, given that it was impossible for the time being to deport naturalized French Jews. The next day he sent a report to the military governor and to other high-level

53. Dannecker: TR.3-59, 1 July 1942; Embassy: TR.3-438, 2 July 1942; Train authorities: TR.10-854, 2 July 1942.
54. Klarsfeld, *Vichy*, pp. 393–6.

German figures in Paris, but since they would hardly be impressed by a report from a mere captain, Knochen signed it.[55]

A little surprise awaited Dannecker during this day of discussions. When he demanded in the morning meeting that the French establish a permanent coordination committee with which he could work, Bousquet agreed, and determined that a representative of the Commissar for Jewish Affairs would head it. Dannecker took note of the reaction of the Commissar, Louis Darquier de Pellepoix, to the new authority that had devolved on him. He looked devastated.[56] Dannecker could hardly comprehend that a man – especially a known Jew-hater – might be reluctant to be an accessory to murder.

Once the immediate goals were agreed upon, Dannecker proceeded to the planning of the first large action. He held a meeting with a number of French officials, including Darquier and Leguay. It was concluded that 22,000 Jews would be arrested in Paris. Within two days (by July 10) the commanders of the different quarters of the city would be given cards on the Jews in their districts from the central Jewish card file; the cards of those who were not arrested would be returned at the end of the operation. The beginning of the roundup was set for Monday morning, July 13. The prisoners would be brought to the Vélodrome d'Hiver hall and from there would be divided between the Drancy, Pithiviers, Compiègne and Beaune-la-Rolande camps. One deportation train would depart from each camp each week, and Dannecker also provided briefings on the trains.[57]

On Saturday, July 11, there was another German–French meeting. The action was postponed to July 16, after Bastille Day. An estimated 24,000 to 25,000 Jews were to be arrested, and their deportation was to begin no later than July 22. The longest section in the minutes of the meeting dealt with pails that were to be put on the trains; the Jews, through UGIF, were to supply 800 of them, 40 for each train. Department IV J considered issuing additional instructions about this. I do not know why this intense preoccupation with pails, but it demonstrates that all those participating in the meeting clearly understood how horrible the conditions on the trains would be.[58]

---

55. Klarsfeld, *Vichy*, p. 397; TR.3-318, 6 July 1942; TR.3-261, 6 July 1942; TR.10-878 pp. 80–2, 400, 7 July 1942.
56. TR.3-318, 6 July 1942.
57. TR.3-699, 8 July 1942.
58. Marrus and Paxton, *Vichy*, p. 249; TR.3-1349.

The high period of deportations from France was July 17 till late November, during which thirty-eight of the total seventy-three trains departed. It was during this period that the Germans came close to the target they had set at the beginning of the year – to deport 40,000 Jews from France. On the face of it, this would seem to have been a success for the SS, in cooperation with all the other German bodies that took part in the operation, and of course the Vichy government and police. This is the story recounted by historians.[59]

The version is correct with regard to the Germans. French collaboration was, however, less unequivocal and more complex. From the moment the possibility of mass deportation was first raised, months before implementation began, the French had reservations. They did not demand that it not be done at all, but were consistently reluctant to take part. In a series of meetings at a wide range of levels, meetings at which the SS men sometimes used threatening language, a certain (temporary) measure of French consent crystallized, in parallel with a certain (temporary) measure of concession on the part of the SS. In mid-July the French were prepared to participate in the arrest, concentration and deportation of non-French Jews from the occupied zone; the fate of the non-French Jews in the free zone was somewhat more vague, and Jewish citizens of France seemed to be protected from deportation throughout France.

Only a few senior French officials discussed the deportation of the Jews. Did they know that deportation meant death? That is hard to determine. From the middle of July 1942, however, a large number of Frenchmen were involved in the deportation operation – policemen, camp guards, transportation workers and the civilian environment. It would be hard to state that, at least during the initial weeks, these people were aware of the full significance of what they were doing. Their willingness to be accomplices would seal the fate of tens of thousands of Jews.

On Sunday, July 12, the bureaucrats rested. All the details had been agreed upon, all the arrangements had been made; ahead of them was the first week of the actual liquidation of French Jewry. And Dannecker was not there.

Knochen – and Hagen, and Oberg – were looking for a way to

---

59. TR.10-878, p. 44; Marrus and Paxton and, of course, Klarsfeld. Richard Cohen, on the other hand, although his subject is somewhat different, portrays Vichy's position in a rather more complex way.

get rid of Dannecker, whose methods were too extreme for their tastes. He put the deportation of the Jews above all else, and had no compunctions about making baseless threats against the French. His superiors preferred to carry out the same policy without creating friction with the French. Once, when Dannecker asked Knochen to check to make sure that the French understood that they were subordinate to the Germans, Knochen responded with evident impatience: "Why all this endless nitpicking?"[60] During the second week of July it was decided that the detention camps in southern France would be examined to estimate the number of deportable Jews they held. The German representatives would be Dannecker and his deputy Ernest Heinrichsohn, accompanied by Schweblin, the French police officer in charge of Jewish affairs, whose own standing in the eyes of his superiors was shaky at the time.[61] Dannecker could not refuse to take on such an important mission, but it meant that during the entire week of the great raid, the pinnacle of all his efforts, to use language that might sound high-flown but is firmly grounded in reality, he had to be far from where the action was.

Dannecker's place in Paris was taken by his new deputy, Heinz Röthke. Röthke arrived in the IV J office on June 1 from his previous position as an official in the administration at Brest.[62] He was supposed to assist Dannecker, but during the course of July he proved that he was capable of replacing him, and Dannecker was rotated out of France in August.

This change is interesting, and its timing even more so. First, because Eichmann was not able to protect his old colleague and friend – when the senior officials in France wanted him out, he was out, and replaced with a new and unknown man. This would hardly have been a reasonable scenario had Eichmann been the omnipotent mover of the Final Solution – as he in fact was not. There is another point, however, which is important. Dannecker had been located in Paris from the beginning of German rule there, and for two years had labored to advance a policy he had been planning as early as the fall of 1937 – the removal of the Jews from their homes and their deportation. Yet even

60. Klarsfeld, *Vichy*, p. 132; TR.3-698, 8 July 1942.
61. Klarsfeld, *Vichy*, p. 403. Regarding Schweblin, see Marrus and Paxton, *Vichy*, p. 245. Heinrichsohn had been a law student in Berlin and was sent to Paris in 1940. He had worked under Dannecker since then. He was 22 years old. Klarsfeld, *Vichy*, p. 593.
62. Klarsfeld, *Vichy*, pp. 63, 133–4.

though this had been his personal project, when circumstances demanded, it was possible to find him an anonymous replacement from outside the system who arrived, learned the material, and did the job – at the climax of activity and its most sensitive moment, the beginning – without the actual accomplishment of the mission being affected in the least. If one were to read the documents from this period while ignoring the symbols of the authors, there would be no way of noticing that Dannecker was out and Röthke in. This is anonymous bureaucracy at its purest. Or does it indicate something else – a large pool of antisemitic Nazis from which it was possible, without difficulty, to find a replacement for someone who had been removed? Is this a universal phenomenon that says something about officials, or a singular phenomenon that says something about the Germans of the period?

Röthke's first days on the job were devoted to an attempt to keep up the pace of deportations that had been decided upon, despite the restriction that only stateless Jews be deported (in fact, there were a large number of these, mostly Jews who had been stripped of their citizenship when they fled Germany). On July 14 he cabled the camps outside of Paris: "Since it is permitted to deport only the stateless, notify me urgently how many of these there are in your districts."[63] He notified Eichmann that this change was making it so difficult for him that he had canceled the departure of a train from Bordeaux scheduled for the next day, and had postponed the departure times of two additional trains. In the future, he promised, he intended to keep to the established train schedule, but there might well be changes in the departure stations.[64]

Eichmann's reply was not long in coming. That same day he telephoned Röthke in a rage. Such great efforts had been invested in obtaining trains, he thundered, and here the men in Paris were giving up one of them with apparent ease. Such a thing had never happened before. In such circumstances, he would have to consider halting the deportations from France. Röthke, apparently shaking in his boots, responded that it was not his fault, and that it would not happen again. In the memo on the conversation that Röthke recorded afterwards, he referred to Eichmann as "Dr Eichmann."[65]

This incident is familiar, and has been described in the literature as

63. Klarsfeld, *Vichy*, pp. 405–6.
64. TR.3-705.
65. TR.3-60.

a demonstration of Eichmann's centrality and power in the deportation of the Jews.[66] But anyone who is acquainted with the way the Security Police worked knows that Eichmann had no way to carry out his threats. Beyond this outburst of anger, which may have been sincere and may have been for show, all it did was make clear to the men in Paris that their excuses would not be accepted and that they had to carry out the mission. There may also be a link between this incident and Dannecker's departure. From Eichmann's point of view, the first thing that Röthke did as Dannecker's replacement was cancel a deportation train. Precisely because Eichmann knew that he could not keep Dannecker in Paris against Knochen's will, he had to make the rules of the game clear to Röthke. The threat to halt the deportation of the Jews of France could frighten only a person who did not know the system, a person who granted the uneducated Eichmann the title of "Dr," and who was prepared to believe also that a lieutenant colonel, simply because he worked in Berlin and traveled around Europe as Heydrich's representative, was capable of deciding which Jews would be deported from which countries. Beyond the terror that Eichmann caused Röthke, he also appealed to his sense of responsibility towards his mission, and to their common interest in getting rid of the Jews.

Support for this interpretation can be found in two additional facts. First, the minute that Dannecker returned to Paris he called Eichmann and assertively defended Röthke[67] – which means that had Dannecker canceled the train, Eichmann would not have called to threaten him, or that the threats would not have made an impression. The second fact is that there is no indication that Eichmann took the matter up with Knochen and, had Eichmann really been thinking of a change in policy in France, he would have discussed the matter with Knochen, not with Röthke. The purpose of the entire exercise was to make an impression on Röthke.

Before dawn on Thursday, July 16, 4000 French policemen set out to arrest 25,000 Jewish residents of Paris in accordance with the cards they had been given from the central card file. The operation was directed by the French police, under the supervision of the German Security Police

---

66. G. Hausner, *Justice in Jerusalem*, New York: Schocken, 1968, p. 106 – but Hausner's description is repeatedly inaccurate. Hilberg, *Destruction* (1961 edn), p. 407, cites this case, but refrains from comment. Arendt, *Eichmann*, shows the best intuition on this point, when she refers to Eichmann's behavior as "a farce," pp. 163–4.
67. Klarsfeld, *Vichy*, pp. 406–7.

– not just IV J.[68] Many Jewish men had gone into hiding in the mistaken assumption that this time, as in the raids of the previous year, only men would be taken. Beginning at 9 a.m. hourly reports of the number of people arrested were made. The operation lasted until 5 p.m. and 11,363 Jews were arrested, most of them in the morning. The action was renewed the next day, but far fewer were arrested – only 1521, for a total of 12,884. Of these, 3031 were men, 5802 were women, and 4051 were children.[69] This was the largest roundup in France during the entire war, but it captured only half of the planned number. One reason was, as noted, that the men fled. Another was that many French policemen appeared in Jewish homes twice – first to give warning, and afterwards in order to find no one home.[70]

Röthke summed up the operation for Knochen the day after it ended, on Saturday July 18. He blamed the small number of people arrested on advance leaks from the French police, and on warnings given during the operation by the policemen making the arrests. He acknowledged, however, that it had not been possible to find a single policeman engaging in such activity. In his opinion, the great identification with the Jews by the French population helped many Jews. Röthke also prepared a second, less detailed report for the military administration. Lischka signed it.[71]

In discussing deeds of an especially criminal nature, one naturally concentrates on crimes committed against the weak – and who is weaker than children? This is not the place to determine whether the murder of a child is a greater crime than the murder of an adult, but we do not relate to the deeds in the same way. For this reason, descriptions of atrocities,

68. See testimony of Kurt Wiedemann, NCO in VI: ZSL 104 AR-Z 1670/61 Bd.XIII, p. 2884. Klarsfeld, *Vichy*, pp. 119–22.

69. Marrus and Paxton, *Vichy*, p. 251.

70. I received interesting food for thought on the events of this day from a conversation I held in my office at Yad Vashem in September 1993 with Mr Serge Rodgold. Mr Rodgold was a boy in Paris in July 1942. His father had been arrested before the action, and he was left at home with his mother and sisters. French policemen visited their apartment twice, but the second time Rodgold and his family were with their neighbors, and so were saved. When I asked him whether he did not appreciate this action on the part of the French police, he responded in the negative. "If we had not hidden with the neighbors, but instead waited in our apartment, they would have arrested us without any pangs of conscience and have sent us to Drancy and from there to our deaths, as they did with the others," he said. This, too, it must be admitted, is a realistic view.

71. Klarsfeld, *Vichy*, pp. 409–11.

including those of the Nazis, often focus precisely on atrocities against children. If a special discussion was conducted on the fate of the children – as was done in France in the summer of 1942 – that does not surprise us: We expect murderers to treat children differently from their parents. Alternatively, had the treatment not differed, we would see that as a clear example of base immorality. In this sense, attitudes towards children are a kind of litmus test whether a shred of humanity remains in bureaucrats who devote most of their time to devastation.

Dannecker was the first to bring up the subject of the children, in the middle of June, during the preparations for the deportation operation. He proposed to Knochen that the operation be called the "resettlement of the Jews." Under such a rubric, he said, entire families could be deported, or children not deported with their parents could be sent later. A practical proposal on the deportation of children (from the southern zone) together with their parents was put forward not by Dannecker, but in fact by Laval, on July 4. On July 6 Dannecker asked Eichmann for instructions, proposing that children be added beginning with the fifteenth deportation train. Eichmann did not respond, and Dannecker tried again, this time with hard data – in the coming action, he wrote, it was expected that 4000 children would be arrested (almost precisely the number that were in fact captured). The French Jewish welfare organizations could not take care of more than a tenth of these. Accordingly, he requested an urgent reply: was it permitted to deport children, beginning with the tenth (no longer the fifteenth) shipment?[72]

When any such initiative reached Eichmann from his forces – in this case, from France – his practice was to submit the matter to his superiors in order to receive approval and cover for his subsequent actions. The decision on the deportation of children from France apparently had serious implications, and Gestapo commander Müller did not want to decide by himself, either. He passed the decision on to Himmler (Heydrich had recently been assassinated).[73] The answer was slow in coming. The delay was the subject of no little correspondence and, most importantly, it caused inestimable suffering.

The day after the big roundup Röthke sent a telegram to Berlin. There were 4052 children under arrest, he stated, and we are awaiting

---

72. First mention by Dannecker, 15 June 1942: TR.3-873; Laval: Klarsfeld, *Vichy*, p. 123; Dannecker (6 July 1942): TR.3-261; Dannecker (10 July 1942): TR.3-64.
73. Eichmann, *Interrogation*, II, p. 702.

your decision. When he briefed Knochen on the same matter, Knochen was actually of the opinion that the RSHA had already approved the deportation of children; nevertheless, they continued to wait. Another day passed, and Eichmann said to Dannecker by phone that the approval of the deportation of children would arrive.[74] But the written order had still not arrived two weeks later. In the meantime, it had been necessary to keep up the pace of the deportations. From a telegram Röthke sent to the top officials at the Pithiviers and Beaune-la-Roland camps it is clear that he knew that the deportation of the children was only a matter of time, but he nevertheless ordered that they be separated from their parents if this was necessary to keep up the pace of the deportations.[75] This should cast entirely new light on the claim of these officials, after the war, that they did nothing they were not ordered to do.

Those who insist on seeing these people as "just bureaucrats" should take a careful look at this telegram and at the practical significance of the order it contains. They should ask themselves whether there is any similarity between this message and myriad other messages created by bureaucrats in the twentieth century. Can any bureaucrat initiate an order to separate children from their mothers so that the mothers could be sent quickly to their deaths, while the children would be sent to their deaths only after a few weeks of horror, all in order to stay on schedule? Do we have enough data to state that each of us could potentially act in this way, were we to be placed in the appropriate circumstances? Perhaps the opposite is true, and the willingness to act this way is the test that can be used to divide the bureaucrats of the world into different groups – a group that is able to act in such a way, and a group that is under no circumstances able to do so?[76]

The go-ahead to deport the children arrived from Berlin on August 7, but for some reason no action was taken on it.[77] Maybe even they needed a special dose of evil to push them over the edge into yet greater moral corruption? On August 11 they asked for additional

74. Röthke: TR.3-1165; Knochen: Klarsfeld, *Vichy*, p. 410; Eichmann: TR.3-65, 20 July 1942
75. TR.10-878, p. 138, 30 July 1942.
76. Billig chose to end his book on the Final Solution in France with testimonies about the transfer of the children through Drancy, immediately prior to their deportation to Auschwitz. The very reading of the descriptions is emotionally difficult. Josef Billig, *Die Endlösung der Judenfrage in Frankreich*, New York: Beate Klarsfeld Foundation, 1979, pp. 219–25.
77. Klarsfeld, *Vichy*, p. 432.

approval, which arrived on August 13.[78] Between August 13 and August 17 about 3000 children were brought from the Pithiviers and Beaune-la-Roland camps to Drancy so that they could be deported from there on trains, together with adults, to their death at Auschwitz. On August 17, 1942 the first train carrying children set out – 323 girls and 207 boys, all under the age of 16. Packed into the cars, they crossed Europe over the space of two days until they arrived at Auschwitz. Eight hundred and seventy-six of the passengers on the train were murdered on the day they arrived at Auschwitz; one adult man remained alive at the end of the war.[79] The final document dealing with the subject is a French one. On August 18 Bousquet told the provincial commanders in the free zone to deport Jewish children between the ages of two and eighteen.[80] The fact that they were Jews was more important than the fact that they were children.

To the best of my knowledge, no comparative study has yet been done on the subject of the persecution of children in the context of comprehensive political murder. Beria's thugs in Stalin's Soviet Union set up orphanages for the children of their victims; Pol Pot used children to murder other children in Cambodia. Rwandan murderers apparently specifically targeted children in the terrible spring of 1994. Yet not all of these examples can lead us to conclusions about bureaucrats, the subject of this study. What is especially important, however, is to comprehend the distinction between the claim that the Nazis were entirely and eternally unique and the very different claim that they were unusual, and that we cannot draw conclusions from them about all of us. The present study does not argue that they were entirely unique, but rather that they were unusual. Even if a few other examples are found of bureaucrats who conducted policies of methodically hunting down and murdering children, it would not be proof that all bureaucrats are capable of doing this. At most it can demonstrate that the Nazis were not the only exceptions.

*

There is no period for which the documentation is more detailed than June and July 1942, and it may be that this reflects the intensity of department IV J's activity leading up to the mass deportations. From this period through the liberation of France by the Allies the men of the

---

78. TR.3-712; TR.3-1212.
79. Klarsfeld, *Vichy*, pp. 149, 330.
80. Klarsfeld, *Vichy*, p. 435.

department occupied themselves with deporting Jews – making arrests, coordinating trains and sending them off. There is not much to be learned from the routine activity of sending trains, precisely because it was routine. The subject of obtaining and coordinating the trains is interesting because it allows us to follow the relations between the field office in Paris and the central office in Berlin, and so to learn about the source of the initiative at various ranks. Another major field of action in 1942–3 was the problematic relations with the French, and especially the growing obstacles that the French placed in the way of the Germans – obstacles that became much more serious after the Italian army entered the picture in November 1942.

On July 19, 1942 Dannecker returned from his tour in the south and called Eichmann in order to defend Röthke's decision to cancel the deportation train the previous week. He blamed the failure on Knochen, since in accepting Bousquet's demand not to deport French Jews he had created a new situation and thereby sabotaged the entire conception that had guided IV J. It would seem from this document that the power of Knochen, the commander in the field, was greater than that of Eichmann in Berlin,[81] at least in the immediate range. However, one must be careful not to take Dannecker's claims too seriously, since he was on bad terms with Knochen. On the other hand, even with such a heavy accusation in hand, Eichmann was unsuccessful in preventing Dannecker's replacement.

Novak also joined the telephone conversation. He notified Dannecker that deportation trains could not be sent to Poland before the end of August.[82] When it came to determining in principle whether trains could be sent at all, Novak in Berlin was the man who saw the general picture, and was, if not the man who made the decision, at least the one who provided the information, as far as the representatives in France were concerned. When the deportations were renewed in August, Röthke discovered that no one was willing to provide the escorts. The Paris headquarters notified him that the Field Gendarmerie would not escort deportation trains any more, and that the job should be assigned to the Order Police. Röthke went to meet representatives of the Order Police,

81. TR.3-65; This is the conclusion arrived at by the prosecution in the case against Lischka, TR.10-878, pp. 82–3.
82. TR.3-65.

who told him that escorting trains was not their job but that of the gendarmerie. Röthke, exasperated, went to Dannecker, who had been temporarily stationed in Dijon, and asked him for policemen to escort a train from the free zone. But these were marginal problems that did not interfere with the implementation of the deportations. That very same day (August 21, 1942) Röthke asked the RSHA for the train schedule for the month of October, so that he could plan accordingly.[83]

Back in June, before the deportations, Dannecker had believed it would be better to use freight cars, which required fewer escorts. A telegram from Berlin on this matter reached Paris on July 23, at the time when prisoners from the big roundup were being deported. Eichmann was signed on it, but apparently it was Novak who wrote it; it was addressed to Knochen, but it was really intended for Dannecker. The RSHA's position was that passenger cars also needed only an officer and fifteen police escorts, so there was no need to switch to freight cars.[84] Later, however, they did, and the subject was raised again towards the end of August, in two very strange documents that can be explained only by using the Orwellian concept of doublethink.

On August 26 Röthke prepared for his assistant, Sergeant Horst Ahnert, a list of points to be clarified in his upcoming visit to IV B 4 in Berlin. The list included requests to increase the pace of the deportations from Paris. The strange parts are items 3, 4 and 7. On the matter of the deportation trains from October onward, would it be possible to receive passenger cars? There would be children on the trains, and it would be cold. On the same matter, perhaps it would be possible to schedule the departures for somewhat later in the morning, since it would still be dark at early hours (item 3)? Yet the next item (4) seems to betray this ostensible concern for the children. Auschwitz is demanding that we send blankets and work shoes together with the deportees, Röthke wrote. We don't have any. Can we send them later?

Item 3 would seem to reflect some sort of humane concern. Item 4 can be read either way. It may reflect humane concern (blankets would be sent for the Jews as soon as possible) — or absolute cynicism (the Jews are going to die anyway, so it doesn't matter if the blankets arrive with them or not, but if Auschwitz needs blankets, we'll send some when we can).

83. Klarsfeld, *Vichy*, pp. 431, 437, 438; ZSL 104 AR-Z 1670/61, Bd.4, p. 83, 21 August 1942.
84. TR.3-709.

What does item 7 reflect? It required Ahnert to find out in Berlin what exactly was happening there. UGIF reported that Parisian Jews were receiving postcards from deportees – was this possible? (Because if the Jews were being sent to their deaths, how in the hell could they be sending postcards?)[85]

Ahnert returned with answers. Yes, it was possible to increase the pace of the deportations in September and October. No, it was impossible for the trains to leave later in the morning. If there was a problem in loading the Jews in the dark, load them on the day before and guard the trains. And Auschwitz insists that the equipment arrive with the deportees.[86] If Ahnert knew Stuschka's postcard hoax, he did not mention it.

What can be learned from these two documents? It would seem to me that even hard-hearted bureaucrats found it easier at times to make use of the ambiguity and euphemisms that were part of their craft in order to hide from themselves the full significance of their actions, precisely because of the dissonance between their comprehension deep down that their work was fundamentally wrong, and their duty to perform it.[87]

General guidelines, such as the categories of Jews that were to be deported, arrived from Berlin. At the end of August Heinrichsohn asked whether it might be possible to "dispose of" stateless Jews married to Aryans.[88] Since the deportations were limited to non-French Jews, they were looking for a way to exploit this category to its limits. This was a question of high policy, so it was referred to the RSHA. Another type of information that arrived from Berlin had to do with the basics of train schedules. One of the most significant things that Ahnert heard at the conference in Berlin was that no trains would be made available to the SS between November 1942 and January 1943.[89] In retrospect, one might have thought that the slowdown in deportations derived from the shortage of trains at the time of the Soviet siege of the German forces in Stalingrad – but that is not the case. SS officers knew about it months in advance.

The way in which quotas were filled was largely the

85. Klarsfeld, *Vichy*, pp. 441–2.
86. TR.3-142, 1 September 1942.
87. The other possible explanation – that they *really didn't know what was going on* – is simply untenable, and flies in the face of everything described here.
88. TR.3-61, 29 August 1942.
89. TR.3-142, 1 September 1942.

responsibility of the local Security Policemen. Sometimes there was a gray area. When Ahnert learned that it would not be possible to deport Jews starting in November, he did some calculations and found that at a rate of three trains a week, with 27,000 Jews already deported, it would not be possible to deport more than 52,000 of the 78,000 stateless Jews. It was thus necessary to increase the pace of the deportations so that a train set out each day from the middle of September. Ahnert initiated this change in the pace of the deportations, not Novak in Berlin. He referred his calculations and recommendations to Hagen, so that through him they would reach Oberg directly. It is hardly surprising, then, that Knochen was angry, and ordered that in the future anything meant for Oberg would go though him.[90]

Dannecker's removal did not end the tension between the Jewish affairs department and Knochen's headquarters. Time and again the department's men appropriated authority to themselves and acted independently. As Dannecker's removal proved, Eichmann was unable to protect them. But the repeated attempts of junior officials in the department to work directly with officials far senior to them indicate a high level of self-assuredness. This derived, apparently, from their intensive work on an issue that was so central to the Nazi regime and its ideology.

Within France the department's men had substantial power. When the need arose, Röthke could change points of departure for trains or send to his death the brother of Léon Blum, who had been France's premier before the war.[91] At the end of September he sent a train carrying only 211 Jews. It may be that he feared a run-in with Eichmann, or perhaps, as he claimed, he wanted to prove to the French that their efforts to stop him would be fruitless.[92] When 3000 Jews were concentrated in Drancy, but the order not to send trains was already ostensibly in force, Röthke asked for permission from Berlin to send four special shipments. An answer from Novak arrived three days later, signed by Günther. It approved the deportations, and coordinated the escort forces.[93] On November 5 Röthke notified Berlin of an additional train — without

90. TR.3-141, 3 September 1942.
91. Léon Blum: TR.3-37, 23 September 1942.
92. TR.3-272, 30 September 1942.
93. Röthke: TR.3-711, 30 October 1942; Novak: TR.3-1261, 2 November 1942.

asking for approval. Novak/Günther approved the train two days thereafter.[94]

Communication and coordination between Berlin and Paris were excellent. Basic implementation guidelines, time frames and categories of deportees were set in Berlin; in Paris, Security Police men oversaw the concentration of the Jews and the filling of the trains. Berlin and Paris collaborated in initiating the trains and there were no cast-iron rules — whoever saw a need for a train arranged one, and whoever was asked to approve approved. The military government received ongoing reports, and the foreign ministry kept things calm on the diplomatic front. In October it even happened that the embassy provided IV J with approval for the deportation of Jewish citizens of Greece residing in France.[95] It was not always clear which German body was providing policemen to escort the trains, but no train was ever delayed because of this.

If trains were delayed it was because of the French. Judging by Nazi documentation, most of the French authorities were less than enthusiastic about the policy, and all in all succeeded in slowing, restricting and curbing the extent of the deportations.[96] The subject preoccupied the Nazis from the time the deportations began, and as time passed it preoccupied them more and more.

Dannecker returned from his trip to southern France on July 19, 1942. He had found, of course, confirmation for his world view in the discovery that 85 per cent of the gamblers in Monte Carlo were Jews. He had been pleased to meet locals, including police officers, who were eagerly anticipating getting rid of the Jews. On the other hand, he was

94. Röthke: TR.3-258; Novak: TR.3-259, 7 November 1942.
95. Klarsfeld, *Vichy*, p. 472.
96. Richard Cohen, summarizing the story of the UGIF, sees two types of antisemites among the bureaucrats of Vichy — those who wished to reduce the Jewish presence in France while protecting the Jews from the extreme Nazi policies, and those who fully accepted the Nazi policies. Xavier Vallat represents the first type, and Cohen notes with some surprise that some Jews even regarded him as a philosemite. Darquier was of the second type. Richard Cohen, *The Burden of Conscience: French Jewish Leadership during the Holocaust*, Bloomington, IN: Indiana University Press, 1985, p. 187. Peschanski quotes a German bureaucrat named Dr Blanke who put his finger on the problem as early as 24 November 1941: "The main objection to M. Vallat is not his lack of energy concerning the Jews. ... What one may hold against him is that, in differentiating between the French and the Jews, he envisages a relatively large number of exceptions favoring Jews who are long-time French residents, war veterans, etc." Quoted in Denis Peschanski, "The Statutes on Jews," *YVS*, XXII, 1992, p. 74.

disappointed that so few Jews had been arrested. He had found that the French authorities were not even strenuously enforcing the French law of the beginning of October 1940, according to which non-French Jews were to be kept in camps.[97] In his next meeting with Bousquet, he pressed for another roundup, more successful than the first, asked for enforcement of the French law on the concentration of non-French Jews, and demanded that the French give up those Jews who had been naturalized since 1927, and perhaps even since 1919.[98]

A week later, on July 27, Röthke met with Leguay. They spoke about the transfer of three or four thousand Jews from the south to Drancy for the purpose of deportation, and the next day Leguay appeared in Röthke's office and explained that it would not be possible to keep up the pace and that the Jews were scattered through many towns. Röthke warned him that this was just the beginning, and that the French had to begin immediately to round up additional Jews. Röthke asked Knochen to work to speed up the change in the French citizenship law, which he wanted passed by the middle of August. Dannecker, efficient as always, proposed that the French pass a law similar to regulation 11 of the Reich citizenship law, so that the deportation of a Jew would automatically lead to the nullification of his citizenship.[99] From the Nazis' point of view, this was a good suggestion – but there is no sign that it was ever raised with the French. The Germans probably understood that the French would view such a proposal as an infringement on their sovereignty.

The level of the talks was raised two days later. Knochen, and perhaps Oberg as well, met with Bousquet. Bousquet actually approved the transfer of 3000 stateless Jews from the French zone, and was optimistic that the citizenship nullification law would get the support of Laval and Pétain, both of whom were interested in solving the Jewish problem.[100]

On August 3 the level of the talks was raised once again, with Knochen and his staff meeting with Laval and his advisers. As befits bureaucrats, Knochen arrived equipped with a list of demands prepared by a junior expert, Dannecker (who was still in his position at that time). During or after these talks Knochen scribbled comments in the margins of the document. Dannecker (in the preparatory document) took an

97. TR.3-706.
98. Klarsfeld, *Vichy*, p. 417, 21 July 1942.
99. Klarsfeld, *Vichy*, pp. 19, 423–4.
100. TR.10-878, p. 120.

aggressive line towards the prime minister of France. The train timetable for the deportations had been set already, he said, and could not be changed. If the French did not keep up the pace the Germans would have to deport French Jews from the occupied zone. The French police would have to become more efficient in capturing Jews. In the free zone it would be possible to stick to what had already been agreed and to deport all Jews who had illegally crossed the border between the zones. Knochen's marginal notes indicate that no special problems were raised in the conversation. The French remained consistent and preferred capturing stateless Jews to capturing those who had crossed the border. They raised no arguments against increasing the pace of deportations beginning in mid-August 1942. The Germans left the meeting with a sense that they had made it clear to Laval that this was an ongoing operation, and that in the end the Jews with French citizenship would also be deported.[101]

The Germans, however, knew their partners, and knew that without continuing pressure there would be no results. Röthke sent for Leguay on August 18 and impressed on him that all the trains planned for September would be leaving full, one way or another.[102] The Germans' arrogance, or perhaps their eagerness, led them to ignore proper protocol. On August 27 Heinrichsohn (a 20-year-old sergeant) met with Leguay and the director of his bureau, Thomas Sauts, and continued to apply pressure. Even Knochen, who is certainly not suspected of wanting to defend the Jews, was angered by this audacity and demanded that in future important matters be discussed on higher levels, and in coordination with him.[103]

The SS men grew increasingly impatient as the French continued to stall. At a conference in Berlin of IV B 4 representatives from the entire continent, on August 28, the representative from France was told that the rate at which the Jews were being removed from France was not sufficient, or as Röthke summed up for Knochen, "There is a lot of catching up to do before the end of October ... this is the Final Solution of the Jewish question in Europe, decided by the Führer and the Reichschancellor." Röthke attached a breakdown of the required rate of deportations, as well as a complaint that the French were not keeping up the pace. He cited, as an example, the raid that had taken place shortly

101. Klarsfeld, *Vichy*, pp. 427–8; TR.3-111, memo by Röthke, written a week later.
102. TR.10-878, p. 108.
103. Klarsfeld, *Vichy*, p. 443.

before in the free zone, in which only 7000 Jews had been arrested, apparently because many of the others had been warned in advance.[104]

Röthke put much hope in an expected meeting between Oberg and Laval. The outcome of the meeting seems to have been a disappointment. Laval asked that he not be presented with new demands on handing over Jews from the southern region, since he had run into difficulties from the church and other institutions. Oberg confirmed that there was no intention of making new demands. On the same day, Ahnert of IV J submitted a position paper to Hagen, with a request to notify Oberg that the situation was serious, and that without a change in the French position, including a revision of their citizenship law, it would not be possible to accomplish the task set by the RSHA.[105] And if Laval's position had not been difficult enough for the Security Police, Bousquet made it clear to Hagen that the French could not commit themselves to supplying Jews for the daily train from mid-September, as the Germans demanded.[106]

Towards the middle of September Röthke submitted several memos to his commanders in Paris. The French are not serious in their efforts to arrest the Jews, he wrote, are not keeping to the agreements, and even many non-French Jews in southern France have not yet been deported. Without a radical and immediate change, it would not be possible to keep up with the pace of deportations that had been set, despite the great efforts required to obtain trains.[107] It is interesting – and perhaps significant – that we possess no mention of any attempt by Röthke to get IV B 4 in Berlin to do anything about this serious problem. Does this indicate that Röthke was aware of the limits of their power? Even if HSSPF Oberg had already accepted the French position, wasn't there anyone in the RSHA who could change it? In any case, in the middle of the month Zeitschel concluded sadly that the pace of the deportations was about to slow down considerably.[108]

---

104. TR.3-315. Laval himself again demonstrated on this date that he understood what the deportations were about, when he asked Oberg to formulate a standard form of explanation, so that he could respond to the diplomatic inquiries he was receiving on the matter. He did not ask what was happening to the Jews, but instead what should be said was happening to them. It was decided to say that the Jews were being sent for labor in the Generalgouvernement. Klarsfeld, *Vichy*, p. 454.
105. TR.10-878, pp. 83–4; Klarsfeld, *Vichy*, pp. 451–2; TR.3-141, 3 September 1942.
106. Klarsfeld, *Vichy*, p. 455.
107. TR.3-1260; Klarsfeld, *Vichy*, pp. 459–61, 12 September 1942.
108. Klarsfeld, *Vichy*, p. 464.

In the light of the unsatisfactory cooperation of the French authorities, it was decided in IV J to conduct a large action against the Jews in Paris, according to a prepared list. The arrangements were made in detail, but were based on French policemen, about 3000 of them. Care was taken not to tell any of them, including their commanders, about the operation in advance.[109] At the last minute it was canceled, but a few days later, on September 24, 1594 Jews with Romanian citizenship were arrested, by French policemen.[110]

Knochen himself reported to IV B 4 towards the end of September. We tried to deport Jews who are French citizens, he wrote; the French authorities resisted, and the matter was discussed at the highest levels. Oberg accepted the French position, and the RFSS accepted his recommendation not to exert pressure on this matter because Pétain's position was uncompromising. This being the case, we have no choice but to satisfy ourselves with deporting Jews of other citizenships, which requires coordination with their governments. I request, he concluded, that the foreign ministry take care of the matter.[111] Two weeks later the Security Police stations throughout the occupied zone carried out a roundup of Belgian, Dutch, Romanian, Bulgarian, Yugoslavian and stateless Jews. There were no limitations on the age of the deportees, with the exception of the bedridden, who were transferred to Jewish institutions; a total of 1965 were arrested. Together with 650 who had been arrested before, they were deported on three trains.[112] A month later there was a special action to capture Jews of Greek citizenship, leading to 1060 arrests. Röthke asked Knochen to commend the French police. This time, it seemed, no one had leaked news of the action in advance. Knochen notified Bousquet.[113]

On December 19 Eichmann asked Knochen at what rate the deportations would be renewed during the first quarter of 1943. At the beginning of January there was supposed to be a meeting at the Ministry of Transportation, and such an estimate was vital in order to receive trains. It is interesting that the men in Paris did not rush to reply, and sent their answer only on December 31 – that is, at the last minute. Knochen's secretaries typed, Ahnert wrote, Röthke is recorded as responsible, and

109. TR.3-715, 16 September 1942; Klarsfeld, *Vichy*, pp. 465–6.
110. Klarsfeld, *Vichy*, p. 468, 24 September 1942.
111. TR.3-270, 26 September 1942.
112. TR.10-878, pp. 57–9, 5 October 1942.
113. Klarsfeld, *Vichy*, p. 473.

Knochen signed a vague telegram to Berlin that did not in fact respond to the question. It said that the deportations should be renewed in mid-February or the beginning of October, at an unspecified rate.[114]

In the light of the limited expectations, they switched to plans for limited deportations. The arrests of Jews in Paris and the provincial cities had never ceased, and in the middle of February Röthke and Knochen wrote to IV B 4. They noted that 1200 deportable Jews had been collected in Drancy, as well as more than 2000 French Jews who had been arrested for various infractions, and asked for permission to send a train or two to Auschwitz. Likewise, they asked for clarification on the issue of French Jews. Günther replied that the matter of the trains had in principle been coordinated with the Ministry of Transportation, but the precise dates would be coordinated in Paris. The Metz station would supply police escorts after receiving advance notice from Paris. He proposed including intermarried Jews on the trains with the criminals, since there was not permission to deport them directly.[115]

Röthke and Knochen wrote the next day to their men in the provinces and told them that, according to the instructions of the RSHA, two trains were about to leave. As many Jews as possible should be sent to Drancy, they ordered.[116] This is a clear instance of making a proposal, getting approval for it, and then acting "on orders." On February 3, 1943, Röthke coordinated by telephone with the Wehrmacht train directorate the assignment of two trains, for February 9 and February 11. The telephone call was confirmed in writing and the information was also provided to the Security Police in Metz. Two days later Knochen signed a letter to the commander of the Order Police in France, and asked for police escorts up to the border. The number of planned trains had in the meantime increased to three.[117]

It may well be that the Department of Jewish Affairs (whose name had in the meantime been changed from IV J to IV B) saw this activity as a possible turning point, an opening that would bring new momentum to the deportations. Röthke asked Berlin for permission to renew the deportations, and of course received it, on February 10.[118] On the other hand, at exactly the same time he wrote to the Seine district police and

114. Eichmann: TR.3-122; Knochen: TR.3-317.
115. Knochen: TR.3-260, 21 January 1943; Guenther: TR.3-1223, 25 January 1943.
116. Klarsfeld, *Vichy*, p. 479, 26 January 1943.
117. TR.3-274; TR.3-434.
118. TR.3-252, 10 February 1943.

asked them to arrest all deportable Jews. He pondered with Knochen the possibility of deporting hundreds of French Jews who had been detained since the end of 1941 at Drancy, since only with them could he fill the third deportation train. The problem was that the French police had made it clear that they would not cooperate with such a deportation.[119]

So as not to display any weakness to the French, the Germans decided to send the third train on February 13 in any case, even without French assistance, and for this purpose called in reinforcements from the German Order Police. The bluff, if that is what it was, succeeded, and when the French saw that the Germans were determined to go ahead, their policemen joined as well.[120]

After the concentrated effort of February 1943, the deportations ceased for a few weeks. Only twice more during the entire war did the Germans manage to send three or more trains in a single month. They never again approached the horrifying pace of thirteen trains a month, as in August and September 1942.[121] The French position prevented this. In a conversation between them, Eichmann demanded of, or notified, Knochen that Jews of French citizenship should be deported. Knochen responded by applying to Eichmann's commander, Müller, in order to explain to him what Eichmann apparently refused to understand. First of all, the French, Pétain at their head, he said, opposed deporting Jews who were French citizens, and would actively resist any such attempt. Second, the direction the war was taking was encouraging the French to toughen their position. They were no longer sure that the Germans would win, and in any case they could profit by an American victory, but not by a German one. Third, the Italians opposed the deportation of Jews, and were dragging the French along with them; in any case, so long as the Italian zone of occupation was safe Jews would continue to stream there to escape deportation.[122]

From the beginning of the deportations there was a difference between the French and the Germans. The French, some of whom were antisemites and others of whom were opportunists, were willing to deport Jews to an unknown but final fate, if this served their political or

---

119. Klarsfeld, *Vichy*, p. 485, 9 February 1943; TR.3-252. This situation partially explains the smugness with which Klaus Barbie announced his arrest of 86 Jews in Lyon. ZSL 114 AR 3616/65 BD.1, pp. 9–12.
120. TR.3-277, 12 February 1943; Klarsfeld, *Vichy*, p. 492, 16 February 1943.
121. March 1943: five trains; May 1944: three trains. Klarsfeld, *Vichy*, pp. 330–1.
122. TR.3-121, 12 February 1943.

other needs. On certain points, such as the subject of the deportation of children, they were even ahead of the Germans. Still, they could be dissuaded from the policy on many points. The opposition of the clergy dampened their enthusiasm; the German demand to transfer Jews (including non-French ones) from the free zone was seen by them as a threat to their sovereignty – not to mention the deportation of Jews who were French citizens, something they never agreed to. What they did not have was a general aspiration to get rid of the Jews in order to achieve some meta-historical objective. The story of the fate of the Jews of France illustrates the practical, indeed crucial, importance of this ostensibly academic distinction.

Historians such as Paxton, Marrus and Klarsfeld have rightly come out against the self-righteous French tone that placed all responsibility for the deportation of the Jews on the Nazis. But the real collaboration, at all levels, between French and Germans was limited. The two groups were not identical, neither in motives nor in behavior. The Germans' behavior was harsher, not only in distant Poland but also in Paris. The Italians, the Germans' allies, took an entirely independent line. As Knochen sensed, but still did not know, they were to become the major factor that sabotaged the deportation of French Jewry in 1943.

Just as Dannecker knew in advance that cooperation with the French would be problematic, Röthke knew in advance that the Italian position would be problematic. On August 21, 1942, he complained to the German embassy in Paris that the Italians were trying to protect their Jewish citizens in France against all German measures. He added insolently that because of their pro-Jewish position, he would in the future refuse to accept communications from them. Let them go to the embassy, not to him.[123]

In November 1942 the Germans took over the French areas that had until then been outside the military government, and the Italians also occupied an area in southeastern France. From this point onward the Germans could capture and deport Jews from southern France as well, without consideration of French sovereignty; on the other hand, the importance of the Italian position grew. This was, first, because of the fear that the Jews would flee to the Italian territory en masse, since there was no border between the two zones. Even more importantly, there was concern that the French would take advantage of the disagreements between their conquerors in order to take an independent position – that

123. TR.3-720.

is, in order to refrain from capturing Jews.

The Italians sabotaged the German efforts. To do so, they made efficient use of the Nazi bureaucracy itself – which applied itself at all levels to the attempt to remove the unexpected obstacle. This chapter of the story is important, then, not only because of the position taken by the Italians, but especially because of the behavior of Nazi bureaucrats.

On January 9, 1943 a memorandum was issued by Oberg's office in the wake of his previous day's conversation with Bousquet. The Italians, it stated, were making it difficult to round up Jews. Four days later Knochen himself wrote to Müller in Berlin. Leguay had informed him of the change in the Italian position – they did not care if the French police wanted to arrest French Jews, but they had better not touch any non-French Jew, Italian or otherwise. Knochen explained to Müller that this position not only protected too many Jews, but also made it difficult for the French to take action even against French Jews. Knochen was also able to relate that Daluege, who had recently been in France, was supposed to inform Himmler himself of this.[124] When the Nazis encountered a serious problem, they responded quickly, and at senior levels. This was not Röthke writing to Eichmann, but rather Knochen to Müller, and apparently Oberg writing via Daluege directly to Himmler.

No time was wasted in Berlin. Only three days later the German ambassador in Rome met with Italian Foreign Minister Galeazzo Ciano, who sidestepped giving an answer. The German embassy in Paris sent a detailed telegram of protest to Berlin.[125]

Oberg protested once again to Kaltenbrunner and Himmler on February 1. The next day Knochen signed a telegram prepared by Röthke, who had somehow obtained a secret report from the commander of the French police in Nice to Laval. The report described the aid the Italians were giving the Jews, and Röthke/Knochen asked Müller to translate it from the French and pass it on to Himmler in order to stress to him the serious nature of the problem. Another day passed and Röthke/Knochen asked Müller to enlist the senior military commander in the West to speak to his Italian counterpart.[126] In addressing this commander, they made use of security–military arguments to the effect that the Jews constituted a security threat – but they also cited the real argument: that Italian policy

124. Oberg: Klarsfeld, *Vichy*, p. 476; Knochen: TR.3-815, 13 January 1943.
125. Rome: Klarsfeld, *Vichy*, pp. 477–8; Paris: TR.3-726, 23 January 1943.
126. Oberg: Klarsfeld, *Vichy*, pp. 539–40; Knochen: TR.3-819, 2 February 1943, Klarsfeld, *Vichy*, p. 481.

was threatening to sabotage the execution of the Final Solution throughout France.[127] They assumed that such an argument would impress the general. On February 4 Knochen signed a long and whining letter of Röthke's to IV B 4, saying that the protection the Italians were giving the Jews was making a joke of the Nazis and their anti-Jewish policy.[128] It is almost entertaining to pick out from the unprecedented flood of senior-level messages from Paris to Berlin the question of the Security Police man in Marseilles, August Moritz, to Röthke: "It looks to us as if the Italians are forbidding the French in Nice to arrest Jews. Do you know anything about this?"[129] While the warning about the danger to the policy, like the impetus to action, went from Paris to Berlin and not vice versa, it was possible for German officials on the local level in France not to know anything about it.

From the beginning of February 1943, and perhaps long before, the top figures in the Rome regime knew the truth about the Germans' Jewish policy. A scholar who has carefully investigated their actions notes that this news contributed to shaping their policy, so that both considerations of Italian interests and clear reservations about the policy of murder were involved. Their goal was to save the Jews.[130]

The Italians played their cards well. They did not admit that they were conducting a deliberate effort to interfere with the German policy. Instead they promised over and over again to look into the matter, but in practice refrained from reporting on the results of their inquiry.[131] There also seem to have been Italian officials who evaded the Germans with the excuse that the complaints were unfounded, since in mid-February an order had been given (from the German embassy in Paris to the Security Police there!) to take action against the Jews in the southern regions, and to submit a detailed description should the Italians interfere.[132] We do not

127. TR.3-489, 3 February 1943.
128. Klarsfeld, *Vichy*, pp. 483 ff.
129. ZSL 114 AR 3617/65 Bd.1, p. 11.
130. Daniel Carpi, *Between Mussolini and Hitler: The Jews and the Italian Authorities in France and Tunisia*, Hanover, NH: Brandeis University Press, 1994, pp. 106–7, 130 and especially p. 133, where he quotes a document from 23 March 1943 that states unequivocally that the intention of the Italian policy is to save the Jews in the Italian zone in France, be their citizenship Italian, French or any other.
131. Achenbach of the embassy to Röthke, TR.3-487, 8 February 1943.
132. Achenbach to Röthke, 11 February 1943, Klarsfeld, *Vichy*, p. 488. And see ZSL 114 AR-Z 3616/65 Bd.1, pp. 14–15, Lyon to Paris, 20 February 1943; or Lischka to Knochen, 22 February 1943, Klarsfeld, *Vichy*, pp. 492–3.

possess all the documentation, but it is clear that after it was collected in Paris it was sent to Berlin, where it served as the raw material for a letter that was prepared by IV B 4, signed by Müller, and sent on to the foreign ministry on February 25. In that letter, Müller detailed five cases in which the Italians sabotaged German efforts, or the French refrained from acting on the grounds that the Italians were interfering.[133] Müller's signature was meant in this case only to impress the foreign ministry; he did not himself handle the matter, as may be learned from Eichmann's telegram to Knochen of the next day, which said that he (and not Müller) had given the information to the foreign ministry for the purpose of preparing a meeting between the two foreign ministers.[134]

A shred of hope was felt by the entire Nazi bureaucracy in France at the end of the first week of March, when their representative in Marseilles, Moritz, announced that the Italians were supposed to evacuate all the Jews from the coastal region into the interior.[135] Disappointment came two weeks later. While the Italians had indeed notified the German ambassador in Rome that the Jews had been evacuated, the consul in Marseilles reported that no change had occurred in the field.[136] The deluge of complaints from Paris against the Italians continued unabated, and Oberg spoke about this directly with Himmler during a visit to Berlin.[137]

On March 9, Ribbentrop sent his ambassador in Rome, Hans Georg von Mackensen, to Mussolini with a long message on the Jewish issue. It began with quotations and descriptions that clearly proved that Italian generals and officials were acting in contradiction of German policy in the Italian zone. Since Mussolini had given Ribbentrop to understand, on the latter's visit two weeks earlier, that he intended to cooperate with the Germans, Ribbentrop had three practical alternative suggestions on how to deal with the problem. First, the matter could be handed over to the exclusive purview of the French police. Second, the matter could be handed over to the Italian police and would be removed

133. TR.3-962, IV B 4/43g(81).
134. TR.3-697, 26 February 1943. The document reached Ribbentrop in Rome too late, as he had already discussed the issue with Mussolini. In the absence of concrete examples of Italian obstruction, his presentation had been rather lame, and Mussolini had brushed it aside. Carpi, *Italian Authorities*, pp. 116–28.
135. ZSL 114 AR 3617/65 Bd.1, p. 14, 6 March 1943. Röthke/Lischka notified IV B 4: Klarsfeld, *Vichy*, p. 502.
136. Röthke to IV B 4, signed by Lischka. Klarsfeld, *Vichy*, p. 507.
137. Klarsfeld, *Vichy*, p. 518.

from the army's hands. Third, the issue could be handed over to the German police, who would handle it with the French without involving the Italians at all. Ribbentrop concluded with a comment that Hitler himself was in the picture.[138]

The Nazis no doubt preferred the third option, but it never had a chance because it clearly violated Italian sovereignty. For this reason, Ribbentrop told Mussolini that he and Himmler preferred the second option. Or as some scholars have suggested, it may have derived from a complete misunderstanding of the Italian position.[139] Himmler and Ribbentrop were used to thinking that in a regime like theirs the police force was more reliable for carrying out ideological missions. If they gave any thought to the matter at all, it would have been to note that the same was true in the Soviet Union and to apply the rule to the Italian case as well, without knowing that the distinction was meaningless there.

It is ironic that it was German pressure that led the Duce to decide that the Italian police would handle the Jews in the occupied zone. When the Italian deputy foreign minister summoned the German ambassador on March 20 to inform him of this, he explained that the decision resulted from what had been learned from experience – that it was impossible to trust the French police to act properly against the Jews. It was better, he said, for the Italians themselves to do the job.[140] Here is an interesting case in which the documentation faithfully reflects the opposite of the truth. A senior police officer named Guido Lospinoso was named to oversee the activity.[141]

The archival research and writing of this book did not bring the author many light moments. If there was any relief, even of humor, it was supplied by the Lospinoso affair. Over the space of months, from April 1943 to the shattering of the Italian-German alliance in September, the Italians succeeded in duping the Nazi officials, as they took efficient – and comic – advantage of the Germans' bureaucratic work procedures. Beyond the breathing space it granted the Jews, the incident presents a challenge to those who would argue that bureaucracies are neutral bodies who do the work assigned them. The Lospinoso affair is an event in which two bureaucratic systems with very clear and opposite conceptions clashed. The story is the result of high awareness of

138. Carpi, *Italian Authorities*, p. 126.
139. Carpi, *Italian Authorities*, pp. 126–7.
140. Carpi, *Italian Authorities*, p. 134.
141. TR.3-727, 20 March 1943.

individuals, rather than of emotionless adherence to performing a task set by higher officials.

Lospinoso received his assignment – apparently in a very sketchy way – from Mussolini himself on March 19. It was to transfer the Jews from the coastal region to locations at least 100 kilometers from the sea. Within less than three days he arrived in Nice, set up his headquarters, and disappeared.[142] At least he did as far as the Germans were concerned.

On March 27 Müller, who seldom left Berlin, was received by Mussolini and asked how the matter would be handled. Mussolini promised cooperation between the two sides. When he returned to Berlin, Müller instructed Knochen to make contact with Lospinoso.[143] On April 5, after three days of searching, Knochen (himself, not Röthke) notified Müller that he could not find him. Two days later Müller asked once again what was going on. Before resuming discussions with the Italians, after all, he had to know whether Lospinoso was even in France, as the chief of the Italian police claimed.[144] The next day Knochen (in a letter by Röthke) wrote to Müller that Lospinoso had apparently returned to Italy. Before leaving he had left a list of questions with a captain named Francesco Malfatti di Montetretto, who was stationed in the Italian embassy in Paris. The questions had to do with German intentions against the Jews. Knochen expressed his position on the matter, or perhaps he signed a letter that expressed Röthke's opinion, which was that it seemed improper to conduct negotiations with a captain, especially given that they had been told to speak with Lospinoso. (This differed from the entirely routine procedure in which Röthke, who was merely a lieutenant, negotiated with French officials of much higher rank than he, such as Bousquet, the French police chief.) Knochen/Röthke added at the end of the letter that Malfatti claimed that the questions had reached him from his commanders in the army, not from Lospinoso.[145]

In an April 9 telegram to Knochen, Müller, in Berlin, stated that he had told the police attaché in Rome to ensure that Lospinoso come to

142. Carpi, *Italian Authorities*, pp. 137 ff.
143. Carpi, *Italian Authorities*, pp. 146–7; TR.3-820, 2 April 1943.
144. Knochen: TR.3-812; Müller: Klarsfeld, *Vichy*, p. 520, 7 April 1943. Francesco Malfatti di Montetretto.
145. Klarsfeld, *Vichy*, p. 581, 8 April 1943. And Carpi adds that, although no one knows who originated the questions, which dealt with past and present German policies towards the Jews, they clearly were not pertinent, and may have been a scam to keep the Germans away from Lospinoso for the time being. *Italian Authorities*, p. 149.

Berlin or make contact with Knochen immediately. Let's wait and see, he suggested.[146] While they waited, Knochen and Eichmann met, apparently in Paris, and discussed the matter.[147] Eichmann sent a message to the Italians via the foreign ministry, in which he proposed a personal meeting with Lospinoso in Paris. The Italians simply failed to respond.[148]

May 24: Röthke wrote a note to Knochen: a German officer named Gudekunst had spoken with Captain Malfatti, and Malfatti said that no one in the Italian embassy in Paris had heard of any plan of Lospinoso's to make a visit to the city. That same day Röthke prepared a letter on the matter to Müller in Berlin, signed by Knochen, stating that "the impression is that Lospinoso is using delaying tactics."[149]

Lospinoso was sighted for the first time on June 22, by the French. He arrived for a meeting with Bousquet and spoke with him about the plans to assemble the Jews. The plans did not win Bousquet's support, and Lospinoso said that if that was the case the Italians would have to continue to discuss the matter, in Italy. Bousquet spoke of this to the Germans, who were, of course, angry. Knochen expressed his incredulity and anger in an urgent telegram to Müller and Kaltenbrunner.[150]

At the end of June 1943 the only hope that SS officers still expressed was that it would be possible to persuade the Italians to halt the flight of Jews into the Italian zone of occupation.[151] Lospinoso's shadow began to darken the work of the local levels also, when an Italian official named Luceri Tommaso announced to the representative of the Security Police in Marseilles, Rolf Mühler, that it would be impossible to take any measures before clarifying the matter with Lospinoso.[152] Towards the end of July Röthke wrote a memo expressing his frustration. The Italians' behavior, he wrote, is harmful and unaffected at all by the fact that we have sent more than twenty reports on the matter to Berlin.

146. TR.3-822.
147. TR.3-826, p. 5, 28 April 1943.
148. TR.3-875. Memo by von Thadden, 1 June 1943.
149. TR.3-825, 826.
150. Klarsfeld, *Vichy*, pp. 536–7, 23 June 1943. It is interesting that we hear of many reports to Müller, and of some to Himmler, but only of a few to Kaltenbrunner. It may well be that the men in Paris had not yet decided how to relate to him – but it is surprising to discover that they were able to express their position in this way.
151. Klarsfeld, *Vichy*, pp. 537–8, 29 June 1943.
152. ZSL 114 AR 3617/65, Bd.1, pp. 19–20. Meeting of 7 July 1943.

Perhaps the commander of the Security Police (Kaltenbrunner) could do something?[153]

In August the Germans in Paris swallowed their pride and Hagen spoke with Malfatti. (This was an interesting choice: Hagen was of low rank – only one rank higher than Malfatti himself – but fairly senior in his job – or perhaps he was only supposed to look that way to Malfatti? Why was Röthke not sent to the meeting?) The Italian promised to convey to Rome the Germans' dissatisfaction.[154] In other words, the meeting failed, because it brought about no change.

During this entire period Lospinoso was in Nice, and labored in broad daylight to transfer Jews from the coastal region to abandoned hotels and confiscated private houses in the inland districts. He later claimed ingenuously that he had had no idea that the Germans were looking for him, but that can hardly be taken seriously.[155] For Lospinoso, ingenuousness was a sophisticated method for avoiding head-on collisions with those whose intentions were the opposite of his.

Then he appeared. Faithful to his methods, his appearance created at least as much chaos among the Germans as had his absence. He showed up in the office of the commander of the Security Police in Marseilles, Mühler, on August 19. The astounded Mühler quickly reported to Röthke: "Lospinoso was here today. He said that the situation has changed because of the change of government in Italy. I told him what we want, and he promised to look into it and to return five days from now." Knochen himself reprimanded Mühler: "I am astonished that you are negotiating with Lospinoso without my knowledge. You are to present me with a report and evaluation of the man immediately. This is a subject of the utmost severity." Mühler, like a schoolchild making excuses, tried to justify his actions: "Lospinoso initiated the meeting, not I. The conversation was of a general nature only – and actually, it seems to me that his purpose was really something different. In the past he gave me a list of Jews, and apparently his instructions have changed, because this time he asked that it be returned to him." Paris to Marseilles: "Did you at least keep a copy of the list?" Mühler to Paris: "We didn't have time. After all, it was he who gave us the list, and suddenly he asked for it

153. TR.3-664, 21 July 1943.
154. Klarsfeld, *Vichy*, pp. 553–4, 18 August 1943.
155. Carpi, *Italian Authorities*, p. 158. Carpi has indications that at least one Sipo officer, stationed at Marseilles, had met Lospinoso in May, in Nice. But there seems to be no echo of this meeting in the German documents.

back. But he promised that he would return the original as soon as he comes back."[156] From the tone of this, it can be assumed that not even Mühler believed this. The simple truth was that for months Lospinoso had made himself scarce in order to sabotage the policy, and now he had appeared – to sabotage the same policy. The whole time he proved himself to be a much smarter bureaucrat than his German colleagues-cum-opponents. He made use of his Italian colleagues and resembled them, but being at the vanguard, he needed to be more clever. And he was.

It was, in fact, the Nazis who requested that the Jews in southern France be handled by the police rather than the Italian army. In Germany the distinction made sense, because there the SS-Police were at the ideological vanguard of the regime. That was hardly the case in Italy. Is it not probable that historians are liable to make a similar logical error and attribute to their subjects unrealistic patterns of thought? The incident illustrates how a careful reading of the documents can lead away from the truth, when the authors of the documents are lying. The Italians lied to the Germans when they said that their intention was to participate in the policy of deporting the Jews, and it took the Germans months to realize this. Could it be that some scholars have been duped by declarations of the murderers who described themselves as low-level bureaucrats who had been without hatred or evil intent?

Finally, there is the question of banality. The Italian officials were not particularly nice people. They had reached the senior levels of the Italian Fascist bureaucracy; human dignity and freedom were hardly the values that guided their daily actions. Still, they had their limits. As has been shown, humanitarian concern was one of their motivations in the Jewish matter. Why can we not conclude from this that as the enormity of the crime increases, so the number of people willing to take part in it will decrease? Perhaps the Italian reflex was so natural (or banal?) that even veteran Fascists had it. Why should we see the Nazis, rather than the Italians, as the prototype of normality?

*

In parallel with the German failure with the Italians, a failure that was undone only when the Italians left France in the summer of 1943, they suffered another failure with the French. As early as 1942 it had been clear that sooner or later the French would have to change their position with regard to Jews who were French citizens, since the Germans obviously

156. Klarsfeld, *Vichy*, pp. 554, 558, 560–2.

intended to deport all the Jews in the country. Their method was to demand that the French revoke the citizenship of naturalized Jews. This would allow the French to preserve the pretense of sovereignty inasmuch as they would legislate the appropriate law, and the Germans could continue to deport Jews who were not (any longer) French citizens. It would also demand of the French that they hand over only the weakest link within the French Jewish public. Of course, there would later be a conflict over the deportation of long-established French Jews, but SS officials did not worry about long-term goals — they concentrated on achievable ones.

After a certain amount of hesitancy, someone in the German Security Police in France decided that the French would be told to revoke the citizenship of all Jews who had been naturalized since 1927, the year in which the French immigration laws had been changed.[157] However, a letter from Knochen to Eichmann written some weeks later indicates that Knochen knew that the French were likely to prefer 1932 as the cut-off year. Even in such a case, Knochen estimated, it would make 100,000 more Jews available to the Nazis.[158]

In the meantime French–German relations grew worse. On March 22, 1943 preparations began for the deportation planned for the next day. Leguay went to Röthke and told him that an order from Pétain himself prevented him and his men from assisting in the deportation of French Jews. The situation in the field was apparently one of great confusion, with the French police joining in the work, leaving and joining again. To Röthke it was clear that he could not count on French assistance in sending trains in the future. Knochen was not in Paris at the time, and Röthke summed up the incident for Lischka and Hagen. He said that Leguay had apologized for the change, and cited his orders, but he also commented that the Germans were demanding more of the French than they demanded from others. After all, the problem of British and American Jewry remain unsolved as well, he noted.

Did Leguay indeed say this? If so, what did he mean when he compared occupied France with the combatant British and Americans? Whatever the case, Röthke's reply is even more fascinating. He argued with Leguay (apparently more to vent his frustrations than to change Leguay's position, since the latter was obeying his orders). And he said

157. TR.3-249, 6 March 1943.
158. TR.3-704, 29 March 1943.

that "The American people will probably soon act even more rigorously against the Jews than we [Germans] ever did." Röthke also explained to Leguay that in all his recent speeches Hitler had reiterated the importance of solving the Jewish question.[159]

Hagen summoned Leguay to Oberg's headquarters, and the conversation repeated itself. Leguay announced that the French police would not cooperate with the deportation of French Jews. Hagen expressed his astonishment – they're only Jews, after all, he exclaimed. He also noted the importance that Hitler attached to the deportations, which he emphasized in his speeches. Leguay explained once again that Laval and Pétain were not prepared to take responsibility, even if the Germans were determined to continue.[160]

In the meantime, Knochen returned to Paris and Röthke placed on his desk a long and detailed memorandum citing many reasons why the change in the French position should not deter the Germans. The last Jew should be removed from France before the end of the war, he maintained. No French leader should have any say in this. The Führer's will should be the only determining factor, and he had made himself clear in his recent speeches. Deportation was important because French Jewry was still strong and was behind the Communists, the terrorists, the Gaulists and the other enemies of the Reich. The most effective war against all these elements was the war against the Jews. Another aspect was that the French public did not understand why antisemitic Germany (so in the original) was not taking action against the Jews, especially against the rich and influential ones. In conclusion, Röthke proposed forcing the French police to cooperate.[161] It is interesting to see the high level of ideological conviction expressed by Röthke in this secret internal document. After a year of working with Knochen on a daily basis, he certainly had no need to put on a show or to justify himself. If he nevertheless wrote this, it must have come out of complete personal identification with the cause. He said what he really thought. Even his citing of Hitler is indirect. He does not refer to a direct order but rather to public speeches. That was enough for him; there was no need for an explicit order directly from Hitler to Paris.

In April Bousquet gave Oberg a draft of a citizenship nullification

159. Klarsfeld, *Vichy* pp. 513–15, quotation on p. 514.
160. TR.10-878 (Ankl), pp. 124–5, 25 March 1943.
161. TR.3-718, 27 March 1943.

law and asked the Germans' opinion. It stated that the citizenship of Jews naturalized after January 1, 1932 would be annulled. Hagen wondered whether the Germans ought to demand that the date be moved back to 1927, or whether it was best not to raise the issue. He explained that in August 1927 the French law had been changed so that it would be possible to become naturalized after spending only three years in the country, as opposed to ten previously. This led to granting tens of thousands of Jews citizenship. It was absolutely necessary for the new laws to negate the citizenship of all of them. Knochen noted that such a position was not practical, and anticipated that the 1932 date would be chosen. Still, he saw some sense in attempting to set 1927 as the cutoff date.[162] The debate between them was pragmatic, not ideological. In contrast, it would seem that Oberg leaned towards agreeing to 1932, as Röthke and Knochen felt it necessary to remind him of the significance of the two dates – since 1932 some 20,000 Jews had received citizenship, whereas 70,000 had since 1927. Oberg was convinced.[163] The entire discussion took place in Paris, and there is no reference to consultations with Berlin.

The working relationship between the French and the Germans seems to have been good during this period. Pétain himself received Oberg, accompanied by Knochen and Hagen, for a get-acquainted conversation. Both Bousquet and the Germans left with the feeling that the atmosphere would improve.[164] Towards the middle of June Leguay came to visit Röthke and informed him that the law (with 1927 as the cutoff) was about to be passed. After this happy announcement, he asked for Röthke's intervention in a personal matter. A Jewish woman married to a relative of his had been arrested – could she be released? Röthke recommended an affirmative response.[165] Even he at times acknowledged pragmatic considerations, especially since French Jews married to Aryans were not generally being deported.

On June 8 Oberg paid a visit to Himmler in Berlin. Himmler demanded that the French be pressured to pass the law immediately and that the Jews be deported by mid-July – an almost impossible schedule. Hagen gave Röthke Oberg's instructions to increase the pace of work,[166]

162. Klarsfeld, *Vichy*, pp. 521–2, 12 April 1943.
163. Klarsfeld, *Vichy*, pp. 526–7, 21 May 1943.
164. Klarsfeld, *Vichy*, pp. 522–3. The meeting took place on 15 April 1943.
165. Klarsfeld, *Vichy*, p. 530.
166. TR.10-878 (Ankl.), pp. 121–2.

and Röthke did so. On June 12 there was a meeting with Hagen to discuss in great detail the practical significance of the change in the French law. It was decided that there would be an extensive and intensive action on the very day the law was promulgated, in order to exploit the surprise factor. Röthke issued a long and detailed document laying out how it would be carried out, expected difficulties, and how to deal with them.[167]

A new participant in the Paris forum was SS-Captain Alois Brunner. In practice, most of Brunner's activity would involve brutally hunting down Jews in hiding, whether working out of Drancy or in southern France. It may seem as if Eichmann had sent him to France in order to speed up the deportations after Röthke had failed.[168] But, given the context, Brunner seems to have arrived, on orders from Himmler, not to scrape the bottom of the barrel, but rather to manage the deportations that everyone expected would be shortly renewed.[169]

In the framework of the preparations for this big roundup Röthke needed reinforcements, so he signed Knochen on a letter to Müller. The revision of the law is expected in mid-July, he wrote. Please send 250 Security Policemen, preferably French speakers. The answer was prepared in IV B 4 but was signed by Müller: no manpower is available. You will have to make do with the officer and three policemen we recently sent (the reference is to Alois Brunner); ask for reinforcements from Oberg.[170] Berlin also left personnel matters to be handled by the men in the field.

All the preparations were for naught. On July 15 Röthke sat with French representatives to coordinate the action; the only thing holding them up was the passage of the law. That same day he sent a telegram to his colleagues in the Security Police in Brussels: "Please deport the French citizens that you have; it will accustom the French authorities to the deportation of their citizens."[171] A week later nothing had yet happened, and Röthke wrote a memo that raised for the first time the possibility that

167. Klarsfeld, *Vichy*, pp. 530–5.
168. Mary Felstiner, "Alois Brunner: 'Eichmann's Best Tool'," *Simon Wiesenthal Center Annual*, vol. 3, 1986, pp. 1–46; Mary Felstiner, "Commandant of Drancy: Alois Brunner and the Jews of France," *Holocaust and Genocide Studies*, vol. 2/1, 1987, pp. 21–47. In "Commandant" she portrays Brunner as having pushed Röthke aside. There does not seem to be clear documentation of this.
169. This is also the reading of Safrian, *Männer*, p. 262. Eichmann's role is not recorded. It seems reasonable to assume that, following Himmler's order to beef up the staff in Paris, it was Eichmann who chose the experienced – and, at the time, idle – Brunner.
170. Knochen: TR.3-1217, 28 June 1943; Müller: TR.3-1218, 2 July 1943.
171. TR.3-1219; TR.3-1522.

the Germans would have to arrest all the Jews, without regard to what group they belonged to, using German forces alone.[172] On August 3 Röthke knew that the signing of the law was being delayed, and he asked for the assistance of the German embassy in order to make sure that it would be signed within the week. On August 6 Leguay confirmed to Hagen that there were doubts.[173] On August 7 Knochen and Hagen met with Laval. The meeting has been described as a dramatic one. Laval concealed his position behind "clouds of excuses," but the message was clear – he refused to accept the Germans' demands.[174]

On August 15 Röthke himself, accompanied by an officer named Geissler and Bousquet, met with Laval. Röthke was 31 years old and a lieutenant. Laval was 60 and the prime minister of France, even if French sovereignty was extremely limited.

We do not have the French summary of the meeting, which is unfortunate. Röthke's report paints Laval as trying to be evasive and to retreat from the positions he had agreed to previously. He claimed that Pétain would not agree to the change in the law, that the French had not known that the change would also apply to women and children, did not know that the Germans were planning to deport everyone immediately, and besides they had to be given the opportunity to appeal before their deportation, something which would take three months in each case. And, of course, the Italians were interfering. Röthke was furious. Hadn't Laval himself already signed the law? Laval responded that every day he had to sign huge piles of documents, that he hadn't checked and had assumed that all was as it should be. Röthke emerges from his own report as taking a determined stand against the prime minister of France, forcing him into making clearly specious excuses. Laval is referred to as a "sly fox" denying things he had long known. His protests should be discarded, as he himself knew. With regard to Laval's comment that French policemen would not in the future be made available for deportation operations, Röthke wrote that "impertinence is becoming a method." As far as he was concerned, a prime minister who did not obey orders from a lieutenant was impertinent, since the Final Solution to the Jewish question was the will of the Führer. At the end of the document Röthke noted that from here on out no aid should be expected from the French for the

---

172. TR.3-664, 21 July 1943.
173. Röthke: Klarsfeld, *Vichy*, pp. 548–9. Leguay: Klarsfeld, *Vichy*, p. 549.
174. Klarsfeld, *Vichy*, pp. 550–1; Marrus and Paxton, *Vichy*, p. 325.

deportations, and that it would be wise to organize an independent German action to arrest all the Jews.[175]

On August 19 Röthke visited the offices of the Commissar for Jewish Affairs and announced that since Pétain was procrastinating on signing the law, the Germans were preparing to deport masses of Jews without consideration of their citizenship.[176] Hagen and Knochen repeated this four days later in an additional meeting with Ferdinand de Brinon, the French representative to the German authorities, who was scheduled to meet with Pétain. Either the French would take action, he was told, or the Germans would find other personnel. De Brinon's only suggestion was that the French examinations (and appeals) be speeded up. Knochen reported on this to Kaltenbrunner.[177]

On September 4 Röthke reported to Hagen on the new policy "on the assumption that the planned operation in the Italian zone succeeds" and that control there passed from the Italian army to the Wehrmacht. This included combing the area and catching all the Jews, with the help of local informers who would get a bounty on each arrest. The main effort would be concentrated on southern France. Brunner would arrive in the region for this purpose within two or three days. If the French demanded sorting the Jews by their citizenship or date of naturalization, this would be done only in Drancy.[178]

As in the Reich, the era of mass arrests in France had largely come to an end. They were replaced by targeted activities on the local level. The activity took place less on the desks of the bureaucrats, and were decided more in the torture chambers designed to produce information on Jews in hiding. Knochen and Röthke retreated from center stage; Alois Brunner and his thugs took their place. The documentation that makes the current description possible becomes scarcer, and it is difficult to follow the bureaucrats as bureaucrats. Safrian calls Brunner's activity from here on out a "manhunt."[179]

At the beginning of this work I noted that the SS officers who were at the heart of the system that murdered the Jews had, in general, come to the SS equipped with ideological identification from home. Their work in the 1930s showed that they took their antisemitism very

175. TR.3-1523, 15 August 1943.
176. Klarsfeld, *Vichy*, p. 555.
177. Klarsfeld, *Vichy*, pp. 556–8. Meeting of 23 August 1943, report of 25 August 1943.
178. ZSL 114 AR 683 Bd.II, pp. 103–5.
179. Safrian, *Eichmann Männer*, pp. 261 ff.

seriously, which qualified them to play a central role in the Nazi policy against the Jews. From the annexation of Austria to the summer of 1941 they participated in shaping the policy, evincing callousness and brutality that were appropriate for their job. They batted no eyelids when it came time to turn words into deeds. In the fall of 1941, when the policy came to fruition, they conducted the operation of deporting the Jews of the Reich efficiently and with sound mind, using brutality when they saw a need for it, and evidencing initiative in overcoming the obstacles along the way. The chapter on Holland showed that the pool from which SS officers could be drawn was a large one, and was not limited to a small group that had been occupied with this policy for years. Those who came in on relatively short notice were also fit for the task, even in conditions that were less than optimal, when the surrounding conquered population made its reservations clear.

The story of the deportation of French Jewry shows that it was possible to replace a senior, experienced SS officer, at a most critical moment, with an anonymous young officer without this having any effect at all on the running of the policy. Yet it would be an error to think that this is an inherent trait of all bureaucracies, since the story of France provides clear proofs that bureaucracies do not function anonymously and neutrally. On the contrary. What was common to all the officials was that they all understood more or less what was happening to the Jews, and because of this their attitudes and willingness to participate differed. The SS did everything to advance the deportations, and benefited from the support of other German elements. The French collaborated when convenient, and delayed matters when it served their purposes. Their hatred of the Jews was of a different quality and nature than that of their German colleagues—opponents. The Italians, who became part of the picture from the fall of 1942, also understood what was going on, and were able not only to sabotage the murder machine, but to do so with such great sophistication it took the Germans months to figure out whom they were facing.

The story of France illustrates another important point – the limits of German power. The more independent the local government was, the less dependent on the Germans, the more restricted was the Germans' ability to harm the Jews without coordination with the locals. In Holland it was necessary to break the population's spirit, which was accomplished at the beginning of 1941. In France it was necessary to break the spirit of the Vichy administration, and this was not feasible in the existing political conditions – which had been determined by the Germans, in keeping with their own interests. As a result, the officials had to fight for their position, threaten, persuade, sometimes even plead. They cannot have done so without understanding the nature of their mission, and without understanding that their interlocutors thought their actions repugnant.

They were bureaucrats of evil. In the spring of 1944 they turned their attention to the only large Jewish community remaining in Europe – that of Hungary. Time was running out, but there was still much work to do.

From the testimony at the Eichmann trial

Georges Wellers

[Referring to Dannecker] He was a man who was perpetually under pressure, perpetually in a rage. He reached for his revolver very easily, he shouted very easily when he came to Drancy.... Several times, for instance, when he came to Drancy, the order was given that nobody was to be in the courtyard of the camp and nobody was to look out of the windows. When Dannecker was walking in the courtyard, as soon as he saw a face in a window he threatened the face that he saw. He sometimes came up into the rooms and I know, I have been personally present at the deportation of a few people who had been picked out by Dannecker at the last minute just as the convoy was leaving the camp; people were included on Dannecker's personal orders and added to the convoy. He was a man who was undoubtedly an evil spirit in the camps in which I saw him ...

[Referring to the arrival at Drancy of about 4000 children in the summer of 1942] They arrived in the camp in buses in the usual way. Everyone was transported that way – in buses guarded by Vichy policemen with Vichy Inspectors of Police. The buses came right into the camp. In the middle of the courtyard there was a place separated by barbed wire, and the buses came into this area very fast. The children were told to leave the bus because one bus followed the next at great speed, and they had to make way for the buses behind them. And so these unfortunate children were completely disorientated and at a loss; they left the buses in silence. They were taken in groups roughly corresponding to the numbers in each bus – sometimes there were fifty, sixty, eighty children. The older ones held the younger ones by the hand. No one was allowed to go near these children apart from a few people among us, including myself, who had special permission. They were taken into rooms in which there were no furnishings but only straw mattresses on the ground – mattresses which were filthy, disgusting and full of vermin.

Q. Mr Wellers, did all these children know their own names?

A. No, there were many infants two, three, four years old who did not even know what their names were. When trying to identify them, we sometimes asked a sister, an older brother – sometimes we simply asked other children if they knew them, in order to find out what they were called. In this way we did find some names, very often no doubt quite a wrong one, and then in the camp we made little wooden discs, and on the discs the name was inscribed which had been established this way, obviously without any certainty that the name was correct, and the discs were then attached with a string to the neck of each child. Unfortunately, some while afterwards, we found boys with discs carrying girls' names and girls with discs belonging to boys. The children amused themselves with these discs and exchanged them.

Q. Mr Wellers, what happened to these children's possessions?

A. Well, these children generally arrived with miserable bundles – very badly made up, naturally – and, as they were forced to get off the buses very quickly, the children usually forgot their miserable baggage in the bus, and then the buses were emptied and the bundles were left in the courtyard on the ground. When the buses left the camp, the children were brought back from the rooms to the middle of the courtyard to look for their belongings.

Q. What was the children's state of cleanliness?

A. Frightful. These children arrived at Drancy after already having been completely neglected for two or three weeks at Beaune-la-Rolande and Pithiviers – they arrived with dirty, torn clothes in a very bad condition, often without buttons, often with one of their shoes completely missing, with sores on their bodies. They nearly all had diarrhea; they were incapable of going down into the courtyard where there were lavatories. So sanitary slop-pails were put on the landings, but the small infants were incapable even of using these sanitary slop-pails which were too big for them, so on the day of the arrival of the first convoy four teams of women were formed to care for them and look after these children – women who themselves were liable to deportation, so that when one of them was deported, she was replaced by another. These women got up very early in the morning, before everyone else; they went to the children's quarters where the children were put 120 to a room, one on top of the other, on dirty mattresses, and they tried to do whatever was possible to mend the clothes as best they could, and to wash the children who soiled themselves throughout the day. There was neither soap nor linen; they did everything with their own handkerchiefs and with cold water in the rooms. At midday they brought them soup. There were no mess-tins in the camp either, so they served them soup out of cans. The infants couldn't hold them in their hands, as the soup was hot, and there were children who were incapable of saying that they had not yet received their ration, and, well, it was these women who looked after them.

Q.   Mr Wellers, I have one question: Was it at all permitted for the adults to be with the children at night?

A.   No, by 9 p.m. no adult had permission to be in the children's rooms apart from three or four people who generally had the right of circulating throughout the camp. I myself had this authorization. At night they were completely alone in these large rooms lit by a single bulb covered in blue paint, because it was wartime and in Paris the air-raid precautions required all visible bulbs to be painted blue. They were thus in semi-darkness, more than semi-darkness; in a place which was hardly lit at all. They slept on the floor, one next to the other. Very often they cried, they became agitated; they called for their mothers. It happened a number of times that a whole roomful of 120 children woke up in the middle of the night; they completely lost control of themselves, they screamed and woke the other rooms. It was frightful!

Q.   Do you remember Jacques Stern?

A.   Yes. It was a small episode, one among many. René Blum [a well-known public figure, brother of former French Prime Minister Léon Blum] was an extremely sensitive person. One day he asked me to take him to visit the children's rooms. I took advantage of a moment in the day when there was no supervisor – immediately after lunch – I took him with me and we went up into a children's room. When we entered this room, right next to the door stood a little boy – I think he must have been seven or eight years old; he was remarkably handsome, with a face which was very intelligent, very lively. He wore clothes which must have been of very good quality, rather stylish, but in a pitiful condition. One foot was bare, he wore only one shoe, he had a little torn jacket and buttons were missing. He appeared rather happy. When we went in, René Blum went up to this child. Blum was a very large man, thin but very tall; the child was small. René Blum asked him how old he was. I think he answered seven or eight years, I don't remember exactly. He asked him what his parents did. The child answered: My father goes to the office and mummy plays the piano. She plays very well, he added.... At that moment, the boy turned to both of us and asked us if he would soon be leaving to join his parents – because I should tell you that we told these children that they would be leaving the camp of Drancy in order to rejoin their parents. We knew very well that it wasn't true, not because we knew what happened to Jewish children at Auschwitz – not at all – but we had seen in what circumstances they had been brought to Drancy and in what conditions they left, and we were sure that they would never rejoin their parents at their place of arrival. So I answered this boy: Don't worry, in two or three days you'll rejoin your mother. He had a little jacket with little pockets, and from one pocket he took out a little half-eaten biscuit in the shape of a soldier which had been given to him. And he told us: "Look, I'm bringing this to mummy." René Blum, no doubt deeply moved, then bent over the little boy who looked very happy, very engaging. He took his face in his hands and wanted to stroke his head, and at that moment the child, who only a moment ago had been so happy, broke into tears ...

Q.   Was Röthke present during several deportations of children from Drancy?

A.   Certainly, during several children's transports. He was present at nearly all the departures from Drancy, and, taking into consideration that at least eight convoys of children left the camp, I am sure that Röthke was present at all eight or at least at six or seven.

Q.   Mr Wellers, did the children leave the camp easily?

A. No, most of the time this, too, was a terrible operation. They were woken at five o'clock in the morning; they were given coffee. They had woken up badly, in a bad mood. At five o'clock in the morning, even in the month of August in Paris, it is still very dark; it is still almost night, and when they wanted to get them to come down into the courtyard, it was usually very difficult. So the women volunteers tried through persuasion to get the older ones to come down first, but several times it happened that the children began to cry and struggle. It was impossible to bring them down into the courtyard of the camp, and so policemen had to go up into the rooms and take in their arms the children who were struggling and screaming. They took them down into the courtyard.

(*The Trial of Adolf Eichmann*, vol. II, pp. 581–5)

Hungary

While there had been several savage actions in the country's border regions, and while many of its Jewish men had been taken for forced labor under conditions that took a heavy toll in lives, at the beginning of 1944 the Hungarian Jewish community was the only group of Jews in the German sphere of influence that had not yet been touched in any major way by the Holocaust. But on March 19 of that year, Germany overran Hungary. By the beginning of July almost all the Jews in the provinces had been deported, most of them to their deaths in Auschwitz; only the community in Budapest remained, largely intact. This was the largest deportation operation during the entire Holocaust, encompassing some 435,000 Jews. Even the deportation from Warsaw in the summer of 1942 could not match it in magnitude, much less in the complexity of the operation.

All this was done under the command of Adolf Eichmann, who on a one-time basis transferred his place of residence from Berlin to the field, locating himself in Budapest. Anyone who wants to see in Eichmann a diabolical figure who turned the gears of the Final Solution will seek corroboration in the events in Hungary. The question before the reader of this book is, however, whether the deeds of Eichmann and his bureaucrats in Hungary can add something to our understanding of them. We also want to know whether the findings so far presented can help to understand the project of liquidating Hungary's Jews.[1]

In examining the beginning stages of the Final Solution, in the Reich the main questions were who knew what and when. I argued that greater significance should be attached to what Eichmann was doing at

---

1.   The following discussion is based primarily on: Randolph L. Braham, *The Politics of Genocide: The Holocaust in Hungary*, vol. 2, New York: Columbia University Press; Raul Hilberg, *The Destruction of European Jews*; Eugene (Jeno) Levai, *Black Book on the Martyrdom of Hungarian Jewry*, Zurich: *Central European Times*, 1948; Jeno Levai, *Eichmann in Ungarn, Dokumente*, Budapest: Pannonia Verlag, 1961; Randolf L. Braham and Nathaniel Katzburg, *History of the Holocaust: Hungary* (in Hebrew), Jerusalem: Yad Vashem, 1992.

the end of the summer of 1941 than to what many other people were saying, since he knew what they did not know. I also showed how Security Police officers learned their mission while they were in action. All this was different in Hungary in 1944 – all the Germans involved had long known that the mission was to kill all the Jews. It is doubtful if it was possible to be a senior official in any Nazi agency without knowing that in the spring of 1944; if there were people who nevertheless managed not to know, they were certainly not the type of people to whom Hitler, Himmler or Ribbentrop would assign jobs of any importance.

This can be illustrated with the senior German figure who was sent to Hungary, the general plenipotentiary Dr Edmund Veesenmayer, a foreign ministry official who also held senior SS rank. In practice he was the Führer's representative in Budapest. Veesenmayer brought some interesting qualifications to his job. In 1943 he had been sent to Hungary twice in order to study the situation there, and had written detailed reports of his findings. In both cases he expressed himself very clearly on the Jewish issue. On April 30, 1943 he attributed the weakness and defeatism that in his opinion characterized Hungary to the Jews' huge influence there; in December 1943 his report to the foreign minister stated that the Jews were a dangerous enemy, that they controlled the political system and the economy, and that they operated an efficient intelligence network. He added that it was inconceivable that such a dangerous center of activity could be allowed to continue to function while the Reich was fighting for its life.[2] This was hardly a man who needed to be told by Eichmann, far inferior to him in rank, what fate awaited the Jews. A historian who stubbornly splits hairs and argues that the absence of the word "kill" in the reports means that Veesenmayer did not know about the Final Solution does not understand the limited role that written documents play in people's lives.

The decision makers in Hungary also knew, at least in general terms, what the Nazi regime was doing to the Jews. There were those in Hungary who had known what was happening since the murder program began, and who asked that at least some of the Jews in their country be included. They used the code phrase "resettlement," but after the "resettlement" of at least 16,000 Jews from Hungary to Kamenets-Podolsk, where they were murdered, in the summer of 1941, it was clear

2. Nuremberg Documents NG–2192, quoted in Levai, *Eichmann in Ungarn*, pp. 65–71; Nuremberg Documents NG–5560, 10 December 1943.

to them what lay behind this formulation. At the beginning of 1942 a Hungarian general named Jozef Heszlenyi proposed continuing the deportations – he spoke of 100,000 Jews who would be deported to the Ukraine – but after contacts that lasted for months the Nazis rejected the proposal. The occasion for the rejection was that Eichmann asked the foreign ministry to say that it had no interest in deporting only 100,000 Hungarian Jews, and that it would be better to deport all the Jews together.[3] Doma Sztojay, then Hungary's ambassador in Berlin, took part in the discussions. In a conversation with a member of the Hungarian parliament, György Ottlik, he spoke of the "resettlement" of at least 100,000 Jews, and admitted to him that what was really meant was their execution.[4] Sztojay was appointed to the head of the Hungarian government after the German invasion.

Hungarian head of state Miklós Horthy had himself heard about the genocide no later than April 1943, when he met with Hitler and Ribbentrop at Klessheim castle. The two Germans told him that Jews were being killed in Poland. Horthy replied afterwards in writing, noting his status as a veteran foe of the Jews.[5] In a confrontation with Hitler on the eve of the German entry into Hungary (Klessheim, March 19, 1944) the Jewish issue was again raised, and Hitler made clear what he was thinking. Horthy described it to the outgoing government immediately upon his return to Budapest: "Hitler was indignant about Hungary not yet having taken the steps necessary to solve the Jewish question. They accuse us of the crime of disobedience to the will of Hitler, and claim that I did not allow the killing of the Jews." Sztojay said that Ribbentrop pressured him on the same point.[6] If that is what was recorded in the minutes, we can only guess what was actually said. But the protocol is clear enough. Hitler told Horthy that the Jews of Hungary had to be murdered.

3. Randolf Braham, *The Destruction of Hungarian Jewry: A Documentary Account*, New York: World Federation of Hungarian Jews, 1963, vol. 1, p. 87. Braham follows the case further, as the idea to use the Hungarian offer as a lever to reach an agreement to deport all Jews from Hungary was bandied around among high Nazi functionaries such as Himmler and Ribbentrop at least until February 1943. See there, pp. 85–95.
4. Braham, *History*, pp. 170–6, claims that the primary motives for the German occupation of Hungary were strategic and political, but both the Germans and the Hungarians were aware of the implications for the Jews.
5. Braham, *History*, p. 228.
6. Levai, *Black Book*, p. 78.

On the other hand, German industry was in a bad state. The army demanded – and received – more and more men, and would soon begin calling up teenagers and the elderly as well. Speer's armaments ministry was desperate for working hands, and was prepared to employ Jews. Hitler himself was involved in the discussions on the expansion of production in the aircraft industry, in the framework of what was called the Jäger program. The temporary need for labor apparently fitted in with the desire to remove all the Jews from Hungary and kill them, so it was decided to demand that the Hungarians transfer 100,000 Jews to the Reich for labor; Horthy agreed to this at Klessheim.[7]

The term "Final Solution" had been in the air since the spring of 1941, and served as a cover code for elements outside the SS who were not party to the secret. At the beginning of 1942 the cover term for the murder of the Jews was "deportation to the East." The central figures involved knew exactly what this meant; others learned during the course of events, each man at his own pace and according to his own circumstances. Both cover terms were commonplace by the spring of 1944. Since the Red Army was advancing rapidly towards Hungary's eastern frontier it was a little difficult to speak of "deportation to the East." It is hard to prove that anyone was making any systematic search for some other euphemism, but a reading of the documents shows that "transfer for labor in the Reich" was one formula in use. At the height of the deportations Eberhard von Thadden of the foreign ministry visited Budapest. He met with his friend and colleague Eichmann, and in his report on his visit, dated May 25, 1944, he wrote that about 116,000 Jews had been "deported to the Reich," and that the intention was to deport about a million Jews by the summer. A third of them could work for the Todt labor and construction organization or other organizations – meaning that the document itself declares that two-thirds of the deportees were not in fact targeted for labor.[8] Veesenmayer used the same formula in his report to Ribbentrop in the middle of June, except that in the meantime the number of deportees had doubled.[9]

Veesenmayer took an active part in determining the composition of the new Hungarian government, which was headed by Doma

7.   Bauer, *Jews for Sale?*, p. 155.
8.   Braham, *Destruction*, pp. 380–5, especially p. 383.
9.   Braham, *Destruction*, p. 403.

Sztojay.[10] He made it clear to the new prime minister that his government would be judged on two issues: supplying goods that Germany needed, and the solution of the Jewish problem. He ensured that the "right" Hungarians got portfolios. The new interior minister, Andor Jaross, appointed two secretaries of state to deal with the Jewish issue. Laszlo Endre was named to head the administrative branch and Laszlo Baki was appointed to head the political arm of the ministry. Both were well-known and active Jew-haters. In the lead-up to his appointment, Baki declared publicly: "My job is connected to the final and utter liquidation of the Jewish and leftist scourge in this country. I am sure that the government will be able to complete this great mission, which is of huge historical importance."[11] Before his appointment Baki had been a member of parliament who had made a name for himself as an extreme antisemite and a supporter of the Nazis. The suggestion that he did not know exactly what he was talking about, or that he edged into carrying out the genocide policy without being entirely aware of its significance, is simply not reasonable. Perhaps this is why those who advocate such explanations do not focus on Hungary.

When Horthy returned from Klessheim to Budapest on his special train, a special car carrying senior Nazis was added. Kaltenbrunner was among them.[12] On March 22, 1944 he met Sztojay. Kaltenbrunner demanded that the Jews of Hungary be handled according to the German model, and assigned the details to Eichmann.[13]

As far as the Security Police was concerned, the technical preparations for the invasion of Hungary had been carried out towards the middle of March. The forces mustered at Mauthausen, and among them was a unit commanded by Eichmann, which was called the Sonder-Einsatzkommando (Special Mission Unit) Eichmann. Most of the men in the unit came from department IV B 4 in Berlin – about 15 officers and 30 NCOs and others. Officially they were under the command of SS-Colonel Dr Hans Geschke. Geschke was appointed BdS after the occupation of Budapest, and his forces were divided into eight subunits according to their field of activity. Eichmann and his men were in a separate unit. On professional issues they were directly subordinate to Kaltenbrunner or

10. Braham, *Destruction*, pp. 318–19, Veesenmayer to Ribbentrop, 2 May 1944.
11. Quoted in Braham, *History*, p. 184. The original article was published on 29 March 1944.
12. TR.3-827, p. 7. Interrogation of Kurt Becher.
13. TR.3-358, Report from the Hungarian courts, April 1946.

Müller in Berlin.[14] This relatively autonomous special unit to take charge of one of the issues discussed between Hitler and Horthy could not have been established without the approval of the most senior levels. The fact that Eichmann was sent need not be taken as an indication of his legendary ability to influence the Reich's policies, but rather as a sign of the great priority his commanders assigned to the issue at the time of the invasion of Hungary. Since his talent had already been proven, and the heads of the Reich saw a great need to destroy the Jews of Hungary, it was decided to send him exceptionally. It was an unusual (but not surprising) solution to an unusual problem.

Horthy made his peace with the change in Hungary's status because of the threat of a violent military invasion by the Wehrmacht. In order to prevent this he agreed to a non-violent occupation. Nazi activity in Hungary relied on military power, and after most of the army units were withdrawn, it relied on the threat of their return. Most of the German soldiers left Hungary within a month, leaving a small force under the command of General Hans von Greifenberg. The army apparently played no role in the anti-Jewish measures.[15]

The top German authority in Hungary was Veesenmayer, who was appointed by Hitler. Among the powers assigned to him were: "to guide the activities of all the German civil agencies and bodies functioning in Hungary and to issue political guidelines to the Supreme Commander of the SS and the police, who will be appointed to his staff for the purpose of carrying out 'SS and police missions that will be accomplished by German agencies in Hungary and especially police missions connected to the Jewish question'."[16] In simple English, this means that he was responsible for the SS as well. Several Jewish affairs experts served on his staff; the ones most involved in the deportations were the referent in the embassy, Adolf Hezinger and, from the end of May 1944, his replacement Theodor Horst Grell.

The commander of the SS forces at the time of the entry into Hungary was Kaltenbrunner himself, but he remained in the country for only three days. The permanent commander of the SS forces in the

14. TR.3-29; 502 AR-Z 150/59, vol. 9, pp. 1305–6. Eichmann and his men began their preparation for Hungary at Mauthausen, on 10 March 1944. Braham, *History*, p. 182

15. Braham, *History*, p. 179.

16. Braham, *Destruction*, p. 304; appointment of Veesenmayer by Hitler, 19 March 1944.

country was SS-General Otto Winkelmann, the HSSPF. The commander of the Security Police forces was, as noted, Geschke, and the head of the forces in Budapest was Lt. Col. Alfred Trencker. It was Trencker's men who arrested large numbers of Jews in Budapest and its environs in the first weeks of the occupation.

Baki headed the interior ministry's department XX, and was responsible for the police and the gendarmerie. Most of the work of concentrating and deporting the Jews was assigned to the gendarmerie's regional units, and a key figure who coordinated their work with Budapest was Lieutenant-Colonel Laszlo Ferenczy (whose rank was the equivalent of Eichmann's). His headquarters was in the Lomnic Hotel in Buda, close to Eichmann's headquarters in the Majestic Hotel.[17] Endre's department (XXI) dealt with hunting down, arresting, and deporting the Jews. The deportation operation was called "rehousing and resettlement," and the department that managed it was called – with brilliant cynicism – the housing department.[18] Ferenczy hung an even more cynical sign on his office door: "International Storage and Shipping Company Inc."[19]

"Every era has its own theoretical-psychic motif, according to which people establish their position and according to which their hypocrisy is determined."[20] In the twentieth century – even in the horrible 1940s – the motif was humanism, the product of the enlightenment. People are not to be killed for no reason; even when a reason is given it is presented in a somewhat apologetic tone. To paraphrase the continuation of the above quote, a society that sanctifies the value of human life will have murderers, but the style of their murders will be different from that in which there is no such sanctification. Atilla the Hun did not hide his deeds behind talk about a state of emergency and the return of national property – he simply pillaged, raped, and murdered. He was no less a murderer for this, but apparently he was less hypocritical. Arendt, who tried to absolve Eichmann and his colleagues of cynicism, ignored such small details – unfortunately. It isn't possible, after all, that Ferenczy chose this sign absent-mindedly. And can it be that he and Eichmann never joked about it?

This is significant. Learned men and women have said that every

17. Braham, *History*, pp. 187–8.
18. Braham, *History*, pp. 180–8.
19. Levai, *Black Book*, p. 115.
20. Haim Hillel Ben-Sasson, *Continuity and Variety* (in Hebrew), Tel Aviv: Am Oved, 1984, p. 365.

person can be a mass murderer, but has it been proven that every person can be hypocritical? Such a statement cannot withstand even the simplest test in human life — the empiric test of the day-to-day. There are hypocrites among us and there are honest people; there are those who lie easily, and there are those who pay a high personal price because of their insistence on being honest. A blanket statement that the reverse is true ignores the ability of every individudal to weigh his actions, choose his own road, to distinguish between good and bad and to prefer one to the other. Such statements ignore a person's ability to be either good or bad, and mean we are nothing more than a dim reflection of the era in which we live. In his choice of doorplate, Ferenczy showed clearly that he was a liar, and hinted that he understood he was a murderer. In other words, his cynicism negates the possibility that he acted in good faith, and good faith is the foundation of the entire school of Hannah Arendt.

Towards the end of the day of their arrival in Budapest, Eichmann's men gathered in the company of Kaltenbrunner at the Kisludlab restaurant. During the meal Kaltenbrunner made a speech in which he wished Eichmann and his staff success in deporting the Jews, and called on the other Security Police men to give whatever assistance they could.[21] A day or two later (March 22), Eichmann met Endre. If we recall that on the same day Kaltenbrunner met Sztojay and made clear to him what the goal of the Jewish issue was, then the purpose of Eichmann's meeting with Endre was clearly to establish rules of protocol between the Germans and the Hungarians. In the unequal partnership between the two countries, the commander of the Security Police gave instructions to the prime minister, and the referent, a lieutenant colonel, advised the secretary of state. Endre asked to see the wording of anti-Jewish laws legislated in Slovakia, and Wislicency was sent to bring them.[22]

Endre worked swiftly. He issued, in the space of just a few weeks, a long series of regulations that constricted Jewish breathing space. Members of the free professions were fired or restricted (with the exception of Jewish doctors, who represented such a large minority in the Hungarian medical community that it was impossible to get along without them). Tens of thousands of Jewish stores and businesses were closed, bank accounts were blocked, land was nationalized. Food rations

21. Claudia Steur, *Theodor Dannecker: Ein Funktionär der "Endlösung"*, Tübingen: Klartext, 1997, p. 132.
22. TR.3-901, pp. 5–6. Wislicency's response to Kastner.

were restricted, as were the permitted purchasing hours. Non-Jews were forbidden to work in Jewish homes. Only ten days after the Germans entered Hungary a yellow Jewish badge was imposed for all Jews from the age of six upwards (March 29). Marking the Jews made it possible to restrict their freedom of movement – they were forbidden to leave their homes at night and their travel was restricted. Their telephones were confiscated and this added another brick to their growing wall of isolation.[23] The police continued to arrest Jews on the streets of Budapest, and by April 28 a total of 8142 were under detention.[24] Developments that took place over eight years in the Reich and two years in France and Holland took less than three weeks in Hungary. Someone – Eichmann, Endre, apparently both of them together – knew exactly what they needed to do to achieve their goal. Furthermore, unlike in other countries, at this point Eichmann enjoyed the full and enthusiastic support of his local colleagues. Without them he would not have achieved what he wished.

Since their central mission had not yet begun, Eichmann's men occupied themselves with confiscating property. Novak, accompanied by two plain-clothes Hungarian policemen, traveled around the city searching out "Jewish objects – especially villas." When the "object" seemed appropriate, the Jewish owners were ordered to evacuate it within three to four hours. Novak did not object to their taking as much as they could with them, which would make the inventory work easier, so long as furniture, bedding and all else required for comfortable living remain on site for the use of the new German tenants. There was apparently a lot of individual corruption, since twenty years later Novak still remembered the "irregularities" (and memory was not Novak's strong point). Hunsche registered all the property.[25]

Two thousand Jews were arrested, at the train station and in the streets, immediately upon the Germans' arrival in Budapest. They were sent to the Kistarcsa camp.[26] The arrests in Budapest and its environs continued. Their purpose was apparently to create an atmosphere of terror among the city's Jews, a feeling that the sword was hanging above

23. For a detailed description of this legislation process, see: Hilberg, *Destruction*, 1st edn, pp. 531–5.
24. TR.3-679, Veesenmayer to AA.
25. Novak: ZSL, RSHA 413 AR 1310/63, pp. 54–5; Hunsche: ZSL, AR-Z 60/58, vol. 1, pp. 372–5.
26. TR.3-347, p. 4, affidavit of Imre Reiner, 5 October 1960.

them by a thread at all times, and to stress the new, inferior status of the Jews in the Hungarian consciousness. They may also have been a kind of test to see whether the Hungarian populace was willing to stand aside while the Jews were removed from among them, and it indeed was. The Jews in detention also served as an accessible and convenient pool for carrying out special deportations. But the Nazis did not intend to base their actions on this pool, because their plan was first to liquidate the Jews in the provinces.[27]

On April 4, 1944 there was an important meeting chaired by Baki. Among those present were senior officers in the German and Hungarian armies, Eichmann and several of his officers, Endre, Ferenczy and Colonel Győző Tölgyesy, commander of the gendarmerie in district VIII, Carpatho-Ruthenia. The subject of the discussion was the concentration and deportation of the Jews. Three days later Baki issued an order summing up what was discussed at the meeting. Its title, "Designation of Jewish Accommodation," directly contradicted its first sentence, and the spirit of the entire document: "The Royal Hungarian Government intends to rid the country of the Jews." The order emphasized that this meant all Jews, of all ages, with the exception of those working in vital war industries. Prior to their deportation the Jews would be gathered together at collection points, and this task would be carried out by the police and the gendarmerie. The German Security Policemen were given the status of advisers, and the Hungarians were to take care to cooperate with them. The order set out the rules applying to the vacated Jewish apartments, and to Jewish property and valuables. Not only would the Jews be deported – they would be forbidden to take more than fifty kilograms of equipment and supplies with them, including blankets.[28]

There are those who have described the meeting and the order as a decision to concentrate and deport the Jews.[29] But the documents can be read otherwise – that there had been a previous decision (whether formally worded or not), and that the meeting of April 4 was a technical discussion of some of the operative details, and perhaps also a presentation of the plan to a broader group. According to this reading, the phenomenon is similar to the Wannsee Conference fifty months previously – following a decision made elsewhere, other officials were

27. Endre demanded to start with the deportation of the Jews of Budapest; Eichmann insisted on starting in the East. Braham, *History*, p. 249.
28. Levai, *Black Book*, pp. 112–13, brings the full text in English.
29. Braham, *History*, p. 243.

updated and the operational principles were coordinated. To continue with this model, the next meeting, which took place in Baki's office on April 6, was something like the meeting of Security Police representatives that Eichmann held on March 6, 1942. Both meetings discussed the detailed operational instructions for the concentration and deportation of the Jews. Eichmann contributed his great experience, and also knew what kinds of meetings needed to be held. His Hungarian partners were eager students, thirsty for knowledge, but this did not mean there was no need for a guiding and experienced hand. Eichmann, with his status, could impose his opinion on Endre with regard to the order in which the Jews would be deported from the different regions. Endre wanted to begin with the Jews of Budapest. Eichmann explained that the Jews closest to the front should be dealt with first, in order to give the action some aura of reasonableness and so as to prevent disquiet among the other Jewish communities.[30]

On April 14 Veesenmayer notified Ribbentrop that Sztojay had given his approval for putting 50,000 Jews at the service of the Reich for labor; another 50,000 could be expected during May. The Hungarian police and the SD were dealing with the technical aspects, Veesenmayer said. The next day he asked where in the Reich to send the Jews that the Hungarian labor authorities were prepared to hand over – 5000 immediately and the rest over three or four days. He reiterated that the SS (in this telegram, Winkelmann) would be taking care of the details. The foreign ministry referred the question to Eichmann that same day – a somewhat strange bureaucratic move, given that Eichmann, like Veesenmayer, was in Budapest. Because of Veesenmayer, who was their man, the foreign ministry was in the picture, but apparently not really at its center. On April 20 von Thadden informed Eichmann that he understood that there was a problem finding rail cars, but that Günther was sure it would be possible to solve this the minute that Kaltenbrunner gave the word. On April 22 von Thadden was able to report to Ribbentrop that the RSHA was handling the matter of trains. On the same matter, Veesenmayer reported to the foreign ministry in Berlin that the SD was working in coordination with Endre, and that his (Veesenmayer's) man (probably Hezinger) was coordinating with the SD.

The chain of events is a bit mystifying, since it looks as if the Hungarian authorities were interested in deporting Jews immediately, that

30. Braham, *History*, pp. 247, 249.

Veesenmayer in Budapest and von Thadden in Berlin were pushing for execution, but that the RSHA was dragging its feet. Furthermore, it is not obvious which Jews are being spoken of. The picture becomes clearer in a telegram from Veesenmayer to Berlin dated April 23. The Jews of the Carpathians, it states, had been concentrated since April 16; 150,000 had already been put into the ghettos, and the estimate was that by the end of the operation, a week hence, the number of those concentrated would reach 300,000. The work would continue in other districts immediately thereafter, until all the Jews were assembled, except those in Budapest. There were contacts about deporting the Jews – first 3000 each day from the Carpathians, and afterwards from the other districts. "They will be deported to Auschwitz. Care should be taken not to harm the interests of the war industry; in order not to put the operation at risk, I suggest putting off the deportation of the 50,000 Jews fit for work from the Budapest area whose deportation I have demanded up until now – in any case there are transportation problems.... It seems to me that this will be the best way, since the roundup of the Jews needs to be total. Request instructions, if you think differently."[31]

The sequence of events was apparently as follows: Veesenmayer wanted to get rid of the Jews as fast as possible, and asked to begin with 50,000 Jewish laborers whom the Hungarian authorities who worked with him were prepared to hand over immediately. The air ministry in Berlin was also expecting these laborers, as is clear from the minutes on the matter of the Jäger plan, dated April 14.[32] The RSHA, on the other hand, was in no hurry. The 50,000 laborers were but a small portion of the Jews of Hungary, and the SS wanted to take care of them all. And the RSHA had heard from its Hungarian contacts – not from the ministry of labor, but from the fanatic antisemites in the interior ministry – that Hungary would soon allow the mass deportation of all the country's Jews. It is in this context that the April 24 message from Günther to von Thadden should be read to mean that the deportation of Jews for labor in open facilities in the Reich was not acceptable, since it would make the policy of purifying the Reich of Jews look ridiculous. If Jewish laborers were to be used in the Reich, it could only be in closed SS facilities – and in any case it would be best to wait for information from Eichmann.[33] Günther

31. Braham, *Destruction*, pp. 242–4, 247–8, 354–6.
32. Braham, *Destruction*, pp. 336–41, especially p. 341.
33. TR.3-213.

needed five days to reply to this inquiry (by cable and by telephone) from von Thadden, and Günther did not delay matters for five days except when it was convenient for him.

The turning point, as the RSHA saw it, was the meeting of April 20. For several days the Jews of Carpatho-Ruthenia had been gathered together in concentration facilities. The commanders of the gendarmerie in the region "complained" about the harsh conditions there. Wislicency transferred this, personally, to Budapest. In a meeting in Baki's office, with the participation of Eichmann, Hunsche, Novak, Wislicency, Ferenczy, Ferenczy's aide Captain Laszlo Lulay, and Colonel Tölgyesy, the commander of the gendarmerie in Marmarossziget in Carpatho-Ruthenia, Eichmann proposed solving the problem by deporting all the Jews out of Hungary. That was in the morning; the official request was submitted at 4 p.m. Eichmann immediately organized a meeting in Vienna to coordinate the trains, with the participation of Novak, Lulay and representatives of the transport ministry, while he cabled Kaltenbrunner about his success.[34]

From the moment it was possible to deport the provincial Jews, Veesenmayer abandoned, without batting an eyelid, his previous position. Not only did he not ask to deport the 50,000, but actually recommended suspending action on their deportation in favor of the general deportation that would begin with the Carpathian district. Everyone agreed that all the Jews should be killed, but Kaltenbrunner, Eichmann and Günther proved to have stronger nerves than Veesenmayer or von Thadden. If there is any need for one last testimony to the cynicism of Eichmann and his crew, it can be found in their work after the three-week delay in which they refused to handle the deportation of the Jews from the Budapest region, and instead waited for approval of the mass deportation that would begin in the provinces. After refusing to take the Jews from Budapest, they now turned around and deported, typically, those Jews who were most available – those detained at Kistarcsa, near Budapest. It was from there that the first deportation train left, on April 23 – for Auschwitz, not to factories in the Reich.[35] Immediately afterwards the methodical deportation of all the Jews from the Hungarian provinces began.

The concentration of the Jews of Carpatho-Ruthenia was

34. TR.3-584, pp. 10–11; TR.3-856, pp. 8–9: two postwar testimonies of Wislicency.
35. TR.3-347, p. 6 (Reiner). Veesenmayer reported two trains, on 27 and 28 April 1944. Braham, *Destruction*, p. 361.

launched in the middle of April, on the 16th at the latest and apparently a few days prior to that.[36] The procedure established there was repeated afterwards in all the other provinces. First the Jews from the villages and small towns were arrested. In many cases they were evicted with only a few minutes' warning. The points of concentration were determined by the local authorities. They were frequently factory yards, brick kilns, quarries and other such facilities never meant for human habitation. The Jews spent several weeks in these places, exposed to the elements and tormented by the Hungarians who tried to extort all their property, sometimes including that which existed only in the imaginations of ignorant neighbors who "knew" that all Jews are rich. The food supply was poor at best, as were the sanitary conditions. By the time they were put on the deportation trains the Jews were exhausted, ill and very frightened.[37] While the Jews of one region were being deported, those in the next region were being concentrated, and the preparations for concentration were begun in a third region. It was all carried out by various Hungarian agencies, but Wislicency and his colleagues closely supervised it, and saw to it that there were enough trains.[38]

A foreign ministry official (first Hezinger, then Grell) visited the concentration points and saw to it that Jews with protected passports were not deported. After the war they presented this as their own small rescue operation in the midst of the inferno,[39] but in fact their job was to contribute to the smooth functioning of the operation by ensuring that the foreign representations had no cause to charge that their citizens were being deported.[40] Hezinger's contribution was so great, and his ties with Eichmann and his men so good, that Veesenmayer was concerned that replacing him would harm the mission. At the end of May he went so far as to ask von Thadden to try to postpone Hezinger's transfer.[41] Eichmann was also afraid of Hezinger's replacement by Grell , in light of the friendly cooperation between them, a relationship it might take weeks to build

36. Braham, *History*, p. 250. There is a certain lack of clarity as to the precise date of beginning the concentration of the Jews in rural areas.

37. Braham, *History*, pp. 250 ff.; Braham, *Politics of Genocide*, pp. 604 ff., Levai, *Black Book*, pp. 115 ff.

38. Levai, *Black Book*, p. 144.

39. Both Grell and Hezinger claimed at Nuremberg (1948) that they had obstructed Eichmann, in their small way. TR.-3977, 985.

40. This is the reason given for their being sent: Thadden to Veesenmayer, 6 April 1944, in Braham, *Destruction*, vol. 1, p. 335.

41. Braham, *Destruction*, pp. 381–2.

with Grell.[42] In retrospect, there seem to have been no problems, and Grell seems to have functioned well. The foreign ministry's active participation stands out in Veesenmayer's ongoing and detailed reports, written in practice by Grell,[43] which included the numbers of detainees, places of concentration and the number of deportees. In the middle of the deportations (June 6) Veesenmayer warned the foreign ministry that if information about them leaked, the Jews were liable to defend themselves. A week later he reported that Jews were fleeing to Slovakia, and suggested that implementation be resumed there as well – since in Slovakia the mission had not yet been completed.[44] The reports of von Thadden, who visited Budapest a week after the deportations began and spoke at length with Eichmann,[45] also reflect the foreign ministry's involvement.

When they dealt with the deportation of the Reich's Jews, the SS officers were forced to cope with political and legal problems, in particular the issue of what categories of Jews could be deported. In Holland there had been similar problems, including Jews who enjoyed the protection of the war industries, or Jews who went into hiding. In France the deportations were affected more by the relations of the French – and Italian – authorities with the Nazis. In Hungary there were no problems like these until the beginning of July 1944. In the absence of problems, and in light of the full cooperation of all those involved, it was possible to deport almost every Jew in the country except for the Budapest community within the space of two months.

Endre, Eichmann, and their entourage went for a first inspection tour of the concentration areas on April 24. Endre summarized his impressions in a newspaper interview:

---

42. TR.3-678, 25 May 1944.
43. ZSL 502 AR-Z 150/59 Bd.VII, pp. 131–2. The reports themselves are to be found in YVA record group TR.3, as well as in Braham, *Documents*. The information about the persecution of the Jews was daily culled from the reports of the SS.
44. TR.3-384; TR.3-385, 14 June 1944. Ribbentrop suggested that Veesenmayer discuss his proposition directly with the German representative in Slovakia, Ludin; he wished to be kept informed about developments. TR.3-798.
45. TR.3-678, 25 April 1944. Following the report by von Thadden, Staatssekretär Wagner had a summary written for Ribbentrop. The report openly discusses the deportation of at least 900,000 Jews "to the East," including the intention to deport the Jews of Budapest sometime in July. TR.3-1342. Wagner's report is dated 16 May 1944.

Table 3 The deportation of Hungarian Jewry[46]

Region	Area of the country	Date of concentration	Date of deportation	Number of trains	Number of deportees
I	Carpatho-Ruthenia	16 April	15 May–7 June	92	289,357
II	North Transylvania	3 May	As in Region I	included in above	included in above
III	Northern Hungary	5–10 June	11–16 June	23	50,805
IV	Southeastern Hungary	16–10 June	25–28 June	14	41,499
V	West and south-west Hungary	30 June–3 July	4–6 July	10	55,741
VI	Budapest suburbs	30 June–3 July	6–8 July	8	none
Total				147	437,402

We took measures that were carried out in a humanitarian way, taking moral factors into consideration. The truth is that nothing bad happened to them [the Jews]. They can live among themselves in one group within the boundaries of the ghetto according to their national and racial laws. We have allowed them to cook with sesame oil, so that they would not have to transgress one of the important precepts of their religion. Ghettoization has been carried out humanely, without rough behavior. I gave an order to protect them well.[47]

Endre was lying. On this point, and on many others. It is hard to dispute the facts. For the historian trying to reconstruct the way decisions were made, it is not always clear when a man is lying, when he does not know what he is talking about, and when he believes what he is saying even if there is no good reason for him to do so. But Arendt's solution is too simple. The genocide of the Jews was not an armchair project conducted from a well-ordered desk in a closed room. More importantly, it lasted a long time and demanded ongoing involvement. The building stones from which it was constructed were millions of relatively small and

46. Braham, *History*, p. 289. The total sum of 437,402 is from Veesenmayer's daily reports. Ferenczy counted on his own, his total sum being 434,351.
47. Levai, *Black Book*, p. 123; Braham, *History*, p. 266.

daily actions – what to say to a journalist, at what speed to respond to a telegram, what to tell the frightened Jews facing you. Arendt argues that the big decision – to be an accessory to murder – was never made at all, since the small man in a large system did not discern any need to make it. In following the actions of the bureaucrats in Berlin, we saw that this is not the way things were. This is a good illustration of the fact that the small decisions, which Arendt refrained from addressing, were indeed banal. The bureaucrat had to decide whether he should lie or tell the truth. It can't possibly be that Endre innocently invented his old wives' tale about the sesame oil, just as it can't possibly be that Eichmann thought his behavior was normative when he first came face to face with the leaders of Budapest's Jews.

The only great unknown during Eichmann's mission was whether he would succeed in duping the Jewish leadership in a way that would ensure the level of cooperation he required of them. He had great experience at his disposal, both theoretical and practical, and the deportation of Hungarian Jewry was the high point of his career. His experience and determination helped him carry out the mission in the optimal way, from his point of view.

Representatives of the Jewish organizations were summoned to a meeting with German representatives that took place on March 20 at 10 a.m. in the offices of the Neolog community (the Neologs were a group similar to Reform Judaism). There were seventeen Jewish representatives present, together with six Nazis: Krumey, Wislicency, an unidentified officer, two civilians (one a woman) and an armed sergeant. The Germans introduced themselves as men of IV B 4 (and not of Sonderkommando Eichmann), and gave instructions that were a combination of general guidelines with technical details, and of threats with reassurances. The community leaders were told that all Jewish–German contacts would be made through IV B 4. Jews were forbidden to leave Budapest or even to change their places of residence. Anyone who had left recently was required to return. Within 24 hours reports were to be submitted describing the structure of the community and the number of Jewish families, and including lists of public property and the names of all office holders. At that time the Jewish representatives would be reconvened, in a more complete forum. A *Zentralrat*, or central Jewish council, would be set up containing no more than six members. It should have a telephone manned at all times, for receiving messages from the SS. Newspapers and all other published material would be submitted to IV B 4 for censorship.

A reassuring article should be published immediately in the Jewish press. Arrests would most likely continue, but they would be of a political (as opposed to racial, apparently) nature; religious, social, and cultural activity could continue as before.[48]

The next day, March 21, in the afternoon, Krumey and Wislicency met with a larger group of about 40 Jewish representatives. The SS officers made it clear that they would recognize only one single Jewish representative body, the *Zentralrat*, which was to be established. Some of the Jewish representatives complained about the confiscation of property and the arrests, and the officers tried to calm them. While these activities would continue, they said, they were not so bad, and after all there was a state of war.[49] On March 28 an additional meeting was held, this time with the representatives of communities outside Budapest. Krumey and Hunsche arranged special travel permits for the Jewish representatives, and worked to reassure them about the coming period as well.[50]

Eichmann deliberately refrained from meeting Jewish representatives during these first days, leaving this to his staff. These first meetings took place on "Jewish territory" – at the offices of the Jewish organizations. Eichmann staged his first meeting with the Jews in a different setting – it took place at his headquarters at the Majestic Hotel, early on the morning of March 31, after the main points of the policy had already been settled with the Hungarians. Hilberg describes the meeting "as one of the best performances of his [Eichmann's] career," and another historian, Levai, wrote that "Eichmann in fact hypnotized the Jewish representatives, and through them all of Hungarian Jewry."[51]

Only Krumey, the most senior of his assistants, was present at the meeting – which underlined to his audience that this time they were dealing with a new level of officers. For most of the meeting Eichmann spoke. He announced the requirement to wear a Jewish badge, beginning that same evening. At first this would be a temporary badge, but it would quickly be exchanged for a permanent one. The Jewish representation would be responsible for its distribution, and he gave detailed instructions on the best way for this to be done. Preparing three million badges would

48. TR.3-813.
49. TR.3-347, pp. 4–5 (Imre Reiner); TR.3-662, pp. 6–7 (Freudiger).
50. TR.3-347, p. 7 (Reiner).
51. Hilberg, *Destruction*, p. 529. Hilberg quotes Levai.

require 70,000 meters of fabric, he told them, suggesting that each badge be sold for three pengö.

Travel: Jews were forbidden to move without special permits, but he would consider issuing appropriate permits for those living far from their places of work. Only he, exclusively, could sign such permits (meaning that only a small number would be issued, and that the Council should be selective in submitting requests).

The detention camp at Kistarcsa: if the detainees were well-behaved, it would be all right. The same applied to the adult Jewish men who would be taken for labor. Industrial production was important and, if they worked properly, they would not be treated badly. If they worked close to their place of residence they would be allowed to return home each night. But it was likely that they would be sent out of Hungary. By presenting matters in this way, Eichmann created the impression that labor was the main concern, and that he did not want to divide families; if this nevertheless happened, it would be for objective reasons having to do with the location of the workplaces. It would be best if Jews volunteered for this work, but if they did not volunteer, the Jewish leadership would have to employ force. When the Jewish representatives replied that they had no authority to draft people against their will, Eichmann chastised them for their liberal instincts.

Then he presented himself as looking out for their best interests. The Jewish Council, or *Judenrat*, that was to be established would also be responsible for Jews who had converted to Christianity, and he suggested levying higher taxes on them, since they were rich. The Council would have a newspaper, the only newspaper that would be allowed the Jews. Every Jewish family would have to subscribe – and this would also be a source of income for the Council. He should be provided with a list of all the Jewish organizations – but they should not be concerned, all these measures would be revoked after the war, when the Germans would once again become good neighbors. Actually, he, Eichmann, found violence repugnant, and in his experience it had been necessary to use violence against Jews only in cases in which they had resisted the Nazis (there was a certain measure of truth in this, if you don't call murder violence). If the Jews helped the partisans, he would slaughter them mercilessly.

Eichmann went on to tell them of his great expertise in Jewish issues, and he was happy to hear that there was a Jewish museum in Budapest – he even promised to visit it later in the week. When one of those present argued that a Jewish badge would be humiliating, and that he was afraid of being molested, Eichmann reassured him: if anyone was molested, he, Eichmann, wanted to be told about it.[52]

Eichmann and his men were experienced, and did not need to be told that they should neutralize the Jewish leadership and use it for their own purposes. Krumey, Hunsche and Wislicency acted accordingly from their first day in Hungary. At the time of the meeting with Eichmann, he could already go as far as to announce measures that required Hungarian approval. At the meeting he presented an interesting combination of authoritativeness – the senior Nazi officer for Jewish affairs – and of preoccupation with fine detail of the kind that would usually be reserved for junior officers. He apparently wanted to be seen as omnipotent, both because of his rank and position, as well as because of his expertise and professionalism. This was also part of a deliberate policy. The Jewish leaders were to realize that they were facing a man who could not be deceived and who could not be circumvented. Eichmann summed up his talk by saying this explicitly: "We already have much experience in handling Jewish affairs, and no one here should get the impression that we can be misled. Anyone who tries to do so will have to deal with Eichmann himself."[53]

All in all, Eichmann's performance achieved its objective. However, there were certain exceptional cases in which Jewish actions had some marginal influence on matters. One of these affairs has found its way deep into Israel's memory of the Holocaust, because of the sensational trial of one of its key actors, Rudolf (Reszo) Kastner, and because of the effect his trial had on Israeli politics in the 1950s and after.

Kastner had been a Zionist activist in Budapest. At the beginning of 1943 he and his colleague, Joel Brand, took part in the establishment of the Relief and Rescue Committee, an organization whose object was to save Jews from the Nazis. The committee was headed by Otto Komoly, another Zionist activist. They had ties with the Working Group, an organization of Slovakian Jews who also tried to engage in rescue activities. The members of the Rescue Committee knew about contacts between the Working Group and the SS, and in particular with Dieter Wislicency, Eichmann's man in Bratislava. The members of the Rescue Committee clearly believed, apparently erroneously, that through

52. TR.3-785, pp. 1–4 (Erno Munkaci).
53. Jeno Levai (ed.), *Eichmann in Ungarn: Dokumente*, Budapest: Pannonia Verlag, 1961, p. 81.

contacts with – and particularly bribery of – Wislicency they could slow down the pace of the persecution of Hungarian Jewry. With the Red Army on Hungary's eastern frontier, slowing down the deportations was a very real way of saving lives.[54]

Just after the Germans entered Budapest, Wislicency presented the members of the rescue committee with a letter from Rabbi Michael Dov Ber Weissmandel of Bratislava, recommending that the Jews negotiate with him, Wislicency. In the weeks that followed there were several meetings between the committee's members and Wislicency and his colleagues, including Otto Hunsche and Hermann Krumey, Eichmann's deputy. Tens of thousands of dollars (mostly in Hungarian currency) were handed over to the SS officers as advances on a broader agreement; Bauer sees these contacts as a Nazi attempt at extortion. But it was more than this: in the critical weeks of shaping the anti-Jewish actions in Hungary, after the German invasion but before the concentration of the Jews, the SS officers thought that the contacts contributed to keeping the Jews calm. The members of the Rescue Committee did not have the standing to incite the Jews of Hungary,[55] but there is no certainty that Eichmann and his men knew this.

On either April 16 or 25, Eichmann summoned Joel Brand to his office and proposed trading Jews for merchandise. Brand later described the meeting:

> "[D]o you know who I am? I am in charge of the *Aktion!* (operation). In Europe, Poland, Czechoslovakia, Austria it has been completed; now it's Hungarian Jewry's turn." ... He had summoned me in order to propose a deal. He was prepared to sell me a million Jews – goods for blood, that was his way of speech at that time. ... "Speak!"[56]

It is doubtful whether these initial contacts were carried out

---

54. The description of the negotiations is based heavily on Yehuda Bauer, *Jews for Sale? Nazi–Jewish Negotiations 1933–1945*, New Haven, CT: Yale University Press, 1994, chapter 9: "Satan and the Soul – Hungary, 1944."

55. Bauer, *Jews for Sale?*, pp. 158–61, 163.

56. The exact date is unclear. Bauer, *Jews for Sale?*, p. 163; Brand at Eichmann's trial, State of Israel, Ministry of Justice, *The Trial of Adolf Eichmann, Record of the Proceedings in the District Court*, Jerusalem, 1993, vol. III, pp. 876, 1020. It is worth watching the videotape made of the trial. Sixteen years after the event, Brand (probably not fully consciously) mimicked Eichmann as he had been that day. The tone of his voice and his body language told of Eichmann's arrogance and his contempt for the Jews. Perhaps Arendt wasn't in the courtroom that day. Yad Vashem Film Archive, collection 791.

without the knowledge and agreement of Eichmann's superiors, since Eichmann was always very careful to cover himself for all his actions. There can be no doubt, however, that the exchange proposal was made. Shortly thereafter Brand set out for Istanbul, together with another Jew, Bandi Grosz, who had served previously as a courier and agent for several intelligence services, including that of the German army. Between the first offer and Brand's departure there were several other meetings between Eichmann and Brand, with the participation of SS officer Kurt Becher (who was involved in the confiscation of Jewish property) and apparently also of Veesenmayer, and perhaps Winkelmann. Others were also involved, since Eichmann, who wanted to persuade Brand that the matter was serious, gave him cash and letters sent to the Rescue Committee from Switzerland, and intercepted and confiscated by the Nazis.[57] There can be no doubt that the matter was carried out with the approval of elements far senior than Eichmann. The question, then, is who did in fact initiate the affair, and why?

It does not look as if Eichmann made the proposal in order to obtain the passivity of the Jewish leadership, for several reasons. First, the Rescue Committee, and certainly Brand, was not the Jewish leadership, and Eichmann, who met the Jewish leadership from time to time, did not discuss the deal with them. Second, prior to the deportation of the Jews of Hungary Eichmann had never tried to engage in this kind of deception; he knew from experience that the truly weak link in the deportation chain was generally the local authorities, especially the police. In April and May the working relationship between the SS and the Hungarians was excellent, and contacts of this type could only have endangered them. Third, no one knew better than deportation expert Eichmann that transferring a million Jews across the continent at the height of a war was an extremely complex operation. Transferring them so that they arrived healthy and whole, as the German army was retreating, was simply not possible. Finally, Eichmann didn't want to free a million Jews, he wanted to kill them. Had it occurred to him, even in retrospect, that he had sought to save Jews and that the endeavor had failed through no fault of his, he would later have gone to great lengths to make sure his Israeli judges knew about it. He certainly took care, for example, to tell the court about his ostensible Zionist sympathies in the 1930s. That he was silent

57. Bauer, *Jews for Sale?*, p. 164.

on the Brand mission indicates that it never even occurred to him that his contacts with Brand and Kastner might really save some Jews.[58]

Eichmann, then, was not the initiator, nor did he see the matter as a way of saving Jews. The initiative seems to have come from Himmler, who was prepared to use the Jews as commodities if in exchange he could advance the Reich's other interests. The most comprehensive description of this line of action can be found in Yehuda Bauer, *Jews for Sale?* He found a latent, and sometimes overt, willingness to trade in Jews when it served Nazi purposes. At no point, Bauer shows, did that willingness, however, involve any concession on the ultimate goal of eliminating the Jews. It was at most a deferment of the genocide. Perhaps Brand's mission fit this model; it may well be that this was an attempt by Himmler to camouflage himself against the German foreign ministry. Brand was accompanied by Bandi Grosz, and Grosz also carried a message, this one meant for foreign intelligence services: "Himmler wants to talk." Sending an emissary in an attempt to trade Jews was within Himmler's competence; conducting contacts with the Western armies for the purpose of affecting the progress of the war went beyond his authority and ran contrary to Hitler's position.[59] By sending Brand, Himmler was able to feel out the Allies "in full daylight."[60]

With regard to Himmler's desire to negotiate there were two deviations from the established policy of deporting the Jews to their deaths. More than 18,000 Jews were sent to labor camps in the Vienna area during the second half of June. At least 12,000 of them survived. Eichmann presented this action to Kastner as part of the negotiations — those who were transferred to Vienna would in the meantime not be at risk of deportation to Auschwitz — but apparently the principal motive was an order from Kaltenbrunner, who wanted Jews to work on

58. In addition to Eichmann, Hunsche, Krumey, Novak, and Wislicency were also tried after the war. It occurred to none of them to get themselves off the hook by claiming that they had been sincerely trying to rescue the Jews, and had been thwarted by the Allies — although Wislicency did come close. This silence alone should be sufficient indication of the fact that the thought never crossed their minds.

59. Bauer, *Jews for Sale?*, p. 166.

60. On 22 July 1944 Veesenmayer cabled Ribbentrop: Winkelmann had told him that Himmler had authorized the sending of Brand, for the purpose of exchanging goods for Jews. Veesenmayer seems unaware of Grosz and his mission. Braham, *Destruction*, p. 630.

fortifications there.[61] The second deviation was allowing a group of selected Jews to escape on what was called the Kastner train. Kastner hoped that when the Western Allies saw that the Nazis really were willing to free Jews they would understand the importance of continuing the negotiations, and would at least conduct them seriously enough to slow the pace of the murder machine. While Eichmann and Becher took advantage of the opportunity to extort large sums of money from the passengers, it can't be that money was their real motivation. The train left Hungary (on June 30, 1944) because Himmler hoped that allowing it to go would advance the negotiations. After a stay of several months at Bergen-Belsen, the train's passengers were sent to Switzerland, but their fate was by then no longer linked to that of their fellow Jews in Hungary.[62]

These contacts between the SS and the Relief and Rescue Committee have been the subject of much controversy, both among historians and in the Israeli public. It is not necessary, however, to delve deeply into the details of the affair to determine that there was no essential contradiction between Himmler's plans and Eichmann's actions. Himmler sent Eichmann and his staff to Budapest to deport the Jews of Hungary to their deaths, and this is what they did, with the assistance of all the relevant German agencies and, especially, of the Hungarians. Had the Hungarians not reversed themselves, all the evidence indicates that Eichmann would have completed his mission. The deportations were cut short not by Himmler but by Horthy.

On June 30, 1944 Veesenmayer first noted that there was a problem with Horthy, who opposed the concentration of the Jews of Budapest. For this reason the action was delayed by ten days, and in the meantime activity centered on the Jews of region V (west of Budapest) and in the more distant suburbs of Budapest. In parallel, gendarmerie forces began arriving in the city, but Horthy ordered that they be removed.[63] On July 4, Veesenmayer sat for two hours with Horthy and did not like what he heard. Horthy criticized the situation, attacked the Sztojay government, and especially Baki and Endre – who were, it will be

61. Kaltenbrunner to the Mayor of Vienna, Blaschke, 30 June 1944: "I hope that these transports will be of assistance to your urgent tasks." The letter was prepared in Eichmann's office (IV A 4b 3433/42g (1446)). Braham, *Destruction*, pp. 415–16; Hilberg *Destruction* (1961 edn), p. 545.
62. Bauer, *Jews for Sale?*, pp. 197–200.
63. Braham, *Destruction*, p. 414; Hilberg, *Destruction* (1961 edn), p. 548.

recalled, the central figures in the anti-Jewish actions. He also spoke of the large amount of international pressure being applied to halt the deportations – from the Vatican, from the King of Sweden, from the Swiss government and the Red Cross. Veesenmayer tried to explain to him that the present policy was simply implementation of the hostile stand on the Jews that had been taken by the Horthy regime for many years. Veesenmayer did not fully appreciate the serious nature of the situation, and he did not send his report on this matter to Berlin for two days.[64]

On July 5, in the evening, Veesenmayer spoke with Sztojay and showed him a telegram from Ribbentrop warning the Hungarians of foreign attempts to save the Jews of Budapest. Sztojay responded bitterly, asking the Germans to reassess their position. The Jews of Romania and Slovakia had not, after all, been deported. Furthermore, the Germans had shown that they were prepared to release Jews when this was profitable for them. The reference was to a deal in which the SS gained control over Hungary's largest industrial conglomerate, the Weiss-Manfred Works. Jewish families were among the concern's owners. Following the German invasion of Hungary, the SS agreed to allow the Jewish owners and their families – some 45 to 47 people – to leave for Portugal with some of their wealth, in exchange for ownership of the conglomerate being transferred to the SS. The Hungarians were clearly not pleased that such an important firm had fallen into German hands.[65]

Sztojay also spoke about pressure from foreign governments, but he was especially upset by the secret messages that had been sent from the American and British missions in Berne to their capitals. These cables had included precise information on the deportations from Hungary, and had called for pinpointed reprisal actions.[66] On the morning of July 7,

---

64. Braham, *Destruction*, pp. 419–24. Horthy had told Veesenmayer that Endre was "a little crazy." Winkelmann, reporting on the conversation directly to Himmler, took umbrage: "Endre is one of Hungary's clearest thinkers." Braham, *Destruction*, p. 432.
65. Randolf L. Braham, *The Politics of Genocide* (revised and updated version), New York: Columbia University Press, 1994, p. 5.
66. Braham, *Destruction*, pp. 425–9. Actually, these messages had been sent by Rabbi Weissmandel to Berne, in an attempt to cause the Allies to act upon the information in them. The Allies didn't, but in the meantime the Hungarians had intercepted them, and, in the words of Hilberg, the Hungarians had "frightened themselves to death." Hilberg, *Destruction* (1961 edn), p. 549.

Sztojay notified Veesenmayer that, in coordination with Horthy, the deportations had been halted.[67]

Despite this official suspension, the deportation from the outskirts of Budapest (region V) was completed on July 6; permission to act against the city's Jews was not, however, granted.[68] In his frustration, Eichmann ordered that 1500 Jews from among those detained at Kistarcsa be loaded onto a deportation train (July 15). The members of the *Judenrat* heard of this and managed to alert Horthy himself, who gave an order to stop the train before it crossed the border and to return it to the camp. On July 18 Eichmann and his men were able to trick both the Jews and Horthy. The members of the *Judenrat* were summoned to Eichmann's office, where they were placed in total isolation. They were forbidden even to telephone out to order food. Hunsche kept them busy all day on various pretexts. At the camp itself Novak and his men loaded the Jews quickly and brutally onto the train and sent it northwards. Novak disconnected the camp's telephone line and forbade the Hungarian staff to leave until he was sure that the train had crossed the border.[69]

The power and creativity of Eichmann and his men had been sufficient to murder an additional trainload of more than 1000 Jews. But this was a unique circumstance, and served mostly as an outlet for their sense of frustration. It did not advance their policy. Rather, it showed that evil and depravity were more important driving forces than were power and efficiency. Despite all his experience and ingenuity, Eichmann could not deport Jews without Hungarian cooperation, and the integrated efforts of the Germans were now directed at changing the decision.

On July 9 Veesenmayer spoke with Jaross, the Hungarian interior minister. Jaross was interested in continuing the deportation of the Jews, even against Horthy's wishes, but proposed to wait a bit and then to deport them first from Budapest to the provinces, and only thereafter from the country. Veesenmayer agreed, and reassured Berlin that the matter was under control. Berlin was not satisfied with this, and the next day Ribbentrop cabled Veesenmayer that he must bring about a change in Horthy's decision.[70] Veesenmayer reported once again on the Hungar-

---

67. Veesenmayer put this announcement into his summary of the discussion of the evening of 5 July 1944, which was then sent on 6 July 1944. Braham, *Destruction*, p. 425.
68. Braham, *Destruction*, p. 436.
69. TR.3-347 (Imre Reiner), TR.3-1445 (Alexander Brody).
70. Braham, *Destruction*, pp. 439–40; TR.3-848, 10 July 1944.

ians' bitterness that the Jews of Romania and Slovakia had not yet been deported, and on all the pressure from the West on Hungary to halt the deportations. He went together with Winkelmann to Horthy and the two of them tried to persuade him to change his mind, but to no avail.[71] On July 13 Veesenmayer reported that Horthy felt himself swamped with petitions to save the Jews, and that he had contacted Hitler directly on the matter. On July 16 Ribbentrop sent Veesenmayer a sharp protest from Hitler to Horthy. Ribbentrop, in Hitler's name, threatened Horthy that Hungary would be occupied if he tried to change his government or sabotage the continued deportation of the Jews.[72] For the next few weeks the situation was unclear. Horthy was expected to change his government; in the meantime Sztojay seemed to be saying what the Germans wanted to hear, without backing his words with action.[73] In mid-July Eichmann and his men left Budapest and waited at Lake Balaton for an opportunity to resume their activity.[74]

On August 10 Veesenmayer reported that the Hungarians were prepared to renew the deportations in the near future. On August 14 there was already a target date: August 25. Eichmann had already been notified, Veesenmayer told Berlin. While Horthy had placed restrictions on the categories of Jews who could be deported, the Germans – Eichmann, and Grell in the embassy – had not paid much attention to this. Eichmann notified the Jewish leaders that they were to begin preparing lists of deportees.[75]

On August 23 Romania left the Axis powers and German air force planes bombed the royal palace in Bucharest. The Romanian army joined the Red Army offensive against the Wehrmacht divisions stationed in Romania. On the day that the Germans hoped to renew the deportation of Hungarian Jews, the government changed. Horthy appointed General Geza Lakatos prime minister. Lakatos equivocated about his predecessor's commitment to the deportation of the Jews, and even asked the Germans to recall Eichmann and his unit. It was clear that

---

71. Braham, *Destruction*, p. 444; TR.3-807, Horthy at Nuremberg.
72. Braham, *Destruction*, p. 449; TR.3-772; Hilberg, *Destruction*, p. 550.
73. Braham, *Destruction*, p. 461.
74. TR.3-901, p. 13. Affidavit of Wislicency, 25 March 1947.
75. Braham, *Destruction*, p. 469; TR.3-156, Veesenmayer to Berlin; TR.3-976, Grell to Berlin, 19 August 1944; TR.3-347 (Imre Rainer).

so long as Lakatos was prime minister there would be no deportations.[76] In light of this state of affairs, Eichmann and his staff left the city towards the end of September, leaving only Wislicency behind.[77]

A good illustration of Eichmann's mood during these months in particular, but also with regard to the mission in general, can be found in a description of his return to Budapest after the Szalasi coup of mid-October 1944. The war in Hungary was coming to an end, and Eichmann had no trains available for deporting Jews. In any case, Himmler was no longer interested in continuing the murder at Auschwitz. Nevertheless, Eichmann summoned Kastner and gave him a fiery speech:

> Here, you see? I'm here again! You thought that the events in Bulgaria and Romania would be repeated here? You forgot that Hungary is always under the Reich's shadow, and our arms are long enough to catch the Jews of Budapest. ... And now, listen: this new government obeys us. I am going to immediately establish contact with Minister [of Jewish Affairs] Kovarcz. The Jews of Budapest will be deported, this time on foot.... You don't like it? You're afraid, ha? Don't tell me American stories! Here we're going to work hard, and immediately![78]

In the weeks that followed many thousands of Jews were deported on death marches in the direction of the Austrian border, or were murdered in and around Budapest by the Hungarian Fascist Arrow Cross organization. As in France, the last stage of the murder of the Jews lost its organized bureaucratic form, and looked more like a frenzied malevolent bloodfest.[79] In keeping with this, the documentation is not particularly organized, but the fury and rabidity of the murderers indicates

76. Hilberg, *Destruction*, p. 551. Bauer notes that Himmler told Winkelmann, on 24 August 1944, not to carry through the deportations planned for the next day; an astonished Veesenmayer had to be informed by Ribbentrop that this was indeed so. Bauer's explanation is that the developing negotiations between the SS and Saly Mayer in Switzerland had made Himmler pause. Bauer, *Jews for Sale?*, pp. 215–21. Given both the fact that Hitler himself had been pushing to have the deportations from Budapest renewed, and the far more momentous news from Romania, in the shadow of which the German–Hungarian relationship was also clearly shaking, this explanation is not convincing. Bauer brings no evidence that Himmler's negotiations might have changed Hitler's mind; we have, however, already seen foreign governments refusing to deport Jews at Hitler's bidding.

77. TR.3-387. Report by Grell, 29 September 1944; Hilberg, *Destruction*, p. 551.

78. TR.3-900, p. 109 (Kastner). When Wislicency was shown this quotation, after the war, he affirmed that it sounded just like the vocabulary Eichmann would have used. TR.3-901, p. 16.

79. Braham, *History*, pp. 320–4.

that the way they ended indeed informs us about they way they began. When it was no longer possible to maintain an orderly bureaucratic system for murdering the Jews, they turned to disorderly, vicious murder.

Our survey, which began with seminars to instill antisemitic consciousness, ends with the death marches of tens of thousands of civilians, most of them old people, women and children, through the snow to the Austrian border. The men who presented their carefully researched papers at the seminars are the same ones who commanded the death marches. They certainly saw the connection between the two – shouldn't we?

From the testimony at the Eichmann trial

Esther Goldstein

Q. You were taken off the freight cars, you were told to leave your personal effects behind?

A. Yes.

Q. Was your sister holding her daughter – a baby and her son, who was five years old?

A. Yes.

Q. An SS man came up to your sister and asked her ...

A. My mother was standing near us. He asked whether she was our mother, and she said yes. Then he said to her: "Give the children to your mother." She said: "No, they are mine, I will not hand them over." There was an argument. Then he called to a prisoner, in prisoner's garb, to translate for her, possibly in Yiddish, perhaps she would understand better. He said to her: "If you want to live, give your children to your mother." She said: "No, they are mine, I will not hand them over." Then the SS man came up to her, took the little girl and gave her to my mother, and he took the boy also by force.

Q. And they no longer are alive?

A. No.

Q.   Nor your mother?

A.   No.

(*The Trial of Adolf Eichmann*, vol. III, p. 1282)

Martin Földi

The moment we reached Auschwitz some people came in – we did not know who they were, for we had never seen uniforms such as theirs. We were given an order to get down, but quickly, and to leave all our effects and belongings inside the freight car. We alighted, and it was in such a hurried manner and at such a fast pace that we did not realize what was happening. They said to us that the men should stand to the right side with children over the age of 14, and the women on the left with the young boys and girls. They, the women, began walking while we were still standing, and suddenly they were almost completely out of view. I stood there with my son who was only 12 years old. After we had started walking forward, I suddenly came up to a certain man. I did not know who he was. He was dressed in a uniform of the German army, elegant, and he asked me what my profession was. I knew that being a lawyer by profession would not be very helpful and, therefore, told him that I was a former officer. He looked at me and asked: "How old is the boy?" At that moment I could not lie, and told him: 12 years old. And then he said: "*Wo ist die Mutti?*" (And where is your mother?) I answered: "She went to the left." Then he said to my son: "Run after your mother." After that I went on walking to the right and I saw how the boy was running. I wondered to myself, how would he be able to find his mother there? There were so many women and men, but I caught sight of my wife. How did I recognize her? My little girl was wearing some kind of a red coat. The red spot was a sign that my wife was near there. The red spot was getting smaller and smaller. I walked to the right and never saw them again.

(*The Trial of Adolf Eichmann*, vol. III, p. 968)

Conclusion: Listening to the Screams

In his dramatic book *Ordinary Men*, Browning describes how the unit of German policemen that is his subject one day reached the Jewish ghetto in Konskowola and liquidated its residents. They shot the sick and the elderly in their homes, in their beds, in the streets. The young people were rounded up at the nearby train station and sent to a labor camp. Everyone who remained was marched to a site outside the town and shot. In the midst of this, says Browning, "One of the policemen chatted with the head of the Jewish council, a German Jew from Munich, until he too was led away at the end."

When I read that sentence, I knew Browning could not be correct in his historical analysis, much less in the title of his book. Did they *chat*? What could they possibly have chatted *about*?[1]

What can be more natural, more universal, than a young man and woman falling in love in the streets of Paris, like Ilse Warneke and Theodor Dannecker? What did they talk about, standing hand in hand on the bridges of the romantic city, watching the waters of the Seine flow beneath them? Perhaps we can get an inkling from a letter Dannecker wrote to his wife near the end of the war, in the midst of the chaos and ruins of Germany. Still hoping for a miracle, he accused the German *Volk* of failing its historical test. "I believe in the eternal Germany and the higher mission of our Führer Adolf Hitler," he declared.[2]

During his interrogation (April 17, 1963), Rajakowitz tried to dodge responsibility for a document he had signed by explaining: "It was

---

1. Christopher Browning, *Ordinary Men: Reserve Police Battalion 101 and the Final Solution in Poland*, New York: HarperPerennial, 1992, p. 117. Interestingly, although we have discussed his book at length, both by mail as well as in person, he has yet to respond to my questions regarding this incident. Would the Jew in the story, had he survived the day, have been in any way willing to accept this description?
2. Claudia Steur, *Theodor Dannecker: Ein Funktionär der "Endlösung"*, Tübingen: Klartext, 1997, p. 225.

August, it was vacation time, and the German occupation forces [in Holland] were no different from the others. Apparently Zöpf was on vacation, so I signed."[3] Sometimes the SS murder bureaucrats seem so similar to the rest of us. They wrote letters, took vacations, sought promotion, worried about what the neighbors would say. They seem so ordinary, it is not difficult to be lulled into thinking that their bizarre actions must have been caused by the harsh historical conditions in which they lived. Had we lived then, we might think, it would have taken a great effort not to act as they did.

But remember what they did. Ordinary Gertrud Slottke participated in a roundup of Jews. In her report the next day, she suggested that someone had better have a look at the immunity certificates held by some of the Jews she saw; they were supposed to be safe from deportation because they were rich and important, but how could that be, if they were wearing rags? She also noted, matter-of-factly, that the action had proceeded quietly except for some women who screamed hysterically.[4] Those screams — how could she report them so calmly? What has to happen to an adult woman for her to scream in public, in front of strangers? If Slottke was unmoved, unshaken in her performance of her duty, is she like any ordinary woman we know?

The German scholar Benno Müller-Hill sensed the danger, even if he did not state it explicitly, when he chose to conclude his book on the murderous Nazi doctors with the following unacademic paragraph:

> I have come to the end of my account. I have tried to describe the actions and behavior of psychiatrists and anthropologists in their own words. I have used the language of a science which also became the science of destruction. I have spoken of asocial individuals, products of racial mixing, idiots, persons of mixed blood, non-Aryans, schizophrenics and Gypsies. None of these individuals called themselves by these names. You will not hear in my sentences the screams of children as the chloroform reached their hearts. Nor will you hear the cries of the resisting patient: "You will rue this with your blood," as the door closed behind him. I have not spoken of those who blew up the crematorium in Auschwitz and who were executed immediately. Who hears the cries of the last of these men hanged in front of fellow prisoners: "Comrades, I am the last." Any hope there was for mankind was not to be found in German scientists but in their resisting victims. The staring eyes of the

---

3.   ZSL 107 AR 518/59 (Raja), p. 52.
4.   ZSL 107 AR 518/59 Bd.II, pp. 364–5. The report was written on 27 May 1943.

murdered rest on us. I have no inhibitions about calling murderers murderers, even when the West German Supreme Court gives rulings such as "manslaughter excluded by the statute of limitations," as in the case of Dr Borm, the director of an extermination centre. Murder remains murder even when the law shows itself to be impotent and the courts are unable to punish even one single person for the genocide of the German Gypsies. All indignation is in vain if it is not based on knowledge of the facts and if it does not endure. "If I do not stand up for myself, who will stand up for me? If I am only for myself, who am I? If not now, when then?"[5]

The author seems to feel that the very language ostensibly common to him and to his subjects defiles him, and he asks to purify himself. After reading him we ask ourselves suddenly, might it be that some of these scholars failed to listen to the testimonies of the survivors before reaching their conclusions? Reading Arendt's book, I am left with no doubt that the witnesses at the Eichmann trial were a nuisance to her; their stories were not relevant to the important matter at hand.[6] Browning, who described a police unit that murdered many thousands and deported tens of thousands, did not find a single survivor – and there were a few – to include in his book. The same is true of many of his scholarly colleagues. What can we say about a historical method that reaches weighty conclusions about a group of men, and through them about all of us, but consistently ignores the testimony of another group no less crucial to the story?

Hans Günter Adler, a survivor and an important investigator of the Nazi bureaucracy, did not fall into this trap. He critiqued Arendt, without naming her, by noting that "Anyone who describes Eichmann as banal does not know what he is talking about."[7] There can be no doubt that *those doing the work did not think they were similar to anyone else; they were an elite*. It was clear to them that even German officials outside their organization might not necessarily be capable of performing their mission. Himmler said so himself:

These measures in the Reich cannot be carried out by a police force made up solely of bureaucrats. A corps that had merely sworn an oath

5. Benno Müller-Hill, *Murderous Science: Elimination by Scientific Selection of Jews, Gypsies, and Others, Germany, 1933–1945*, Oxford: Oxford University Press, 1988, p. 104.
6. See her discussion of the witnesses, pp. 233ff.
7. Adler, *Verwalteter Mensch*, p. 119.

of allegiance would not have the necessary strength. These measures could be borne and executed only by an extreme organization of fanatic and deeply convinced National Socialists. The SS regards itself as such and declares itself as such, and therefore has taken the task upon itself.[8]

We don't need either testimonies of survivors or the repugnant declarations of Heinrich Himmler whose commitment to Nazi ideology no one denies. After all, we have seen these people in action. They were antisemites long before they were Nazis, and many were Nazis before this was necessary or desirable for careerists. We have seen them in the 1930s, tracing the threads of the threatening and completely imaginary international Jewish conspiracy. They were already then contriving plans – original plans, one should note – to exploit the Jewish leadership to advance their own policy. We have taken note of the bestiality and brutality that characterized their treatment of the Jews of Vienna in the spring of 1938, and which did not wane in the years that followed in Berlin, or in Amsterdam. And we have not even related the fiendish deeds of Alois Brunner and his henchmen in Greece, France and Slovakia, because they were so fundamental to his way of working that it is hard to view him as a bureaucrat, even though he was one of Eichmann's most important officers.[9] We have heard them declaring of themselves that "All of us, and not just the Führer, are Jew-haters." We have sat with them in their offices in Berlin as they talked and sometimes joked among themselves about the contemptible Jews who were finally getting what they deserved. In Budapest we saw how they were able to lie, not only flagrantly but also artfully, in order to sow confusion and uncertainty among the Jewish leaders, making it easier to send the Hungarian Jews to their deaths. We have not seen them doing their job without understanding it. They knew what they were doing; they chose to do it. At each stage they ran into constraints, difficulties and obstacles, and always devoted their full energies to removing everything that stood in the way of achieving their goal.

They were wholeheartedly in accord with their mission, and that in itself is enough to discredit the suggestion that there was something

8. Quoted in Adler, *Verwalteter Mensch*, pp. 868–9.
9. He is repeatedly one of the central characters in the descriptions by Safrian in *Eichmann Männer*; and see also Mary Felstiner, "Alois Brunner: 'Eichmann's Best Tool'," *Simon Wiesenthal Center Annual*, vol. 3, 1986, pp. 1–46; and Mary Felstiner, "Commandant of Drancy: Alois Brunner and the Jews of France," *Holocaust and Genocide Studies*, vol. 2/1, 1987, pp. 21–47.

banal about them. But the foundation of Arendt's argument was not that they were not diligent, but rather that they did not comprehend that this diligence was criminal. But in this she erred as well. They worked alongside other bureaucracies, with other officials who sometimes did not agree with German policy. They could not have dealt with these opponents and simultaneously believed their behavior was the only possible option. We have heard – especially in France – how they preached to the French on the importance of deporting the Jews. Is it really possible that French authorities never responded in kind, never argued about the need to rid the continent of Jews – even when leaders of the French church asked these questions aloud, in broad daylight? And the correspondence with the foreign ministry on the atrocity propaganda that was liable to be directed against Germany if anyone were allowed to return alive – can that be evidence of ingenuousness? And Bosshammer, one of whose jobs was to keep track of this "propaganda" in the foreign press – could he and those around him really not understand that there were people who viewed the Reich's policies as blatant evil? And their strict classification of the documents? Not to mention the descriptions of doubts they felt – Hunsche and his secretary in Berlin, Dannecker and Röthke hesitating for one last minute before beginning the murder of children. Even Dannecker.

Only those who trust bogus versions of the events, such as the one Eichmann presented in Jerusalem, could possibly believe these men did not know they were doing something the rest of the world thought was wrong. In fact, even someone reading only trial interrogations could know their consciences were not clear. There was that astounding ability of theirs to remember the fine details of every period of their lives except for the part about which they were interrogated; about that they could not remember even what could be proven. This interesting psychological phenomenon shows better than a thousand witnesses that they, like other human beings, clearly discerned the black flag flying over their deeds.[10]

10. As a member of the staff of the Yad Vashem Archive I have repeatedly had the occasion to read large quantities of the files of interrogations of Nazi criminals in the Zentralestelle der Landesjustizverwaltungen in Ludwigsburg, Germany. The pattern here described is to be found in thousands of cases. Members of Einzatsgruppen who would have us believe they first heard of the murder of the Jews in the late 1940s; administrators in conquered territories who were not aware there had ever been any Jews in their localities. I have repeatedly found it intriguing (better: nauseating) to see how they suddenly *do* remember, with certainty, that they were on vacation precisely on the date 22 years earlier for

During the interrogation in the 1960s of one of the murderers from the Einsatzgruppen, the investigator asked a non-legal question. "Tell me, if they had ordered you to shoot your son, would you have carried that out as well?" Without a moment's hesitation the murderer gave him the obvious answer: "Of course not!"[11] They weren't stupid, after all, nor blind. The advantages they saw in the murder of Jews simply outweighed the disadvantages; but this was inconceivable when it came to the murder of their own children.[12] Apparently even SS men knew the difference between good and evil when they wanted to.

Scholars are in danger of delving so deep that they overlook what an intelligent viewer sees at once. Dr Gerald Weissman described his colleague Dr Eduard Pernkopf, who was appointed to head the Vienna medical school after the *Anschluss*:

> No explanation of the behavior of Pernkopf and his friends is satisfactory. They were "evil" (à la Hannah Arendt) but no worse than Heidegger or Heisenberg, and they were by no means "banal." Pernkopf, Eppinger, and Rizak were eminent Viennese academicians. Cultivated in art and science, they could distinguish Hindemith from Schoenberg after ten bars, or lues from cirrhosis at ten paces. They were purposeful men who knew the kind of society they wanted for their country and found a politics that would give it to them. It seems to me that these men were not suddenly seized by mass paranoia: Their personality did not suddenly "double" (à la Robert Jay Lifton). No, in the center of Europe, mistaken men, certain and arrogant, planned a

cont.
    which the prosecution seems to have documents proving crimes committed by their unit. When they returned to the unit, three days after the danger had passed, no one even told them about what had transpired. Lest the reader think that this was merely a standard stratagem to save oneself from prosecution, I must add that in conversations I have had with hundreds of Germans of my own generation, they have told me that this peculiar form of memory (shall we call it "un-Arendtian memory?") is most common, even in the face of the questions to parents from murderers' children, and even on their deathbeds.

11. ZSL II 206 AR-Z 46/61 Bd.15, p. 702. Vernehmung ggn. Angeklagten Joseph König, 8 October 1962.

12. Which should remind us that precisely this point − "The criminal Allies are killing our children" − was the kind of thing the Nazi propaganda machine used to bolster its spirits. As if to say: we are doing some rather ugly things, but we have the right to do so, given what we're up against. Feigning innocence can be done only when one accepts their definition of innocence and guilt.

broad racial experiment, told their students – and the world – what they planned to do, and went about doing it.[13]

If everything is so clear, why isn't it? What is the source of the great attraction to Arendt's idea, and why has it been developed and elaborated to the point that it has become a permanent fixture of Western consciousness, a staple of modern culture?

Aharon Appelfeld, Holocaust survivor and novelist, wrote in an essay entitled "Interim Account":

> The Jew saw himself as involved in the great endeavor of progress, in which nationalism and sectarianism disappear, and the world renews itself in some sort of new human unity. This faith, one of whose first spokesmen he was, made him blind. He did not see, he could not see, that forces of darkness and evil that had been lying in wait for him for years were now about to burst out of the undergrowth and eat him alive.[14]

Enlightenment, rationalism, universality, humanism – all these failed when faced with the "forces of darkness and evil," and could not defend the Jews (in fact, faith in them contributed to their destruction).

During years of research on this book, I tried to follow the precept of the English historian Collingwood: re-enact the past.[15] The attempt failed. The more I understood the SS officers who were my subject, the less I knew them. Not that they cannot be explained, but scholarly empathy did not help me. I found that rational explanations are shallow and unpersuasive, since they remove from the SS officers their chief characteristic – their evil.

The memory of the Holocaust threatens us, the rationalists. If we do not see the Nazis as ordinary, like us, must we not accept their own assumption that there are fundamentally different types of people? Even more threatening is the fear that if we really want to explain them, we

---

13. Gerard Weissmann MD, "Springtime for Pernkopf," in *They All Laughed at Christopher Columbus: Tales of Medicine and the Art of Discovery*, New York: Times Books, 1987, p. 60. I wish to thank Professor William Seidelman for bringing this essay to my attention.

14. Aharon Appelfeld, "Interim Account," *Yediot Aharonot*, 29 September 1995 (Rosh Hashannah 5755/1995).

15. R. G. Collingwood, *The Idea of History*, Oxford: Oxford University Press, 1966, pp. 282 ff. "History as Re-Enactment of Past Experience". Collingwood died in 1943, and probably was unaware of the full depravity of Eichmann and his ilk. Had he lived, would he still have wanted me "to re-enact the past"?

have no choice but to use non-rational concepts, such as evil. "Evil" is not an accepted entry in the academic lexicon. The job of a scholar, we assume, is to study what can be measured and explained, not amorphous entities borrowed from the world of religious values. To demonstrate this I conducted a small and unscientific experiment. I opened the indexes of all the books on my shelf dealing with the Holocaust. The word "evil" appeared in only one of them, a theological work. These books, it should be recalled, are about the murder of millions of innocent people.[16]

To Arendt's credit it may be said that she was not deterred by the word "evil." Her greatness lies in her success in neutralizing all the word's threatening connotations, and this is why she has won such massive recognition. She made it possible for people who consider themselves liberals and humanists to address the Holocaust, to integrate it into their consciousness, without having to examine the foundations of their world view. But the findings of this study show that her brilliant conceptual exercise lacked all historical foundation. Eichmann and his colleagues knew exactly what they were doing, did it wholeheartedly, and afterwards regretted only being caught. The word evil fits them in its full awesome sense.

Ideology played an important role in shaping Eichmann and his comrades. They said this themselves, again and again, so why should we let them off the hook? Even their contemporaries who did not say these things often held similar positions. Benno Müller-Hill conducted interviews with the children of leading figures in German medicine who collaborated with the Third Reich's policy of murdering the mentally ill. Listen to one of them, Gertrud Fischer, daughter of Professer Eugen Fischer, who had been rector of the University of Berlin until 1942. On June 20, 1939, her father said in a lecture:

> The Jew, as such, is an alien and, therefore, when he wants to insinuate himself, he must be warded off. This is self-defense. In saying this, I do not characterize every Jew as inferior, as Negroes are, and I do not underestimate the greatest enemy with whom we have to fight. But I reject Jewry with every means in my power, and without reserve, in order to preserve the hereditary endowment of my people.[17]

16. Actually, the word *may* appear in one or two of the books, but it was not deemed worthy of an entry in the index. See, for example, Bauer, *Jews for Sale?*
17. Müller-Hill, *Murderous Science*, p. 12.

By the early 1980s things looked different to his daughter:

M.-H.: Did he ever have doubts about National Socialism?

G.F.: "My father was a completely apolitical person. Early in life, he was a Catholic, but later he left the church. He was no National Socialist. He was a nationalist and a conservative, but they all were at the time, that's not a matter of politics. He joined the Party late, when pressure was brought to bear on him." About 1938, she thought.

"Was your father an anti-Semite?" I ask.

"No, no," she says. "He worried a lot about what happened to his Jewish colleagues and their wives." "Did you discuss the persecution and extermination of the Jews with him, either during the war or afterwards? Did he ever question himself about his involvement?" "No," she says, "we never spoke about that. I didn't know anything about it during the war. Von Verschuer and he must have known. But we didn't discuss it. ... In any case, why are you picking on him in particular? They were all guilty. He didn't do anything special." "Was von Verschuer an anti-Semite?" "No, certainly not. He was just like my father. He never said 'The Jews are bad,' he said 'the Jews are different.'" And she smiled at me. "He supported the segregation [*Trennung*] of the Jews. You know what it was like, when he came to Berlin in 1927. Cinema, theatre, literature, it was all in their hands. He was for segregation. But he wasn't an anti-Semite."[18]

If we are to believe this, not only was her father certainly an antisemite, but she was as well, and remained one even forty years later.

This should tell a historian that, when a person declares, after the war, that he never had anything against Jews, he may simply be lying. Pre-existing antisemitism (not only in Germany) is not a sufficient cause for understanding the Holocaust. More answers must be searched for. It is possible to discuss the historical context that adversely affected the lives of millions of Germans; it is possible to analyze totalitarian structures, as Hannah Arendt did; and there is no a priori reason to avoid cultural explanations.

But the most significant question raised by the present study is: What can be learned from Eichmann about a murderous potential existing in us all? A lot, Arendt said, because there are people like Eichmann everywhere. Very little, Hausner might have said, except for the need to know how to defend ourselves.

18. Ibid., p. 108.

I propose to distinguish among four kinds of evil in man.

The first kind can be called indifference. This is the ability to live one's life while ignoring the suffering of others, when this suffering is not the result of our own actions. This is the least of the four types of evil, since the fate of the Tibetan exiles or the persecuted citizens of Burma is far from us, and our ability to do anything about them is nil or very small. The greater our ability to have an effect, the closer we get to the second type.

The second kind of evil is selfishness, the ability to cause suffering without intending it, but also without being bothered by it. An example could be selling arms to a dictatorship in order to provide employment for our own citizens. There is more evil here than in indifference, but less than in the next level, since here we have no intention of causing suffering, and merely ignore it so as to advance our own interests.

The third kind of evil is heartlessness. The heartless are those who are able to cause suffering consciously in order to advance their interests. There is a large measure of evil here, since here we first encounter the active desire to cause suffering. It might be proper to divide the heartless into two subcategories: those who are willing to cause limited suffering to an entire community, such as through a policy of confiscation and impoverishment, and those who are willing to cause absolute suffering on a small scale, such as terrorist organizations that murder individuals in order to advance their goals.

The fourth type of evil might be called malevolence. The malevolent are those who devote all their powers to causing as much suffering as possible. There can be no doubt that a person willing to search out his victims in all corners of the continent and to enter into conflict with his own allies in order to advance the operation is infected with evil of a different kind than those who are willing to make do with the murder of those at hand.

The principal criterion for measuring evil, according to this classification, is the intention of the actor, not the results of his actions; his decisions, which are his own, and not their outcomes, which are affected by external factors. It is more serious to murder an individual in cold blood than to live a serene and selfish life while masses of people are being persecuted at the far end of the world, even if the latter is not something to be proud of. The heartless person who could have murdered thousands but held himself back and made do with a few is different from the person who tried with all his might — and malevolently — to murder thousands, but who was prevented from doing so by some external factor and managed to murder only a few.

In Arendt's understanding, the modern world enables a person to reach the fourth level of evil without realizing that this is what he is doing, since the combination of technology and bureaucracy means that many of the perpetrators never have to face the consequences of their actions and, if they do think about them, ideology conceals the meaning of their actions from them. This explanation absolves us of the need to search for anything unique about the malevolent Nazis, since the model is universal, and only the specific historical circumstances led it to be realized. It releases us from the requirement of coping with non-academic and irrational concepts such as hatred and evil, for the same reasons. And it diminishes the humanity of the murderers, while minimizing their crime.

There is a common metaphor used to describe the "descent" into evil: a slippery slope. Because it is slippery, the more we move on it, the faster our descent, the harder it becomes to pull ourselves back up. Someone who finds it difficult to lie will not easily confiscate property; a person who finds it hard to confiscate property will not easily take life; a person who finds it difficult to kill one man will not effortlessly kill an entire community. But a person who makes a habit of lying will find it easier to steal, and the rest is clear.

Arendt's students use this metaphor with greater abandon than she might have herself. She did not say that a person who lies will in the end murder; rather even one who is careful about small things may be sucked into a system that will turn him into a murderer.[19]

An examination of the facts has shown that this is not the way things were, and I would like to devote the final paragraphs of this study to proposing an alternate model: mountain-climbing.

Let us assume for a moment that malevolence actually exists on the high peak of a steep cliff, high up where there is eternal cold and oxygen is scarce. Most human beings spend their lives below. Every

19. And its fallacy can be easily described by choosing the "wrong" slope. Contemporary liberals adhere dearly to the assumption that a gentler language will form gentler people, hence the current fad of political correctness. In essence, they create euphemisms. One doesn't talk about the crippled, but rather about the physically challenged. One doesn't mention the poor, only the economically disadvantaged. And so on. The Nazis were great fans of euphemisms — yet nobody that I am aware of has ever thought to warn that political correctness could lead to Nazism. Slippery slopes are obviously to be found only beneath phenomena of which we don't approve.

healthy person can climb stairs, and walk up a small hill; but not everyone can climb mountains. Only a rare few are capable of ascending higher than 5000 meters, and they will succeed only after receiving proper training and the right equipment. You can't climb to the top absent-mindedly. You must work at it.

The metaphor is clear. All of us, apparently, are infected with indifference. Many of us are guilty of selfishness. Heartlessness, on the other hand, is not so common; the higher we go, the fewer people there will be. Each of us can do an injustice, and many of us are capable of being fairly nefarious. But this can teach us nothing about our ability to commit murder, much less mass murder – and much less than that, a holocaust. Malevolent people do not come out of nowhere; they decide to be that way.

Along the way from antisemitism, common to German Dannecker and to French Xavier Vallat and his colleagues, to the summit of wholesale deportation of Jews to death, which separated German from French, there were many points at which one had to decide whether to continue. We saw that the operation of sundering the Jews from everyone else bringing them to the murder facilities was complex, lengthy, full of small details which had large effects on the outcome. The decision to become murderers was not a one-time matter, as has been assumed by historians who search for a date on which the decision was made by Hitler or his officials. It was a long and steep climb, lined with red lights and black flags. Just as a man does not reach the peak of Mount Everest by accident, so Eichmann and his ilk did not come to murder Jews by accident, or in a fit of absent-mindedness, nor by blindly obeying orders or by being small cogs in a big machine. They worked hard, thought hard, took the lead, over many years. They were the alpinists of evil.

Compare them with the righteous gentiles who endangered their own lives to save Jews. Generally, they were people who did not stand out, and they apparently knew like everyone else, how to be indifferent, even selfish. Some of them, Oskar Schindler being the most famous, were even heartless at first. The mountain-climbing metaphor is a way of describing the change he underwent. The higher he climbed with his Nazi colleagues, the broader became his field of vision and the clearer his sight, until he refused to climb further and went back down.

Instead of trying to explain that we are all capable of doing what the SS did, it would be better to ask what made them into such aberrations.

I have no answers, only the certainty that it is important to look for them, and the sense that it would be best to look not only with historians but also with psychologists, philosophers, theologians – and writers. Had Joseph Conrad or William Shakespeare been in that Jerusalem courtroom, they would never have mistaken Adolf Eichmann for a small, drab man.

From the testimony at the Eichmann trial

Leslie Gordon

Once we got down from the trucks, they put up two machine-guns on each side of the road and told us: "Go eastwards. Don't come back or don't even look back." Some of the people had to do their hygienic doings on the side, and they were shot right on the spot.

Q. By whom?

A. By the SS.

Q. What did you do? Tell us just what you yourself did.

A. Well, we were together. My father was 58, my mother – she was 43. My brother was 22, I was 21, my sister was 19, my brother was 16, another brother was 14, a sister was eight, and my little brother was five. We were trying to keep together and go along the road – as has been told by the "brave" SS.

Q. Who, of all those members of your family, remained alive?

A. Only myself.

(*The Trial of Adolf Eichmann*, vol. III, p. 1128)

Bibliography

Books

Adam, Uwe D., *Judenpolitik im Dritten Reich*, Düsseldorf: Droste, 1972.

Adler, Hans G., *Verheimlichte Wahrheit*, Tübingen: Mohn, 1958.

Adler, Hans G., *Der Verwaltete Mensch*, Tübingen: Mohn, 1974.

Adler, Hans G., *Theresienstadt*, Tübingen: Mohn, 1960.

Adler, Jacques, *The Jews of Paris and the Final Solution: Communal Response and Internal Conflicts, 1940–44*, New York: Oxford University Press, 1987.

Aly, Götz and Roth, Karl Heinz, *Die Restlose Erfassung: Volkszählen, Identifizieren, Aussonderung im Nationalsozialismus*, Berlin: Rotbuch, 1984.

Aly, Götz and Heim, Susanne, *Vordenker der Vernichtung: Auschwitz und die deutschen Pläne für eine neue europäische Ordnung*, Frankfurt/M: Fischer, 1993.

Aly, Götz, *"Endlösung". Völkerverschiebung und den Mord an den europäischen Juden*, Frankfurt/M: Fischer, 1995.

Aly, Götz, Chroust, Peter and Pross, Christian, *Cleansing the Fatherland: Nazi Medicine and Racial Hygiene*, Baltimore: Johns Hopkins University Press, 1994.

Arendt, Hannah, *Eichmann in Jerusalem*, New York, 1963. Some of the quotations are from the latest edition, New York: Penguin Books, 1992.

Arendt, Hannah, *The Origins of Totalitarianism*, 2nd edn, New York: Meridian Books, 1958.

Aronson, Shlomo, *Heydrich und die Anfänge des SD und der Gestapo*, Stuttgart: Freie Universtät, 1971.

Aronson, Shlomo, *The Beginnings of the Gestapo System: The Bavarian Model in 1933*, Jerusalem: Israel Universities Press, 1969.

Avni, Haim, *Spain, the Jews and Franco*, Philadelphia: Jewish Publication Society, 1982.

Bankier, David, *The Germans and the Final Solution: Public Opinion under Nazism*, Oxford: Blackwell, 1992.

Bauer, Yehuda, *Jews for Sale? Nazi–Jewish Negotiations 1933–1945*, New Haven, CT: Yale University Press, 1994.

Bauman, Zygmunt, *Modernity and the Holocaust*, Ithaca, NY: Cornell University Press, 1989.

Benz, Wolfgang, *Dimension des Völkermordes*, Munich: R. Oldenburg, 1991.

Billig, Josef, *Die Endlösung der Judenfrage in Frankreich*, New York: Beate Klarsfeld Foundation, 1979.

Birn, Ruth Bettina, *Die Höheren SS- und Polizeiführer: Himmlers Vertreter im Reich und in den besetzten Gebieten*, Düsseldorf: Droste, 1986.

Black, Peter, *Kaltenbrunner*, Princeton, NJ: Princeton University Press, 1984.

Blau, Peter M. and Meyer, Marshall W., *Bureaucracy in Modern Society*, 3rd edn, New York: Random House, 1987.

Bower, Tom, *Klaus Barbie, Butcher of Lyon*, London: Michael Joseph, 1984.

Bracher, Karl Dietrich, *The German Dictatorship: The Origins, Structure and Effects of National Socialism*, London: Weidenfeld & Nicolson, 1971.

Braham, Randolph L., *The Politics of Genocide: The Holocaust in Hungary*, New York: Columbia University Press, 1981.

Braham, Randolf, *The Destruction of Hungarian Jewry: A Documentary Account*, 2 vols, New York: World Federation of Hungarian Jews, 1963.

Brecht, Arnold and Glaser, Comstock, *The Art and Technique of Administration in German Ministries*, Boston: Harvard University Press, 1940.

Breitman, Richard, *The Architect of Genocide: Himmler and the Final Solution*, New York: Knopf, 1991.

Broszat, Martin, *The Hitler State: The Foundation and Development of the Internal Structure of the Third Reich*, London: Longman, 1981.

Broszat, Martin, *Nationalsozialistische Polenpolitik, 1939–45*, Stuttgart: DVA, 1961.

Broszat, Martin, Buchheim, Hans, Jacobson, Hans-Adolf and Krausnik, Helmut, *The Anatomy of the SS-State*, London: Collins, 1968.

Browder, George C., 'Sipo and SD, 1931–1940: Formation of an Instrument of Power', unpublished PhD thesis, University of Wisconsin, Madison, WI, 1968.

Browder, George C., *Foundations of the Nazi Police State: The Formation of Sipo and SD*, Lexington, KY: University Press of Kentucky, 1989.

Browning, Christopher, *The Final Solution and the German Foreign Office*, New York: Holmes & Meier, 1978.

Browning, Christopher, *Fateful Months: Essays on the Emergence of the Final Solution*, New York: Holmes & Meier, 1985.

Browning, Christopher, *Ordinary Men: Reserve Police Battalion 101 and the Final Solution in Poland*, New York: HarperPerennial, 1992.

Browning, Christopher, *The Path to Genocide: Essays on Launching the Final Solution*, Cambridge: Cambridge University Press, 1992.

Bullen, R.J., *et al.* (eds), *Ideas into Politics*, London: 1984.

Caplan, Jane, *Government Without Administration: State and Civil Service in Weimar and Nazi Germany*, Oxford: Clarendon Press, 1988.

Carpi, Daniel, *Between Mussolini and Hitler: The Jews and the Italian Authorities in France and Tunisia*, Hanover: Brandeis University Press, 1994.

Chary, Friedrich B., *The Bulgarian Jews and the Final Solution, 1940–44*, Pittsburgh, PA: University of Pittsburgh Press, 1972.

Cohen, Richard I., *The Burden of Conscience. French Jewish Leadership during the Holocaust*, Bloomington, IN: Indiana University Press, 1985.

De Jong, Lois, *Het Koninkrijk der Nederlanden in de Tweede Werldoorlog*, Amsterdam: RIOD, 1975.

Dicks, Henry, *Licensed Mass Murder: A Socio-Psychological Study of Some SS Killers*, New York: Basic Books, 1973.

Eichmann, Adolf, *Ich, Adolf Eichmann: Ein historischer Zeugenbericht*, Hrsg. von Rudolf Aschenauer, Leoni: Druffel Verlag, 1980.

Fein, Helen, *Accounting for Genocide: Victims and Survivors of the Holocaust*, New York: 1976.

Fischer, Conan, *Stormtroopers: A Social, Economic and Ideological Analysis 1925–1935*, London: Allen & Unwin, 1983.

Fleming, Gerald, *Hitler and the Final Solution*, Los Angeles: University of California Press, 1984.

Flood, Charles B., *Hitler, the Path to Power*, Boston: Houghton Mifflin, 1989.

Friedlander, Henry, *The Origins of Nazi Genocide: From Euthanasia to the Final Solution*, Chapel Hill, NC: The University of North Carolina Press, 1995.

Friedländer, Saul, *Nazi Germany and the Jews*, Vol. I: *The Years of Persecution, 1933–1939*, New York: HarperCollins, 1997.

Furet, François, *Unanswered Questions: Nazi Germany and the Genocide of the Jews*, New York: Schocken, 1989.

Gay, Peter, *Weimar Culture*, Harmondsworth: Penguin, 1958.

Gellately, Robert, *The Gestapo and German Society: Enforcing Racial Policy 1933–1945*, Oxford: Clarendon Press, 1990.

Goldhagen, Daniel Jonah, *Hitler's Willing Executioners: Ordinary Germans and the Holocaust*, New York: Knopf, 1996.

Gordon, Bertran N., *Collaborationism in France during the Second World War*, Ithaca, NY: Cornell University Press, 1980.

Gordon, Sarah, *Hitler, Germans and the 'Jewish Question'*, Princeton, NJ: Princeton University Press, 1984.

Graf, Christoph, *Politische Polizei zwischen Demokratie und Diktatur*, Berlin: Colloquium Verlag, 1983.

Hausner, Gideon, *Justice in Jerusalem*, New York: Schocken, 1968.

Hays, Peter (ed.), *Lessons and Legacies: The Meaning of the Holocaust in a Changing World*, Evanston, IL: Northwestern University Press, 1991.

Heer, Hannes and Naumann, Klaus (eds) *Vernichtungskrieg: Verbrechen der Wehrmacht 1941 bis 1944*, Hamburg: Hamburger Edition, 1995.

Herbert, Ulrich, *Best. Biographische Studien über Radikalismus, Weltanschauung und Vernunft, 1903–1989*, Bonn: Dietz, 1996.

Hilberg, Raul, *The Destruction of the European Jews*, New York,: Holmes & Meier, 1985.

Hildebrand, Klaus, *The Third Reich*, London: Allen & Unwin, 1984.

Hillgruber, Andreas, *Hitlers Strategie, Politik und Kriegsführung*, Frankfurt/M: Bernard & Gräfe, 1965.

Hirschfeld, Gerhard (ed.), *The Policies of Genocide: Jews and Soviet Prisoners of War in Nazi Germany*, London: Allen & Unwin, 1986.

Hirschfeld, Gerhard and Kettenaker, Lothar, *The Führerstaat, Myth and Reality: Studies on the Structure and Politics of the 3rd Reich*, Stuttgart: DVA, 1981.

Höhne, Heinrich, *The Order of the Death's Head*, London: Secker & Warburg, 1969.

Housden, Martyn, *Helmut Nicolai and Nazi Ideology*, London: Macmillan, 1992.

Jäckel, Eberhard, *Hitlers Weltanschauung, A Blueprint for Power*, Middletown, CT: Wesleyan University Press, 1972.

Jäckel, Eberhard and Rohwer, Jürgen, *Der Mord an den Juden im zweiten Weltkrieg*, Stuttgart: DVA, 1985.

Kempner, R.M.W., *Eichmann und Komplizen*, Zurich: Europa Verlag, 1961.

Kershaw, Ian, *The Nazi Dictatorship*, London: Edward Arnold, 1985.

Klarsfeld, Serge (ed.), *Die Endlösung der Judenfrage in Frankreich*, Paris: Beate und Serge Klarsfeld, 1977.

Klarsfeld, Serge, *Vichy-Auschwitz: Die Zusammenarbeit der deutschen und französischen Behörden bei der 'Endlösung der Judenfrage' in Frankreich*, Nördlingen: Delphi Politik, 1989.

Klarsfeld, Serge and Steinberg, Maxime, *Die Endlösung der Judenfrage in Belgien – Dokumente*, Paris: Beate Klarsfeld Foundation, 1980.

Koehl, Robert L., *The Black Corps: The Structure and Power Struggles of the Nazi SS*, Madison, WI: University of Wisconsin Press, 1983.

Koehl, Rober L., *RKFVD: German Resettlement and Population Policy 1939–1945*, Cambridge, MA: Harvard University Press, 1957.

Kogon, Eugen, *Der SS-Staat. Das System der deutschen Konzentrationslager*, Frankfurt/M: Büchergilde Gutenburg, 1959.

Krausnik, Helmut, *et al.*, *The Anatomy of the SS State*, London: Collins, 1968.

Krausnik, Helmut and Wilhelm, Hans-Heinrich, *Die Truppe des Weltanschauungskrieges*, Stuttgart, DVA, 1981.

Kren, George N. and Rappoport, Leon, *The Holocaust and the Crisis of Human Behavior*, New York: Holmes & Meier, 1980.

Kushner, Tony, *The Holocaust and the Liberal Imagination: A Social and Cultural History*, Oxford: Blackwell, 1994.

Kwiet, Konrad, *Reichskommissariat Niederlande: Versuch und Scheitern Nationalsozialistischer Neuordnung*, Stuttgart: DVA, 1968.

Laqueur, Walter, *Fascism: A Reader's Guide*, Los Angeles: University of California Press, 1976.

Levai, Jeno (Hrsg), *Eichmann in Ungarn*, Budapest: Pannonia Verlag, 1961.

Levai, Jeno, *Black Book on the Martyrdom of Hungarian Jewry*, Zurich: Central European Times, 1948.

Liang, Hsi-Huey, *The Berlin Police Force in the Weimar Republic*, Berkeley: University of California Press, 1970.

Maaz, Joachim, *Der Gefühlsstau: Ein Psychogramm der DDR*, Berlin: Argon, 1990.

Mann, Reinhardt, *Protest und Kontrolle im Dritten Reich: Nationalsozialistische Herrschaft im Alltag einer rheinischen Grosstadt*, Frankfurt/M: Campus, 1987.

Marrus, Michael and Paxton, Robert O., *Vichy France and the Jews*, New York: Basic Books, 1981.

Merkl, Peter, *The Making of a Stormtrooper*, Princeton, NJ: Princeton University Press, 1980.

Merton, Robert, *Reader in Bureaucracy*, New York: Free Press, 1952.

Michaelis, Meir, *Mussolini and the Jews*, Oxford: Clarendon Press, 1978.

Milgram, Stanley, *Obedience to Authority: An Experimental View*, New York: Harper & Row, 1974.

Mitscherlich, Alexander und Margarete, *Die Unfähigkeit zu Trauern*, Memmingen: Serie Piper, 1977.

Mommsen, Hans, *Beamtentum im Dritten Reich*, Stuttgart: DVA, 1966.

Mommsen, Hans, *From Weimar to Auschwitz: Essays in German History*, Cambridge: Polity Press, 1991.

Mosse, George L., (ed.) *Police Forces in History*, London: Sage, 1975.

Müller-Hill, Benno, *Murderous Science: Elimination by Scientific Selection of Jews, Gypsies, and Others, Germany, 1933–1945*, Oxford: Oxford University Press, 1988.

Mulisch, Harry, *Strafsache 40/61: Eine Reportage*, Köln: DuMont Schauberg, 1962.

Peterson, Edward N. *The Limits of Hitler's Power*, Princeton, NJ: Princeton University Press, 1969.

Pohl, Dieter, *Nationalsozialistische Judenverfolgung in Ostgalizien, 1941– 1944: Organisation und Durchführung eines staatlichen Massenverbrechens*, Munich: R. Oldenbourg Verlag, 1996.

Proctor, Robert H., *Racial Hygiene: Medicine under the Nazis*, Cambridge, MA: Harvard University Press, 1988.

Presser, Jacob, *The Destruction of the Dutch Jews*, New York: Dutton, 1969.

Ramme, Alwin, *Der Sicherheitsdienst der SS: Seine Stellung in der faschistischen Diktatur unter besonderer Berücksichtigung seiner Besatzungspolitischen Funktionen im sogenannten General Gouvernement Polen*, Berlin: Deutscher Militärverlag, 1970.

Ringel, Erwin, *Die österreichische Seele*, Wien: Europaverlag, 1991.

Robinson, Jacob, *And the Crooked Shall Be Made Straight: The Eichmann Trial, the Jewish Catastrophe, and Hannah Arendt's Narrative*, New York: Macmillan, 1965.

Rosenkranz, Herbert, *Verfolgung und Selbstbehauptung: Die Juden in Österreich, 1938–1945*, Vienna: Herold, 1978.

Rückerl, Adalbert, *The Investigation of Nazi Crimes, 1945–1978: A Documentation*, Hamden, CT: 1980.

Rürup, Reinhard (ed.), *Topographie des Terrors: Gestapo, SS und RSHA auf dem 'Prinz-Albrecht-Gelände': Eine Dokumentation*. Berlin: Willmutt Arenhörel, 1987.

Rummel, Rudolf J., *Death by Government*, New Brunswick, NJ: Transaction Publishers, 1994.

Rummel, Rudolf J., *Democide: Nazi Genocide and Mass Murder*, New Brunswick, NJ: Transaction Publishers/Rutgers University, 1992.

Safrian, Hans, *Die Eichmann Männer*, Wien: Europaverlag, 1993.

Schellenberg, Walther, *The Labyrinth: The Memoirs of Walther Schellenberg*, New York: Harper, 1986.

Schleunes, Karl, *The Twisted Road to Auschwitz*, London: Deutsch, 1972.

Segev, Tom, *Soldiers of Evil: The Commandants of the Nazi Concentration Camps*, New York: McGraw-Hill, 1987.

Seidler, Horst and Rett, Andreas, *Das Reichssippenamt Entscheidet: Rassenbiologie im Nationalsozialismus*, Wien: Jugend & Volk, 1982.

Sereny, Gitta, *Into That Darkness*, London: 1974.

Speer, Albert, *Inside the Third Reich*, New York: Macmillan, 1970.

Speer, Albert, *The Slave State*, London: Weidenfeld & Nicolson, 1981.

Stachura, Peter (ed.), *The Shaping of the Nazi State*, London: Croom Helm, 1978.

Staub, Ervin, *The Roots of Evil: The Origins of Genocide and Other Group Violence*, Cambridge: Cambridge University Press, 1989.

Stern, Frank, *The Whitewashing of the Yellow Badge – Antisemitism and Philosemitism in Postwar Germany*, Oxford: Pergamon, 1992.

Steur, Claudia, *Theodor Dannecker: Ein Funktionär der "Endlösung"*, Tübingen: Kartext, 1997.

Sweets, John F., *Choices in Vichy France: The French under Nazi Occupation*, Oxford: Oxford University Press, 1986.

The Trial of Adolf Eichmann: Record of Proceedings in the District Court, Jerusalem: State of Israel, Ministry of Justice, 1993.

Totgeschwiegen 1933–1945: Zur Geschichte der Wittenauer Heilstätten, seit 1957 Karl-Bonhoeffer-Nervenklinik. Herausgeber: Arbeitsgruppe zur Erforschung der Geschichte der Karl-Bonhoeffer-Nervenklinik. Berlin: Wissenschaftliche Beratung: Götz Aly, Edition Hentrich, 1989.

Weber, Wolfram, *Die Innere Sicherheit im besetzten Belgien und Nordfrankreich 1940–1944*, Düsseldorf: Droste, 1978.

Wildt, Michael, *Die Judenpolitik des SD 1935 bis 1938: Eine Dokumentation*, Schriftenreihe der Vierteljahrshefte für Zeitgeschichte, München, Oldenbourg, 1995.

Yahil, Leni, *The Holocaust: The Fate of European Jewry, 1932–1945*, New York: Oxford University Press, 1990.

Yahil, Leni, *The Rescue of Danish Jewry: Test of a Democracy*, Philadelphia: Jewish Publication Society, 1982.

Zucotti, Susan, *The Italians and the Holocaust: Persecution, Rescue, Survival*, New York: Basic Books, 1987.

Articles

VjHfZG   *Vierteljahresheft für Zeitgeschichte*
YVS   *Yad Vashem Studies*

Aly, Goetz and Heim, Susanne, "The Holocaust and Population Policy: Remarks on the Decision on the 'Final Solution'," *YVS*, XXIV, 1994, pp. 45–70.

Ball-Kadouri, Kurt J., "Berlin Is 'Purged' of Jews," *YVS*, V, 1963, pp. 271–316.

Bankier, David, "On Modernization and the Rationality of Extermination," *YVS*, XXIV, 1994, pp. 109–30.

Bankier, David, "Jewish Society through Nazi Eyes, 1933–1936," *Holocaust and Genocide Studies*, vol. 6, no. 2, 1991, pp. 11–128.

Bauer, Yehuda, "Who Was Responsible and When? Some Well-known Documents Revisited," *Holocaust and Genocide Studies*, vol. 6, no. 2, 1991, pp. 129–50.

Bierman, John, "How Italy Protected the Jews in the Occupied South of France, 1942–1943," in *The Italian Refuge: Rescue of Jews During the Holocaust*, ed. Herzer, Ivo with Voigt, Klaus and Burgwyn, James, Washington, DC: The Catholic University of America Press, 1989, pp. 218–30.

Breitman, Richard and Büchler, Yehoshua, "Documentation: A Preparatory Document for the Wannsee 'Conference'," *Holocaust and Genocide Studies*, vol. 9, no. 1, Spring 1995, pp. 121–9.

Broszat, Martin, "The Genesis of the Final Solution," *YVS*, XIII, 1979, pp. 73–126.

Browning, Christopher R., "German Memory, Judicial Interrogation, and Historical Reconstruction: Writing Perpetrator History from Postwar Testimony," in Friedlaender, Saul, *Probing the Limits of Representation: Nazism and the Final Solution*, Boston: Harvard University Press, 1992, pp. 22–36.

Diner, Dan, "Rationalization and Method: Critique of a New Approach in Understanding the 'Final Solution'," *YVS*, XXIV, 1994, pp. 71–108.

Felstiner, Mary, "Alois Brunner: 'Eichmann's Best Tool'," *Simon Wiesenthal Center Annual*, vol. 3, 1986, pp. 1–46.

Felstiner, Mary, "Commandant of Drancy: Alois Brunner and the Jews of France," *Holocaust and Genocide Studies*, vol. 2/1, 1987, pp. 21–47.

Friedlaender, Saul, "The 'Final Solution': On the Unease in Historical Interpretation," in Peter Hayes (ed.), *Lessons and Legacies: The Meaning of the Holocaust in a Changing World*, Evanston, IL: Northwestern University, 1991, pp. 23–35.

Friedlaender, Saul, "Dimensions of the Holocaust: Remarks on Two Studies," *YVS*, XXII, 1992, pp. 1–16.

Friedman, Phillip, "The Lublin Reservation and the Madagascar Plan: Two Aspects of Nazi Jewish Policy During the Second World War," in Friedman, Phillip, *Roads to Extinction: Essays on the Holocaust*, New York: Jewish Publications Society of America, 1980, pp. 34–58.

Goshen, Seev, "Eichmann und die Nisko-Aktion im Oktober 1939. Eine Fallstudie zur NS–Judenpolitik in der letzten Etappe vor der 'Endlösung'," *VjHfZG*, 1981, vol. 1, pp. 74–96.

Grabitz, Helga, "Problems on Nazi Trials in the Federal Republic of Germany," *Holocaust and Genocide Studies*, vol. 3, no. 2, 1988, pp. 209–22.

Hildebrand, Klaus, "Monokratie oder Polykratie? Hitlers Herrschaft und das Dritte Reich," in Hirschfeld, Gerhard and Kettenacker, Lothar (eds), *Der Führerstaat: Mythos und Realität*, Stuttgart: DVA, 1981, pp. 73–97.

Hillgruber, Andreas, "The Extermination of the European Jews in Its Historical Context," *YVS*, XVII, 1984, pp. 1–16.

Jochman, Werner, "Die Ausbreitung des Antisemitismus," in Mosse, Werner E. und Paucker, Arnold, *Deutsches Judentum in Krieg und Revolution, 1913–1916*, Tübingen: 1971, pp. 409–510.

Jülich, Dierk, "Die Wiederkehr des Verdrängten – Sozialpsychologische Aspekte zur Identität der Deutschen nach Auschwitz," in Schreier, Helmut und Heyl, Matthias (Hrsg.), *Das Echo des Holocaust, Pädagogische Aspekte des Erinnerns*, Hamburg: Verlag Dr R. Kramer, 1992, pp. 57–72.

Jülich, Dierk, "Erlebtes und Ererbtes Trauma," Lecture given at Akademie Frankenwarte, Würzburg, 15 May 1993.

Kempner, R.M.W, "Der Mord an 35,000 Berliner Juden," in *Gegenwart in Reuckblick: Festgabe für die jüdische Gemeinde zu Berlin*, 1970, pp. 180–208.

Laborie, Pierre, "The Jewish Statutes in Vichy France and Public Opinion," *YVS*, XXII, 1992, pp. 89–114.

Levai, Jeno, "The Hungarian Deportations in the Light of the Eichmann Trial," *YVS*, V, 1963, pp. 69–104.

Lösener, Bernhard, "Als Rassenreferent im Reichsministerium des Innern," *VjHfZG*, 1961, pp. 262–313.

McKale, Donald M., "Traditional Antisemitism and the Holocaust: The Case of the German Diplomat Curt Prüfer," *Simon Wiesenthal Center Annual*, vol. 5 (1988), pp. 61–76.

Mason, Tim, "Intention and Explanation: A Current Controversy about the Interpretation of National Socialism," in Hirschfeld, Gerhard and Kettenacker, Lothar (eds), *Der Führerstaat: Mythos und Realität*, Stuttgart: DVA, 1981, pp. 23–42.

Michman, Joseph, "The Controversial Stand of the *Joodse Raad* in the Netherlands," *YVS*, X, 1974, pp. 9–68.

Michman, Joseph, "Planning for the Final Solution against the Background of Developments in Holland in 1941," *YVS*, XVII, 1986, pp. 145–80.

Milchman, Alan and Rosenberg, Alan, "The Holocaust as Portent: Hannah Arendt and the Etiology of the Desk Killer," in Colijn, G. Jan and Littell, Marcia S., *The Netherlands and Nazi Genocide: Papers of the 21st Annual Scholars Conference*, Lewiston/Queenston/Lampeter: Edwin Mellon Press, 1992, pp. 277–305.

Mommsen, Hans, "Die Realisierung des Utopischen: Die 'Endlösung' der Judenfrage im Dritten Reich," in *Der Nationalsozialismus und die deutsche Gesellschaft; Ausgewählte Aufsätze*, Reinbek bei Hamburg: Rohwohlt, 1991, pp. 184–232.

Peschanski, Denis, "The Statutes on Jews, October 3, 1940 and June 2, 1941," *YVS*, XXII, 1992, pp. 65–88.

Rosenbaum, Ron, "Explaining Hitler," *New Yorker*, 1 May 1995.

Shelach, Menachem, "The Italian Rescue of Yugoslav Jews, 1941–1943," in *The Italian Refuge: Rescue of Jews During the Holocaust*, ed. Herzer, Ivo with Voigt, Klaus and Burgwyn, James, Washington DC: The Catholic University of America Press, 1989, pp. 205–17.

Spector, Shmuel, "Aktion 1005 – Effacing the Murder of Millions," *Holocaust and Genocide Studies*, vol. 5, no. 2, 1990, pp. 157–74.

Watt, Donald Cameron, "Hitler's Sticky Fingers," *New York Times*, 7 August 1994 (review of Lynn H. Nicholas, *The Rape of Europa*, New York: 1994).

Wieseltier, Leon, "Final Comments," in *The "Willing Executioners"/ "Ordinary Men" Debate*," Symposium at the United States Holocaust Memorial Museum, Washington DC, April 8, 1996, pp. 39–43.

Witte, Peter, "Zwei Entscheidungen in der 'Endlösung der Judenfrage': Deportationen nach Łódź und vernichtung in Chelmno," *Holocaust and Genocide Studies*, vol. 9, no. 3, 1995, pp. 318–45.

Yahil, Leni, "Madagascar – Phantom of a Solution for the Jewish Question," in Mosse, George L. and Vago, Bela, *Jews and Non-Jews in Eastern Europe 1918–1945*, Jerusalem: Israel Universities Press, 1974, pp. 315–34.

Yahil, Leni, "'Memoirs' of Adolf Eichmann", *YVS*, XVIII, 1987, pp. 133–62.

Film

Yad Vashem Film Archive:
Proceedings of the Eichmann Trial, collection 791.
Daniela Schmidt, *Rosenstrasse — wo Frauen widerstanden*, 1990. V–1038.

Index

Adolf Eichmann does not appear in the index, as he is mentioned on almost every page.

Abetz, Otto   179, 182–3, 185, 186, 191
Ahnert, Horst   207–9, 213–14
Albert, Dr Wilhelm   28, 76
Amen, John H.   128
Amsterdam   6, 129, 143, 145–52, 154–6, 159, 161, 168–72
Anders, Karl   98
Apeldoorn   162–3, 165
Arendt, Hannah   1–4, 8, 9, 39, 56, 128, 141, 177, 244–5, 253–4, 270, 272–4, 276, 278
Asche, Kurt   152
Asscher, Abraham   148
Auschwitz   92, 107, 115, 129, 132, 138–9, 159, 161, 164, 166, 168, 175–8, 189, 193–4, 205–8, 215, 235, 238, 249–50, 260, 265, 267, 269

Badoglio, Pietro   135
Baki, Laszlo   242, 244, 247–8, 250, 261
Balaton, Lake   264
banality of evil   3, 4, 9, 133, 273
Barneveld   168, 169, 171, 174, 176
Beaune-la-Rolande   186, 197, 204–5, 234
Becher, Kurt   259, 261
Bene, Otto   144, 153, 156, 158, 160–1, 167, 174, 176
Bergen-Belsen   96, 121, 173–4, 261
Berlin   5, 35–8, 40, 41, 85, 97, 102, 107, 112, 113, 126, 132, 137, 151, 173
Besançon   180
Best, Dr Werner   12, 15, 26, 183–4, 186
Birkenau   138
Blobel, Paul   137
Blum, Hans   97
Blum, Léon   23, 209, 235

Blum, René   235, 236
Böhmker, Dr Hans   147–8, 151
Bomelburg, Karl   179
Bondy, Alexander   123
Bondy, Heinz   123
Bonhoeffer, Karl   60
Bordeaux   180, 200
Bormann, Martin   176
Bosshammer, Friedrich   6, 96–7, 116, 119, 133–5, 139, 140, 272
Bousquet, René   194–7, 205–6, 211, 213, 218, 222–3, 227–8, 230
Brand, Joel   257, 258, 259, 260
Brandt, Rudolf   54
Bratislava   104
Breslau   28
Brinon, Ferdinand de   231
Brunner, Alois   229, 231, 271
Brussels   119, 152, 229
Bucharest   264
Buchenwald   121, 147
Budapest   238–9, 241–2, 244, 246, 248–50, 255–7, 261, 264–5

Calmeyer, Dr Hans Georg   164–5
"Calmeyer Jews"   174
Chelmno   86
Ciano, Galeazzo   69, 218
Cohen, David   153, 155
Cohn, Benno   40
Columbia Haus (prison)   30
Compiègne   186, 188–9, 197
Conti, Dr Leonardo   163
Cozzi, Jenni   53,   123

Dachau   15, 36
Daluege, Kurt   13, 14, 179, 218

Dannecker, Theodor   5, 29, 30–1, 33, 38, 66, 69, 71, 74, 115, 133, 150–2, 181–201   203–4, 206–7, 209–11, 217, 233, 268, 272, 279
Danzig   65
Darquier, Louis de Pellepoix   197
De Gaulle, Charles   184
Deppner, Erich   153
Diels, Rudolf   12
Dijon   180, 207
Dischner, Josef   153
Drancy   186, 188, 197, 209, 211, 215–16, 229, 231, 233–5
Düsseldorf   101, 111, 122, 180

Eicke, Theodor   15
Endre, Laszlo   242, 244–5, 247, 248, 252–4, 261
evil   177, 204, 225, 233, 263, 275, 277–9

Ferenczy, Laszlo   244–5, 247, 250
Fiala, Fritz   139
Fingernagel, Erna   130
Fischböck, Dr Hans   144
Fischer, Eugen   275
Fischer, Gertrud   275
Földi, Martin   267
Frank, Anne   178
Frank, Hans   144
Franken, Adolf   95, 97
Frick, Wilhelm   14, 16, 17
Friedman, Yisroel   57
Fünten, Ferdinand aus der   145, 153, 155, 161–4, 168–9, 171–2, 175

Gemmecker, Albert   153–4, 163, 164–5, 175
Geschke, Dr Hans   242, 244
Giersch, Margarete   134
Goebbels, Josef   73, 74
Goering, Hermann   12, 51–2, 67, 68, 75–7, 80, 89, 182–4
Goldstein, Esther   266
Gordon, Leslie   280
Greifenberg, Hans von   243
Grell, Theodor Horst   243, 251, 264
Grosz, Bandi   259, 260
Grotefend, Dr Ulrich   176
Günther, Rolf   5, 53, 55–6, 66, 85, 94–7, 100, 102–7, 112, 113, 121, 123–4,

129–34, 138, 140, 161, 166, 209, 210, 248–50
Gurs   72
Gurwitsch, Max, 120
Gutterer, Leopold   73–4, 96
Guttman, Viktor   124,
Gutwasser, Richard   95–6

Hagelman, Helmut   28
Hagen, Herbert   5, 20, 26–7, 31, 35–8, 181, 196, 198, 209, 213, 224, 226–8, 230–1
Hague, The   124, 140, 145, 152, 154, 159
Hanke, Rudolf   129
Harster, Dr Wilhelm   6, 145–6, 148–51, 154, 156–8, 161, 163, 167–8, 170, 172, 173–4
Hartenberger, Richard   96, 139
Hartl, Albert   47
Hartmann, Richard   5, 52, 67, 74, 84–5, 95–6, 98, 104, 122, 136, 139
Haselbacher, Dr Karl   20
Hassel, Elisabeth   164
Hausner, Gideon   1, 2, 4
Heidegger, Martin   2
Heidelberg   123
Heinrichsohn, Ernst   199, 208, 212
Henlein, Konrad   32
Hering, Luise   128
Hess, Rudolf   19, 70
Heszlenyi, Jozef   240
Heydrich, Reinhard   11–17, 19, 22, 25–6, 28, 46–7, 49–52, 63, 65–6, 69–70, 74, 76–7, 79, 81–2, 85, 88–90, 95, 109–10, 136, 179–81, 184, 201, 203
Hezinger, Adolf   243, 248, 251–2
Himmler, Heinrich   11–17, 19, 21, 29, 34, 46, 48–51, 54–6, 63, 68–70, 72, 77–9, 83–5, 107–8, 119, 126, 148, 160–1, 174, 179, 181–2, 184, 186, 194, 203, 214, 218, 220–1, 228, 239, 260–1, 270–1
Hitler, Adolf   12–14, 34, 36, 38, 43, 58–9, 61, 63, 68–71, 74, 78–9, 81, 83–4, 91, 144, 149, 176, 181–3, 185–6, 189, 212, 227, 230, 239, 240–1, 243, 264, 268
Höppner, Alexander von   67
Höppner, Rolf-Heinz   76, 81
Horthy, Miklós   240–1, 243, 261–4

Hrosinek, Karl 95–6, 98
Hüls, Gustav 97
Hunke, Gudrun 128
Hunsche, Otto 95–7, 100, 102, 111,
    115–21, 123, 130, 135, 138, 246, 250,
    255–6, 258, 263, 272

Istanbul 259
Izbica 99

Jäger plan 249
Jänisch, Rudolf 50, 51, 70, 94, 105, 137
Jaross, Andor 242, 263
Jerusalem 1, 4, 27, 272
Jeske, Willy 97, 98

Kaltenbrunner, Ernst 50, 52, 54–6, 108,
    113, 117, 118, 128, 175, 218, 223–4,
    231, 242–3, 245, 248, 250, 260
Kamenets-Podolsk 239
Kastner, Rudolf (Reszo) 257, 260–1, 265
Katowicz 63
Kistarcsa 246, 250, 256
Klessheim 240, 242
Klingenfuss, Karl Otto 116, 124
Knispel, Marie 128
Knochen, Dr Helmut 6, 52, 54, 179–81,
    184, 187, 189, 191–6, 198–9, 201–4,
    206–7, 209, 211–12, 214–20, 222–4,
    226–31
Knolle, Friedrich 148, 159
Kolrep, Otto 97
Komoly, Otto 257
Korherr, Richard 92
Kovner, Abba 9, 93
Krieger, Friedrich Wilhelm 66
Krumey, Hermann 254–6, 258
Kryschak, Werner 55, 96, 122–6, 129,
    130, 137–8
Kube, Karl 95, 97–8, 123

Lages, Willy 145, 152, 154–5, 161, 171–2
Lakatos, Geza 264
Laval, Pierre 184, 196, 203, 211–13, 218,
    230
Leefmans, Jacob 128
Leefsma, Jacob 129
Leguay, Jean 194–5, 197, 211–12, 218,
    226, 227–8
Levy, Leah 138

Lichtenstein 111
Liepelt, Hans 96
Lischka, Kurt 6, 180, 185, 187, 196, 202,
    226
Lobstein, Dr Jacques 163
Łódź 67, 76, 84, 86
Lösener, Dr Bernhard 87
Lospinoso, Guido 221–5
Lublin 99
Lulay, Laszlo 250
Luther, Martin 51, 68–9, 90, 136, 188

Mackensen, Hans Georg von 220, 221
Madagascar 67–8, 70–3, 80, 81, 127, 146
Malfatti di Montetretto, Francesco 222–4
Maly-Trostinets 91
Mannel, Herbert 95
Marks, Elisabeth 129
Marseilles 223–4
Martin, Friedrich 129
Mauthausen 147–8, 151, 156, 160, 242
Melkman, Joseph 177
Menkes, Sara 93
Metz 215
Miethling, Erna 130
Mildenstein, Leopold von 20
Minsk 91, 111
Mischlinge 91–2, 95–6, 98, 110, 111, 113,
    122–3, 132, 176
Mischke, Alexander 97, 98
Monte Carlo 210
Morgenstern, Tsherna 93
Moritz, August 219–20
Mös, Ernst 55, 95–6, 98, 122–6, 129, 130,
    136–8, 173, 175
Mühler, Rolf 223–5
Müller, Heinrich 17, 46, 47–8, 50, 52,
    63–4, 66, 74, 84, 101–2, 107, 112–13,
    116–18, 121, 187, 194, 203, 216, 218,
    220, 222–3, 229, 243
Mussolini, Benito 69, 70, 124, 135, 220,
    221, 222

Nancy 180
Nebe, Arthur 46, 86
Naumann, Dr Erich 145, 174–5
Neumann, Liona 141
Neumann, Max 29
Nice 222, 224
Nisko 64

Novak, Franz 5, 55, 95–7, 102–5, 107,
    111–12, 115, 122, 161, 189, 193,
    206–7, 209, 210, 246, 250, 263
Nuremberg 32, 113
Nuremberg Laws 108, 111, 112, 145, 151

Oberg, Karl 181, 189, 195–6, 198, 209,
    211, 213–14, 218, 220, 227, 229
Ohlendorf, Otto 46, 66
Oranienburg 31
Orléans 180
Orwell, George 124
Oslo 106
Ostrava 64
Ottlik, György 240

Pachow, Max 96
Palestine 1, 26–7, 30–1, 36, 67, 75, 133,
    175
Paris 104, 115, 152, 179–81, 184–6,
    193–7, 199–201, 207–8, 213–15,
    228, 268
Pétain, Phillipe 179, 196, 211, 214, 216,
    227–8, 230, 231
Pfeifer, Paul 97, 98
Pithiviers 186, 197, 204–5, 234
Ponary 93
Prague 5, 85–6, 97, 101, 102, 109–10
Preuss, Paul 97, 98

Quandt, Johanna 131

Rademacher, Franz 68–9, 70, 90, 109, 111,
    115–16, 135–6, 152, 157, 188
Rafael, Gideon 67
Rajakowitz, Dr Erich 6, 66, 70, 108,
    150–1, 157, 159, 268
Rasch, Dr Otto 86
Rauter, Hans Alvin 74, 143, 147–9,
    156–63, 167, 169–71, 173
Ravensbrück 121, 151
Reichsbahn 104
Ribbentrop, Joachim von 51, 67, 69, 70,
    110, 220–1, 239, 240–1, 248, 262–4
Richter, Gustav 133
Riga 132, 141–2
Rome 36, 219, 220, 223
Röthke, Heinz 6, 47, 52, 54, 125, 191,
    199–204, 206–7, 209, 211–15,
    217–19, 222–4, 226–31, 236, 272

Rothschild, Alfonse 39
Rothschild, Louis 39
Rouen 180

Salonika 104
Sauckel, Fritz 113
Sauts, Thomas 212
Schellenberg, Walter 52, 74
Schindler, Oskar 279
Schleier, Rudolf 185
Schmidt, Fritz 144, 149, 157, 158
Schöngarth, Dr Eberhard 145
Schröder, Kuno 20, 22
Schwamenthal, Hildegard 119
Schwebblin, Jacques 189, 199
Seidl, Dr Siegfried 85
Seyss-Inquart, Artur 66, 144–5, 148–9,
    151, 156–63, 167–9, 174–5
's-Hertogenbosch, *see* Vught
Silberman, Dora 131
Six, Dr Franz 26, 28
Slottke, Gertrude 54, 150, 165–7, 171–2,
    173, 175, 269
Sonderbehandlung 127–8, 130
Sonderkommando 1005 137
Speer, Albert 43, 73, 113, 241
Stahlecker, Franz Walter 37
Stalingrad 107
Stange, Otto 104
Stein, Edith 159
Stephan, Ilse 128
Stern, Jacques 235
Stettin 66, 106
Stockholm 134
Stojay, Doma 240, 242, 245, 261–3
Streckenbach, Bruno 47, 49, 66
Streicher, Julius 22, 32
Stulpnagel, Karl-Heinrich 181, 184, 187
Stulpnagel, Otto von 179, 180
Stuschka, Franz 95, 96, 139, 208
Stuttgart 31
Suhr, Friedrich 53, 82, 88, 95–7, 100, 102,
    109, 111, 115–16, 135

Tel Aviv 27
Thadden, Eberhard von 119–20, 135, 140,
    241, 248, 249, 250, 251–2
Theresienstadt 54–6, 85, 91, 96, 100–4,
    106–7, 110, 112, 124, 133, 139,
    159–60, 166, 175

Thierack, Otto   126
Thomas, Dr Max   179–80
Tölgyesy, Gyözö   247, 250
Tommaso, Luceri   223
Transnistria   134
Treblinka   91
Trencker, Alfred   244
Tulard, André   189

Vallat, Xavier   186
Vatican   159, 262
Veesenmayer, Dr Edmund   239, 241,
    248–52, 259, 261–4
Vienna   6, 21, 35–9, 41, 64, 73–4, 76, 86,
    91, 101, 119, 141, 260
Vught   145, 160, 168–71, 174

Wagner, Ellen   132
Waldsee   140
Walzertraum   128
Wannsee Conference   56, 85, 89, 96, 100,
    110, 152, 247
Warneke, Ilse   181, 268
Warsaw   114, 238

Wassenberg, Hans   97
Weill, Rabbi Jullian   184
Weiss-Manfred Works   262
Weissmandel, Michael Dov Ber   258
Weizmann, Chaim   23
Wellers, Georges   233–6
Werner, Alfons   120, 166, 173–4
Westerbork   145, 153, 155–6, 159, 161–4,
    166, 168–73, 175–8
Wimmer, Dr Friedrich   144, 146, 147
Winkelmann, Otto   244, 248, 259, 264
Winzerstube   128
Wisliceny, Dieter   5, 20–7, 34–6, 38, 69, 81,
    139, 245, 250, 251, 254–5, 257–8, 265
Wöhrn, Fritz   55, 95, 96, 97, 109, 111, 114,
    120, 121, 124–7, 130–3, 136, 140
Wolff, Leo de   155
Wurm, Paul   69

Zeitschel, Karl-Theo   179, 185, 191, 192,
    213
Zöpf, Wilhelm   6, 54, 145, 150–4, 158,
    163–7, 170–5, 269
Zurich   26